Media and Society into the 21st Century

A Historical Introduction

Second Edition

Lyn Gorman and David McLean

WILEY-BLACKWELL

A John Wiley & Sons, Ltd., Publication

This second edition first published 2009
© 2009 by Lyn Gorman and David McLean

Edition history: Blackwell Publishing Ltd 2002, published as Media and Society
in the Twentieth Century

Blackwell Publishing was acquired by John Wiley & Sons in February 2007.
Blackwell's publishing program has been merged with Wiley's global Scientific,
Technical, and Medical business to form Wiley-Blackwell.

Registered Office
John Wiley & Sons Ltd, The Atrium, Southern Gate, Chichester, West Sussex,
PO19 8SQ, United Kingdom

Editorial Offices
350 Main Street, Malden, MA 02148-5020, USA
9600 Garsington Road, Oxford, OX4 2DQ, UK
The Atrium, Southern Gate, Chichester, West Sussex, PO19 8SQ, UK

For details of our global editorial offices, for customer services,
and for information about how to apply for permission to reuse the copyright material
in this book please see our website at www.wiley.com/wiley-blackwell.

The right of Lyn Gorman and David McLean to be identified as the author of this
work has been asserted in accordance with the Copyright, Designs and
Patents Act 1988.

Library of Congress Cataloging-in-Publication Data

Gorman, Lyn.
Media and society into the 21st century : a historical introduction / Lyn Gorman
and David McLean. – 2nd ed.
  p.   cm.
Includes bibliographical references and index.
ISBN 978-1-4051-4935-8 (pbk. : alk. paper) 1. Mass media–History–20th century.
I. McLean, David. II. Title.
P90.G577 2009
302.2309'04–dc22

2008039271

A catalogue record for this book is available from the British Library.

Set in 10/13pt Palatino by SPi Publisher Services, Pondicherry, India
Printed by TJ International Ltd, Padstow, Cornwall

04   2013

Media and Society into the 21st Century

Contents

Acknowledgments

We would like to acknowledge the importance of our experience in developing and teaching subjects in media history to students at Charles Sturt University. Such experience provided the incentive to write this book, because no single work provided a satisfactorily comprehensive and up-to-date history of mass media.

We thank Ross McKibbin, Neville Meaney, and Therese Taylor for their helpful comments on sections of the manuscript. Lyn Gorman would like to thank David Levine for access to a very special library; Bill Fitzwater for constructive critique and some "gems" on British television history; Nancy Blacklow for insights and resources for the revised edition; and Caroline for the support and inspiration only a daughter can give. David McLean would like to thank Wendy, Jessica, and Simon for their patience and support.

1

Introduction

The pervasiveness of media in the early twenty-first century and the controversial question of the role of media in shaping the contemporary world point to the need for an accurate historical perspective on media and society. Here, as in all other aspects of human experience, the benefits of historical understanding include an awareness of alternatives (a reminder "that the choices open to us are often more varied than we might have supposed" if we were to focus exclusively on the present situation); the exposure of myths – of misleading and sometimes dangerous beliefs based on a distorted view of the past; and a clear appreciation of "what is enduring and what is ephemeral in our present circumstances."[1] Discussion of the role of the media in society has too often been characterized by assumptions that present-day media arrangements are somehow natural and unavoidable, by too limited an awareness of the range of possibilities for media structure, content, and influence, and by questionable and erroneous ideas about the "lessons" of media history.

In recent decades a burgeoning scholarly literature has provided the basis for a sound historical perspective on media and society. It is true, as Kevin Williams has observed in a fine survey of the history of mass communications in Britain, that the "historical development of the mass media, and how media forms and representations have changed over time, have been traditionally of less interest in the growing amount of research, writing and musing on the mass media and modern society and culture."[2] Nonetheless, there is now a substantial body of works on aspects of media history, with newspapers, the film industry, radio, television, new media, advertising, and propaganda the subjects of first-rate works by historians and other scholars. Yet, with few exceptions,[3] we have lacked a survey that brings together the findings of specialized research on media history in a number of countries, attempts to make sense of developments since the emergence of mass media, and provides an introduction for readers unfamiliar with the field. This book is designed to meet that need. It draws on the considerable body of historical writing on media now available and provides historical perspective on the rapid and extensive developments in media and communications since the 1980s.

The book begins with the emergence of the mass press in the late nineteenth century and ends with globalization and media in the twenty-first century. Within that broad framework it takes up various themes. These include the importance of the context – political, social, cultural, economic – in which mass media have developed and been adopted; the interaction between technological and social change; the relationships between media institutions and the state; and the interrelationships of different media. Our main focus is on the development of newspapers, film, radio, television, and the new media that arose at the end of the twentieth century; on their use for purposes of information, persuasion, and entertainment; and on their cultural and political impact. Chapters 2, 3, and 4 examine the emergence and development of the three main mass media before the Second World War. Chapters 5, 6, and 7 deal with the use of media for purposes of economic and political persuasion through advertising and propaganda. The post-1945 history of television and older media is the subject of Chapters 8 and 9. Chapters 10, 11, and 12 are concerned with recent developments concerning the role of media in war and international relations, the rise of new media, and globalization. The study does not claim to be comprehensive. Limits on length have not allowed a fuller treatment of magazines and book publishing, or of links between media and the popular music industry, for example. We hope nonetheless that the final choice of media to be covered and themes to be pursued satisfies readers in relation to the dominant mass media and the major issues that have arisen concerning their role in society.

The study is comparative as well as historical: it is based on the firm conviction that an understanding of media and society requires not only an analysis of change over time but a comparison of the experience of different societies. Evidence is presented from a range of countries, although particular attention is given to the United States and

Great Britain, partly because of limitations of space, and partly because of the global influence of US and British media developments.

The role of the media in society has been contentious since the beginning of the mass-circulation press and the film industry in the 1890s. It is a controversy that has been evident both in popular discussion and in various theoretical approaches that have emerged. These provide a backdrop to this work. "Mass-society" approaches have been especially influential. The term "mass" gained currency just as communications possibilities were expanding rapidly at the end of the nineteenth century. As Williams notes: "The history of mass communication is in one sense a history of the fear of the masses ... [who became] increasingly visible with the growth of the media and communication industries."[4] The concept of a "mass society" created by the products of the mass media was part of the pessimistic assessment of the impact of industrialization that developed early in the twentieth century. This approach dominated critical thinking for a long time. Writers such as T. S. Eliot and F. R. Leavis drew negative conclusions about the effects of mass media. They distinguished high from low culture, considered "packaged" popular culture inferior, and deplored the undermining of individual cultural experience by media products.[5]

Members of the Marxist "Frankfurt school," including Theodor Adorno, Max Horkheimer, and Herbert Marcuse (who left Nazi Germany for the United States in the 1930s), developed another version of mass-society theory in their efforts to explain why capitalism had survived. Extending Marx's theory, which he had developed before the advent of mass communications, they suggested that the mass media had encouraged the working class to be passive, thereby diminishing the likelihood of proletarian revolution to overthrow capitalism. According to this view, capitalist society maintained social control and cohesion through ideology; the culture industry reproduced the values necessary to maintain capitalist society; and the mass media made people passive recipients of the dominant ideology.

There have been other variants of this "ideological-control" thesis, which depict media messages or particular media as supporting those in power and subordinating working people. Thus television is portrayed as a tool of capitalism, a means of maintaining ideological control. It gives a false view of reality, makes viewers unquestioningly accept existing social conditions; its programs reduce critical consciousness and encourage hypnotic passivity. Louis Althusser and other theorists developed these views in the 1960s, arguing that the maintenance of capitalism depended on manipulation of the ruling ideology so that workers would submit to it. An opposing view of the media has also been influential: the idea that they are important in ensuring freedom and democratic rights, and in providing channels for popular participation. This was especially influential in relation to newspapers as they developed on a mass scale. The press was seen as "the fourth estate," playing a watchdog role as a check on government. Similar views feature in discussion of the potential of new media, such as the Internet, to offer citizens means of active participation and unrestrained access to information.

Research on the effects of mass media – some of it based on "moral panics" about the alleged impact of media – drew attention to audience responses to, and uses of, mass media. Much of this research failed to reach firm conclusions of wide applicability, but it was useful in demonstrating how audiences are active rather than passive, and in encouraging research on longer-term impacts (such as the effects of the omnipresent images of consumer culture).

Concern with the political economy of the media has remained influential, contributing to research on media organizations, issues of ownership and power, and to analysis of media hegemony, cultural imperialism, and media in the context of globalization. Interdisciplinary approaches have been valuable in work on the complexities of twenty-first-century global media. Terry Flew, for example, has drawn on institutionalism, cultural policy studies, and cultural and economic geography to provide a better understanding of global media – and the economic and cultural dimensions of globalization – than that afforded by narrower critical political economy or cultural-studies approaches.[6]

The growth of new media has stimulated new theoretical approaches. Manuel Castells has been influential in focusing attention on the importance of networks in the "information age;" and some analysts now treat media as subsumed within information and communications technologies in networked (as opposed to mass) society. Studies of the nature and significance of new media have included debates about virtual cultures and cyberspace; and the rapid uptake of online social networking possibilities has drawn attention away from media and mass society to the individual as the basic unit in a networked society and to individual use of social media.[7]

Notwithstanding this recent tendency to emphasize individual engagement with twenty-first-century media, questions about the relative importance of "mass culture," of the influences that shape mass-media products, and of the impact of media messages – whether associated with political ideology or with the values and aspirations of consumer culture – remain relevant. This study advocates a skeptical view of extreme conceptualizations of the role of mass media – either as a means of social control, or as ensuring democratic freedoms. The emphasis here is on the need to examine the broad range of factors that influence both the particular medium and its role in society during a specific period. The corollary of this is that relations between media and society do not remain static. This is pertinent, not only to discussion of new media, when technological change has facilitated rapid developments, but to the entire period studied here.

2

The Press as a Mass Medium

Newspapers had existed long before the press developed as a mass medium. However, social and economic change in the late nineteenth century, together with various technological developments, led to the emergence of newspapers directed to, and attracting, a mass readership. Powerful owners emerged – the "press barons," of whom Stanley Baldwin said: "What proprietorship of these papers is aiming at is power, and power without responsibility – the prerogative of the harlot throughout the ages."[1] The press barons were responsible for substantial changes in the economic organization of the press from the late nineteenth century into the early decades of the twentieth. Their mass-circulating newspapers also attracted attention during wartime, as vehicles for propaganda and means of sustaining national morale. Thus the history of the press in this period sheds light on some central questions regarding the role of the media in society.

This chapter concentrates on British and American experiences particularly, because of the extent of industrialization of the press in these countries, and because these two country studies illustrate the growth of a national mass press, significant changes in economic organization, and changes in journalism, all of which remained important into the twentieth century.

Early Newspaper Development

The earliest predecessors of the modern newspaper appeared soon after the invention of the printing press. In the mid-fifteenth century there were forms of printed material carrying news of events. By the seventeenth century there were small publications called "corantoes" (news sheets), containing items of news for a given period, gazettes that commented on public affairs, and newsbooks and almanacs. The first daily newspaper to be published in Europe was the *Leipziger Zeitung* in 1660. During this period the term "newspaper" came into common use, denoting a publication carrying recent news and appearing regularly. The first English newspaper, the *London Gazette*, appeared in 1665, and the first daily in London in 1702, the *Daily Courant*. By the mid-eighteenth century there were five daily and five weekly papers in London. These were popular in the coffee houses that developed from the mid-seventeenth century. In both the seventeenth and eighteenth centuries, when few individuals could afford to buy a newspaper, locations such as coffee houses, public houses, and barbers' shops provided access to newspapers to an increasingly literate public. Greater access was also provided by English provincial newspapers, which increased in numbers from 24 in 1723 to about 50 in 1782.[2]

None of these publications had a wide circulation, and the significance and influence of the eighteenth-century press should not be exaggerated.[3] Nonetheless, the growth of newspaper publishing, particularly because of the perceived importance of newspapers as vehicles for radical political ideas, attracted official attention. Governments took steps to limit the press, lest it become a means of spreading radical or revolutionary sentiments that might undermine established authority. In England the Stamp Act of 1712 provided that a newspaper proprietor had to pay one penny per sheet printed and one shilling for every advertisement inserted. These rates increased during the period to 1836, although such measures did not stop the publication of radical ideas in the nineteenth century when an "unstamped press," defying the various duties, campaigned for suffrage reform, for example.[4]

In the American colonies newspaper expansion had been rapid. An early publication, in 1690, was *Publick Occurences*. It was short-lived, but soon after, in 1704, a *Boston News-Letter* was published weekly and distributed to subscribers through the postal service. Colonial newspapers developed during the eighteenth century, and the first daily, the *Pennsylvania Evening Post*, appeared in 1783. By the late eighteenth century other daily newspapers such as the *Pennsylvania Packet* and the Philadelphia *Daily Advertiser* were established. The burgeoning press was guaranteed freedom in the First Amendment to the US Constitution, ratified in 1791.

In the nineteenth century social and economic change created circumstances conducive to the growth of wider-circulation newspapers. Increasing industrialization and urbanization, technological innovation, and changes in transportation and in education all had an impact. In England, for example, the Education Act of 1870, and subsequent reforms that made elementary schooling compulsory and progressively raised the school leaving age, created a wider reading public. Opportunities to read increased with the invention of the kerosene lamp. The extension of the franchise led to a growing demand for information, and the growth of cities also tended to increase demand for information in urban areas. In the 1830s and 1840s passenger trains carried London newspapers to provincial English towns; by the 1870s special newspaper trains were operating, making possible more rapid circulation of metropolitan papers in the provinces.

In the American colonies, newspapers that earlier in the century had catered to the economic and political elites, covering matters such as shipping, business, and finance, began taking advertisements and expanding in size, but they had only low circulations. Technological and social changes in the 1830s and 1840s, including the emergence of a middle class and a skilled labor class, provided the context for low-priced, larger-circulation, popular newspapers with broader appeal than the political and mercantile papers. In New York the *Sun* (1833), the *Herald* (1835), the *Tribune* (1841), and *The Times* (1851) began publication, sold by street vendors for one or two cents. By about 1860 some of these papers had daily circulations of 50,000, with the New York *Herald* probably the largest, with a daily circulation of 77,000.[5]

The establishment of international news agencies in the 1830s–1850s – Havas in Paris, Reuter in London, Wolff in Berlin – extended news-gathering internationally and provided previously inaccessible content to newspapers. In America Associated Press was established, a confederation of local and regional news-gathering organizations that distributed a daily telegraphic news report to association members, making it possible even for smaller newspapers to afford access to reasonably comprehensive reports.

Companies such as the news agencies became increasingly important as mass circulation newspapers developed and public demand for news increased. They reflected trends toward big business and commercialization that in turn came to characterize the newspaper industry. News agencies also had an effect on journalism and reporting, placing greater emphasis on objectivity and "facts" rather than opinion, signaling a move away from the central role of opinion in many early newspapers, whose proprietors or editors saw them primarily as vehicles for the expression of their own views on contemporary issues.

Technological developments had an impact on nineteenth-century news-gathering. In 1844 Morse transmitted the first telegraph message, establishing a means of transmitting news quickly for reporters. In the 1850s the first transatlantic cable was laid, facilitating more rapid communication between Europe and North America, and from the 1870s telephone communications became possible. In the 1890s Guglielmo Marconi's experiments with wireless telegraphy and the transmission of radio signals laid the foundations for a worldwide radio telegraph network (see Chapter 4).

Other technological changes influenced newspaper production, with advances in papermaking techniques and in printing being particularly important. Previously paper had been made mainly from rags; but from the 1850s a new process based on wood pulp was introduced, making mass production of paper simpler. Steam power was applied to the printing press, and the cylinder press was developed. The change from the pre-1850s flatbed printing press to the cylinder press meant that many more newspapers could be printed quickly. The typewriter also came into common use in newspaper offices after the 1860s, while the Linotype machine revolutionized typesetting with the use of keyboards and other typographical improvements in newspaper page composition.

Finally, the abolition of previous restrictions on the press had a considerable impact. In England the eighteenth-century imposition of duties had restricted newspaper circulation, keeping prices high enough to limit sales and acting as a disincentive to advertisers. In 1853 the advertisement duty was abolished, followed by the stamp duty in 1855 and the paper duty in 1861. (As noted above, freedom from such restrictions had been considered fundamental in America and the 1791 First Amendment to the Constitution had ensured freedom of the press.) The removal of duties in nineteenth-century England opened the way for considerable change. Cheap daily papers appeared in the provinces, initially costing twopence and soon only one penny. In London the *Daily Telegraph*, aimed at a mass readership, began publication in 1855, priced at a penny. Within five years its circulation was 141,000, and by 1890 it had daily sales of 300,000.[6]

Thus social and economic change had produced conditions conducive to the development of newspapers to satisfy larger literate audiences. Various technological developments made it possible for news stories to be transmitted more rapidly and for newspapers to be produced more easily and in greater numbers. Policy changes removed obstacles and disincentives to relatively cheap newspaper production. Finally, changes in economic organization were crucial to the emergence of a mass press in the late nineteenth century.

Changes in the Economic Organization of the Press

Two changes in economic organization, specific to the press industry, were crucial to the growth of newspapers that appealed to, and were accessible to, much broader audiences than the earlier publications. The first was the rise of advertising – which made it possible to sustain a cheap popular press; the second was the development of newspaper and magazine chains – which produced a different pattern of newspaper ownership, led to the emergence of "press barons" at the turn of the century, and made it possible to achieve "economies of scale." These newspaper owners were less interested in elite opinion and political leaders than in reaching larger groups in society, providing content that appealed to mass audiences, who in turn would attract advertisers whose expenditure would ensure the profitability of the publishing companies.

In America war provided an important stimulus to newspaper development: during the Civil War (1861–5) public hunger for news led to extensive war reporting, particularly by the northern press. Between the end of the Civil War and 1900, urbanization and rising literacy increased the demand for newspapers. Political instability also provided a context for editors such as Horace Greeley (New York *Tribune*) and Charles A. Dana (New York *Sun*) to engage in criticism of political parties. Major newspapers became big business, relying on advertising revenue and aiming for mass circulation. While New York had more newspapers than any other city, there were also flourishing newspapers, aimed at a mass readership, in Washington, Philadelphia, Boston, Chicago, and elsewhere. Also significant in nineteenth-century America was the growth of the black press, reflecting the growth of urban black communities. The ethnic press also grew, and by 1917 there were 1,323 newspapers in various languages, including German, Spanish, and Italian.[7]

In Britain national papers with mass appeal, such as the *People* (1881), the *Daily Mail* (1896), the *Daily Express* (1900), and the *Daily Mirror* (1903), were established, and dailies, weeklies, and Sunday papers became more numerous, many aiming at a large middle market. Whereas in 1850 the number of copies per capita sold to people over the age of 14 was six, by 1920 the figure was 182; and annual newspaper sales in Britain rose from 85 million in 1851 to 5,604 million in 1920.[8]

Most of these new ventures differed from previous newspaper publishing in the relative importance of commercial concerns. Earlier newspapers had been run mainly as small family businesses or by a proprietor who was also interested in writing as editor, often publishing opinions on a range of political or social issues, but generally not expecting to reach a very wide audience. In the late nineteenth century the popular press was commercialized, and newspapers became large businesses whose owners were essentially interested in making a profit.

While technological change enabled mass production of daily newspapers, increasingly this was possible only with large capital investment. Whereas it was possible to start a London daily in the 1850s with approximately £20,000 sterling, the capital required for the buildings, machinery, and so on for the *Daily Mail* in 1896 was approximately half a million pounds.[9] National newspapers became substantial enterprises with large staffs, requiring significant capital investment and with high ongoing operating costs.

Nonetheless, although establishment and production costs were rising, the cost of daily newspapers to the public fell. A key factor was the growth of advertising; this was central to the development of a cheap mass-circulation press. Advertising provided the revenue without which late-nineteenth-century newspapers, printed on a large scale, could not have continued. In Britain, for example, the rise in advertising began after the repeal of the advertisement duty in 1853. Increasingly, in an era of mass production and the development of surpluses of goods, it became important for manufacturers to bring their products to the attention of potential consumers. From the advertiser's point of view, it became more and more attractive to advertise in newspapers, as their circulation increased; the newspaper press provided an ideal means of promoting goods aimed at a popular market.

Advertisers were interested in reaching not only a wide audience but also an audience with sufficient spending power to be able to respond to advertisements by buying.

The rise of advertising agencies and the emergence of major national advertisers were important related developments. Relationships of dependence developed: of manufacturers on advertising agencies to prepare attractive material to be placed in newspapers; of advertisers on the newspaper press as a means of promoting products; of newspaper proprietors on advertisers for the finance that enabled them to run their large enterprises yet at the same time reduce the price of their newspapers to the public.

A second significant change was the development of chains of newspapers (and often magazines) owned by increasingly powerful owners. In the United States Joseph Pulitzer and William Randolph Hearst were dominant; in Britain Lord Northcliffe (and his brother Harold, later Lord Rothermere) developed an extensive newspaper "empire" comprising mass-circulation daily newspapers, Sunday papers, and magazines.

By the 1880s Pulitzer had acquired various newspapers, including the *New York World* (a forerunner of modern tabloids). Pulitzer's newspapers were dependent on advertising for revenue; they were low priced, with appealing layout, illustrations, and popular content designed to appeal to a mass audience. Hearst emerged as a competitor to Pulitzer in the 1890s. He had taken over the *San Francisco Examiner* from his father in 1887, in 1895 acquired the *New York Morning Journal*, and in the following year established the *Evening Journal*. Hearst went on to establish a national chain of newspapers and periodicals (inspiring Orson Welles's 1940s film *Citizen Kane*). Another important figure in American newspaper publishing was Adolph Ochs. He took over the *New York Times* in 1896 and over the next twenty years oversaw its growth as a leading newspaper.[10]

While Pulitzer and Hearst were consolidating their role as "press barons" in the United States, in Britain Alfred Harmsworth/Lord Northcliffe accomplished "the Northcliffe revolution." In the late nineteenth century he had developed a number of small magazines for specific audiences – including *Answers, Comic Cuts, Halfpenny Marvel, Boy's Friend, Bicycling News* – and by the mid-1890s his journals were enjoying a circulation of more than two million. In 1894 he moved into the larger arena with his acquisition of the London *Evening News*, a paper that included a women's column to broaden its market. In May 1896

Harmsworth began publication of the *Daily Mail*, a morning newspaper published in London and selling for a halfpenny.

The *Daily Mail*, "the first truly national newspaper,"[11] rapidly became popular with a mass audience, and sales exceeded those of other British newspapers. It attracted advertisers because of its mass clientele, and Harmsworth encouraged this by publicizing the scale and nature of his audience. He began to provide statistics on circulation and fixed advertising rates according to the number of readers. This provided advertisers with a degree of certainty about how widely their product would be promoted and contributed to a considerable rise in advertising expenditure – around £20 million annually in Britain by 1907.[12]

The success of the *Daily Mail* was due to Harmsworth's understanding of the interaction between circulation and advertising, linked with efficient production and distribution, plus the generally populist political outlook of the newspaper.[13] Harmsworth established overseas offices in New York and Paris, taking advantage of cable transmission to convey news rapidly; he made effective use of railway distribution, so that the morning paper was widely available throughout the United Kingdom; and by the late 1890s his printing operations had expanded to more rotary presses than any other newspaper (making possible economies of scale in newspaper printing). By 1899 the *Daily Mail* had a circulation of approximately one million, its sales having been boosted in particular by the public appetite for news during the Boer War. In 1905 three Northcliffe publications, the *Daily Mail*, the *Evening News*, and the *Weekly Dispatch*, were incorporated as Associated Newspapers Ltd, and shares in this public company sold rapidly.

Alfred Harmsworth and his brothers also invested in provincial papers and continued to publish magazines. In 1908 Lord Northcliffe (Alfred Harmsworth became Lord Northcliffe in 1904) fulfilled a long-held ambition when he acquired *The Times*, a newspaper that could trace its lineage back to the 1780s. *The Times* had dominated British newspapers in the mid-nineteenth century under the "astute commercial policy and editorial flair" of John Thadeus Delane. It acquired a reputation for objectivity and independence and was referred to as "the Thunderer" for its willingness to challenge politicians and policy. Still strongly identified with the governing classes and enjoying considerable prestige, *The Times* had, nonetheless, by the early twentieth century suffered from competition from cheaper newspapers and the expanding provincial press, and from a decline in political patronage.

As Ken Ward points out, when Northcliffe acquired the newspaper there was apprehension about "what he might do to a paper which was seen as a national institution;" but the fears were unjustified, and *The Times's* importance as a voice in public affairs only grew.[14]

By the early twentieth century Northcliffe's newspaper empire was an outstanding example of the concentration of ownership – the second main feature of the immense changes constituting "the Northcliffe revolution." By 1921, the year prior to his death, Lord Northcliffe controlled the *Daily Mail, The Times*, the *Weekly/Sunday Dispatch*, and the London *Evening News*. His brother Lord Rothermere controlled the *Daily Mirror*, the *Sunday Pictorial*, the *Daily Record*, the *Glasgow Evening News*, and the *Sunday Mail*. They jointly owned the magazine group, Amalgamated Press. Another brother, Sir Lester Harmsworth, had a chain of papers in south-west England. Together the Harmsworth brothers owned newspapers with an aggregate circulation of more than six million.[15]

Thus by the early years of the twentieth century newspaper publishing in the United States and Britain had become a major industry, paralleling more general developments in business and industry. The changes in the economic organization of the press underpinned the emergence of newspapers on a mass scale and as important components of economic systems because of their reliance on advertising. Moreover, ownership of important newspapers and magazines had been concentrated in the hands of a small number of "media barons." The power of the press seemed to be exemplified by proprietors such as Pulitzer, Hearst, and Northcliffe. Political leaders of the time attributed considerable influence to the popular press, and they took care to court media owners. The extent to which newspaper proprietors could exert influence on national leaders and policy became an important issue during the First World War (see below). Northcliffe's biographer claims that there can be "no doubt as to the influence of Northcliffe in the calculations and policy decision of the nation's leadership."[16]

Developments in Popular Journalism and Newspaper Mass Appeal

Newspaper formats that would remain substantially unchanged throughout the following century – the broadsheet and the tabloid – were well established by the end of the nineteenth century. Examples of broadsheets were *The Times* of London and the *New York Times*. Larger in format than the tabloids, they were noted for their authoritativeness, comprehensive news coverage, and emphasis on accuracy, which gave them the status of newspapers of record. The tabloids, the inexpensive, mass-appeal newspapers that developed rapidly in the final decades of the nineteenth century, were smaller in format, made greater use of photographs, and relied on a particular style of journalism to achieve mass circulation.

Magazines were also well established, having emerged in the early eighteenth century. In England examples included Daniel Defoe's *Review* (1709), Richard Steele's *Tatler* (1711), and Steele and Joseph Addison's *Spectator*, and, in America, Andrew Bradford's *American Magazine* (1741) and Benjamin Franklin's *General Magazine*. Early magazines were directed at the literate elite, carrying short stories and poems, essays on philosophy, religion, and natural science, and political and social commentary. In the nineteenth century magazines remained popular alongside the emergent mass press, offering affordable and varied content, and in some cases targeting more specialized markets (including women, with content on fashion, taste, manners, and household matters). In the United States magazine sales boomed in the second half of the century, titles including the *Saturday Evening Post*, *Harper's* and *Atlantic Monthly*, *Collier's*, *Cosmopolitan*, and *McClure's*. These publications were sold cheaply, they attracted large readerships, and they proved attractive to advertisers. They were to remain an important means of developing content for niche markets.

While the style and content of the popular newspaper press of the late nineteenth century did not represent a complete break with newspapers from earlier periods, several characteristics were important: new approaches to presentation and layout, changes in journalistic style, and shifting priorities in content. As indicated above, the relative importance of advertising was one of the key changes and was fundamental to the economic viability of a mass press. Changes in technology facilitated new styles of presentation – with developments in typography and in photogravure came the use of different typefaces, new layouts, greater use of illustrations, producing newspapers that were more appealing than earlier publications with their monotonous, single-column layout.

Different styles of journalism were a feature of late-nineteenth-century newspapers – although historians have pointed out the "new journalism" was not really new. However, the approach known as "new journalism" was important in ensuring that newspapers such as those owned by Pulitzer and Hearst in the United States and Northcliffe in Britain gained wide appeal. It was lighter in tone, used headlines and shorter paragraphs, was more sensationalist in style, gave greater coverage of "human-interest stories" (a term coined by Charles Dana, editor of the New York *Sun*),[17] and intentionally aimed at a broad, popular audience. During the final years of the century the reporting in Hearst's New York *Morning Journal* was described as "yellow journalism," an approach that thrived on sensationalism, emotive headlines, pictorial material, and campaigns for particular causes, all in the search for large audiences and maximizing profit from newspaper sales.

As far as content was concerned, the increase in the volume of advertising was crucial, but there were also other trends. The content of early newspapers had catered to dominant groups in society, covering trade and commerce, wars, religion, politics, literature. Such content did not disappear as a mass press developed, but relative importance changed. For example, party politics and use by politicians declined while news taken from the expanding news agencies gained ground (and came to feature more prominently on the front page of popular newspapers); reporting of sporting events (including horse racing, cricket, football, rugby, baseball) increased, particularly from about 1890. Some types of news were not new – police news/crime and scandal had been commonplace in Sunday papers earlier in the century – but they became relatively more important. During this period the importance of entertainment relative to news and information in newspapers increased.

However, the "serious role" of newspapers must not be forgotten: it was in the nineteenth century that the notion of the press as a "fourth estate" emerged, and, as the press was freed of individual and party political ties, this role as a check on government remained an important ideal. Furthermore, the press was important in relation to the development of public opinion (a term that emerged in the second half of the eighteenth century in various European countries), the emergence of a "public sphere," an arena in which debate on important issues takes place (as conceived by Habermas), and the evolution of political culture. Particularly during times of upheaval, newspapers contributed to changing political culture. Briggs and Burke cite the "explosion of new publications" during the first six months of the French Revolution in

1789 as a striking example. Newspapers, together with other forms of oral and visual communication, helped destroy old traditions and construct a "new community of citizens."[18] In Britain in the late nineteenth century the mass press was seen increasingly as reflecting public opinion and representing the people. Similarly, American newspapers performed "cultural work," with readers using journalism to engage in community and civic life.[19] At the beginning of the twentieth century the increasingly industrialized mass press had economic, social, political, and cultural importance. Perceptions of its role during war illustrated thinking of the time.

The Popular Press and War

The growth of widely circulating newspapers in the context of more literate and urbanized populations raised questions about the power of the press in relation to public opinion, especially at times of national emergency. In turn, the role of war correspondents became more important. The war correspondent has long been recognized in literature. Those who reported battles in classical and medieval times (for example, Xenophon, Caesar, Homer) are sometimes referred to as forerunners of the war reporters of modern times. The development of mass-circulation media was, of course, critical to any broader impact of reporting from battlefronts.

The period between about 1865 and the outbreak of the First World War in 1914 is sometimes referred to as a "golden age" for war correspondents because of the rise of the popular press, technological developments leading to use of the telegraph, the lack of censorship, and the popularity with popular-press readers of stories of wartime "adventures" abroad. One early war correspondent was William Howard Russell, who wrote for *The Times* in England during the Crimean War of 1854–6. In his reports he drew attention to British bungling, to the inadequacies of the British command, and the appalling conditions in which wounded British troops suffered. Russell's "revelations about the conduct of the war, backed up by the editorials written by Delane himself [John Thadeus Delane, editor at *The Times*], aroused public opinion to such an extent that it led to the fall of the Aberdeen government in 1855,"[20] showing how damaging press revelations could be, and how political/military and media interests could diverge significantly. After the Crimean War, governments tried, with varying degrees of success, to control newspapermen during war.

In other wars in the second half of the nineteenth century war reporters played roles of some significance. In the American Civil War they released information of value to the enemy. In various imperialistic wars and expeditions of the late nineteenth and early twentieth centuries war correspondents helped stimulate jingoistic and nationalistic sentiments. The Spanish–American War of the late 1890s provided an example of the manner in which mass-circulation newspapers, particularly the New York newspapers owned by Pulitzer and Hearst, could be used to influence opinion during war, encouraging nationalist and pro-war sentiments.

In 1897 these papers waged a campaign for the United States to go to war against Spain over Cuba, when Cuban nationalists staged a rebellion against Spain. For the New York press the Spanish–American War was a convenient one – it was not too close; it was relatively short (April–December 1898); it made limited demands on men and materials; and for the United States there were no defeats, no stalemates, and a relatively low casualty rate (385 dead and 1,662 wounded).

One of the main questions about the role of the newspapers in this conflict is whether their reporting did contribute substantially to American involvement. The traditional view is that powerful newspaper proprietors provoked American intervention by promoting national hysteria, and that this was an early example of media involvement in military matters. Hearst and Pulitzer certainly encouraged war; they stirred up xenophobia, publishing violently anti-Spanish stories (some apparently completely fabricated), and indulging in newspaper jingoism. Hearst is said to have sent the artist Frederick Remington to Havana to provide illustrations of the war. When Remington reported that everything was quiet and expressed a wish to return to New York, Hearst reportedly advised him: "Please remain. You furnish the pictures and I'll furnish the war."[21] The reporting by the New York papers also had a potentially widespread impact, as other regional newspapers took many stories from them.

The US Congress voted for war on April 19, 1898. However, the impact of the press should not be exaggerated, as other factors were important. The United States wanted to end Spanish and European colonialism on the American continent, and war was likely, regardless of the role of Hearst or Pulitzer.[22] The question about newspaper influence might be put in another way: were the Hearst and Pulitzer papers reflecting existing national extremism and pro-war sentiment, or were they leading and shaping public opinion? The relationship between mass media and public attitudes has been a continuing theme in histories of the mass media in the twentieth century. In general it seems safe to say that views expressed in newspapers are unlikely to strike a chord in readers unless there are pre-existing dispositions or attitudes favorable to their reception.

In the history of the mass-circulation press the Spanish–American War was significant for reasons additional to the proprietors' use of the medium to express bellicose and nationalist sentiments. The result of the sensationalist reporting was that circulations of New York papers increased dramatically to more than one million per day. The war also encouraged more extensive reporting of foreign affairs by the large American newspapers and wire services (although reporting costs were so high that proprietors failed to make a profit).[23] Through arousing interest in war reporting, the Spanish–American War set the scene for newspaper reporting of the First World War. Even before active American involvement in the First World War, by 1915 there were about 500 American correspondents in Europe, and many more joined them after the United States declared war against Germany in April 1917. The public thirst for news during wartime contributed to a growing demand for newspapers.

The popular press continued to thrive in the United States during and after the First World War. Hearst established an "empire" comparable to that of the Harmsworths in Britain. After the First World War he owned thirty-one newspapers, six magazines, and two wire services, as well as having interests in the film industry. In the early years of the twentieth century the American newspaper press as a whole was at a peak numerically. By 1910 there were 2,433 daily newspapers with an aggregate daily circulation of 24.2 million, and by 1918 some 2,600 dailies.[24]

Reporting of the Boer War (1899–1902) in the English press also illustrated the importance of mass media during war. New media technologies and growth of the mass press enabled reporting of this colonial war in a manner and on a scale not previously possible. The press helped create a climate of public opinion for war and was used for propagandist purposes. Stephen Badsey notes: "Another common theme which found its first expression in the Boer War was the military belief that recent changes to press behaviour, public sensibilities and media technology posed a new and dangerous threat to their ability to carry out military operations." However, he concludes cautiously:

> it is not necessary to overdraw parallels, nor to project back onto a previous age the obsessions of our own, to show beyond dispute that the role of the mass news media in the Boer War was, and was recognised at the time to be, of central importance to its conduct. The Boer War was a media war, just as much as it was a political war, or a soldier's war, or a people's war.[25]

Just over a decade later the media assumed greater significance during war, as entire populations became involved in "the Great War."

The Mass Press and Total War

The large-scale control and presentation of information became vital during the First World War, when civilians, as well as the military, were critical to the conduct of "total war." The manipulation of information was directed to two main ends: first, to maintain morale among the home-front population; and, second, to influence opinion in neutral and enemy countries. Censorship and propaganda were central in these efforts.

There is debate about the role of the mass press during the lead-up to war. One view is that the press created a climate of opinion favorable to war. Some of the British newspapers conducted campaigns that were anti-German, highly patriotic, and jingoistic. Some journalists encouraged militarism and promoted an unreasoning hatred of Germany, contributing to the highly charged pre-1914 international atmosphere. Northcliffe's *Daily Mail*, with its own foreign news service and wide coverage of international affairs, was anti-German and "scaremongering."[26] When Northcliffe acquired *The Times* in 1907, it is said that he left the newspaper a large degree of independence, promising no editorial interference, but with one proviso: the editor would have unrestricted control unless he should fail to warn the British people of the coming German peril. Northcliffe insisted "upon that duty being discharged."[27]

An opposing view is that the press was merely reflecting dominant views rather than leading public opinion. Moreover, even if one could prove the link between mass public opinion and the views expressed in the daily press, the relative significance of public opinion in the decision to go to war – compared with the decisions of politicians, diplomats, and military leaders – should not be exaggerated.

While the contemporary consensus is that the role of the media in the lead-up to the First World War should be assessed within the broader context of politics and foreign policymaking, it is worth noting that at the time many politicians and journalists shared an exaggerated belief in the abilities of the press to shape public opinion. As a result, the mass press did wield considerable influence: wartime magnified the power of journalists, and Lord Northcliffe was influential in his campaigns on censorship, recruitment, conscription, munitions supply, war strategy, air power, propaganda, and peace terms, among other things.[28]

During the First World War, "the national news and propaganda media, recognised as potent war weapons, indispensable for manipulating the truth so as to sustain Home Front morale and influence neutral opinion, were … rigorously harnessed."[29] In Britain legislation gave the government more powers to intervene in communication. A Press Bureau was set up to monitor telegrams and dispatches in 1914, to issue to newspapers the official war news supplied by the War Office and Admiralty, and to censor war news obtained independently by the newspapers. The Defence of the Realm Act gave the government powers to limit press freedom. As the war dragged on, as the need for fighting manpower increased, and, as conscription became an issue, civilian morale and active contributions to the war effort assumed greater importance. Here the popular press played a role in encouraging enlistment, carrying advertisements for munitions workers, encouraging food economy, and so on.

While the maintenance of morale at home was one important function of the press during wartime, propaganda was another. In Britain a War Propaganda Bureau was established in 1914 and placed under the general direction of the Foreign Office in 1916. While contemporary opinion considered propaganda in neutral countries to be vital to the war effort, historians debate just how much it achieved. Some say that British propaganda in the United States during the early years of the war and until US entry in 1917 stimulated sympathy for the Allied cause and broke down American isolationism. Others question its impact: appeals to informed American opinion may have reinforced pro-British sentiment, but Ward maintains that the key factor was the cutting of the telegraphic cable between Germany and the United States in August 1914.[30] This meant that war news from Europe was routed through London to the United States and was subject to censorship under the Defence of the Realm Act regulations. Thus the United States received its European war news with a British slant.

In relation to this debate, it is evident that a decision to go to war is always based on many factors in a complex situation, and that any explanation that relies solely on a single reason, such as the impact of propaganda, is likely to be too simple. The United States went to war for various reasons, including unwillingness to see Britain replaced by Germany as a major power, the impact of German submarine warfare on US interests, and the evolution of opinion concerning American involvement, not simply because of British propaganda.

Nonetheless, at the time propaganda continued to be considered important. In Britain a new Department of State, responsible directly to Prime Minister Lloyd George, was established in London to deal with propaganda in early 1917. In the following year Lord Beaverbrook, the owner of the *Daily Express* from 1917, was appointed Minister of Information. Thus a "press baron" was given an important wartime portfolio, with responsibility for propaganda at home and in the United States, France, and other neutral countries.

As well as propaganda directed at neutrals, propaganda directed at the enemy began to be organized more methodically when Lord Northcliffe was appointed Director of Propaganda in Enemy Countries in 1918. (His brother Lord Rothermere served as Secretary of State for the Air during the war.) Northcliffe, too, enjoyed direct access to the Prime Minister. He initiated a stream of propaganda, engaging in psychological warfare by leaflet. By October 1918 Britain was dropping 167,000 leaflets per day over enemy lines to spread Allied propaganda and to raise hopes among German troops of a just peace for a democratized Germany. The importance attributed at the time to such psychological warfare can be gauged by a comment in the German press in 1918: "Had we shown the same activity in our propaganda, perhaps many things would have been different now. But in this, we regret to say, we were absolutely unprepared."[31] Thus the expertise of press magnates – Lords Northcliffe, Rothermere, and Beaverbrook – and of the popular press in Britain was harnessed to the government's wartime propaganda efforts. Lloyd George appears to have had considerable faith in the power of "press barons" to stimulate and maintain popular support for the war effort. Nonetheless, recent research that integrates work on the "high politics" of British grand strategy and on the "low culture" of the role of propaganda and media has highlighted failures such as the "propaganda neglect of the Western Front" in 1918 when the great victory of the British Army was undervalued and "never properly told" in the British press.[32]

In the United States too steps were taken to influence public opinion in support of the war effort. A Committee of Public Information was set up within a week of the declaration of war in 1917 to "sell the war to the American people." This was accompanied by censorship and other measures, including the Espionage Act (June 1917), the Trading with the Enemy Act (October 1917), and the Sedition Act (May 1918). One result was that Hollywood films on the American Revolution were banned because they portrayed Britain in a bad light, an undesirable message about an ally in the First World War. The cumulative impact of such measures was considerably to restrict the freedom of US media during wartime.

In summary, during total war, when psychological warfare supplemented active military engagement, the mass press was seen as an ideal vehicle for stimulating nationalist sentiment, maintaining home-front morale, attempting to win over neutrals, and spreading disenchantment among enemy soldiers. It is worth noting that journalists were largely in sympathy with government policy during the war, and there was little conflict between the mass circulation newspapers and political and military intentions: "controls were largely unnecessary, since the overwhelming patriotism and sense of duty among the media in the field resulted in total commitment to the government's war aims." More negatively, the part played by the media in total war has been described as the "beginnings of a great conspiracy," with media conscripted to the purposes of the state, and news treated as a strategic commodity.[33] Although film was not yet widely available, the First World War also saw the beginnings of its use for patriotic and propagandist purposes. In Britain *The Battle of the Somme* was shown to mass audiences, contributing to patriotic sentiment concerning the losses in the battle of 1916. In subsequent conflicts other media – radio, film, television – would be used for similar purposes.

Concentration and Competition

In the early twentieth century "the familiar modern newspaper industry structure with mass circulation tabloids and broadsheets, populars and qualities and with chain ownership was established."[34] During the two decades after the First World War there were minor rather than major changes in the mass press: first, although there was a growth in circulation, there was a contraction in the number of national dailies in both Britain and the United States; second, the trend toward concentration of ownership continued, with the interwar years described as the "era of the press barons;"[35] and, third, the commercial nature of the newspaper enterprise was confirmed, with growing dependence on a substantial proportion of revenue coming from advertising. During this period newspapers, the oldest of the mass media, began to face competition from other emerging popular media, radio broadcasting and the film industry.

The growth in newspaper circulation can be illustrated from British statistics: in 1918 the total circulation of national dailies was 3.1 million; by 1926 this had risen to 4.7 million, and by 1939 to 10.6 million. National dailies such as the *Mail*, the *Express*, and the *Daily Herald* engaged in "circulation wars," using gimmicks and the services of door-to-door salesmen to increase circulation. However, during the same period the number of newspaper titles declined, with thirty daily and Sunday newspapers in Britain ceasing publication between 1921 and 1937.[36]

Similarly in the United States, which experienced considerable population growth and urbanization between 1910 and 1930, daily newspaper circulation increased from 22.4 million copies a day in 1910 to 39.6 million copies in 1930, with Sunday newspaper circulation more than doubling in the same period. Yet there too there was a net loss of 258 daily newspapers over those twenty years.[37]

Concentration of ownership came to dominate the national publishing scene. In Britain Northcliffe's death in 1922 was followed by various changes in ownership. For the remainder of that decade and into the 1930s five main companies controlled newspaper production – Associated Press, Amalgamated Press, Westminster Press, the Beaverbrook and Cadbury groups. A major factor in the concentration of ownership was the cost of establishing and maintaining newspapers as large-scale industrial concerns.

What the Northcliffe revolution had begun in relation to advertising was consolidated during this period, with the press dependent on advertising revenue for a substantial proportion of income, supplemented by large circulations based on low prices. In the United States total newspaper advertising revenue tripled in the period 1915–29 from approximately $275 million to $800 million.[38] This predominantly commercial aspect of newspaper enterprises had an impact on the nature of much of the popular press, with entertainment values dominating over news and information.

Tabloids, of which early examples had been published by Hearst and Northcliffe at the end of the nineteenth century, came to enjoy great popularity in the 1920s and 1930s, finding expanding audiences among the less well educated. In New York in the 1920s, for example, three new tabloids, the *New York Daily News*, the *Daily Mirror*, and the *Daily Graphic*, circulated to more than 1.5 million readers without making any significant impact on existing daily newspaper circulation statistics. These small-format newspapers relied on sensationalist journalism (the "jazz journalism" of the 1920s) and "gossip, sin, and scandal." Their use of photographs to enhance their appeal did much to encourage photojournalism in the 1920s.[39] The bleaker environment of the Depression decade saw a decline in popularity of the tabloids. Nonetheless, this newspaper format was to retain varying degrees of popularity throughout the twentieth and into the twenty-first century.

Finally, during this period newspapers faced competition from radio broadcasting and from the emerging film industry as media of information and entertainment. In particular the press had to compete with commercial radio for advertising revenue. Subsequent media history would demonstrate that there was scope for diverse mass media to emerge and flourish, without extinguishing earlier forms; but there was concern in the 1920s about the likely impact of competition on the newspaper press, and in the 1930s newspapers tended to be overshadowed by radio, which was by then enjoying its "golden age."

By the beginning of the twentieth century, therefore, the main characteristics of the modern press had been established. Development over several decades of cheap, mass-circulating, advertising-supported newspapers, many in chains owned by a single proprietor, and the experience of newspaper reporting in the lead-up to, and during, war, had also raised fundamental questions about the role and influence of media in modern societies. These included the relationship between media and public opinion, the power of media to influence policy-making, the links between the press and commercial concerns, the importance of print media in cultural life, and the role of media owners whose power was seen to derive from a concentration of ownership of many media outlets. These have remained important considerations in the history of mass media.

3

The Development of the Film Industry

The economic and social transformations that underlay the development of the mass press in the late nineteenth century also formed the context for the emergence of film as a mass medium. Significantly, mass-circulation newspapers and cinema began at the same time; the 1890s, the decade of "yellow journalism" in New York and the publication of the first mass-circulation daily newspaper in Britain, saw the first commercial screenings of motion pictures in a number of countries. Both film and the mass press catered to the need for cheap entertainment for the vast audiences created by urbanization. But, while the reach of newspapers was confined to city, region, or nation, film crossed cultural and national boundaries and created the basis for a global mass culture with the United States at its center. "Far more people today are reached by the moving picture than by the daily press," a reporter observed in 1908, "and while we read the newspaper only in parts, the moving picture we see complete."[1] Firmly established by 1914 as the most popular medium of mass entertainment, it remained so until the late 1940s. From the outset, and continuing to the present day, film was controversial; and anxieties about its social and political influence frequently led to attempts to exert political control over the medium.

This chapter examines film's emergence as the main form of mass entertainment. The economics and organization of the US film industry before the 1950s, and the international ascendancy of that industry, are considered. The chapter also examines the efforts of politicians and middle-class reformers to censor and control film content, and the effects of these campaigns. Finally, the question of the ideological influence of American movies is discussed.

Origins and Early Development

Film emerged in the 1890s as the culmination of experiments and inventions that took place through the nineteenth century in the United States, France, Germany, and Britain. Techniques of projecting moving images had existed as early as the seventeenth century in such forms as popular "magic-lantern" shows, involving the use of a candle or lamp, lens, and glass slides with pictures to simulate movement. The crucial new development was the projection of photographed moving images. Advances in the application of electricity, the development of photography and celluloid film, and the invention of the motion picture camera and new techniques of projection laid the foundation for the technology of film. The American inventor and entrepreneur Thomas Edison exploited some of these innovations when between 1891 and 1894 he and his assistants invented the "kinetoscope," a "peepshow" machine that ran a 50-foot loop of film past a light source, to be viewed in a piano-sized box in penny arcades. The next step, the projection of motion pictures to be seen by large audiences rather than one person at a time, was the work of a number of inventors. The brothers Auguste and Louis Lumière developed a combined camera and projector, the *cinématographe*, which they used for the first presentation of a motion picture for the general public on December 28, 1895 at the Grand Café on the Boulevard des Capucines in Paris. The *cinématographe* was a commercial success internationally. Within weeks the Lumières had taken their machinery to Britain, other parts of Europe, and the United States. Within a year the *cinématographe* had been used for public motion picture screenings in Egypt, India, Japan, and Australia.[2] Meanwhile film projectors were developed by Max and Emil Skladanowsky in Germany, Birt Acres in Britain, and Charles Francis Jenkins and Thomas Armat in the United States. Armat's invention, the vitascope, was used by Edison for the first public screening of a motion picture in the United States at Koster and Bial's Music Hall in New York on April 23, 1896.

Development of the technology of moving pictures occurred despite the absence of clear and generally accepted ideas on the purpose for which these inventions might be used. That film became above all a form of popular entertainment was the work not of scientists or inventors but of small entrepreneurs who saw its profit-making potential. Often these were disreputable characters with backgrounds in vaudeville theater, music halls, or fairs; and it was in these settings that film screenings usually took place. For ten years after 1895 films were rarely more than a minute in length; the idea of building a whole evening's entertainment around the new medium was scarcely feasible. Instead, films were normally screened during intervals on vaudeville or music-hall programs, as sideshows at fairgrounds, or as features in travelling shows. The appeal of these early films lay mainly in the novelty of moving images. Their content was simple, consisting of actual footage or re-enactment of scenes relating to public events – including Kaiser Wilhelm reviewing his troops, President McKinley taking the oath of office, troops marching off to war, or scenes from everyday life – typically trains arriving at stations, trains going into tunnels, and men playing cards. In many cases the early filmmakers used subjects that drew directly on the entertainment tradition of the fairground and vaudeville, especially boxing matches, slapstick comedy, cockfights, and belly dancing.

Throughout the world, film was mainly an urban phenomenon, and audiences were drawn overwhelmingly from the urban working class. Film provided these people with an affordable and easily understood escape from the reality of their harsh lives. Even language was no barrier to enjoyment during the era of silent film, an observation that has particular significance for the rise of cinema in the United States. Between 1890 and 1914 eighteen million immigrants entered the United States, most of them from southern and Eastern Europe. In the formative years of the film industry, therefore, the American working class was an ethnically diverse, predominantly immigrant community, the members of which often had little grasp of English. The role of film in presenting American myths and customs to immigrant audiences demonstrated the new medium's potential as a force for cultural integration.

Between 1905 and the First World War film rose above its downmarket origins and established itself as a respectable form of mass entertainment, extending its appeal to middle-class audiences. This development, which would be consolidated in the 1920s, was made possible by major innovations in film production and exhibition. The first step was the simultaneous development in a number of countries of film as a medium for telling stories. Between 1896 and 1906 a French magician, Georges Méliès, made over 500 narrative films that were innovative in their use of professional actors, trick photography, animation, and detailed storylines. His pioneering work pointed to the potential of narrative film and provided a foundation for other filmmakers. In the United States Edwin S. Porter's *The Great Train Robbery* (1903) moved beyond the constraints of Méliès' fixed-camera approach, employing realistic plots, tight editing, and shots from different locations. Similar techniques were used in Britain in Cecil Hepworth's seven-minute film *Rescued by Rover* (1905). These filmmakers established film's claim to be an art form in its own right rather than a mere extension of vaudeville, the fairground, or the theater. From the mid-1900s until the late-1910s the one-reel film of about ten to fifteen minutes' duration was the staple of cinema.

Important changes in exhibition accompanied the increasing sophistication of film production. In the middle of the first decade of the century the first permanent movie theaters were established; they quickly replaced the primitive means of screening films that had prevailed since the 1890s. In the United States a proliferation of cinemas began in June 1905 when a Pittsburgh vaudeville magnate, Harry Davis, converted a store for the purpose of continuous daily film screenings and, charging a nickel for admission, called it a "nickelodeon."[3] By 1910 there were 10,000 moving-picture theaters throughout the United States, and twenty-six million people in a population of ninety-two million attended the movies each week. In Western Europe, too, the conversion of stores into cinemas proceeded at a rapid rate. In Germany there were 2,446 theaters by 1914; in Britain there were nearly 4,000 with a weekly attendance of between seven and eight million. Worldwide, there are estimated to have been 60,000 theaters by 1913.[4] Meanwhile, modern methods of distribution were introduced, replacing the system by which exhibitors bought films directly from producers. Now the producers sold or leased prints to distributors, who in turn rented them to exhibitors, allowing a rapid turnover in cinema programs.

The trend toward permanent theaters for film exhibition arose from pressures from two opposite parts of the social order.[5] For the working class, including the immigrant population in the United States, cinema attendance for as little as 5 cents offered a more affordable form of entertainment than a music hall or vaudeville theater. In 1907 a writer in the *Saturday Evening Post* observed of nickelodeons that "in cosmopolitan city districts the foreigners attend in larger proportions than the English speakers," with "the Latin races" particularly prominent.[6] At the same time the movement toward permanent cinemas was an essential step in the effort to gain the new medium respectability and attract middle-class audiences. Film could be freed, to a large extent, of its early association with disreputable forms of entertainment, and film screenings could take place in better neighborhoods, away from the world of the fairground, vaudeville, and the music hall. The next step, from around 1908, was an attempt to increase film's middle-class appeal by building more comfortable and sumptuous theaters, some equipped with full orchestras. The trend would culminate in the construction of ornate, luxurious "picture palaces" in the 1920s.[7]

Coinciding with these changes in exhibition and distribution, developments in filmmaking confirmed film's status as both a unique artistic form and a highly successful commercial product that could attract middle-class as well as lower-class audiences. A more sophisticated approach to narrative film paved the way. The great American director D. W. Griffith worked within the limitations of the one-reel film to bring together a number of advances in narrative technique pioneered by other American and European directors. Rapid cutting from one location to another, flashbacks, close-ups of characters' faces, fade-ins and fade-outs, shooting on location, and a more natural acting style were all part of this new "language" of film. From 1908 Griffith directed over 400 films for the Biograph company. His resignation from Biograph in 1913, in protest at the company's refusal to allow him to make longer films, was symptomatic of the growing desire of filmmakers, supported by public demand, to move beyond the one-reel format.

Two- and three-reelers, and eventually feature-length films, became increasingly common. The world's first feature film, *The Story of the Kelly Gang*, of more than an hour in length, had been made by the Australian director Charles Tait in 1906. More influential internationally were a one-hour French film, *Queen Elizabeth* (1912), starring the famous actress Sarah Bernhardt, and three Italian epics, Mario Caserini's *The Last Days of Pompeii* (1913), Enrico Guazzoni's *Quo Vadis?* (1913), and Giovanni Partrone's *Cabiria* (1914). Inspired by the success of these European features, Griffith set out to make his own epic. *Birth of a Nation* (1915), Griffith's best-known film, is the story of a southern family during the Civil War and Reconstruction periods. The film is informed by stereotypes that reflect Griffith's own southern background: it presents Ku Klux Klansmen as heroes, blacks as brutes, their white allies from the north as corrupt and rapacious. A controversial film because of its racial and political assumptions, it was also a great commercial success. Nearly three hours long, it featured on a large scale those narrative techniques that Griffith had developed in his years at Biograph. More than anyone else, as Robert Sklar has written, Griffith made these techniques "the norms of filmmaking practice and spectator expectation."[8]

By 1920 other principles of the film industry had also been established. Audiences had come to expect films to be organized into separate *genres* – categories or styles of film – such as comedy, melodrama, and Western. Public interest in the films themselves came to be closely associated with fascination with the lives of film stars. The star system, initiated in the United States, was carefully manufactured by film proprietors as a means of promoting their films. The stars "acted as known quantities; like brand names they guaranteed the quality of the product."[9] By as early as 1915, film stars – Mary Pickford, Douglas Fairbanks, Charlie Chaplin, Theda Bara, and William S. Hart were the most prominent – were not simply actors but public personalities. Both the stars and their films were supported by mass publicity. Meanwhile, major organizational changes had begun in the American industry that had far-reaching implications for the development of cinema internationally.

The Hollywood Studio System

In the United States the important developments in production and exhibition of the decade from 1908 coincided with intense competition in the film industry. As the profit-making potential of the medium became clear, many new production companies were established. An early attempt to create a monopoly over the industry was made in 1908 when Edison formed the Motion Picture Patents Company (MPPC) to pool patents on cameras, projectors, and celluloid film, aiming to control film production, distribution, and exhibition. The MPPC waged war against independent producers and foreign imports, but by 1915, when a federal court ordered its dissolution for violation of anti-trust laws, the company was already a spent force.

Yet the MPPC's defeat did not assure the triumph of market forces. The same pressures towards consolidation and concentration that were evident throughout the American economy, including the newspaper industry, proved irresistible. Large amounts of capital were required to exploit the new technologies. The introduction of the expensive technology of sound to American movies between 1927 and 1930 accentuated that requirement. Enormous advantages were to be gained from economies of scale and the elimination of competition. There was an inescapable logic in concentrating film production, distribution, and exhibition in the same hands: production companies wanted to guarantee distribution and exhibition of the films they made, while exhibitors needed a guaranteed supply of good films to screen.

By 1920 the more successful of the independents had laid the foundation for domination of the film industry through a cartel far more successful than the MPPC. Almost all the men who created these companies were Jews of Eastern European or German origins: Carl Laemmle, Adolph Zukor, Jesse Lasky, Samuel Goldwyn, Marcus Loew, Louis B. Mayer, William Fox, the Warner brothers (Harry, Albert, Jack, and Samuel). Most of them began their careers in film as small cinema owners, when the industry was shunned by Anglo-Americans, and they developed a keen appreciation of audience tastes.[10] These men established the principles of the "Hollywood studio system." Oligopoly (control of the market by a small number of firms) and vertical integration (the undertaking by a single firm of all stages in the process of production, distribution, and retail) were central to the success of this system. Consolidated by 1930, it prevailed through the golden age of Hollywood in the 1930s and 1940s.

The shift of film production from the east coast to southern California was part of this development. By the early 1920s most production activity was centered in or around Hollywood, on the outskirts of Los Angeles. The area offered a number of attractions: a sunny climate for outside filming, space for expansion, geographical variety – especially useful for filming Westerns – and a large pool of non-unionized labor. Yet the term "Hollywood studio" is misleading. The "studios" were in fact large corporations, with headquarters not in Hollywood but in New York. Company executives in New York decided annually on the number of films to be made and the budget for each. Moreover, these organizations depended heavily on financial support from Wall Street banks, a dependence that was increased by the large costs of converting to sound after Warner Bros. produced the first "talkie," *The Jazz Singer*, in 1927, and by additional financial pressures created by the Great Depression from 1929.

Film production was only one part of the major companies' activities; distribution and exhibition were also of central importance to the success of the eight corporations that dominated the industry in this period. The five largest, the "Big Five," were fully integrated, involved in film production, distribution, and exhibition: Paramount Pictures, 20th Century Fox, Warner Bros., Loew's Inc. (parent company of the production subsidiary Metro-Goldwyn-Mayer), and Radio-Keith-Orpheum (RKO). Of the others, the "Little Three," Universal and Columbia were involved in production and distribution, while United Artists, formed in 1919 by Mary Pickford, Douglas Fairbanks, Charlie Chaplin, and D. W. Griffith, played the unique role of providing a distribution network for independent producers. These eight companies accounted for the production of about three-quarters of all feature films made in the United States during the 1930s and 1940s.[11] Through collusion, these firms minimized the risk of significant competition entering the industry.

The Big Five's control of exhibition was of particular importance. Ownership of 2,600 first-run theaters in the main cities accounted for 94 percent of investment by these companies during the studio era, production a mere 5 percent.[12] Although these theaters comprised only 16 percent of the total in the United States, they consistently took in three-quarters of box-office revenues.[13] For purposes of exhibition the Big Five divided the country into spheres of influence: Paramount dominated first-run theater ownership in the South, New England and the upper Midwest, 20th Century Fox controlled the far west, RKO and Loew's shared New York, New Jersey, and Ohio, and Warner Bros. controlled the mid-Atlantic states. Of the 100 feature films screened in first-run theaters each year, a Big Five company would screen forty to sixty of its own films in the cinemas it owned and make up the rest with the best films from the other four companies. Independent exhibitors depended on the cooperation of the major firms. Through their employment on long-term contract of the biggest stars and the best producers, directors, and writers, the majors provided the films that most Americans wanted to see. Control of the first-run theaters also gave them crucial leverage: independent exhibitors were reluctant to rent films that had not had a first run, with the free advance publicity that this involved. The system of "block-booking," by which independents were obliged to rent packages of films, including the worst as well as the successful, assured the major companies of a return on every film made. Similarly, independent producers depended on the majors' willingness to distribute and exhibit their films.

Douglas Gomery, the leading economic historian of American film, has placed the film industry in the context of developments in the broader American economy. Approaches to film exhibition employed by the Big Five were derived from retailing techniques developed by the leading chain stores of the period. Large chains of theaters, with centralized management, accounting, and advertising, could spread fixed costs over a large number of operations, ensuring economies of scale. The Big Five adapted these techniques to the changing economic circumstances of the interwar period. The ornate picture palaces built during the 1920s – theaters in which film screenings were accompanied by lavish stage-show presentations – gave way, with the onset of the Depression, to simpler theaters. To reduce costs further, the major firms employed fewer ushers and introduced double features as an enticement to the public. The sale of in-house refreshments, especially popcorn and soft drinks, became a significant source of revenue from the 1930s. By the 1940s the double-bill program, with an intermission for the sale of food and drink, was the norm in American movie exhibition. Along with the successful exploitation of sound technology, adaptation of the Big Five's exhibition practices to new economic circumstances assisted the American industry to survive the Depression.[14]

The International Dominance of American Film

The full measure of the success of the major American firms is that their domination of film markets extended well beyond the borders of the United States. Year after year in the interwar period, US firms produced 75–85 percent of all films shown in the world. This international phenomenon, which began in the mid-1910s, continued to have a profound effect on international cinema and mass culture for the remainder of the century. So pervasive was American influence on filmmaking styles and on public expectations of feature films that the very terms "Hollywood" and "the movies" came to be synonymous globally.[15]

American ascendancy in world cinema was established at such an early stage that it is easy to overlook the fact that it did not always exist. Before the First World War, France dominated international film markets. In 1908 one French company, Pathé, sold twice as many films in the United States as all American production companies put together. By 1910 up to 70 percent of all films exported worldwide were produced in France.[16] Historians have identified a number of reasons for the success of the major American companies in overtaking the French lead in a very short period and in establishing a long-term domination of world film. The most immediate reason can be found in the effects of the First World War. From the outbreak of war in August 1914 European film production was severely reduced, as personnel and resources were diverted to the war effort. With the United States remaining neutral until April 1917, American film exporters took full advantage of the war by moving into markets in South America, Australia, and Europe itself – markets previously dominated by French and Italian companies. The American majors capitalized on this advantage by opening offices in each of the main foreign markets, instead of selling through agents in London as they had done before. An effective global distribution network was established that would serve American film exporters well after the war's end in 1918.[17]

The effects of the First World War and the implementation of global distribution procedures account for the American industry's international expansion from 1915 but not for its long-term ascendancy. In themselves these factors formed no insurmountable obstacle to a postwar European recovery and challenge to US hegemony. The American companies' dominant position stemmed from important advantages over the film industries of other countries. The most fundamental was the large American domestic market. Unlike their foreign competitors, the US majors were assured of a profit from domestic exhibition. They could afford the high levels of investment necessary to make feature films of the highest quality. In smaller national markets, investment in film production was more fraught with risk.

Superior production values, made possible by lavish expenditure, largely account for the universal appeal of American film. Also, the complexity of American society, with its ethnic, religious, and regional diversity, prepared Hollywood filmmakers to cater for a wide range of audiences. The ability of American movies to cross ethnic and class lines was a great advantage in world film markets. Moreover, the American studios' international ascendancy was self-reinforcing: starting in the 1920s, some of the most talented foreign film professionals, including art directors and cinematographers as well as actors and directors, were drawn to Hollywood. The wave of foreign talent that helped make Hollywood not only the center of American film production but the capital of international filmmaking included Greta Garbo, Marlene Dietrich, Pola Negri, Sonja Henie, Maurice Chevalier, Charles Boyer,

Errol Flynn, Basil Rathbone, Charles Laughton, Laurence Olivier, Vivien Leigh, Olivia De Havilland, David Niven, Leslie Howard, Erich von Stroheim, Joseph von Sternberg, Fritz Lang, Ernst Lubitsch, Billy Wilder, and Alfred Hitchcock. Year after year a wide range of American films – Westerns, gangster movies, comedies, melodramas, mysteries, historical dramas, horror films, adaptations of literary classics, and, with the advent of sound, musicals – proved enormously popular throughout the world, as did the stars who featured in them.

By contrast, the productions of other film industries usually enjoyed a narrower appeal. Constrained by limited budgets and characterized by inferior production values, they often dealt with pessimistic themes that undermined their popularity even with home audiences. The British documentary-maker John Grierson identified the problem when he observed in 1928 that American films were optimistic in outlook and characterized by a "spirit of bubbling vigour and unchastened self-confidence," while British films were marked by a pessimism and "drabness" that "do not serve them well in the larger cinema market."[18] Even in the 1930s, when far more British films were made than in the previous decade, "English picture-goers, when asked, almost invariably said they preferred American films to British," giving reasons that included American films' energy, the glamour of Hollywood stars, the naturalness of the actors, and the films' celebration of competitive individualism and democracy.[19]

Any prospect of European film industries challenging the postwar American domination of international film markets hinged on their capacity to offset the American majors' domestic advantage with exports to the United States. This had been the basis of the prewar success of French and Italian firms: by 1908 over three-quarters of leading European film producers' profits came from the American market.[20] A return to such access after 1918 proved impossible. The same oligopoly that, through its control of distribution and exhibition, placed huge obstacles in the path of independent American production companies also ensured that few foreign films were imported. In the 1920s, with the crucial American market denied them, a group of German, French, and Swedish companies planned "Film Europe," a cartel intended to break down national barriers to film distribution through Europe. By treating Europe as one market, it was hoped to offset the advantage enjoyed by the American majors through control of their large domestic market. An ambitious proposal in any circumstances, Film Europe was effectively killed by the coming of sound. Language barriers that could be ignored while films remained silent now created an insurmountable obstacle to hopes for a European equivalent of the American film market.

The American film industry's international dominance aroused widespread concern and resentment in many countries, not only from film industries threatened by American competition but from others who worried about the content and influence of Hollywood films. Concerns were frequently expressed about Hollywood's promotion of violence and immorality, the vulgarity of its films, their emphasis on the importance of wealth and glamour, their subversive effect on established social relations, the unflattering depiction of particular national and racial groups, "product placement" (the use of movies to advertise American consumer products, especially cars, furniture, and clothes), and the "foreignness" of American movies – a concern typified by a 1921 London *Times* editorial which complained that American films show actors "of a decidedly Dago cast of countenance" in "purely foreign or cosmopolitan" situations.[21] These anxieties were often subsumed under a more general fear of "Americanization." An English writer, Arthur Weigall, lamented as early as 1921 that the world "is being trained to see life as it is seen by a certain group of kinema producers and writers congregated in a corner of the United States. The world is being Americanised by the photoplay ..."[22] In 1927 an article in the London *Daily Express* expressed similar fears and could well have spoken for many newspaper editors and politicians throughout the world: "the bulk of picturegoers are Americanized to an extent that makes them regard a British film as a foreign film ... They talk America, think America, and dream America. We have several million people, mostly women, who, to all intent and purpose, are temporary American citizens."[23]

The American industry's business interests required it to portray its products abroad as non-ideological, to downplay their American features, and to portray them as an entertainment medium emphasizing universal themes. Throughout the interwar period, the eight majors obtained an average of 35 percent of their gross revenue from foreign trade.[24] They saw it as vital to cultivate export markets; and they sought to assuage foreign anxieties about Hollywood movies. The formation of the Motion Picture Producers and Distributors of America (MPPDA) in 1922, to protect the common interests of the eight majors, was prompted partly by an action of the Mexican government. In that year Mexico banned the import of films from American companies deemed guilty of making Westerns that featured Mexican villains, invariably depicted as violent, treacherous, and temperamental "greasers."[25] Since the whole industry stood to suffer in such cases, the MPPDA during the 1920s developed procedures for overseeing movie content, negotiating with studios to eliminate material likely to give offense to foreign audiences. Particular attention was given to the sensitivities of crucial markets.[26]

By the mid-1920s, therefore, German heroes started to appear in Hollywood films, while Russian villains replaced the sinister "Huns" who had flourished in 1918, a reflection of the relative importance of Germany and the Soviet Union as sources of foreign revenue for the American industry.[27] The same sensitivity continued even after the Nazi Party had gained power in 1933. Despite the Nazi regime's increasingly brutal and systematic persecution of German Jews, and despite its restrictions on American film imports (the number of Hollywood films allowed into Germany declined to a mere 30 in 1936 from a peak of 205 in 1928 and 59 in 1932),[28] Hollywood movies before the Second World War refrained from any hint of sympathy for Jews or criticisms of Hitler's Germany. MGM, Paramount, and Fox kept their Berlin offices open as late as 1938 or 1939. In mid-1939 MGM head Arthur Loew rebuked actress Myrna Loy for her public criticism of Hitler's treatment of the Jews. The commercial importance of the German market largely accounts for this policy, though concern by the studio heads to downplay their own Jewish background and therefore avoid provoking American anti-Semitism, and anti-Semitic influence in the industry's Production Code Administration (see below), may also have been important.[29]

During the 1920s European governments attempted to protect their film industries from American competition by imposing quotas on film imports. These measures had only limited success. To a large extent American firms were able to circumvent protectionist legislation by the production of "quota quickies" – inferior films made for the sole purpose of meeting quota requirements – through US production subsidiaries abroad. Moreover, such legislation was often built upon shaky political foundations, for exhibitors and the movie-going public tended not to share the producers' opposition to American imports. The fate of a French quota of 1929 highlighted this weakness. In response to a proposal to reduce the ratio of imported to domestically produced films to three to one, the American majors imposed a total boycott on the French market. After six months the French backed down, and an older ratio of seven to one was restored.[30]

With the limitations of protectionist legislation apparent by the end of the 1920s, the introduction of sound to film from 1927 nonetheless raised foreign hopes of ending American hegemony. European companies centering on the German consortium Tobis-Klangfilm used patents over sound systems to delay the entry of American "talkies" into European markets. While language posed no barrier to the American industry's international expansion during the silent era, the introduction of sound raised the prospect that US domination might be restricted to English-speaking countries. Yet by 1931 the US majors had largely overcome the threat that sound had posed to their domination of world film markets. Satisfactory techniques of subtitling and dubbing had been developed, the sound patents struggle had been resolved, and Film Europe was dead. The Hollywood studios made such effective use of sound technology, for music and effects as much as for dialogue, that in the long term the advent of sound accentuated the superiority of the American product. The years 1927–31 were the last period in which the US industry's foreign opponents seriously entertained hopes of ending its global preeminence. In the decades that followed, American hegemony in cinema would for the most part be taken for granted as a fact of international cultural life.

Censorship and Control

International anxieties about the effects of American movies reflected a common assumption that film is a particularly persuasive medium. In this vein the Russian Bolshevik leader Leon Trotsky noted film's peculiar power as a medium "which is accessible to everyone, which is attractive, which cuts into the memory …"[31] Similarly, in Britain in 1916 the National Council of Public Morals observed that films "are having a profound influence upon the mental and moral outlook of millions of our young people – an influence the more subtle in that it is subconsciously exercised."[32] Fear of film's influence being used for harmful purposes was as widely held in the United States as elsewhere. With regard to sex and crime, international and American concerns about the influence of Hollywood movies overlapped. The overwhelming dominance of the United States in world film markets ensured that

American controversies about the moral content of Hollywood's products shaped the kinds of films that the rest of the world saw.

Concerns about film's moral influence are virtually as old as the medium itself. A belief in film's persuasive qualities, the fact that cinema bypassed the traditional authority sources of family, school, and church, its early image as a working-class and, in the United States, immigrant form of entertainment, and the early discovery by filmmakers and exhibitors of the great value of violence and sexual titillation in attracting audiences, all led middle-class reformers from the first years of the twentieth century to decry the harmful effects of film, especially on the behavior of children and youth. The first three decades of the century saw the adoption of more liberal attitudes to sexual behavior and the removal of much of the traditional taboo that had surrounded discussion or artistic depiction of sexual themes. Since films reflected these changing values and helped define new forms of personal and social behavior, many concluded that film was responsible for a wholesale decline in moral standards.

In some countries this reaction led to film censorship at the national level, but in the United States, Britain, and France municipal authorities implemented censorship, supplemented in America by some state government bodies. For the American and British film industries, self-regulation was an attractive alternative to such systems. The British Board of Film Censors was set up by the industry in 1912 and issued certificates to companies that chose to submit their films for scrutiny. Although producers were not obliged to gain the Board's approval nor local authorities prevented from imposing their own censorship standards, this approach came to be accepted not only by the industry but also by the British government and most local governments. In the United States a 1909 experiment in self-censorship by a National Board of Censorship (later the National Board of Review) proved less successful. The National Board's critics claimed that it too often erred on the side of leniency toward filmmakers. Its existence failed to stem the expansion of local and state censorship during the 1910s or demands for censorship at the federal level.

Pressures for governmental control of the movies were a response to developments during the silent era. The pre-First World War tendency of filmmakers to portray and exploit the breaking-down of older moral values, especially where sex was concerned, was more fully developed in the 1920s. The leading female stars of the postwar decade – Pola

Negri, Clara Bow (the "It Girl"), Gloria Swanson, and Greta Garbo – played characters who embodied the period's liberal attitudes to sexual pleasure. Among male stars, none was more popular than Rudolph Valentino and Erich von Stroheim, who exuded sexuality in their screen roles as exotic foreign lovers. The most successful director of the period, Cecil B. DeMille, based a series of comedies on the general message that consumption, fun, and sexual passion can strengthen marriage, giving his films suitably suggestive titles: *Old Wives for New* (1918), *Male and Female* (1919), *Don't Change Your Husband* (1919), *Why Change Your Wife?* (1920), *Forbidden Fruit* (1921), and *The Affairs of Anatol* (1921). He followed these with two biblical epics that afforded ample opportunity to exploit the box-office appeal of violence, orgies, and female nudity: *The Ten Commandments* (1924) and *King of Kings* (1927).

The hostility of the film industry's critics to such movies was exacerbated by Hollywood's reputation for extravagance and debauchery. Based initially on the palatial homes, conspicuous consumption, and glamorous images of the stars, such impressions were encouraged by a series of scandals in 1922. The trial of comedian Roscoe "Fatty" Arbuckle for manslaughter after the death of an actress during a wild party, the murder of a director in circumstances that implicated two actresses, the death of an actor from drug abuse, and public disapproval of Mary Pickford's divorce and quick remarriage, all highlighted to industry leaders the need to create an effective form of self-regulation if calls for federal government intervention were to be silenced.

It was chiefly for this purpose that the MPPDA was established in 1922 with Will Hays, a prominent Republican Party figure, as president. Hays introduced measures to improve the industry's public image and resist federal censorship. Lobby groups were invited to advise the MPPDA on film content, signaling the industry's apparent readiness to listen to public concerns. Producers were encouraged to submit films to the "Hays Office" for scrutiny before their release. In 1927 a set of guidelines for studios, the "Don'ts and Be Carefuls," was introduced. By 1928 the MPPDA was playing an active role in negotiating with filmmakers over synopses and scripts before films reached the production stage. Yet at the end of the 1920s state and local censors were as active as ever and pro-censorship groups still vocal. The problem lay in the lack of enforcement machinery. Studios were neither obliged to submit scripts and films for review nor, if they did so, to accept MPPDA recommendations.

The coming of sound to the movies accentuated the problem. Risqué and profane dialogue, and on-screen discussion of love affairs and criminal behavior, gave the censors and industry critics additional reasons to object to Hollywood's products. Yet sound movies, while more vulnerable to censorship than silent films, were also far more expensive to modify. This was a time, moreover, when the costs of conversion to sound, emerging competition from commercial radio, and, from 1929, the Depression placed the industry under serious economic pressure. By the end of the 1920s, therefore, it was more than ever in the industry's interest to make censor-proof movies. In 1930 the MPPDA revised its guidelines to take account of the introduction of sound, producing a formal Production Code. The Code listed in detail those subjects or forms of behavior that were forbidden (including prostitution, homosexuality, miscegenation, obscenity "in word, gesture, reference, song, joke, or by suggestion," nudity, "excessive and lustful kissing," profane language) or were to be treated carefully (including murder, bedroom scenes, and adultery). From 1931 the studios were compelled to submit scripts to the MPPDA's Studio Relations Committee (SRC) for approval before production. But provision for the studios to appeal against SRC decisions to a panel of producers undermined the new Code's effectiveness. As the impact of the Depression became clear, with weekly attendances falling from an all-time high of ninety million in 1930 to sixty million in 1932, and with profits dropping sharply in 1931 and continuing to fall in 1932–3, producers explored all avenues to bring in revenue.[33]

Between 1930 and 1934, despite the Code, American filmmakers exploited even more than before the box-office appeal of sex and violence. The former Broadway star Mae West reached the peak of her movie career in *She Done Him Wrong* (1933) and *I'm No Angel* (1933), films that abounded in ribald humor and flaunted female sexuality. Cecil B. DeMille returned to the biblical epic genre with *Sign of the Cross* (1932), a film that surpassed even his own previous efforts to cram as much violence, nudity, and salaciousness as possible into a feature film. Hollywood's two leading foreign female stars were cast as prostitutes: Marlene Dietrich in *Blonde Venus* (1932), Greta Garbo in *Anna Christie* (1930), *Susan Lennox (Her Fall and Rise)* (1931), and *As You Desire Me* (1931). Many other films dealt with adultery, promiscuity, and prostitution in ways that often proved popular but attracted the ire of Hollywood's critics. Meanwhile a wave of gangster movies, including the highly successful *Little Caesar* (1930), *Public Enemy* (1931), and *Scarface* (1932), elicited widespread concern about their feared influence on impressionable youth.

A series of studies sponsored by the Payne Fund and based on social-science research conducted between 1929 and 1933 gave ammunition to the critics. The Payne Fund studies' cautious conclusions – that movies, along with other cultural factors, did influence children's behavior – were themselves a source of concern. The distortion of those findings in Henry James Forman's alarmist best-seller *Our Movie-Made Children* (1935) lent plausibility to the view that the movie industry posed a direct threat to public morals – a threat so great that Hollywood was "subversive to the best interests of society … nothing less than an *agent provocateur*, a treacherous and costly enemy let loose at the public expense."[34]

In addition to renewed threats of federal government intervention and the strengthening of local and state censorship, the industry faced the growth of Catholic opposition, culminating in the formation of the Catholic Legion of Decency in 1934. More than anything else, the threat of a movie boycott by twenty million American Catholics persuaded the MPPDA to give teeth to its Code. In 1934 it replaced the SRC with a Production Code Administration (PCA) under the direction of Joseph Breen, a conservative Catholic who took as guiding stars the convictions that most movie-goers were "nit-wits, dolts and imbeciles," and that most of the film industry's problems could be blamed on "lousy Jews" who "seem to think of nothing but money making and sexual indulgence."[35] Studios were obliged to submit both scripts and completed films to Breen's office. Heavy fines, exclusion from the Big Five's theaters, and condemnation by the Legion of Decency were the penalties for release of a film without a PCA seal of approval.

From 1934 until the 1950s the Production Code, enforced by the PCA, heavily influenced the content of American films. Studios took it as axiomatic that in the movies sexual relations outside marriage were never justified and vice and crime must always be punished. Filmmakers were careful to exclude offensive language and accepted strict limits on displays of bare flesh on the screen. The sexual suggestiveness that had flourished in the movies between 1930 and 1934 became a thing of the past. Yet, while filmmakers often complained about these restrictions, they did retain the freedom to deal with sexual themes, though these now had to be approached obliquely. In the form of "romance," sexuality remained a staple of Hollywood cinema. Despite the impact of the Code, Hollywood continued to make films that were extremely popular among both American and foreign audiences – films that were often artistic as well as commercial successes.[36]

Ideology and Influence

Although the censorship movement in the United States was motivated mainly by anxieties about Hollywood's treatment of sex and crime, both the scope of the MPPDA's activities and the range of community complaints about film content were far more varied. The SRC and PCA considered objections from professions, trade associations, and other groups, each of which asserted that its image or interests had been harmed by particular films or the movies in general. Thus social workers resented their portrayal as heartless and interfering. Anthracite coal producers organized a boycott of Fox because of a comedy showing a householder's troubles with his coal furnace. A circus tent fire in one film led circus operators to threaten legal action. Businessmen in Atlantic City objected to the depiction of their city as "the place to take one's secretary for a week-end." The men's undershirt business complained of a drastic drop in sales after Clark Gable removed his shirt and revealed a bare chest in *It Happened One Night* (1934).[37]

The industry sought to mollify aggrieved groups and pre-empt organized opposition by removing potential causes of offense. In 1938 the PCA codified this approach in a statement of policy on handling sensitive issues not covered by the Code. One result was that Hollywood films tended to feature a utopian social background in which, as Ruth Vasey has written, "doctors, lawyers, and bank managers were motivated by altruism, and the police force pursued wrongdoers largely untroubled by graft and corruption."[38] By the mid-1920s it became less common for the movies to adopt a sympathetic view of radical politics or take a pro-labor position on relations between workers and employers. If financial dependence on Wall Street bankers and the predispositions of company executives and studio bosses were not in themselves enough to ensure the triumph of conservative political views, the commercial imperative of obtaining the approval of state, local, and foreign censors, supported by the MPPDA's role in the production process, reinforced the tendency.[39]

Ideological assumptions about nationality, ethnicity, and race were also embedded in Hollywood's products. Films that featured foreign villains or gave unflattering views of other countries were frequent causes of complaint from representatives of foreign governments. As products of mass culture, American movies expressed cultural stereotypes that were highly influential in the English-speaking world during the first decades of the twentieth century. Brutal and treacherous Mexicans, inscrutable and cunning "Orientals," and emotional and undisciplined Europeans, all found their way into motion pictures and all generated protests. The MPPDA worked to persuade the studios to remove offensive stereotypes, but success depended on the importance of the market in question for the distribution of particular films. Not all films were made for international distribution, and, of those that were, some markets were more significant sources of revenue than others, as the contrast between Germany and the Soviet Union shows. Despite the MPPDA's efforts, cultural stereotypes remained. Moreover, even when Hollywood responded to foreign pressures by avoiding an explicit association of such stereotypes with particular national groups, the effect was not to achieve a more sophisticated view of the world but to present a universe populated by "Americans" and "foreigners," the former governed by middle-class values, the latter an undifferentiated mass characterized by their adherence to alien customs – often quaint or exotic, sometimes sinister, but always different from the American norm.[40]

In another way, too, the universe of Hollywood movies diverged from reality. While the pressures of international film distribution led the MPPDA to work to reduce the role of cultural stereotypes in the movies, the entrenched racial prejudice of US society had a very different effect where the portrayal of the American black population was concerned. The treatment of race in American movies in the interwar period is a two-part story. In these years independent black filmmakers sought to express "the colored man's viewpoint"[41] in movies that screened in black neighborhood theaters. Chronically hamstrung by limited funding, these "race movies" nonetheless included such works of artistic value as *Body and Soul* (1925), made by Oscar Micheaux, the most successful African American director, and featuring the famous black singer and actor Paul Robeson.[42] These films gave a prominence to the depiction of black life that stood in stark contrast to the content of mainstream American cinema.

In its approach to race, as in the treatment of sex and crime, the MPPDA saw its primary task as eliminating controversial film content likely to antagonize state and local censorship boards. A policy of not offending white sentiment, including that of the segregated South, governed Hollywood's approach. In an era when the African American population of the southern states endured a system of apartheid, when black men were frequently lynched by white mobs, and blacks through-out the United States lived in a condition of social and economic inferi-ority, the MPPDA steered Hollywood clear of stories and characters that seemed subversive of the status quo in race relations. In pre-Second World War movies, African Americans were seldom persecuted, and miscegenation did not occur. It was unusual for blacks to appear outside the traditional roles of servant, railway porter, or entertainer, and strong black characters were seldom portrayed. The "sambo" stereotype – the black as servile, childlike, and happy – was as much a part of Holly-wood's universe as the Mexican bandit and the evil Chinese villain.[43]

Although, therefore, the Hollywood bosses insisted that their films were intended merely to entertain – "If you want to send a message, call Western Union," Samuel Goldwyn is reputed to have said – the movies did present a coherent worldview, based on distinctive attitudes to politics, race, ethnicity, and "Americanism." They did, in other words, send "messages." How much this mattered – to what extent audiences were influenced by these messages – is a central problem concerning film's role in society. Early twentieth-century critics saw the media as enormously powerful institutions with an unlimited capacity to shape public attitudes (see Chapter 1). Even in the early twenty-first century, this view of the media as a determinant of "mass society" con-tinues to influence popular attitudes. Yet the history of the film indus-try points to the limitations of such a view. Even the world's most successful film industry – the oligopoly of eight major US firms – was in one perspective merely the mirror of its society. The adoption and implementation of the Production Code, following years of controversy over the moral content of films, highlights the extent to which Hollywood was vulnerable to societal pressures. Moreover, the cultural stereotypes that abounded in American movies were not invented by Hollywood or employed for the purpose of indoctrinating the public. Rather they predated the invention of film and appealed to filmmakers partly because these people were themselves products of time and place, partly because such images drew upon attitudes and beliefs that were widely shared and therefore easily appreciated by audiences. Nor should it be assumed that audiences passively absorbed onscreen messages. Continuing objections to film content from many sources, both in the United States and abroad, underline the power of movie-goers to accept or reject the ideas conveyed by films.

Yet it would be wrong to conclude that film did no more than mirror society and that anxieties concerning the medium's influence were entirely misconceived. At the very least, American films exerted a powerful influence on language, fashion, and consumer behavior. Moreover, the US industry's global dominance ensured that this influence extended to most parts of the world. Within the United States, it is true that the movies did not create prevailing attitudes toward race and class. Nor did they create the national myth of American exceptionalism – the idea that America is a unique nation, the embodiment of liberty, entrusted with a providential mission to carry the benefits of democracy to all peoples. Yet the movies' mass appeal ensured their importance in sustaining and disseminating these attitudes. By the Second World War film had established itself not only as the most successful medium of mass entertainment but also as a social force of fundamental significance. In the context of total war, as we shall see in Chapter 6, national governments of diverse political complexions would acknowledge this phenomenon as they attempted to exploit film's potential as a medium of mass persuasion.

4

The Growth of Radio Broadcasting

In the 1920s radio developed as a mass medium, and radio broadcasting evolved as a means of bringing entertainment into private homes. According to Herbert Hoover, the radio boom was "one of the most astounding things that [has] come under my observation of American life".[1] Like other "inventions," radio drew on a range of earlier technological developments, on the pioneering work of individuals in various countries, and in this case on enthusiastic experimentation by amateurs. The 1930s and 1940s are considered to have been radio's "golden age," when it became an integral part of the domestic environment, a key supplier of entertainment, and a trusted source of information. During these decades radio enjoyed a popularity that was challenged only by the advent of another mass-entertainment medium, television, in the 1950s.

During this time institutional forms evolved in the United States and Britain – commercially based network broadcasting and public-service broadcasting respectively – that provided models for the development of radio broadcasting elsewhere. A variety of program formats evolved, some drawing on earlier forms of entertainment, others developing to take advantage of the special qualities of the new medium. During this period radio's relationship with other mass media stabilized after initial suspicion, antagonism, and competition. On the eve of the Second World War not only was radio poised to play an important wartime role as a source of information and entertainment and as a powerful tool for propaganda, but the manner in which radio broadcasting had developed provided a basis for the development of an equally pervasive medium in the second half of the twentieth century – television.

Early Radio Development

Radio as a means of mass communications, broadcasting to sizable audiences, developed in the 1920s, but technological developments during earlier decades, experimentation by pioneering individuals, and rather different uses of the technology formed an important background to the relatively quick take-up of radio after the First World War.

Radio communications had existed for more than twenty years before radio broadcasting on a large scale began. It began as wireless telegraphy, using Morse code as a means of communications, with each letter of the alphabet represented by a series of dots and dashes signaled by electrical impulses. One of the pioneers of radio development was the Italian Gugliemo Marconi. In the 1890s he carried out experiments at his father's estate in Italy, transmitting wireless messages using Morse code. He moved to Britain in the mid-1890s and established the Marconi Wireless Telegraph Company, then in 1899 set up the Marconi Wireless Company of America. In 1901 the first transatlantic wireless signal was sent from England to Newfoundland. Marconi began to use wireless telegraphy in ship-to-ship and ship-to-shore communications (with Marconigrams), and the British Navy became interested in his work.

Across the Atlantic Lee De Forest (who claims in his autobiography that he was the "father of radio") made an important advance with the "audion," a three-electrode vacuum tube used to amplify voice transmissions. He interested the United States Navy in his work on wireless telegraphy. In 1903 the US Signal Corps became involved in experiments, in 1905 President Theodore Roosevelt used wireless on the warship *West Virginia*, and in 1908 De Forest's radiotelephone equipment was installed on ships of the North Atlantic Fleet. In the same year De Forest broadcast phonograph records from the Eiffel Tower in Paris, and two years later he was responsible for a live opera broadcast from the Metropolitan, New York, drawing attention to the entertainment potential of radio. In 1912 the sinking of the *Titanic* had some significance for wireless development, as the rescue operation was coordinated by Marconi wireless telegraphy.[2] The work of pioneers in the United States such as De Forest, Reginald Fessenden, and Frank Conrad was important in moving beyond wireless telegraphy and the transmission of information through the use of Morse code to wireless telephony and the transmission of voice and music.

During the early years of the twentieth century enthusiastic amateurs began to focus attention on radio as a technology with potential for entertainment purposes. From about 1906 in the United States there was an amateur radio boom, with enthusiasts building their own crystal sets, locally broadcasting brief items such as weather reports, using Morse code, or making occasional or weekly broadcasts of news bulletins and music. In some instances music stores provided phonograph records in return for advertising, but this practice was stopped in 1922 when a clause in amateur radio licenses prohibited the broadcasting of "entertainments."

The outbreak of war in 1914 temporarily halted any development of radio as a source of entertainment or as a means of mass communications. (The armed services took over Marconi's American operations, and a ban was imposed on amateur radio.) However, technical progress during the war years (for example, in the production of valves) contributed to improvements in the quality of radio broadcasting in the 1920s. After the war radio became more popular. In Britain, where the Post Office had control over radio communications and issued licenses to users, the growing popularity of amateur radio was evident from the number of licenses issued: by 1921 in Britain 150 amateurs were licensed to transmit and 4,000 to receive radio broadcasts.[3]

In the postwar years commercial interests became involved in radio broadcasting. In England in 1920 the Marconi Company began transmitting speech from Chelmsford to test radio telephony. An early example of cross-media collaboration occurred in June that year when Northcliffe's *Daily Mail* sponsored a half-hour recital by opera singer Dame Nellie Melba. In the United States the Westinghouse Corporation took out licenses and began broadcasting regularly with a published weekly schedule. These early programs drew on newspaper and magazine publishers, music publishing houses, and dance orchestras in New York hotels.

By the 1920s radio had moved from being primarily a means of maritime communications to a medium capable of providing entertainment to large audiences in their homes. No longer just the concern of amateurs, it was increasingly attracting commercial attention.

Technology and Society

A key question regarding developments in radio, and indeed in any other mass medium, concerns the relationship between technological and social change. Does technology shape society or cause social change; or is the main determinant the way in which society uses technology or controls technological change?

Technological determinism is the view that technology is the agent of social change; it implies that technological change occurs autonomously. The opposing view is that social forces shape technology. For example, corporate decisions to finance research and development may have a crucial impact on technological change, or state decisions concerning the form in which a technology is to be developed may be critical.

With respect to radio development it is insufficient to focus simply on technology. Rather, the interrelation between technology and society is important. It is evident that various technological developments in the late nineteenth and early twentieth centuries were essential in enabling the transmission of messages by wireless telegraphy or telephony. However, the development of radio broadcasting as a mass medium depended on other factors as well as technological change.

For example, wireless sets had to be produced on a large scale and marketed. This became possible partly because of expertise developed during the First World War, but a changing social context was also important in increasing public receptiveness of radio as a new medium. Increasing urbanization and mobility created a need for more efficient communications systems, and there was considerable emphasis on the private sphere, on the family home, as a center of social life. Thus a suitable social context existed for a medium that brought news and entertainment into the home. Context was also important for the institutional models of radio broadcasting that developed. In Britain attitudes to the role of the state, influenced by the recent experience of war, favored some state involvement, but there were also strong public-service ideals. In the United States commercial concerns and support for free enterprise affected the way in which radio broadcasting developed.

Thus it is important to consider the development of radio in its broad socio-economic–cultural context. According to Hugh G. J. Aitken, "broadcasting did not result from the inexorable unfolding of a technological imperative latent in radio technology; it burst on the scene when continuous wave radio finally found a mass market." Susan Douglas's work on the "pre-history" of radio broadcasting between 1899 and 1922 analyzes not only technological but also social, economic, ideological, and cultural frameworks that influenced the enduring shape of American radio broadcasting – for example, the role of the business community and large corporate concentrations.[4]

Susan Smulyan, examining the commercialization of American broadcasting, argues that a range of factors influenced the choice of a particular technology to provide radio broadcasting services: "Wired networks had a deciding influence on the development of broadcast radio because network radio brought expensive charges to rent wires and thus the need for broadcasting, as well as receiver sales, to make money." Programming had to be centralized to save money and to attract advertisers who wished to appeal to a national audience. The attempt by the developing networks to attract advertisers affected the form and content of radio broadcasting and was fundamental to the American commercial broadcasting model: "Radio became a way to sell products, and most programs merely filled the time between commercials."[5]

Other socio-economic changes were important: for example, the spread of electricity in rural areas in 1930s in the United States made feasible the purchase of radios, which became the center of family entertainment. The emergence of radio as a mass medium illustrates well the importance of contextual as well as technological factors. The institutional forms that emerged in different countries illustrate how different contexts and values shaped radio broadcasting. The contrasts between the United States and Britain exemplify the impact of specific socio-political–cultural environments on the development of this mass medium in the 1920s and 1930s.

Institutional Models

Two contrasting institutional forms of radio broadcasting emerged in the United States and Britain after the First World War: commercial broadcasting and public-service broadcasting (on totalitarian models of radio broadcasting see Chapter 6). These provided not only models for the development of sound broadcasting elsewhere but also frameworks for the establishment of television as a mass medium later in the twentieth century. It is worth noting, however, that some state broadcasting systems that developed (in Europe, for example), although similar to the British Broadcasting Corporation in being owned and funded by the state, enjoyed much less independence than was the case in Britain.

The Commercial Model

The institutional arrangements for radio broadcasting that developed in the United States reflected the needs of commercial groups, which saw radio broadcasting primarily as a means of profit-making.

In 1919, partly to consolidate patents needed for further development, the Radio Corporation of America (RCA) was formed, comprising the companies General Electric, Westinghouse, and American Telephone and Telegraph (AT&T). Another reason for establishing RCA was to avoid foreign control of the emerging industry via the British Marconi Company.[6] The formation of RCA set a pattern for American radio broadcasting, one in which commercial entrepreneurs dominated, with the main stakeholders in the company being wireless-equipment manufacturers and cable owners.

The Westinghouse company had been involved in developing transmission equipment and crystal sets. In 1920 it had made the first scheduled, non-experimental public radio broadcast from KDKA station in Pittsburgh, a broadcast of the US presidential election results. After this experiment the members of RCA acquired or established stations in many major cities. In 1922 AT&T withdrew from RCA and established the first advertising-supported station, WEAF in New York. The first paid radio advertisement, for property from a Long Island real-estate firm, went to air on WEAF that year.

The number of broadcasting stations in the United States grew swiftly in the early 1920s. By 1922 thirty licenses to broadcast on the bandwidth designated by the Secretary of Commerce had been issued to businesses, institutions, and wealthy individuals. By the following year there were more than 550 stations, with at least one in every state. Crystal sets and early model radios, most requiring headphones, became available. Within two years of the KDKA broadcast it is estimated that there were 1.5 million radio sets in the United States.[7] There were problems as a result of this rapid expansion, as competition for limited wavelengths for broadcasting developed. This American experience had an impact in Britain, where there was a desire to avoid such chaos and impose greater regulation.

One important innovation was the use of telephone lines to broadcast across large distances. AT&T had a monopoly of US telephone lines in the early 1920s. It proposed to link selected radio stations into a network, allowing members to use the system on payment of a "toll." Station owners then let out time to sponsors, who organized program content. This opened the way to creating chains or networks of stations, broadcasting the same program simultaneously. The networks became the characteristic institutions of American radio, and subsequently television, broadcasting. In addition, advertising revenue became the means of financing radio broadcasting. This was to have a lasting impact on the content of programming.[8]

In 1926 the first of the networks was formed, the National Broadcasting Company (NBC). Led by David Sarnoff, president of RCA, the parent company of NBC, this network began broadcasting with twenty-four stations. By 1931 it had expanded to sixty-one stations for each of its two components, the "Red" and "Blue" networks. NBC took over AT&T broadcasting facilities and used AT&T landlines.

In 1927 the US Congress established the Federal Radio Commission to regulate radio, to ensure that stations operated in the public interest and that monopolistic control was avoided. In 1934 this became the Federal Communications Commission (FCC), with powers extended to include telephone as well as radio. Ken Ward points out that the FCC was unable to interfere in the basic organization of broadcasting in the United States, network control, and that there was no real government intention of interfering in sound business practice. Smulyan demonstrates how these developments in broadcasting occurred in a society already accustomed to integrating new technologies such as the railroad, the telegraph, and telephone. Precedents such as these helped to shape the relationship between radio and the federal government, and existing forms of economic organization influenced radio development. After patent issues had been resolved, private control of radio technology production – and private control of broadcasting itself – seemed "normal" in the American context.

A second network emerged in 1927, the Columbia Broadcasting System (CBS), initially with forty-seven stations but by 1931 comprising seventy-nine affiliates.[9] The networks continued to expand throughout the 1930s, making national radio programming possible. Another was added in 1934, the Mutual Broadcasting System (MBS), which, by the mid-1940s, had more than 300 affiliate stations. In 1943 NBC, after charges of monopolistic practices, sold off the stations of its "Blue" network, and these formed the American Broadcasting Company. NBC, CBS, and the ABC remained the dominant American network broadcasters throughout the twentieth century.

Financially, the essential characteristic of US broadcasting was that the networks relied on selling time to advertisers who made or sponsored programs. The impact of commercial sponsors on radio programming content in turn became an important issue in the interwar period (and later). As radio became an increasingly lucrative business, advertising agencies established radio departments and supplied radio programs. They took over responsibility for developing, writing, and packaging complete programs and series for sponsors, and they sold program packages to the networks as part of sponsorship arrangements.

The amounts spent on advertising increased substantially. In 1935 NBC had a net advertising income of $3.7 million and CBS of $3.2 million; five years later the respective figures were $5.8 million and $7.4 million. By 1944 CBS customers included thirteen who bought more than $1 million worth of time each, and three who spent more than $4 million on advertising.[10]

The development of audience rating services in the 1930s (at a time when market research and public relations were assuming greater importance in industrialized societies) increased the power of sponsors and agencies. In the 1930s the Crossley ratings and the Hooperatings (succeeded in the late 1940s by ratings research by the A. C. Nielsen Company) provided data to prospective advertisers on listening audiences. If a program did not rate well, it was highly likely that the sponsor would withdraw and the network drop the program. Thus the commercial environment, and more specifically radio advertisers, were powerful influences in the history of American broadcasting, having considerable impact on program content (see also Chapter 5).[11]

Because the networks relied financially on selling time to advertisers, commercialization pressures were apparently irresistible. J. Fred MacDonald supports the argument that American radio could not have escaped commercialism: "It was an instrument of electrical entertainment aimed at a commercial democracy – a world of independent, average people who preferred an occasional advertising announcement to the implications of a broadcasting system fully regulated by governmental bureaucrats."[12] However, there were reservations about the commercial organization of broadcasting; in 1932 a Senate resolution authorized the FCC, in the light of the British experience, to study the "possibility of government ownership and operation" of radio, as well as ways to reduce or even eliminate radio advertising. (Certainly, the case of the BBC – see below – shows that there were alternatives to a commercial broadcasting model.) Smulyan, in her detailed analysis of the commercialization of American broadcasting between 1920 and 1934, does not accept "commercial inevitability" but rather notes the range of economic, organizational, and cultural factors that shaped American broadcasting.[13] In contrast to Britain, these factors included a less stratified society, the dominance of economic considerations, and greater diversity rather than a tendency to elite national cultural leadership.

In summary, the broad context in which radio broadcasting became technically possible and in which radio was adopted on a mass scale was important. The lack of agreement in the 1920s about using radio for advertising purposes (see Chapter 5) indicates that there was, indeed, no "inevitability" about commercial broadcasting being the norm. Rather, factors such as the relative power of commercial interests during the early decades of radio development, the strength of American consumer culture, and public reluctance to support high levels of government intervention were important in favoring a commercial model. The history of radio development in Britain illustrates the impact of a different set of socio-economic–political circumstances.

The Public Service Broadcasting Model

In Britain a public-service broadcasting model was adopted. In the 1920s the British Post Office, responsible for such matters, authorized the Marconi Company to broadcast to wireless enthusiasts, first locally (at Chelmsford), then more widely from a London station 2LO in 1922. As in the United States, pressure from amateur radio enthusiasts (who in 1922 established a Radio Society of Great Britain) encouraged this decision. However, the British Postmaster General, aware of developments in the United States and fearful of chaos and congestion on the wavelengths, declined to license other wireless manufacturers to conduct broadcasts. Instead he proposed a consortium of leading manufacturers (including Marconi, Metropolitan-Vickers, Western Electric, and General Electric). This resulted in the formation of the British

Broadcasting Company, which received a license from the Post Office and began transmissions in November 1922 from 2LO (London), followed by transmissions from other stations in major centers of population such as Manchester and Birmingham.

In contrast to the situation in the United States, in Britain finance for radio broadcasting came from royalties on wireless sets sold by the companies, plus part of the revenue from broadcast-receiving licenses – that is, a license fee.[14] Advertising revenue was not the financial basis for British broadcasting.

By October 1923 the British Broadcasting Company was operating eight stations, and about half the population could pick up a signal strong enough to operate a crystal set, with this rising to about 85 percent by 1925.[15] After some financial problems, and after investigations by the Sykes and Crawford committees in 1923 and 1925, the company became a corporation, the British Broadcasting Corporation (BBC), established on January 1, 1927 by a Royal Charter, generally avoiding domination by either commercial and manufacturing interests or by government, and emerging as a national institution, promoting the national interest and culture.

The responsibilities of the BBC, as set out in its charter, were to "inform, educate and entertain." It was neither to advertise nor to editorialize. It was promised a guaranteed income from licenses, and it enjoyed editorial independence. This situation was in marked contrast to that in the United States. In Britain the BBC had a monopoly; it was publicly funded; it was not dependent on advertising or sponsorship; and it had "public-service" responsibilities under its charter. If there were any constraints on its independence, they did not come from advertisers or program sponsors but rather from Parliament, where the level of license fees was determined. There was also potential for government influence through its power to appoint to the board of governors; and the influence of expectations about BBC alignment with British establishment values and priorities should not be ignored. Nonetheless, the "BBC had a cultural freedom of manoeuvre almost unknown elsewhere."[16]

There is debate about the origin of public-service broadcasting concepts in Britain. Ken Ward contrasts Britain with the United States, arguing that the development of public-service broadcasting in the former showed that greater consideration was given to political and social needs. Paddy Scannell and David Cardiff put a rather different view: "Public service was a concept grafted onto an initial pragmatic set of arrangements between the Post Office and the British radio industry to establish a broadcasting service that would create a market for radio-receiving apparatuses; the definition of broadcasting as a public utility to be developed as a national service in the public interest came from the state."[17]

As in the United States, so too in Britain, various factors explain the adoption of this particular institutional model of radio broadcasting. The creation of the BBC, a public corporation with public funding and a monopoly over radio broadcasting, was understandable in the inter-war period. The First World War had led to higher levels of government intervention and centralized control. This continued to have an impact in the 1920s. "The development of the public corporation depended on the rejection of both market forces and politics in favour of efficiency and planned growth controlled by experts.... There was a widespread dissatisfaction with the *ad hoc* nature of industrial competition." In the British context there was less support for market forces, capitalist competition, and unrestrained commercialism; there was greater support for traditions of public service; and there were many precedents for public corporations to be established under royal charter, free from both private control and direct state management.[18]

In addition to these broad influences on British broadcasting, one individual stands out for his impact on the developing character and ethos of the BBC and for his imprint on public-service radio broadcasting. John Reith was appointed managing director of the British Broadcasting Company in 1922, general manager of the newly created British Broadcasting Corporation in 1926, and its director general between 1927 and 1938. Reith (knighted in 1927 to become Sir John Reith) considered that broadcasting carried with it a high moral responsibility. Rather than seeing radio as a commercial enterprise, he led the BBC during its first decade as a respectable national institution providing a public service. He believed that the BBC should lead and shape rather than follow public taste; and he stressed the educative function of the public broadcaster. Reith's approach reflected the confidence of an upper class in a stratified society, where there was support for national institutions and cultural leadership.

The public-service model did not go unchallenged in the 1930s. Rather than serving British society generally (as suggested by Ward), the BBC came to be identified with the "establishment" as an authoritative institution whose programming captured state and royal events rather than catering to all social classes and conveying more comprehensive images of British society during the Depression decade.[19] Discontent with the BBC monopoly and with Reith's leadership became apparent, and pressure mounted for the BBC to be more responsive to audience demands. Reith's resignation and then the Second World War ushered in substantial change in BBC programming, although the public-service ethos remained strong.

In summary, by the 1930s two different models for radio broadcasting had emerged in the United States and Britain. Competing networks were the basis of commercial radio in the United States; they depended on income from advertising and sponsorship, and provided programming designed to appeal to mass audiences and emphasizing entertainment values. The BBC had a monopoly over radio broadcasting in Britain. This public-service broadcaster was publicly funded, did not take advertising, and enjoyed considerable independence within broad charter obligations to provide news, information, and entertainment, but with an emphasis on educational rather than entertainment values. These models – or combinations of the two – provided frameworks for radio broadcasting in other countries, and in the second half of the twentieth century for the development of television broadcasting.

Radio Programming in the "Golden Years"

In the interwar period radio spread rapidly and was taken up with enthusiasm. In the United States access to radio in the 1920s had been confined to a few densely populated areas, but by 1938 more than 90 percent of urban households and 70 percent of rural households contained at least one radio set. In Britain by the mid-1920s some 85 percent of the population was able to receive national or regional programs, and by the end of the 1930s approximately 9 million radio sets were licensed. In these countries and elsewhere the extension of electricity was important in making possible the take-up of radio in private homes.

When radio broadcasting began, listening involved using crystal sets with headphones and was, therefore, a solitary activity. Technological change and experimentation during the First World War resulted in valve receivers with loudspeakers becoming available in the postwar years. Group and family listening became the most common means of enjoying radio. Development of cheap utility sets made radio more widely accessible. During the "golden years" radio listening was, therefore, most commonly a feature of the home, with radio sets as large pieces of furniture dominating living areas. During the Depression years and during the Second World War radio fulfilled an important role in cultural and social life as many people found themselves with hours of involuntary leisure time or a desire for escapism or solace. Radio ownership and listening increased during the Depression years, and polls in the United States in the late 1930s found that radio listening was overwhelmingly preferred (over reading and movie-going) as an inexpensive leisure activity.[20]

A rich variety of radio programs developed during the 1920s and 1930s for these expanding audiences. Some accounts of these "golden years" nostalgically celebrate particular programs and the contributions made by individual radio personalities: *The Jack Benny Program, Amos 'n' Andy, Fibber McGee and Molly,* Orson Welles's *Mercury Theater of the Air, The Bob Hope Show, The Lux Radio Theatre,* among many in the United States; *Music Hall, In Town Tonight, Band Waggon,* and *The Children's Hour* among BBC programs. In the field of entertainment, early radio tended to draw on existing forms such as vaudeville and theater, broadcasting stage plays, variety shows, public lectures, and concerts, without any significant adaptation to take advantage of the features of radio as a medium. This borrowing was not without problems. For example, theater owners initially saw radio as a competitor and refused to cooperate, putting pressure on actors not to work on radio. Broadly speaking, one can contrast the greater "seriousness" of BBC programming, with its educative and informing intentions, with American programs dominated by entertainment values, exemplified by radio serials, soap operas (so called after the soap companies that were major sponsors of this format), and "sit coms." However, BBC programming did not lack diversity, with popular music, comedy shows, plays, and sporting broadcasts complementing "serious" programs.

One type of programming that played an important role in early radio, and was relatively uncontroversial, was music. In the 1920s the foundations were laid for an enduring relationship between radio and the music industry. Music not only became an important component of radio programs, but radio in turn had considerable impact on music, making it possible for music to be heard at a distance and by a theoretically limitless number of listeners. It became "both a unique populariser of minority music (including classical music) and by far the most powerful means for selling records. Radio did not change music, but the role of music in contemporary life is inconceivable without it."[21]

Initially music was important partly because of a lack of other types of program, and partly because of the idea that radio programming should flow, be continuous, without breaks or silences. Music was easily incorporated into programming; it was uncontroversial; it did not have to be adapted (unlike drama, for example); it was not subject to the sorts of pressures exerted by theater owners. It also offered opportunities for mutually satisfactory arrangements in the commercial environment of early American radio. De Forest refers to the first sponsored radio program in 1916, when recordings from the Columbia Gramophone Company were broadcast.[22] Radio and music seemed to be obvious partners in the 1920s: early radio broadcasting coincided with the craze for dancing, and dance music became a very popular component of radio programs.

In the 1930s the American networks featured dance music (including "swing" and "jitterbug"); big-band leaders had regular series; and a weekly program featured the top ten in record sales. In Britain the BBC's use of music was partly driven by Reith's paternalistic approach, preferring "high culture" to popular taste, and aiming to raise levels of musical appreciation among the listening public. Classical music formed an important part of British broadcasting. The BBC established its own Music Department in 1927, took over sponsorship of the Henry Wood Promenade Concerts (the "Proms"), and in 1930 established its own Symphony Orchestra.

However, the BBC repertoire did extend beyond classical works. Music such as comic and light opera and light orchestral works, other popular forms such as military band music, musical comedy, revue numbers, and ballads, as well as the music of popular dance bands, helped to fill BBC airtime. In the 1920s British radio reached agreements with large hotels such as the Savoy in London to broadcast dance-band music directly; the success of bands such as the Savoy Orpheans led to their recording with companies such as His Master's Voice and helped to popularize this type of music. In 1928 the Corporation established its own dance orchestra.

Stephen Barnard has argued that the BBC exerted pressure as a major contractor of bands, influencing the form, content, and repertoire of dance-band music and legitimizing this type of music to the exclusion of other contemporary forms of popular music such as accordion playing and community singing.[23] In the 1930s the BBC came under pressure to broaden its programming in music and other areas. British listeners began to have access to American-style music programs when, in 1931, Radio Normandie started to operate from the north coast of France; and in 1933 Radio Luxembourg opened an unauthorized wavelength, playing light music and operating on the American model. This gave impetus to demands for the BBC to be more responsive to audience tastes. (However, even under Reith the BBC had not been entirely insensitive to listener opinion; according to Ross McKibbin, "in the formulation of programmes the corporation had to take into account listener preference."[24])

Radio's use of music for entertainment had an immense impact on the music industry. The demand for sheet music increased as radio popularized particular songs and dances. Radio came to be a major factor in the spread of particular styles of music beyond their regional sources, including country and Western music, gospel music, and jazz. Developments in recorded music led to higher-quality recordings in the 1930s. During the war years, 1939–45, broadcasters increasingly relied on gramophone records, because conscription limited the number of bands and musicians available, and as music came to play a large part in wartime programming as a means of bolstering morale.

In addition to music, other program formats evolved during the "golden years." Sporting events became important, sports commentating for radio developed, and sport provided both a popular and a relatively cheap form of content (as it would continue to do in later decades). Radio drama developed, particularly as radio's special power to stimulate the imagination came to be appreciated. The most striking example of the power of radio drama in the 1930s was the broadcast by Orson Welles of his *War of the Worlds* in 1938. Welles's "clever manipulation of the various conventions of radio was responsible for inciting a nationwide panic" that Martians had landed, as listeners mistook drama for factual reporting.[25]

As well as music, drama, and sport, American radio programming provided a rich offering of comedy and variety shows, Westerns and detective programs, soap operas, and quiz shows. Radio was also used for political purposes by Presidents Harding and Coolidge in the 1920s, and later by other political leaders, including President Roosevelt in the 1930s (see below).[26]

By the end of the 1930s radio was an established and popular medium. Program formats had been developed to take advantage of its particular qualities. It was also a serious competitor for the newspaper press as a source of news, and for the film industry as a source of entertainment.

Radio and Other Media

As radio developed in the 1920s, its relationship with the newspaper press and with another emerging mass medium, the film industry, evolved. Information programming, specifically news broadcasting, illustrates one aspect of the relationship between established and emerging mass media.

In Britain in the 1920s newspaper owners were hostile toward radio, which was seen as a competitor in providing news to the public. The Newspaper Proprietors' Association attempted to prevent the broadcasting of news bulletins before 7.00 p.m. to protect newspaper sales and to prevent radio comment on public events. However, particular events helped to establish radio as a news medium. One was the General Strike of 1926 in Britain. Because of the strike very few newspapers were published, so audiences nationwide received news from the radio, showing the potential of the medium for news broadcasting. As a consequence, the BBC developed its own news service. In the following decade the Crystal Palace fire, in 1936, highlighted radio's advantages of immediacy and impact. BBC reporter Richard Dimbleby gave an on-the-spot telephone report, complete with background sound of fire-bells and the crackle of flames. The fire occurred after the evening papers had gone to press, so timing gave radio an advantage in this instance.

In the United States newspaper interests played an important part in early radio development. Michele Hilmes cites examples of newspapers in Chicago and Detroit that used radio to advertise and enhance their profile with the public. She points to the complementarity of these media, with radio being used to draw readers to newspapers for schedules, promotions, comics, and advertising tied to popular radio features. However, by the 1930s cooperation had given way to competition, as a long-running battle developed between the newspaper press and radio over control of news-distribution channels.

The economic depression of the early 1930s added to growing journalistic concerns about radio as a competing source of news, as the press began to lose advertising revenue to radio. In the United States the Biltmore Agreement of 1933 attempted to prevent the supply of news to radio by the newspaper press and wire services. Under the terms of this agreement the radio networks were to dismantle their news divisions and receive just two brief news bulletins from a Press–Radio Bureau. This was to be established after the Biltmore Conference to take wire service news bulletins from press associations and provide copy to be read over the air. News bulletins were to be broadcast only at certain times of day, when they would not provide serious competition for newspapers, and news services were to be broadcast without sponsorship. However, the agreement broke down, and the Press–Radio Bureau was disbanded in 1938.

Gwenyth L. Jackaway argues that this period of "media warfare" came to an end for a number of reasons. In the mid- to late 1930s some newspaper proprietors, rather than continuing to treat radio as a competitor, decided to take a stake in the new medium and gained an interest in radio stations. There was also increasing pressure to use sponsorship not only for entertainment programs but also for news broadcasts, because they too represented a potentially lucrative source of advertising income. The agreement collapsed partly because it did not have comprehensive support from broadcasters, as some independent radio stations had not participated and were able to take news from other wire services and engage in sponsored news bulletins. Thus by about 1937 newspapers had abandoned their antagonism toward radio and accepted it as an established institution. In the late 1930s the networks re-established their own news divisions.[27]

Between radio and the film industry mutually supportive arrangements developed in the 1930s. For example, in the United States popular radio drama programs such as *The Lux Radio Theater* used Hollywood stars. The program was based on Hollywood movies, and the broadcasting site was even moved from New York to Hollywood. Thus for mass audiences new media expanded the range of information and entertainment programming available, and new and emerging media found ways of working together.

The Impact and Significance of Radio

There was relatively little serious historical study of the significance of radio as a mass medium before the 1990s. Hilmes in 1997 claimed that no other medium had been "more thoroughly forgotten by the public, historians, and media scholars alike." Television had been the subject of many studies, but radio had attracted little scholarly attention.[28] Douglas too noted that "radio as an invention, and a cultural force, is regarded as mattering very little now in the grand scheme of things, especially in the face of cable TV, blockbuster movies, and the Internet. It is low-tech, unglamorous, and taken for granted."[29] The work of Hilmes, Douglas, and others did much to advance historical understanding of radio broadcasting beyond earlier studies of technological changes that made radio broadcasting possible and celebratory accounts of early program genres. Jean Seaton, in a recent study of both radio and television, provides a multi-layered perspective on broadcasting as "a distinct and pervasive cultural form that frames much in contemporary life." The "layers" take account of "broadcasting conventions, markets, innovations, choices, values and perceptions of audiences [that] themselves mutate." They embrace institutional histories, policy and market pressures, political decisions and the relationships of broadcasting institutions with governments, technological change, programming, scheduling, and sources of creativity (including "case studies in cultural history"), and "creative dialogue" with audiences.[30] Interpretations of radio's broader significance in the late 1930s can be illustrated by reference to three areas: politics, consumerism, and national and cultural identity.

Very early radio broadcasts included political messages: the 1920 pioneering broadcast by KDKA, Pittsburgh, covered the results of the US presidential election. As national networks developed in the 1920s and 1930s, political candidates could reach national rather than local audiences. The relationship between the media and politicians became increasingly important throughout the twentieth century, with the amounts of money spent on political campaigning increasing exponentially. President Franklin D. Roosevelt made effective use of radio in the 1930s with his "fireside chats." He used radio as a political instrument to win elections, silence opponents, and sell his domestic- and foreign-policy measures to the American public, including the New Deal agenda at home and anti-isolationist messages concerning American involvement abroad.[31]

The development of radio as a commercial mass medium in the United States was also intertwined with expanding consumerism in the twentieth century. Advertising and sponsorship provided the financial basis of American radio broadcasting, and audiences received "free-to-air" services as a result. Advertisers reached huge national markets by way of the broadcasting networks. The fact that the institutional framework developed for American radio also applied to television in the second half of the twentieth century meant that broadcasting delivered an extraordinarily powerful tool to commercial and corporate interests, with the audience as potential consumers. Douglas claims that radio hastened "the shift away from identifying oneself – and one's social solidarity with others – on the basis of location and family ties, to identifying oneself on the basis of consumer and taste preferences."[32] The increasing importance of commercialism has been a recurring theme in the history of mass media in the twentieth century and beyond (see Chapter 5).

Finally, radio exercised a powerful influence socially and culturally at the national level and for particular groups. Douglas, writing of the American context, states: "Radio played a pivotal role … in helping us imagine ourselves and our relationships to other Americans differently. It constructed imagined communities … and thus cultivated both a sense of nationhood and a validation of subcultures.… Radio did indeed … bring the country together … [and] the radio networks cemented New York City's role as the cultural capital of the nation." Scannell and Cardiff have highlighted the social impact of broadcasting in Britain, particularly in producing "communities."[33] Similar arguments could be made for the role of radio in other national settings. Historians have indicated the role of radio in catering to specific audiences such as women – for example in daytime programs, including the popular serials and soap opera that developed in the 1930s.[34] Radio has also been important at the local level in fostering and sustaining community identity, and community radio has retained widespread popularity, even as new media have emerged.

By the late 1930s radio had "blurred the boundaries between the private domestic sphere and public, commercial, and political life."[35] It had revolutionized home entertainment, introducing a hitherto unknown variety of entertainments. A mutually beneficial relationship between radio and music had been established, and previously unimagined audiences had access to whatever styles of music broadcasters chose to include in their programming. Arrangements for commercial broadcasting – and the role of advertisers and sponsors – provided easy access to vast markets of listeners as consumers. The existence of national networks had made possible an "intimacy" between political leaders and electorates impossible in previous periods. As a source of information, radio offered an immediacy and scope in terms of audience reach unmatched by any other medium at that time. The Second World War would enhance the reputation of radio as a source of information and entertainment, and radio would continue to thrive, despite later competition from television and new media.

5

The Rise of Advertising

"When the historian of the Twentieth Century shall have finished his narrative, and comes searching for the sub-title which shall best express the spirit of the period," commented *Printer's Ink* in May 1915, "we think it not at all unlikely that he may select 'The Age of Advertising' for the purpose."[1] Those developments in media and society that were the cause of such observations are the subject of this chapter. It examines the emergence of modern advertising from the late nineteenth century. Changes in the techniques and content of advertising after the First World War, including the application of "psychology" and use of the new medium of radio, are then considered. Finally, the chapter discusses the question of advertising's influence, giving particular attention to the problem of advertising's role in the creation of consumer culture and its effects on consumer behavior.

The Origins and Development of Advertising

Modern advertising is a product of the late nineteenth century; its origins are to be found in broader changes in the economy and communication that occurred at that time. A response to the Industrial Revolution, advertising's early development was inextricably linked to that of the mass-circulation press. Its chief characteristics are best understood by looking at forms of advertising that existed before the late nineteenth century. British and American newspapers had published paid advertisements since the seventeenth century, but these were mostly short, closely printed factual notices of the kind now called "classified" advertising. Some of these early advertisements had a persuasive element, especially in the case of patent medicines. As early as 1758 Samuel Johnson complained of the exaggerated claims of advertisers: "Advertisements are now so numerous that they are very negligently perused, and it is therefore become necessary to gain attention by magnificence of promises and by eloquence sometimes sublime and sometimes pathetick. Promise, large promise, is the soul of an advertisement."[2] Yet most advertisements in this period were intended simply to inform potential customers of the availability of goods and services. This remained the case for newspaper and magazine advertising well into the second half of the nineteenth century. Display advertising – non-classified advertisements with a visual appeal – became increasingly common from mid-century, but in outdoor forms: posters, billboards, sandwich boards, and eventually advertisements on streetcars, buses and trains, and electric signs. Display advertising at first lacked respectability, being associated with circuses and sellers of patent medicines, men whose reputation was akin to that of used car salesmen in later years. Usually, therefore, the reputable press shunned this kind of advertising.

The situation changed in the last two decades of the nineteenth century. In these years, throughout the West, the press was transformed, with the emergence of mass-circulation newspapers and magazines supported by advertising revenue (see Chapter 2). In these publications small factual notices gave way to larger advertisements – incorporating large print, pictures, even color – to the point where full-page advertisements became common. Such a fundamental change in the physical appearance of advertisements reflected a major shift in intention: the main purpose of advertising was now to persuade buyers, rather than simply to provide information.

The readiness of the press at the end of the nineteenth century to embrace forms of advertising once regarded as disreputable arose from major changes in economic life. Department stores, which began in the United States and Europe in the 1860s and 1870s, expanded their operations in the following two decades and advertised extensively in newspapers.[3] In the same period large national manufacturing companies emerged and began to advertise directly to the public. Previously consumer goods had been in chronic short supply; there had, therefore, been a ready market for such goods. A vast increase in productivity, made possible by the mechanization of manufacturing, fundamentally altered older patterns of production and distribution.

Periods of depression between the mid-1870s and mid-1890s highlighted the new problem of overproduction, which industrialists began to define as one of underconsumption. To minimize their risks, they sought to control the market, partly by advertising to ensure demand for their products.[4]

Some of the goods advertised in this way were new inventions, such as bicycles, typewriters, sewing machines, and photographic film and equipment. Advertising was also used extensively where there was little difference between the products of different manufacturers. This was true of soaps, breakfast cereals, beverages, cigarettes, and electric light bulbs. Not surprisingly, manufacturers of such products figured prominently in the ranks of advertisers at the turn of the century: Pear's, Ivory, Sapolio, Colgate-Palmolive, Kellogg, Quaker Oats, Bovril, Nestlé, Cadbury, American Tobacco Company, General Electric. Where competing products were more or less identical, distinctions had to be planted in the minds of consumers by advertisements that said little about the products' intrinsic merits. In the 1880s brand names started to be used for this purpose. Brand-name advertising aimed to persuade the public to regard a particular brand as synonymous with quality, even to regard the brand as synonymous with the product. Slogans or catchphrases served the same purpose. "Good morning! Have you used Pears' Soap?," Ivory soap's "It floats," and National Biscuit's "Lest you forget, we say it yet, Uneeda Biscuit," provide early examples of how effective slogans could be in creating popular awareness of a particular product that, to all intents and purposes, differed little from the products of the manufacturer's competitors.[5]

The transformation of the purpose and content of advertising brought with it the emergence of a modern advertising industry. The period 1890–1914 saw the development of fully-fledged advertising agencies, which employed specialist copywriters and designed and prepared advertisements rather than simply buying space in the press, as earlier agencies had done. Advertising campaigns were introduced, involving the careful coordination of newspaper and magazine advertisements with outdoor advertising and storefront displays. Advertising overcame much of its previous lack of respectability and was increasingly seen as an attractive profession for ambitious young men and women.[6] The total annual volume of advertising in the United States grew rapidly from an estimated $682 million in 1914 to $1,409 million in 1919 and $2,987 million in 1929.[7]

The rise of advertising was closely intertwined with the development of consumer culture. In the United States between the 1880s and the 1920s the vast expansion in consumer goods and their greater afford-ability, along with a steady reduction in working hours and the increased availability of inexpensive entertainments, transformed attitudes to consumption and leisure. The rapid growth of the film industry was one aspect of this development; increased expenditure on a wide vari-ety of consumer products was another. The decade from 1919 saw a huge growth in Americans' ownership of cars, radios, telephones, washing machines, vacuum cleaners, refrigerators, silk stockings, and other goods.[8] In this context a traditional emphasis on the virtues of self-denial, frugality, and hard work was increasingly challenged by a preoccupation with acquisition, material comfort, individual indul-gence, and pleasure as the way to happiness. The term "consumer culture" refers to this new set of values and beliefs. (The terms "con-sumerism," "consumer society," and "consumption ethic" are also used by writers on the subject.) The advertising industry that expanded so quickly from the last two decades of the nineteenth century aimed on one level to persuade the public to purchase the goods that industry was now capable of producing in vast numbers. On another level its aims were more ambitious, involving no less than the overturning of traditional values of self-denial and simplicity and the promotion of consumption as a way of life.

This important historical development was not as straightforward as has sometimes been claimed. In recent years historians have shown that the origins of consumer culture can be found well before the 1880s. Even by the eighteenth century, in Britain and the North American col-onies, a fondness for commercially marketed clothing, furniture, and other consumer goods was widespread among the middle classes and even those below them in the social order. Yet even in the 1920s, despite the general prosperity of the decade, many Americans remained too poor to take advantage of the expansion of consumer products, while others, even among the affluent, resisted the values of consumer cul-ture. The final triumph of these values in the United States occurred only after the Second World War. Nonetheless, there can be no doubt that the forty years from 1880 saw a major change in American patterns of consumption, and that in these years a shift toward the values of consumerism, although incomplete, also took place.[9] These changes were most fully developed in the United States; similar trends would occur in other countries at different stages of the twentieth century. The relationship between the emergence of consumer culture and the growth of mass advertising is a central historical problem.

The Techniques and Content of Advertising

Just as significant as the rapid expansion of advertising after the First World War were changes in advertising techniques. In these years "psychological advertising" was fully developed, inspired by wartime propaganda and by the influence of behavioral psychology, with its claims to hold the key to the manipulation of human desires. The rise of the mass media seemed to confirm the lessons of psychology: advertisers looked to the popular appeal of movies, tabloid newspapers, and confessional magazines as evidence that consumers were best reached through emotional appeals rather than reason.[10] In the 1920s the main trends in twentieth-century advertising were firmly established. Advertisements, especially in the United States, increasingly focused on the consumer rather than the product. They moved beyond prewar reliance on brand names, slogans, and catchphrases as methods of persuasion and aimed to convince consumers that health, social success, sex appeal, and marital happiness would result from the use of Ipana toothpaste, Palmolive soap, Chesterfield cigarettes, and countless other mass-produced goods. The advertiser took on the role of the consumer's friend, confidant, or adviser. Many advertisements invoked the advice of fictional or real-life "experts" on medical matters, home economics, child rearing, interpersonal relations, interior decoration, and dress sense. Consumers were encouraged to distrust their own inexpert judgment and to welcome the advertiser's assistance in dealing both with sources of discontent inherent in the human condition – illness, loneliness, frustration – and with many other causes of unhappiness identified by the advertising industry, including wrinkled skin, body odor, dandruff, "halitosis" (bad breath), "intestinal fatigue" (constipation), and "homotosis" (poor home furnishings). Central to this approach was the aim to create a perpetually insecure, dissatisfied consumer, anxious about status and personal well-being and ready to embrace consumption as the solution to life's problems.[11]

These approaches were first developed in the traditional advertising media of magazines and newspapers. From the late 1920s American advertisers increasingly supplemented their use of the printed press by exploiting the new medium of radio. They did so after initial hesitation. In its early years radio was viewed as a dignified, culturally uplifting medium, presenting a stark contrast to the downmarket appeal of the movies and tabloid press – a perception that stemmed largely from the affluence of radio's initial audience. Even the leaders of the advertising industry shared Secretary of Commerce Herbert Hoover's belief in 1922 that it was inconceivable that "we should allow so great a possibility for service, for news, for entertainment, for education, and for vital comercial purposes, to be drowned in advertising chatter, or used for commercial purposes." Advertisers feared that the intrusion of commercial messages into such a lofty medium would breed audience resentment toward all kinds of advertising.[12]

But radio's advantages as a vehicle for persuasion proved irresistible, all the more so when the medium gained nationwide coverage with the creation of broadcasting networks (see Chapter 4). In 1928 the American Tobacco Company drew attention to this potential when it increased sales of Lucky Strike cigarettes by 47 percent in two months after a radio advertising campaign.[13] With growing concerns that the public was becoming saturated with advertisements, and with fears of overproduction that came to a head with the beginning of the Depression in 1929, radio provided a new way to try to grab the consumer's attention. Its advantages included intrusiveness: the radio listener, unlike the magazine reader, could not easily ignore advertisements. More than print advertising, radio allowed the commercial to be blended easily with entertainment. Product names could easily be interwoven into the plots of radio drama and comedy programs or mentioned in passing in musical variety shows. Dramatized commercials – commercials in the form of brief mini-dramas, of the kind now familiar from television – also appeared. By the 1930s, as the radio audience expanded, advertisers revised their earlier view of listeners' elevated tastes and discarded many of their reservations about the medium's suitability for salesmanship. Radio advertising became more direct, hard-hitting, and ubiquitous. Radio "personalities" – whether announcers, comedians, or singers – took on the combined roles of showman and salesman, their effectiveness accentuated by the ability to seem to speak personally to each listener. Radio advertising was now so closely integrated with entertainment that the newly created radio departments of advertising agencies scripted and produced both the commercials and the shows.[14]

American advertisers were attracted to radio partly because they were persuaded of its value as a means to reach women through day-time programs. They had long been convinced, correctly, that consumers were overwhelmingly female.[15] Advertisements designed for a mainly female audience highlight advertisers' adeptness in exploiting social change. In an era of major advance in women's rights – women gained the vote in the United States in 1920 – advertising portrayed consumption as the expression of female freedom and autonomy and as the path to fulfillment. Through their purchasing decisions and loyalty to the brands of their choice, women were told, they would exercise their sovereign rights. Through the purchase of new home appliances they would be freed from the slavery of domestic labor. Cigarette advertisements portrayed these products as symbols of female emancipation.[16]

Advertisements often combined an emphasis on progress with appeals to traditional values of domesticity. Thus a widely distributed General Electric advertisement of 1925 presented an image of a mother reading to her two children, accompanied by a text that explained that electrification had freed mothers to do more important things than housework. It was, the advertisement insisted, a mother's duty to delegate to electricity as much household labor as possible: "Human lives are in her keeping, their future is molded by her hands and heart. No lesser duties should interfere with the supreme duty of having plenty of time with the children."[17] In American advertisements generally in the interwar period the "modern" woman remained above all a homemaker. The chief benefit of the vast array of consumer goods now available, advertisements suggested, was that they would assist women to become "better wives and mothers." A woman's "duty" was to make full use of advertised products to run the household efficiently and stay beautiful.[18]

The treatment of women's role in society is a good example of ideological messages conveyed through advertising. Another concerns questions of social class. American advertising of the 1920s and 1930s, in marked contrast to European advertising, appealed to middle-class values and aspirations.[19] To reach as large an audience as possible, American advertising obscured class differences and portrayed an affluent, classless society. Advertisements conveyed a clear message, reflected in such catchphrases as "any woman can" and "every home can afford": those who purchased the advertised product, regardless of occupation or means, would assert their equality in a middle-class world through possession of the same products as the very rich. A young housewife's inability to afford a $780-a-year maid like her neighbor, Ivory Soap declared in a typical advertisement of the kind, could not deny her the possession of "nice hands" by using Ivory.[20] Class resentment and proposals to redistribute wealth were to be frowned on, since "equality," it was asserted, already existed in the form of a general availability of inexpensive consumer goods. In the advertisements of the 1920s, therefore, could be seen the beginnings of an idea that reached its peak in the 1950s: America as a middle-class consumer society.[21] Outside the United States, too, the identification of ordinary people as "consumers" rather than "citizens" became increasingly common in the four decades after 1920.[22]

The Influence of Advertising

In the depiction of women as subservient to men and of US society as classless, advertisements presented as self-evident and permanent what were in reality historically conditioned and questionable assumptions. The effects on cultural values and attitudes of such portrayals of social relations represent one of the most important forms of advertising's influence. As in the case of cultural stereotypes in the movies, the ideological messages conveyed by advertisements reinforced prevailing views on social roles and helped to perpetuate forms of behavior favored by dominant groups.

Also important was the far-reaching influence that advertising exerted throughout the twentieth century by virtue of its central role in the economics of the media. By 1900 advertising provided the bulk of revenue for newspapers and magazines. By 1930 it provided almost 100 percent of the revenue for radio in the United States; this would later be the case also for television. The importance of these facts of economic life is difficult to overstate: in a fundamental way the print media and commercial broadcasting shaped their content with a view to maximizing advertising revenue, usually by seeking mass appeal. At the very least, the result was media content that differed markedly from that of public service and government-controlled media systems. Viewed optimistically, advertising's dominant role generated programs and publications that responded to popular taste and were free of political interference. Yet in some respects the results were clearly deleterious, although often in ways that involved sins of omission rather than commission. Above all, media dependence on advertising has threatened freedom of expression, by fostering reluctance on the part of media firms to publish articles or broadcast programs seen as likely to offend some members of the audience and therefore deter advertisers, and by encouraging an unwillingness to criticize companies with advertising money to spend. Significantly, for many years *Reader's Digest* was the only mainstream American publication to campaign against the tobacco industry on the basis of steadily mounting evidence of the lethal consequences of smoking. As the one popular magazine that did not accept advertising, *Reader's Digest* was not deterred by fear of losing revenue from cigarette advertising.[23]

Equally contentious is the question of advertising's influence on consumer behavior. The advertisers of the 1920s and conservative critics of "mass society" had in common a belief in the passive nature of the mass audience. The public, they assumed, was easily manipulated by advertising, as it was by movies and other forms of mass culture.[24] The apparent success of advertising campaigns was taken as proof that the public accepted at face value the emotional appeals of advertisements. Particularly instructive, it was thought, was the Lambert Company's marketing of Listerine antiseptic. After 1920 Listerine achieved a spectacular increase in sales, apparently as a result of a series of advertisements that persuaded the public to discover a new need: to use a mouthwash to combat "halitosis." Lambert capitalized on this success by inventing other uses for the same product: a cure for dandruff, an after-shave lotion, a cure for colds and sore throats, and a deodorant. The Listerine advertisements, which included such famous lines as "She was often a bridesmaid but never a bride" and "Even your best friend won't tell you," were models of the new advertising approach with its association of the product with love, social success, and happiness.[25]

After the Second World War the same assumptions about the power of advertising formed the basis of a liberal critique of the institution. Especially influential in the 1950s and 1960s, and most clearly stated by the historian David M. Potter and the economist John Kenneth Galbraith, this view maintained that the industry had been central to the creation of consumer culture in the early twentieth century. It lamented the allegedly powerful influence of advertising in the United States (and, by implication, in other Western countries). So convinced was Potter of the all-important role of advertising in building a consumer culture that he identified it as one of those institutions that wields immense influence in American society, comparable in this respect to the church, the education system, and business. Unlike these other institutions, however, Potter maintained that "advertising has in its dynamics no motivation to seek the improvement of the individual or to impart qualities of social usefulness, unless conformity to material values may be so characterized."[26] In particular, liberal critics condemned two aspects of advertising's economic role. First, they argued that advertising raises the prices of products – because manufacturers need to recoup the costs of advertising – and that it works against rational consumer choice and the efficient use of resources. Consumers, they maintained, choose products not on the basis of quality and price, as should be the case in an efficient economy, but because of the persuasiveness or manipulative influence of advertisements. Second, these critics accused advertising of creating "false needs," of persuading consumers that they need products that, in any objective view of things, they do not.

Marxist writers, notably the social philosopher Herbert Marcuse, also made the distinction between real and false needs.[27] Like the liberal critics, Marxists emphasized the powerful and manipulative nature of advertising. For the Marxists, advertising was essential to the survival of capitalism. Without advertising, they argued, the problem of over-production would have led to a state of permanent depression, causing the collapse of the capitalist system. Marxist critics also argued that advertising had functioned as a mechanism for control of the working class by the capitalist ruling class. By instilling in the masses a preoccupation with the illusory attractions of consumption, advertising was intended to turn workers' minds away from the exploitative nature of capitalism and the oppressive conditions in which they live and work, and in this way to protect the capitalist system from working-class unrest and revolution.[28]

Since the 1960s the liberal and Marxist critiques have been increasingly questioned by other scholars, who have argued that advertising is not as powerful as previous writers had believed, that advertising did not create consumer culture, and that the influence of advertising can be understood only by examining its interaction with other developments. An appraisal of advertising's role in the history of the twentieth century must take these recent perspectives into account.

That advertising undermines efficiency by often rewarding persuasiveness, at the expense of price and quality, is undeniable. On the other side of the ledger, advertising may well contribute to economies of scale. In the final analysis the longstanding debate as to whether advertising's overall economic impact is harmful or beneficial probably cannot be resolved. By contrast, the view that advertising affects brand choice is largely uncontested. As early as the 1880s the successful campaigns of major soap manufacturers demonstrated that advertisements could indeed persuade consumers to purchase a particular brand rather than another brand or a generic (and equally effective) product. In the early twentieth century the history of the cigarette reinforced the point: the success of the R. J. Reynolds brand Camel, the American Tobacco Company's Lucky Strike brand, and Liggett and Myers' Chesterfield in the 1920s owed much to effective advertising.[29] The history of advertising provides many such examples of the impact of advertising campaigns on brand choice.

Whether advertising's influence extends to the primary demand for products – whether many people buy, say, cigarettes at all only because of advertising – is a more controversial question. Although the Listerine campaigns of the 1920s suggest that, in that period at least, advertising may well have had the power to persuade consumers to purchase products that otherwise they would not have considered, the case of cigarette marketing highlights the complexity of the issue. Between 1910 and 1930 cigarette sales in the United States increased tenfold. The increase coincided with heavy investment in advertising by the major tobacco firms, leading many observers at the time and since to conclude that advertising had caused the jump in sales. But it is more likely that the growth in cigarette retailing resulted from the interaction of advertising with social and cultural changes, assisted by the production of milder forms of cigarette than those available before the First World War. The war encouraged many young men to take up smoking as a means of relief from the horrors and tedium of warfare. After the war the cigarette was linked to the movement toward greater social and civic equality for women: cigarettes became a cheap and convenient symbol of equality. Michael Schudson points out that tens of thousands of women began smoking in the 1920s before any cigarette advertisements were directed specifically at women. He concludes that it would be "more accurate to observe that cigarette smoking among women led tobacco companies to advertise toward the female market than to suggest that advertising created the market in the first place." For Schudson, the example of cigarette advertising illustrates a broader truth: "That advertising has played a role since the late 1920s in promoting smoking among women should not blind us to the fact that this change in consumption patterns, like many others, had roots deep in cultural change and political conflict that advertising often responds to but rarely creates."[30]

Other evidence supports the suggestion that cigarettes had an appeal independent of the influence of advertising. While American advertisers made far-reaching claims for their ability to manipulate human emotions, their normal practice was first to determine who was likely to buy the product and then to tailor an advertising campaign accordingly. At the outset they excluded from their calculations between 30 and 65 percent of the population; this was the range of estimates of those who were not sufficiently well-off to achieve consumer status. Invariably, before the late 1940s, the potential market was viewed as affluent, white, and of north and west European origins. Blacks and other ethnic minorities never appeared in advertisements as consumers – as opposed to servants and menial workers – because these groups were not seen as part of the market. By targeting those who were viewed as predisposed to buy, advertisers implicitly recognized the limitations of manipulation.[31]

A predisposition to purchase consumer goods was often based on the intrinsic merits of those products. Whatever the role of advertising in increasing sales of electrical appliances, it was also the case that, as David E. Nye reminds us, "electric stoves were far cleaner than coal and wood stoves; electric washing machines eliminated a backbreaking chore; electric irons made ironing faster and cooler work in the summer."[32] Many low-priced, packaged goods – soaps, breakfast cereals, biscuits, canned food, and similar products – offered the advantage of convenience. Yet in other cases – cosmetics and such multipurpose products as Listerine are good examples – the utility of consumer goods was questionable. In such cases the suspicion arises that sales depended on the success of advertising in manipulating the emotions of the audience. The issue of advertising as the creator of "false needs" therefore arises.

Here, too, recent scholarship has questioned one of the central ideas of older critiques of advertising. Where Potter, Galbraith, and Marcuse assumed that there is a useful distinction between "real" needs, which can somehow be determined objectively, and false needs, artificially whipped up by advertising or some other social influence, subsequent writers have emphasized the difficulty of establishing objective, generally accepted criteria that might be used to determine which needs are "real" and which "false," which products are necessary and which not. Beyond the most basic biological requirements, they argue, all human needs are socially constructed: the needs of people in one society differ from those in another. To show that a particular need has been stimulated by advertising is therefore not to demonstrate that it is false; it simply shows that advertising has contributed to a redefinition of needs.[33]

These insights do not amount to an apologia for advertising. Thus Schudson, one of the leading critics of older interpretations, nonetheless regards advertising as "the art form of bad faith," claiming that "it features messages that both its creators and its audience know to be false and it honors values they know to be empty." Whether it sells products or not, it "often promotes bad values."[34] But Schudson argues that advertising's liberal and Marxist critics, in emphasizing its central role in the creation of consumer culture and in the stimulation of "false needs," have underestimated the complexity of the historical process. Both advertising and consumer culture, he suggests, have their origins in changes in the market in the late nineteenth century. It was not a matter of advertising causing consumer culture; rather, both developments were part of a more fundamental social transformation. Seen in this light, advertising "is but one factor among many in shaping consumer choice and human values."[35] Such conclusions are consistent with those of recent scholarship on the history of the press, film, and radio, replacing earlier assumptions about the all-powerful impact of media content on public attitudes and values with a more complex picture – one that emphasizes the need to understand media influence as the product of interaction with broader cultural factors.

6

Propaganda in Peace and War

The word "propaganda" was originally used in a religious context when, in the seventeenth century, Pope Gregory XV established the Sacred Congregation for the Propagation of the Faith ("de Propaganda Fide"), a body with a missionary role. Later the word was used to describe not only religious proselytizing but also the dissemination of political beliefs. The development of media of mass communications from the end of the nineteenth century provided new and vastly expanded channels for propagandists. As demonstrated in Chapter 2, the First World War showed how modern media could be used on a large scale for propagandist purposes. Governments in the belligerent countries used the media to bolster patriotic and nationalist sentiment, to sustain morale at home, and to wage psychological warfare against the enemy.

In the twentieth century the exploitation of media for political purposes became commonplace. Totalitarian states such as the Soviet Union and Nazi Germany provided striking examples, but propaganda was by no means absent from democratic societies. A major difference in official approaches to use of propaganda was willingness as opposed to reluctance to "label" activities aimed at persuading or influencing the minds and political behavior of others. In Germany in the 1930s, for example, the Nazis viewed propaganda in a very positive light and made no effort to disguise the fact that it was to be employed as a tool of the regime. When Hitler came to power in 1933, he established a Ministry for Popular Enlightenment and Propaganda. By contrast, in the democracies there was reluctance to admit to the use of propagandist activities, and these tended to be described as "information," "education," or, rather more aggressively, "psychological warfare."

Whatever terms proved most acceptable in specific political contexts, propaganda does involve an effort to persuade, to manipulate opinion. Therefore, it is likely to be most effective if people do not have access to multiple sources of information and if they are discouraged from thinking critically. Michael Balfour has suggested that the "best touchstone for distinguishing propaganda from science is whether a plurality of sources of information and of interpretations is being discouraged or fostered." David Welch has noted that, although propaganda is often seen as the art of persuasion, more often than not it reinforces existing trends and beliefs. Furthermore, according to a common view of propaganda, it appeals to irrational instincts; but Welch notes that, to be effective, propaganda must also appeal to rational elements.[1] Most importantly in relation to modern media, historians have pointed to the importance for propagandists of technological developments. Jacques Ellul in the 1960s drew attention to propaganda as a sociological phenomenon in technological societies, stressing the importance of mass media in the psychological manipulation characteristic of propaganda. Garth S. Jowett and Victoria O'Donnell defined propaganda as "the deliberate and systematic attempt to shape perceptions, manipulate cognitions, and direct behavior to achieve a response that furthers the desired intent of the propagandist," emphasizing the importance of propaganda as communication and persuasion as part of propaganda.[2] Twentieth-century mass media provided channels for disseminating content intended to influence, persuade, convert, and harness populations to particular political causes on a scale previously unknown.

This chapter examines the use by both totalitarian and democratic regimes of modern media for propagandist purposes. Bolshevik and Stalinist activities between 1917 and 1945 illustrate the extensive use of propaganda within the highly centralized political system of the Soviet Union, where visual media were particularly important in a society with a high level of illiteracy. The propagandist activities of the Nazi regime in Germany from 1933 to 1945 – and of the Nazi Party during its rise to power – illustrate a systematic effort to control and exploit modern media to disseminate political and ideological messages. The use of propaganda by democratic governments such as those of Britain and the United States during the Second World War demonstrates that propaganda should by no means be seen as confined to single-party, centralized, totalitarian political regimes.

The Context of Soviet Propaganda

In the Soviet Union under Lenin and Stalin (as in Germany under Hitler) propaganda was vital to the regime as it set out to politicize vast areas of life. After the Bolshevik Party had seized power in Russia in 1917, mass indoctrination was an important means of transforming society along communist lines. Institutions of mass mobilization and propaganda became central to the Soviet system. The Bolsheviks paid great attention to persuasion, using new symbols, rituals, and visual imagery to instruct Soviet citizens and to transform popular attitudes and beliefs.[3] Under Vladimir Ilich Lenin, Bolshevik revolutionary leaders attempted to manage the revolution through a highly centralized and disciplined party structure and to educate the proletariat. They were ruthless in not tolerating opposition and in manipulating opinion for the sake of the revolution. Propaganda was of central importance to the Bolshevik Party (subsequently the Communist Party), particularly simple forms of propaganda that conveyed easily understood messages to a population with low literacy levels.

The main aims of Soviet propaganda evolved with changing circumstances between 1917 and 1945. The revolution of 1917 was followed by a period of civil war, lasting to 1922, when the regime struggled for survival against various enemies both internal and external (including the supporters of the deposed Tsar, the Whites, national groups seeking independence, and armies of the Western powers that sought to influence events in Russia). The Bolsheviks triumphed in the Civil War, but the regime was still insecure. The New Economic Policy of 1921–9, which allowed for a degree of moderation and for a mixed economy, was intended to reconcile to the regime various alienated groups, especially the peasants who comprised a majority of the population. Throughout the 1920s a main task of propaganda was to persuade the unconverted and remind those loyal to the new regime that the revolution and its results were legitimate and that sacrifices should be endured for the sake of a better future.

From the power struggle following Lenin's death in 1924 Joseph Stalin emerged as the dominant figure in the Communist Party and leader of the Soviet Union. His policy of building "socialism in one country" and modernizing the Soviet economy included the collectivization of agriculture and rapid industrialization. Stalin's Five-Year

Plans, beginning in 1929, resulted in extraordinary hardship for Soviet citizens and were implemented only with the brutal use of force.

The peasantry resisted collectivization. There was a full-scale military campaign and virtual civil war in the Soviet countryside from 1929 to 1933. Millions died from the fighting, in executions and mass deportations, and as a result of artificially created famine, especially in the Ukraine in the winter of 1932–3. In this context the role of propaganda was to persuade the peasants to accept a new, state-controlled agricultural order, and to portray to urban populations what was happening in the countryside in a positive manner. Despite falling living standards, rationing, the devastation of agriculture, and the upheaval created by massive migration to urban areas, propaganda had to convey the message that the regime was responsible for significant accomplishments.

Industrialization, implemented by means of the Five-Year Plans, which imposed unachievable objectives on heavy industry, led to deplorable living standards in the rapidly expanding urban areas and involved rigid labor discipline, enforced by the People's Commissariat of Internal Affairs (the NKVD or secret police), which, by the end of the 1930s, employed some 366,000 people. This period saw the expansion of the Gulag (GULAG is an acronym meaning "Main Camp Administration"), which became a vast network of labor camps, following Stalin's decision to use forced labor to speed up industrialization and to exploit natural resources in the northern parts of the Soviet Union. From 1929 control of the camps was taken over by the secret police.[4] Propaganda was used in conjunction with coercion to persuade workers and their families that the great hardships of the Five-Year Plans were a necessary cost in building a strong, modern country capable of defending itself against powerful external enemies. Stories popularized by the regime in the 1930s included ideas of a "radiant future" (holding out the hope that sacrifice and hardship in the present would lead to a future socialist state of abundance) and "out of backwardness" (with the regime overcoming the legacy inherited from tsarist Russia and becoming a modern, industrialized economy).

In the 1930s coercion and terror, along with Stalin's cult of personality, were dominant aspects of Soviet life. Hundreds of thousands were executed and millions sent to the labor camps. The victims, depicted as "class enemies," included surviving leaders of the revolution of 1917, wealthy peasants ("kulaks"), priests, private businessmen from the New Economic Policy years, party officials who had fallen out of favor with the Stalinist administration, and the bulk of the officer corps of the Red Army and Navy. Applebaum estimates that, at any one time, there were around two million prisoners in Soviet labor camps, but that the total number of citizens who "passed through this massive system", as political or criminal prisoners, between 1929 and the year of Stalin's death, 1953, was around eighteen million.[5] The terror culminated in show trials in 1936–8 involving high-profile public and military figures such as Zinoviev, Kamenev, Bukharin, and Marshal Tukhachevsky, when some of Stalin's victims "confessed" to conspiring with foreign powers to overthrow the Soviet state.

Part of the context for these developments was the rise of Nazi Germany, stimulating fear that Hitler's regime posed a threat to the survival of the Soviet Union and raising the possibility of another war. Thus propaganda emphasized the need for vigilance and personal sacrifice to defend the Soviet Union against fascism or Nazism; it attempted to convince the public that the Soviet Union was surrounded by enemies; that these enemies were assisted by traitors within the country; and that the most extreme measures were necessary to destroy them. In August 1939 a dramatic adjustment was required when Hitler and Stalin signed the Nazi-Soviet Non-Aggression Pact. However, less than two years later, in June 1941, Hitler turned against his ally and invaded the Soviet Union. The central function of propaganda then became the harnessing of the total population to a single-minded war effort against the Nazi aggressors. Russian nationalism and the fight against fascism were central themes during what was referred to as "the great patriotic war."

Media and Methods of Soviet Propaganda

After the revolution of 1917 the Bolsheviks moved quickly to exploit existing media for propagandist purposes, nationalizing the publishing industry in 1917, taking control of the main newspapers *Pravda* and *Izvestia*, banning private advertisements, nationalizing the Petrograd Telegraph Agency, taking over news production by establishing the All-Russian Telegraph Agency (ROSTA) in 1918, and establishing press censorship. Newspapers played a dominant role in Soviet propaganda. According to Jeffrey Brooks, "party leaders shaped all modes of expression through the central press, and local publishers reproduced the Party's message."[6]

Lenin also attempted to use radio. As an emerging mass medium, it had propagandist potential, especially because of widespread illiteracy (by 1926, despite Bolshevik efforts at education, some 50 percent of the rural and 20 percent of the urban population of the Soviet Union were still basically without literacy skills). The Bolsheviks used radio broadcasts to spread party political messages from 1922, but the potential of radio as a propaganda tool remained limited by its relative expense in a poor economy. In the 1930s the regime used loudspeakers to broadcast in factories, clubs, and collective farms to reach wider audiences. However, the print media remained more important than radio: whereas there were some seven million radio sets in the Soviet Union by 1940, newspaper circulation figures were of the order of thirty-eight million.[7]

The problem of illiteracy and the expense of other forms of communications in a vast and poor country meant that mass meetings and "agitation" were important methods of Soviet propaganda. In the 1920s, under the supervision and tight control of the Agitational-Propaganda Section of the Central Committee of the Communist Party (Agitprop), party "agitators" went from the city to the countryside to "sell the revolution," and special "agit-trains" and ships were used for propagandist purposes. Party-controlled groups such as the trade unions and the Komsomol, the Young Communist League, the Party's main youth organization, mobilized mass support for the Party's goals and were a source of active propagandists. Forms of mass mobilization and propaganda included carnivals and parades, and in the 1930s the "public theater" of the show trials. The show trials were given intensive media coverage as public theatrical performances used by the Central Committee of the Communist Party as entertainment-cum-agitational tools.[8] Even the Gulag had a "Cultural-Educational Department" (the *Kulturno-vospitatelnaya chast*, KVCh) whose main role was to propagate the value of work but also organized theatrical performances, concerts, political lectures, and discussions.

Posters were an important form of visual propaganda in the Soviet state. They were simple in form and suited a society with a highly visual traditional culture and low literacy levels; they could be produced in long print runs; and messages could be altered to respond quickly to a changing political context. Poster art stressed conflict and opposition: good and evil, worker and capitalist, peasant and landowner, revolutionary and counter-revolutionary. Early posters depicted revolutionaries as breaking all ties with the old bourgeois world, as bold and heroic defenders of the revolution. They disseminated the Bolshevik slogan of "peace, bread and land" and the theme of class war. They exhorted the people to fight and work harder, and they exposed and ridiculed foreign and domestic enemies. During the Civil War posters circulated on a massive scale, and during the Five-Year Plans they depicted the new era of collectivization and industrialization. In the 1930s poster production was centralized under the State Publishing House. Dominant images included Stalin as uncontested and all-powerful leader, and overachieving workers ("shock workers") promoted under the Stakhanovite campaign (named after a coalminer who far exceeded his quota for coal-mining shifts and became a national hero). They conveyed the atmosphere of threat and fear during the purges, as Stalin became increasingly paranoid about potential opposition. They emphasized the need for vigilance to detect enemies at a time when denunciation became commonplace during the show trials and the great purge. Similar to posters were "wall newspapers," used, for example, in the labor camps, where they were displayed on special noticeboards. While there is evidence that prisoners paid them little attention, the Gulag administration took them seriously, using them to "portray the best examples of work, popularize the shock workers, condemn the shirkers."[9]

The Bolsheviks also valued film as a propaganda tool. As another visual medium, film had the potential to surmount the problems of widespread illiteracy and differences of language and culture in the Soviet Union. Unlike theater, it allowed the central government to exert tight control over political messages that could be reproduced and exhibited in all parts of the country. The Bolsheviks aimed to harness cinema to the purposes of the state, using it to persuade and educate rather than to entertain.

In practice the Bolsheviks were not able to exploit film's propaganda potential extensively in the 1920s. The production and exhibition of feature films throughout such a huge country were very expensive, so resources were largely devoted to making newsreels or brief films with acted parts called "agitki." During the period of the New Economic Policy much film production, distribution, and exhibition remained privately controlled, and the Party was not sufficiently in control to impose complete film censorship. Imported films were permitted from 1924 as a revenue-making measure, and until 1927 most full-length films shown in Soviet cinemas were foreign, especially American. Cinema remained a predominantly urban form of entertainment in the 1920s.

Nonetheless, some feature films made by directors such as Sergei Eisenstein and Alexander Dovzhenko are now considered classics of the Soviet period, including *Battleship Potemkin, October, Arsenal,* and *Earth.* These sought to legitimize the revolution and the Soviet regime, portraying a contest between good and evil in a world in which historical forces, rather than individuals, were all-important. Richard Taylor observes that the Soviet worldview "led to a hero who fell clearly into an ideologically respectable category, be he worker, peasant, soldier, sailor, revolutionary or Party worker, while the villain included all potential sources of dissent or opposition, being characterized (and frequently caricatured) as capitalist, bourgeois, landowner, kulak, priest, officer, spy or counter-revolutionary."[10]

Soviet filmmakers of the 1920s worked under political constraints; nonetheless, within these limits they were allowed considerable artistic freedom. They developed innovative techniques such as *montage,* the juxtaposition of images to elicit a specific emotional response from the viewer, which had an impact beyond the Soviet Union. Directors such as Eisenstein and Dovzhenko were committed Bolsheviks, so their "propaganda" was the product of conviction rather than compulsion. Yet their films, although containing politically sound communist messages, lost favor with the regime. They appear not to have been popular with Soviet audiences, who preferred good stories and recognizable characters. The films therefore presented the Party with a dilemma: it wanted films to provide both entertainment (and revenue) and propaganda, but films that ordinary Russians could not understand or did not enjoy were unlikely to be effective. At the end of the 1920s the films of the great directors were increasingly criticized within the Party for being artistically advanced and tainted with bourgeois ideas.

Under Stalin there was greater restriction on artistic freedom in the film industry, reflecting growing centralization and ideological rigidity, and leading to artistic sterility. Film did become more accessible, as collectives acquired film projectors; but choice was limited in the 1930s, there were virtually no foreign imports, and the number of domestically produced films fell from about 130 per annum in the late 1920s to 35 in 1933. The 308 films made in Soviet studios between 1933 and 1940 were subject to increasing control and censorship. Stalin personally viewed and approved films for exhibition, maintaining tight control over distribution. In 1932 Soviet authorities decreed that "socialist realism" was the only acceptable style for artists and writers. This approach glorified ordinary workers undertaking everyday tasks as proletarian heroes. It was intended to advance the goals of the revolution and was an extreme example of the state attempting to dictate the purpose and form of creativity. There was great emphasis on Stalin's cult of personality. Pictorial representations of his political opponents were altered, as Stalin manipulated the photographic record to erase the memory of his victims. Airbrushing and cropping techniques were used to obliterate all traces of those who fell out of favor or disappeared during the purges of the 1930s; and techniques such as photomontage were used to magnify Stalin's image and importance.[11]

With the beginning of the Second World War propaganda served the purposes of the state during another total war. After the Nazi invasion of the Soviet Union in 1941, all Soviet media were mobilized to support the struggle against Germany. An example of the blatant use of film for propagandist purposes was *Alexander Nevsky*. In 1938, when Germany's foreign policy was increasingly threatening, Sergei Eisenstein had produced this historical epic, intended to rouse patriotic Russian sentiment against the German danger. When Soviet policy changed in 1939 with the Nazi-Soviet Non-Aggression Pact, Stalin banned the film; but it was re-released in 1941 after the Nazis had invaded the Soviet Union. This film – as did other media, press, and radio – emphasized themes of patriotism, national unity, and the despicable nature of the enemy. As the war went on, newsreels and documentaries attempted to persuade Soviet citizens that the German army was not invincible. Soviet wartime propaganda from 1941 depicted the struggle against Nazi Germany as a clash between two ideologies, with the Soviet people united in a struggle for a no-compromise victory.

The Soviet Union in the Stalinist period provided an example of the mass media being used as tools of the state, with the regime having achieved an effective monopoly on public expression. Newspapers, radio, and film were used to spread propagandist messages about the cult of the leader, the successes of a progressive and modernizing policy at home, and, insofar as they gave attention to events beyond Soviet borders, the dangers of enemies abroad.

Nazi Propaganda and Control of the Media

As in the Soviet Union under Stalin, so too in Germany under Hitler and the Nazi Party between 1933 and 1945, the mass media were vital to the regime's propagandist activities. Propaganda – again supplemented by repression and terror – was highly valued by the Nazis, although in the very different context of an industrialized and more literate society than the Soviet Union.

Before becoming chancellor of Germany in 1933, Adolf Hitler had written about the importance of propaganda and employed it to facilitate the rise to power of the *National soczialistiche Deutsche Arbeiterparte* (National Socialist German Workers' Party, NSDAP, abbreviated to Nazi Party). In his political manifesto, *Mein Kampf*, completed in 1925 during a period of imprisonment, he discussed the aims and means of propaganda (his chapter 6 deals with "War Propaganda"). He admitted to having been heavily influenced by enemy propaganda during the First World War, expanding upon the brilliance of the British as propagandists. He was convinced that propaganda was a powerful weapon and should be addressed to the broad masses of the people (not to elites or "the intellectual classes"). His view of propaganda was that it should be simple, concentrating on a few key essentials, expressed in stereotyped formulae and slogans that are repeated persistently. He viewed the mass audience, the targets of propaganda, as having limited intelligence and enormous "power of forgetting," so simple messages were essential. (His assumptions about the audience and his views on propagandist methods and messages were not unlike those of American advertisers – see Chapter 5.)

Hitler began to implement his ideas about propaganda at party functions in the 1920s. Kershaw notes that by 1928 Hitler was Party Propaganda Leader for the NSDAP and was already making his mark as a masterly propagandist. He proved to be a very skillful public speaker, adept at establishing rapport with his audience and appealing to listeners' emotions. Hitler's approach suited the mass meetings that contributed to the Party's rise to power, using propaganda as a key to mass mobilization.[12]

The first of the Nuremburg party rallies was held in 1926, and the emotive torchlight parades and night events became a feature of this annual event. The party experimented with techniques of political agitation and adopted what became powerful symbols (the swastika, the eagle, the *Horst Wessel Lied* as a "theme song"). William S. Allen, in a detailed study of the central German town of Northeim, has shown how the Nazis used propaganda at the local level to strengthen their influence. The party gained control of the press, developed a newspaper, and in the first six months after coming to power subjected the town "to a veritable barrage of propaganda." The Weimar flag was burned and replaced by the Imperial flag, the swastika and other Nazi symbols; there were mass demonstrations, parades, speeches, a celebration of Hitler's birthday, the Day of German Labor, a book-burning day, various SA and SS events, Hitler Youth meetings, plays, and movies. The Nazis were so successful in orchestrating events and engendering a "state of excitement" that popular energy in Northeim for other activities was diminished.[13] In addition, propaganda combined with violence to focus attention on the NSDAP. For example, when Nazi meetings ended in violence – with the *Sturmabteilungen* (the SA, storm troops) or the *Schutzstaffel* (the SS, Hitler's personal bodyguard) breaking up communist or socialist meetings – this heightened their propaganda value and attracted more publicity.

While propagandist tactics drew some to the Party, they did not win unanimous popular support. In 1930–2 pro- and anti-Nazi voters tended to divide along class, regional, and denominational lines. The Social Democratic Party (SPD) and the German Communist Party (KPD) retained strong support among the urban working class and the Center Party among German Catholics. However, by 1932 the Nazis had made striking gains, drawing mass support from the lower middle class, including "young people, many without jobs, voting for the first time, and from those who had not voted before, but had been stirred by events and by propaganda to come to the polls this time."[14]

In the 1930s the emergence of new techniques of mass communications assisted Nazi propagandists. Z. E. B. Zeman has noted: "until 1929 the technical equipment at the disposal of Nazi propagandists was rather primitive. The means of mass communications – large-circulation press, films, radio, and television – ... were usually absent during the rise to power."[15] Once in power, Nazi leaders were able to take advantage of new ways of disseminating propaganda (for example, cheap radio sets).

While Hitler realized the importance of propaganda as a tool in the Nazi rise to power, he thought that the need for it would decline once the party had gained control of the German state, and that organization would be more important than propaganda. In fact Nazi Germany was very much a propaganda state, and Josef Goebbels was a key figure in making it so. In March 1933 Hitler appointed Goebbels Minister of Popular Enlightenment and Propaganda. The importance of propagandist activities to the Party can be gauged not only by the establishment of the ministry – and the overt reference to propaganda in its title – but also by the fact that more than 14,000 people were involved in the party propaganda apparatus by 1934. Goebbels "felt that propaganda should continue to play an important role even after the Nazis had come to power. Propaganda would be necessary to mobilize the masses in support of the new state and its ideological foundations."[16] Propaganda was considered a vital means of converting citizens to Nazi ideology; however, as in the Soviet Union, terror supplemented propaganda as an instrument of the state.

Goebbels had specific ideas on the role of different media. The press was a means of informing and instructing the German people about reasons for government policy; radio provided a link between the individual citizen and the nation. These media were vehicles for propaganda designed to win active commitment, to mobilize total support for the Nazi state. Propaganda was "at the heart of all contact between Government and people, indeed at the heart of all political activity." The fundamental aim of Nazi propaganda, to mobilize the German people behind Nazi policies, implied a restructuring of values, and truth was important only insofar as it served the interests of the state. Old loyalties had to be replaced with selfless service to the national community; racial purity had to be recognized as indispensable; the German people had to develop a hatred of Germany's enemies, while unquestioningly trusting German leadership.[17]

Party control of German media was a necessity, given Nazi propaganda ambitions. Goebbels, as Minister for Popular Enlightenment and Propaganda, had considerable power to implement measures to align the media with Nazi priorities, supervising radio, film, the press, and theater, as well as organizing propaganda abroad. In relation to the press he did not attempt to achieve instant "coordination" (*Gleichschaltung*) with Nazi objectives, but he gradually eroded the independence of German newspapers. He banned or suppressed communist and social democratic papers, then Catholic and middle-class democratic dailies. A 1933 law ended editorial independence, specifying who could be appointed as an editor and how he or she should act (and an Act passed in October prohibited any Jew, or Aryan married to a Jew, from being appointed as an editor). Goebbels acquired the power to veto any journalist entering the profession. Official press conferences were given regularly, ensuring that journalists were exposed to government views. Jeffrey Herf also points to the importance of

Otto Dietrich, the Reich press chief, and his press directives. Dietrich was in daily contact with Hitler and played an important role in conveying his messages (especially radical anti-Semitic propaganda) to the press. By the end of the decade the Nazi Party's publishing house, Eher Verlag, had assumed control of the majority of the German press; a single, state-controlled news agency had been formed, enabling Goebbels's ministry to control newspaper content; and Goebbels had imposed Nazi control over much of German publishing.[18]

The Nazis also used forms of propaganda often associated with less literate societies. Herf argues that wall newspapers, displayed in public places such as metro stations, bus stops, factory cafeterias, post offices, and street kiosks, were an important form of visual propaganda in a society "whose daily rhythms were characterized by walking and mass transit." These conveyed the *Parole der Woche* (Word of the Week), combining newspaper editorial, political leaflet, political poster, and tabloid journalism. They were "an effective method of diffusing political propaganda on a mass scale."[19]

With respect to radio, it was relatively easy for the Nazi Party to take control of the broadcasting system, which had been state-regulated since the mid-1920s. However, whereas prior to 1933 German broadcasting had relied on a network of regional companies loosely controlled by the German Broadcasting Company, from 1933 the Nazis centralized control. Goebbels placed considerable importance on the power of radio, using it as a tool for political purposes and ideological education, as an "instrument to create uniformity and guide public opinion toward the Nazi concept of national community."[20] He encouraged the production and distribution of cheap and more powerful radio sets (sets that could receive only German, not foreign, broadcasts). By 1939 more than 70 percent of German households had wireless. In addition to using radio to broadcast in the domestic environment, the Nazis encouraged community listening. Loudspeakers were installed in public squares, factories, offices, schools, and restaurants. Radio wardens were appointed to ensure that people listened to important speeches and announcements. Political broadcasts were an important part of programming, and by 1935 Hitler's speeches were reaching a radio audience of more than fifty-six million. Welch credits the Nazis with creating a "mass listening public" and notes their "remarkable accomplishment" in using radio to disseminate National Socialist ideas and create a "single public opinion."[21]

Goebbels also used short-wave broadcasting to reach German minority populations beyond German borders. For example, in the Saar cheap receivers were distributed to Germans and used for propaganda broadcasting. Foreign-language broadcasting, using short wave to the United States and medium wave to the United Kingdom, was also developed in the 1930s. Horst J. P. Bergmeier and Rainer E. Lotz have demonstrated how music, including popular music, swing, and jazz, was exploited in Nazi-controlled radio broadcasting to attract listeners to propaganda broadcasts.[22]

Goebbels also experimented with television broadcasting in Germany in the 1930s. Rather than using television sets as a domestic medium, the Nazis made sets available in public places, initially in Berlin, using them to broadcast party messages to viewers. However, television did not become a mass medium under the Nazis.

The film industry was important to Nazi propaganda efforts, and both Hitler and Goebbels were obsessed with cinema. Goebbels placed great importance on film as a means of entertainment, while also considering entertainment a very effective means of propaganda. For him the cinema was a tool to reinforce existing values and beliefs as well as moving people's thinking toward key aspects of Nazi ideology. Films of the Nazi period included themes such as German nationalism, the supremacy of the Aryan race, the Volk community, and militarism.

Even before 1933 film had been important for the Nazi Party. A film had been made of the 1927 Nuremberg party rally and screened to closed party gatherings, and in the early 1930s Goebbels had established a film distribution unit in Berlin. As minister, Goebbels began to establish control over previously independent companies. A Nazi nominee was appointed head of the Cinema Owners' Association in 1933, the official film industry trade union was dissolved, and in July a *Reichsfilmkammer* (Reich Film Chamber) was established. This enabled Goebbels and his ministry to exert control over filmmakers and the industry, as the *Reichsfilmkammer* had power to license films and to decide on the release of completed films, on film financing and on tax concessions.[23]

Another law in February 1934 enabled Goebbels to supervise films from the early stages of production, with compulsory script censorship centralized in Berlin. The Nazis established a film finance bank; and the bank could stop production of undesirable films simply by refusing credit. Jews and "degenerate" artists were removed from German cultural life. Art criticism and film reviews (other than purely descriptive) were banned in 1936, and critics needed a special license from the *Reichsfilmkammer*. Not surprisingly, few foreign films were imported. Nazi organizations distributed films for Hitler Youth organizations, with mobile film units traveling to rural areas and providing a mixture of entertainment and indoctrination to German youth. Between 1937 and 1942 nationalization of the German film industry was achieved, with the state taking over remaining film companies under an umbrella organization, *Ufa-Film*. The result was "enormous concentration of a mass medium in the hands of the National Socialist State and, more specifically, the minister for popular enlightenment and propaganda."[24]

Film historians have provided detailed analyses of specific Nazi films, demonstrating how they disseminated elements of National Socialist ideology. For example, *Hitler Youth Quex*, an early Nazi film first shown in Munich in September 1933 and estimated to have reached an audience of ten million, influenced young Germans with ideas of heroism, comradeship, sacrifice, and the notion of the hero-martyr. The brilliant "documentaries" of Leni Riefenstahl demonstrate the power of Nazi propaganda. *Triumph of the Will*, commissioned by Hitler and released in 1935, portrayed the Nuremberg rally as a Nazi propaganda spectacular, with its themes of leadership and the Führer cult, the national community, the submergence of individual will in the will of the German nation, the triumph of a strong Germany, as well as its powerful use of symbols – the swastika, eagles, and banners. Hitler also commissioned Riefenstahl to record the 1936 Olympic Games in Berlin. Riefenstahl's film *Olympia* – the opening scenes of which depict the Nazi innovation of a torch relay from Olympia in Greece to the Olympic Games venue – was released in 1938. While documenting the games, it was also a powerful advertisement for the achievements of the "new Germany."[25]

Historians have pointed to the significance of propaganda in explaining the great tenacity of the German home front during the Second World War. Goebbels made special use of film to sustain home-front morale and fighting spirit. Even toward the end of the war, as Germany's military situation deteriorated, he continued to commission films. For the historical drama, *Kolberg*, about German resistance to Napoleon's army, he diverted 187,000 soldiers and 4,000 sailors from active duty to act as extras at the very time when Soviet forces were moving into Germany.[26] Such an extraordinary action was a measure of the importance of propaganda for the Nazi regime. Blatantly racist films were also produced in an attempt to win support for this component of Nazi ideology and policy. Hitler initiated *Der Ewige Jude* (*The Eternal Jew*), a crude effort that was a box-office disaster. Goebbels's anti-Jewish film, *Jud Suss*, had more success, and Himmler ordered all under his command, including guards in the extermination camps, to see the film.

As well as feature films, Goebbels and his ministry coordinated the production of newsreels. From 1938 legislation made it compulsory to show a newsreel with all film programs, and newsreels were widely and cheaply distributed. During the Second World War newsreels were used to instill obedience and encourage belief in German victory. By 1940 all other newsreel production companies had been dissolved, and production of the war newsreels was centralized in the *Deutsche Wochenschau*. The films were used not only within Germany but also in efforts to intimidate populations in countries about to be attacked, showing resistance to the German forces as futile.

In summary, in Germany under Hitler, as in the Soviet Union under Lenin and Stalin, control of the media was centralized, and newspapers, radio, and film were used by the regime for propagandist purposes. While it is evident that both regimes exploited the media, it is more difficult to assess just how effective these propagandist efforts were.

The Effectiveness of Propaganda

Totalitarian states regarded propaganda as of central importance in mobilizing mass support and establishing total control over society. Because of this emphasis, and because of the sheer extent of totalitarian propaganda, it is tempting to conclude that it must have been successful. In the Soviet Union the Bolsheviks and subsequently the Communist Party succeeded in consolidating the revolution, extending political control throughout a vast area, and surviving the turmoil of the 1930s and the crisis of the German invasion in 1941. The Nazis in Germany in the 1930s have been viewed as masters of modern propaganda techniques, employing them in an ambitious bid to re-educate the German people for a new society and new value system. It is important to question the extent to which propaganda did assist in achieving totalitarian ends. Where there is tight state control over mass media, omission and suppression can be as important as the content that does appear, and there is a view that, when access to other points of view is denied, people may simply come to take for granted the worldview that is presented so that their perceptions of reality are altered.

The debates are complex, but it is generally accepted that it is simplistic to consider propaganda as a single-factor explanation of political "success." In these totalitarian systems terror and repression accompanied propaganda, and it can be argued that the former played a larger role in destroying opposition and forcing opponents into submission than did propaganda. There were certainly instances of the failure of policy and propaganda: Stalin's collectivization campaign and famine created enormous hostility to the Communist Party in the Ukraine, to the point where the German invaders were at first welcomed as liberators in 1941; the Stakhanovite movement provoked objections from, and resentment among, workers; at the time of the show trials workers and peasants were more concerned with bread shortages and reacted to official information about the trials and terror with skepticism.[27]

As new sources have become accessible, as historians have focused on resistance and the experiences of individuals under totalitarian rule, it has become apparent that a more nuanced appreciation of the impact of propaganda is needed. For example, although official mass culture had a monopoly of Soviet mass media, popular tastes could not entirely be ignored, unofficial popular cultural forms continued to flourish beneath the surface, and "the cultural hegemony of the regime was far from all-embracing." Sources such as letters, memoirs, and diaries indicate that "the hitherto neglected body of dissonant opinion … distorted, subverted, rejected, or provided an alternative to the official discourse." Despite the regime's promises of future abundance and massive propaganda about its achievements, even in Russian towns there was a degree of popular skepticism. Furthermore, the working class had changed so much that its coherence as a class and any workers' sense of special connection with the regime had become questionable.[28]

Applebaum has posed the larger question about the relationship between Soviet propaganda and Soviet reality: did any of its leaders ever believe in what they were doing? In the labor camps she describes the "absurdity" of the gap between propaganda and reality, puts the argument that camp propaganda, "like all Soviet propaganda, was pure farce, that no one believed it …", but notes, on the other hand, that the Gulag administration expended considerable time and money on propaganda. This may have resulted from "rigid bureaucracy," but "perhaps there is no good explanation" and only the paradox of slave laborers being expected to enjoy their work.[29]

Another paradoxical aspect has been explored in recent work based on diaries written under Stalin: rather than resisting the regime's demands, some diarists struggled to understand and embrace them, seeking self-transformation and a sense of belonging. This is reminiscent of arguments developed by Catherine Merridale that, even though they knew Soviet propaganda was based on lies, Soviet citizens were helped by the sense of common purpose and collectivism to endure the tragedies of Soviet history in the twentieth century.[30] This remains an area in which general conclusions are difficult, with different types of sources providing varying insights into individual and collective responses to propaganda.

To understand what predisposes people to receive propagandist messages, Ian Kershaw's work provides insights relevant to both the Soviet Union and Nazi Germany: the effectiveness of propaganda "was heavily dependent upon its ability to build on an existing consensus, to confirm existing values, to bolster existing prejudices."[31] In the Soviet Union propaganda was most likely to be successful when it built on existing fears and prejudices such as memories of tsarist and aristocratic oppression in pre-revolutionary days and fears of Russia's vulnerability to foreign invasion. In Germany propaganda that built on existing values – anti-Marxism, anti-leftism, hostility to the Weimar Republic and the postwar settlement, support for a strong leader (encouraging personal loyalty to Hitler and belief in the Führer myth) – was also largely successful.

Where a consensus did not exist, propaganda tended to be less successful. Kershaw cites the Nazi attempt to promote the idea of a national community; this was not achieved, as social and class divisions did not disappear. Anti-Slav/Russian propaganda and propaganda in support of a racial-eugenic policy of euthanasia in Germany were also largely unsuccessful. As the gap between propaganda and reality became apparent, particularly as the war went on and Germany was no longer victorious militarily, disbelief set in among German citizens. For example, from 1941 it became more and more difficult for German newsreels to convince, as their effectiveness depended on being able to report military victories. Rather than providing factual war reporting, they became unrealistic and relied on irrational themes. German audiences responded negatively, with crowds lingering outside cinemas until the newsreels (first on cinema programs) had finished. Despite Goebbels's unremitting efforts to create a mentality of struggle and endurance, Welch argues that the war newsreels finally failed to combat growing German disillusionment or to produce a suspension of disbelief. Once German military successes had come to an end, Germans tended to associate the newsreels with myth rather than reality.[32]

In relation to the effectiveness of Nazi propaganda a particularly contentious area is the anti-Jewish propaganda. Kershaw classifies this as propaganda "in a vacuum" and concludes that it failed to strike a chord with many Germans, although it did succeed in creating a "Jewish question" and depersonalizing the Jew. Herf extends the argument about anti-Jewish propaganda, claiming that Hitler's attacks were not only on racial but also on political grounds. From 1939 he repeatedly asserted that international Jewry was guilty of starting and prolonging the Second World War, and "the ordinary and daily experience of all Germans included exposure to radical anti-Semitic propaganda whose unambiguous intent was to justify mass murder of Jews." Questions about the extent to which "ordinary Germans" absorbed such propagandist messages and were complicit in what was occurring from 1942 – especially in the death camps – became an important part of historical debate in the 1990s particularly after the publication of Daniel Goldhagen's *Hitler's Willing Executioners: Ordinary Germans and the Holocaust.* Goldhagen argued that longstanding and deep-seated anti-Semitism permeated German political culture and society; that the Nazis were only moving from ideology to reality with "eliminationist" anti-Semitism; and that ordinary Germans became "willing executioners" of Hitler's will in the genocidal program against the Jews. Perhaps the key point here is that the details of the Final Solution were suppressed. The fact that the regime hid, rather than publicized, the "solution" to the "Jewish problem" can be interpreted as evidence of the failure of Nazi propaganda on racial ideology. The main "successes" of Nazi policy against the Jews can be attributed to "industrialized mass murder" rather than to propaganda (although this raises further complex questions about the large numbers required to implement this "solution"). While it is clear that mass media were manipulated to serve the ends of the regime, it remains difficult to unravel the complex relationships between propaganda and public opinion, and terror, repression, and propaganda. Historians caution against taking a simplistic view of a "vertical and monolithic dictatorial state and its society."[33]

Wartime Propaganda in Liberal Democratic Societies

The Soviet and Nazi regimes, because they aimed to politicize all aspects of society, afforded propaganda a central role in political and social life. Governments in liberal democratic countries also engaged in propaganda; indeed, if propaganda is viewed simply as the attempt to influence political attitudes and behavior, it can be understood as a normal part of the activities of government. But the need for systematic propaganda comparable to that of the totalitarian regimes was recognized by the democracies only in wartime. During the First World War they employed propaganda to mobilize the domestic mass support essential for the prosecution of total war and to influence opinion in neutral and enemy countries. For the same purposes, at the start of the Second World War Allied governments established propaganda agencies: these included the Office of War Information (OWI) in the United States and the Ministry of Information (MOI) in Britain. Use of the euphemism "information" in these cases reflected the negative view of propaganda prevailing in liberal democratic societies: it was regarded as something that could be justified only in extreme circumstances and only as a necessary evil.

The reluctance of officials in Allied governments to admit that their "information" activities were indistinguishable from propaganda went hand in hand with a highly influential view of how propaganda should be conducted. Propagandists in Western countries agreed that the most effective propaganda is that which is subtle, indirect, and, indeed, invisible. In other words, it was believed that people are more likely to accept a propaganda message if they are unaware that they are being propagandized. A restrained approach, presenting factual information in a rational way and avoiding lies and highly emotional appeals, was thought more likely to produce that effect. Allied propagandists therefore aimed to achieve a "strategy of truth" or "propaganda with facts." British propaganda in the war with Germany represented the most successful example of this approach. Yet a "strategy of truth," although generally accepted in principle at the time as the most effective approach, did not always prevail. At the other extreme was propaganda that sought to demonize and generate hatred toward the enemy; it came to the fore especially in the war with Japan.

US Propaganda in the Second World War

Whereas in Nazi Germany and Soviet Russia the content of propaganda was directly controlled by the regime, in liberal democratic societies the propagandist's task was more complicated. Democratic governments did not usually enjoy the benefits of direct control of the media but relied instead on censorship and regulation, on such other pressures as they could bring to bear, and on appeals to the good sense and patriotism of media owners and personnel. In such societies, too, not all propaganda was government propaganda. People who controlled and worked in media organizations often had their own ideas as to what messages were best calculated to encourage public support for the war. These aspects of the relationship between media and society in time of total war are exemplified by the experience of the United States between 1941 and 1945.

Those officials given responsibility for US wartime propaganda enjoyed potential advantages. By the 1940s the American press, radio, and film had achieved a degree of penetration of the population that was unequalled in any other country, providing the means by which the propaganda message could be broadcast readily to a mass audience. On the other hand, these institutions were entirely in private hands; there was no system of public-service broadcasting, susceptible to direct government influence in times of national crisis, as in Britain. Censorship was employed to some extent, but it had only negative uses (denying news and information), and the practical need for media cooperation, congressional oversight of the executive arm of government, and a powerful tradition of freedom of the press counselled against its overuse: information was regulated to a lesser extent in the United States than in Britain.[34]

Moreover, US industrial strength and geographical isolation, and a tradition of isolationism in world affairs, created powerful obstacles to the mobilization of mass support for the war. Unlike Britain, the United States did not face a direct German threat to its physical survival; nor was it threatened in any plausible way by the prospect of Japanese invasion, notwithstanding the attack on Pearl Harbor. In 1940–1 the America First movement, supported by many influential Americans, campaigned strongly against US involvement in the war. Its appeal was shattered by the Pearl Harbor bombing and Germany's subsequent declaration of war on the United States in December 1941. Yet, even so, government and military leaders worried about the effects on morale of lingering doubts about the extent of America's interest in the European conflict. Providing the American public and servicemen with a clear rationale for the nation's involvement in the war, especially the war in Europe, was one of the main aims of US propaganda.

Race relations within the United States also posed problems for propaganda officials. Lack of enthusiasm for the war among America's black population, 13 million strong in a total population of 132 million in 1940, caused concern for US leaders both because it threatened to undermine the war effort and because such disunity provided food for enemy propaganda. In the context of entrenched discrimination and prejudice against blacks, including institutionalized segregation in the southern states, many African Americans felt uneasy about a war with another non-white people, the Japanese. This was especially the case since that war seemed to hold little promise of improvement in the position of America's black population and was often justified by white Americans in racial terms. An early 1942 survey, which asked blacks whether they would be better off under Japanese rule, indicated that 18 percent of respondents thought the Japanese would treat them better than did American whites, 31 percent thought their treatment would be the same, and only 28 percent believed they would be worse off.[35] Horace Cayton, a Chicago black leader, put succinctly the dilemma facing many blacks: "Am I a Negro first and then a policeman or soldier second, or should I forget in any emergency situation the fact that … my first loyalty is to my race?"[36]

The OWI was the principal government agency responsible for overcoming such doubts and marshalling mass support for the war effort, as well as ensuring that domestic disunity and disaffection did not harm America's image abroad. Created in June 1942, the OWI sought to harness the media to the purposes of government propaganda. Its attempts to do so often led to antagonism on the part of media organizations, which were often supported by congressmen suspicious of liberal elements in the OWI and of President Roosevelt's administration in general. As a result the OWI was only partly successful in securing media cooperation with its requests.

Much of the US government's propaganda effort was directed toward the use of film. Government propagandists understood well the advantages to be gained from harnessing the resources of the world's leading film industry. Filmmakers, for their part, contributed willingly to the war effort, convinced of the power of their medium to mobilize public support. They did so out of conviction, but it was also the case that such collaboration served the film industry's interests. For the studios not to be seen pulling their weight in support of the war effort would have jeopardized the support of the public – and therefore cinema attendances – and of the banks on which film companies depended for financial backing. Another incentive for collaboration lay in the need for the cooperation of the US military, which often assisted the studios by giving access to its facilities and equipment. Moreover, the OWI, although lacking powers of direct censorship, controlled film exhibition in liberated areas and enjoyed considerable influence with the Office of Censorship, which issued export licenses for films. Since exports accounted for a large part of the industry's profits, government officials held significant bargaining power with the film companies. Overall the major film companies profited from their part in the war effort: despite wartime shortages, the number of movies produced during the war was only slightly below the peacetime level.[37]

Hollywood's contribution to wartime propaganda took a number of forms. Five of the major studios – Paramount, 20th Century Fox, RKO, MGM, and Universal – produced newsreels (usually around eight minutes long) that played a vital role in satisfying the public's demand for visual information about the war and therefore in sustaining morale. Newsreels took on a new importance in the appeal of cinema.[38] The major film companies also gave assistance to government agencies in making propaganda films. Some of Hollywood's leading directors enlisted in the armed services for this purpose. John Huston, while in the army, made a celebrated trilogy of documentaries dealing with the behavior of American soldiers in battle and the emotional impact of war on these men: *Report from the Aleutians* (1943), *The Battle of San Pietro* (1943), and *Let There Be Light* (1946) (the latter film was so graphic that the War Department withheld it from public exhibition). John Ford served as a commander in the navy and made *The Battle of Midway* (1942), in which the American forces "seem to achieve victory because of their moral strength expressed in Ford's folksy style, not because of their superior tactics or armaments."[39] Frank Capra served in the army's signal corps and supervised production of the important *Why We Fight* series, seven orientation films designed to give recruits a clear rationale for American participation in the war (and influenced by Leni

Riefenstahl's *Triumph of the Will*). The first of these films, *Prelude to War* (1943), was also released for civilian viewing in cinemas throughout the United States. Capra also played a major role in the production of the army documentary *The Negro Soldier* (1944), released both to military and – at the OWI's urging – civilian audiences. The film aimed to promote racial unity and black support for the war by celebrating the contribution of blacks to American history and the war effort.[40]

In the United States, as elsewhere, feature films were widely assumed to offer the most effective means of mass persuasion, a consequence of their visual appeal and facility for blending political messages with entertainment. Many Hollywood feature films dealt with war-related themes, typically celebrating the bravery of American fighting men. The OWI prepared an "Information Manual" for Hollywood in 1942, giving guidelines on how to present the war. It reviewed film scripts from all the major studios except Paramount. The OWI's role was not unwelcome to many writers and some directors, who shared the liberal political views that tended to prevail in that organization; but it was often resented by proprietors and producers. While happy to assist the government in making films for propaganda purposes, they were never reconciled to the idea of government agencies telling Hollywood how to make movies. Their suspicions were fuelled by an anti-trust suit filed by the Roosevelt administration in 1938 – suspended in 1940 but revived in 1944 – against the eight major companies for violation of laws on restraint of trade. Above all, the studios were wary of any OWI interference that called for departures from their entrenched practice, reinforced by the 1930 Production Code, of avoiding controversial political and social subjects. They were especially wary on the subject of race relations, where they feared that compliance with the OWI's attempts to improve the portrayal of black people in the movies would produce an adverse reaction from censorship boards in the South. On this question the film companies were supported by southern congressmen and other conservatives in Congress.

Such resistance imposed limitations on the OWI's achievement. That agency did succeed in bringing about minor changes to many scripts. At the OWI's urging, the studios made films that portrayed the United States as a harmonious, unified nation, in which its diverse ethnic groups were as one in their devotion to American ideals of liberty and their determination to defeat fascism. Combat films, accordingly, made a point of presenting ethnically diverse battle units, with, say, Italian,

Irish, and Jewish Americans fighting side by side. In a few films the principle was even extended to blacks: in *Bataan*, *Sahara*, and *Crash Dive*, all released in 1943, black characters appeared in racially integrated combat units (in real life the American armed forces – including supplies of blood plasma – were racially segregated until 1948, and black units were usually limited to non-combat roles). However, in general the OWI had only modest success in persuading Hollywood to move beyond the stereotyped portrayal of blacks that had always prevailed in the movies. Only a handful of Second World War films – including *Casablanca* (1943) and Alfred Hitchcock's *Lifeboat* (1944) – featured strong black characters.[41] For the most part American feature films continued, as the writer Dalton Trumbo put it, to make "tarts of the Negro's daughters, crap shooters of his sons, obsequious Uncle Toms of his fathers, superstitious and grotesque crones of his mothers, strutting peacocks of his successful men, psalm-singing mountebanks of his priests, and Barnum and Bailey side-shows of his religion."[42]

The historian Thomas Cripps has identified two separate impulses behind the treatment of race in American wartime propaganda films. First, blacks and their white liberal allies (including those in Hollywood) saw the war as an opportunity to bring about radical change in the position of blacks in American society and regarded film as a vehicle for that purpose. Second, the main concern of government officials was to encourage black support for the war. On the whole, Cripps argues, Second World War propaganda films satisfied the latter group rather than the former. Only after the war, from 1949, were the ideas of the "Hollywood conscience-liberals" realized in a general way with a series of films that depicted black characters integrated into mainstream American society.[43]

The tensions revealed by film propaganda's treatment of race relations were also evident in radio. Like film, radio played an important part in US wartime propaganda. By 1940 all Americans had access to radio, and a majority of the population relied on the medium as the main news source.[44] Both the federal government and the national broadcasting networks recognized radio's value as a vehicle for promoting national unity. The broadcast of war news, messages from federal agencies intended to boost morale and promote civilian preparedness, and propaganda blended with entertainment were all part of radio's contribution to the war effort. The OWI recognized the medium's potential for raising black Americans' morale and building their enthusiasm for the war. Yet relatively little racial propaganda was initiated, either by the OWI or the War Department. The capacity of government propaganda agencies to use radio creatively to respond to the position of African Americans was severely limited by officials' inability to reconcile two conflicting aims. One was to boost black morale; the other was to avoid offending southern whites, and especially southern congressmen, by not mentioning the racial segregation and discrimination that were the causes of low morale among African Americans.[45]

Finally, the American case highlights a dilemma that confronted all propagandists: that of striking a balance between messages that engender hatred of the enemy and those that are so graphic in their treatment of the horrors of war as to undermine morale. American military and civilian officials, usually with the full support of the media, played an active role in restricting the release to the public of photographs and film footage depicting war casualties, as well as evidence of racial conflict on military bases and conflict between American servicemen and those from Allied nations. These restrictions were eased from 1943, when political and military leaders began to worry about public complacency about the war. American newspapers, magazines, and films in 1943–5 therefore tended to give a more vivid portrayal of wartime horrors than those in the earlier stage of the war. Publications in 1944–5, for example, were permitted to give much fuller coverage of Japanese atrocities.[46]

Great Britain and the "Strategy of Truth"

A reluctance to exploit Nazi atrocities for propaganda purposes was one aspect of Britain's wartime "strategy of truth." Here the lessons of the First World War were important. As a result of the earlier conflict, British propaganda had gained a reputation for exaggeration and lies in the form of anti-German atrocity stories. In their determination to live down this reputation, the officials of the MOI were careful to avoid any suggestion of fabrication. Therefore, although Britain was now at war with one of the most barbaric regimes in modern history, the subject of Nazi atrocities was handled cautiously. The full scale of Nazi barbarism, including the genocide against the Jews, was not clearly understood until the end of the war, but the determination of propaganda officials not to risk inviting public disbelief, either at home or abroad, was an important influence on British propaganda.

The techniques of a successful strategy of truth were not at first obvious to British officials. In the early stages of the war the principle that no news is good news was allowed to prevail; the needs of military secrecy were taken to extremes and allowed to override the demands of good propaganda. Thus in 1939 newsreels were prevented from showing scenes of British troops leaving for France, and newspapers were confiscated for reporting the arrival of British troops in France, so that opportunities to combat impressions of the invincibility of the German army were lost.[47] Incorporation of the censorship machinery of the Press and Censorship Bureau into the Ministry of Information (MOI) in April 1940 was an important organizational reform that reflected recognition of the need to integrate the control of news with the generation of positive propaganda. In working to mobilize the press, broadcasting, and the film industry behind the war effort, the MOI gave top priority to news – "the shocktroops of propaganda," as Sir John Reith described it.[48] Britain's propaganda officials applied three main principles. The first was that it is not enough to suppress news; the public demands news, especially in wartime, and to deprive it is bad for morale. Second, the news must be true and accurate: propaganda "with facts, if not *the* facts, truth, if not the *whole* truth." Otherwise the public are bound to learn that they are being manipulated and will therefore trust neither government nor the media. Third, it was taken as axiomatic that censorship is best when invisible and that, therefore, pre-censorship (control of the news at the point of generation) is far more valuable than post-censorship.[49]

These principles were implemented so successfully that, as Nicholas Pronay states, "the press, the BBC and other organs of 'news' managed to maintain the trust of the British public at home and gained a reputation for Britain abroad for having even in wartime an honest, free and truthful media, yet which gave practically nothing of significance away to an ever-vigilant enemy."[50] Goebbels himself paid tribute to the British approach, observing of a MOI booklet "The Battle of the Atlantic" that "it does so much justice to the German point of view that you get the impression of it having been written by a Swedish Professor who is on the side of neither England nor Germany but only of truth."[51] The BBC, especially, although it worked closely with the MOI and was central to the operation of British propaganda, gained a reputation both at home and abroad for the accuracy and reliability of its news services. As George Orwell observed: "The BBC as far as its news goes has gained enormous prestige since about 1940.... 'I heard it on the radio' is now almost equivalent to 'I know it must be true'."[52] A comparison with Germany's wartime propaganda, which increasingly lost credibility in the eyes of the German public, highlights the effectiveness of the British approach to propaganda.

Propaganda and the Pacific War

Where Britain's war with Germany epitomized a moderate, truthful form of propaganda, the war with Japan often involved a very different approach, one that sought to mobilize popular support for the war by emphasizing differences between Us and the Other, by portraying the enemy as the devil's disciples or as subhuman. In Allied propaganda of the Pacific War this approach was reflected in the frequent use of racial stereotypes. In cartoons, films, magazines, newspapers, posters, and radio broadcasts the Japanese were commonly depicted as apes (typically as savage, buck-toothed monkeys or menacing gorillas), vermin, or subhuman monsters. This tendency to dehumanize the Japanese – to treat them as not only politically but biologically separate from the people of Allied countries – found no parallels in anti-German propaganda, in which the Germans were invariably portrayed as human beings, even if evil, and distinctions were sometimes made between good Germans and Nazis.[53] The racial aspect of Allied propaganda in the Pacific War raises complex issues concerning the effects of propaganda and the relationship between propaganda and society.

Demonization of the Japanese was sometimes the purpose of official propaganda. In early 1942 the Australian government's Department of Information launched its "Know Your Enemy" drive, a "multi-media package of posters, radio broadcasts, newspaper articles and community-based speeches" that departmental memos referred to openly as a "hate campaign."[54] Drawing on the services of journalists, academics, and commercial advertising agencies, and enlisting the cooperation of the press and radio, it was characterized by highly emotional appeals and crude racial stereotypes. One radio script, for example, referred to the Japanese as "a despicable, ape-like race that lent colour to the theory

of evolution," and as "the little monkey-men of the North."[55] Such viru-
lent propaganda attracted a strong public backlash. Criticisms included
the charge that "Know Your Enemy" was blatant, and therefore poor,
propaganda, that it was "unchristian," that it encouraged a "fear complex," and that it would endanger Australian prisoners of war.[56]

The same criticisms of crude racial propaganda were common in
the United States, but with the significant difference that the main official propaganda agency, the OWI, generally sought to restrain, rather
than generate, such extremism. In addition to the reasons that motivated Australian critics of the "Know Your Enemy" campaign, OWI
officials were concerned about the effects of racially based propaganda
on African Americans' support for the war and on attitudes to Asian
peoples other than the Japanese. These officials also feared, with good
reason, that such blatant evidence of white American racism would be
exploited by Japanese propaganda. Hoping to steer hatred of the
enemy into "properly directed" channels, the OWI tried, with only
limited success, to persuade the Hollywood studios to produce films
that promoted hatred of totalitarian and militaristic systems rather
than individual leaders or the German and Japanese peoples. On the
question of Japanese atrocities, the OWI's advice revealed a tension
between the desire to restrain excessively hostile treatment of the
enemy and the aim of deterring public complacency in the last two
years of the war.[57]

That crude, racially based propaganda thrived as it did, despite
official qualms, is evidence of the peculiar nature of Western public
attitudes toward Japan. While Australian criticisms of the "Know Your
Enemy" campaign serve to remind us of the complexity of public
attitudes, it remains the case that, in those Western countries involved in
the Pacific War, the media both reflected and helped bring about a degree
of hatred of the Japanese that even surpassed hostility toward Germany.
Scholars such as John Dower have documented the extent of these
hatreds and have pointed to the savagery of the conflict in the Pacific,
evidenced, for example, by the ruthless determination of Allied soldiers
not to take prisoners. Dower, in a controversial interpretation, argues
that the hatreds, and the racial imagery in which they found expression,
stemmed from longstanding racist attitudes, established well before
1941 and reflected before the Second World War in fears of the "Yellow
Peril," restrictions on Asian immigration in the United States and
Australia, and discrimination against Japanese (and other Asian)

immigrants in those countries. These attitudes were matched by a Japanese sense of superiority to Westerners, reflected in images of foreign demons, depicted as impure, decadent, arrogant, and barbaric.[58]

The value of Dower's work is to remind us that propaganda cannot succeed in a vacuum. Western racial images of the Japanese were appealing in part because they fed upon pre-existing stereotypes. A belief in white superiority to non-Europeans had prevailed in the West since at least the fifteenth century. It received pseudo-scientific support from Social Darwinism in the late nineteenth century. The anti-Japanese racial stereotypes that flourished in the Second World War grew out of these beliefs; they were not invented during the war itself. Nonetheless, Dower underestimates the extent to which the experience of the Pacific War, as opposed to pre-existing racial prejudices, caused hatred toward the Japanese and led to crude Allied propaganda. To a large extent American, Australian, and British hostility to the Japanese was a response to Japan's actions after 1937: its aggression and atrocities in China, its attack on Pearl Harbor in 1941, and its subsequent brutality and cruelty toward Allied prisoners of war and civilian internees. To the extent that the Japanese were more the target of Western hatred than the Germans, this experience, at least as much as racism, provides the explanation. Of course, during the Second World War Germany committed acts of barbarism on an even greater scale than Japan. However, it was crucial to Western attitudes that German atrocities involved mainly Jews and Eastern Europeans, whereas Allied servicemen and civilians were among the victims of Japanese atrocities (although not on the same scale as Chinese, Indians, Koreans, Indonesians, and other Asians).

The more convincing conclusion, therefore, is that racial propaganda directed at Japan appealed to many Americans, Australians, and Britons because it fed both on longstanding prejudices, reflected in the stereotyped wartime portrayal of the Japanese as apes and vermin, and on the experience of the war itself. This kind of propaganda contributed to wartime hatreds, but only in a secondary way. To a greater extent such propaganda should be seen as mirroring, rather than causing, anti-Japanese hostility.

These examples of the use of propaganda in peace and war, by both totalitarian and democratic regimes, illustrate the importance of mass media when exploited in the interests of the state. As media evolved during the twentieth century, they were used for the purposes of persuasion both at home and abroad. However, the effectiveness of such propagandist use of the newspaper press, radio, and film varied not only according to the extent of media penetration but also with other factors such as pre-existing attitudes and beliefs, the extent to which propagandist messages confirmed or diverged from social "realities," and the degree to which the state resorted to other measures such as terror and repression to supplement propaganda to realize official purposes.

7

Cold War and Communications

The defeat of Nazi Germany and Imperial Japan was soon followed by the start of a conflict that President Harry S. Truman described in 1950 as a "struggle, above all else, for the minds of men," one in which the American people would eventually prevail by getting "the real story across to people in other countries" – in other words, by propaganda.[1] His successor, President Dwight D. Eisenhower, shared this view, identifying America's "aim in the Cold War" as "to get the world, by peaceful means, to believe the truth." The means by which this was to be done, he explained, were summed up by the term "psychological warfare," which he defined as "the struggle for the minds and wills of men."[2] Like the Second World War, this struggle for hearts and minds demonstrated again the inextricable links between media and politics at both domestic and international levels.

The Cold War dominated international politics for four decades. Its violent rhetorical clashes, the reluctance of the United States and the Soviet Union to negotiate their differences, and above all their engagement in a highly dangerous nuclear arms race, encouraged a widespread fear that the conflict would lead to total annihilation. The Cold War was at its height from 1947 to 1962, and especially, within that period, until Stalin's death in 1953. But tensions between Washington and Moscow were renewed in the 1980s, and the whole period from 1945 to 1989 was one of US–Soviet rivalry. The era ended with the disintegration in 1989 of the empire acquired by Moscow in Eastern Europe at the end of the Second World War, and the collapse of the Soviet Union itself in 1991.

Although the Cold War had important political, strategic, and economic dimensions, an ideological clash between Soviet communism and American nationalism was central to the conflict. The universalistic nature of the conflicting ideologies was crucial: each claimed to represent the aspirations of humanity, regarded the other as the devil's disciple, and allowed no room for compromise with its rival. This aspect of communism is well known: the communists asserted that the masses of the world aspired to rid themselves of the chains of feudalism and capitalism and embrace communism, and that only the wicked designs of the class enemies of ordinary people could prevent the realization of this utopia. The importance of ideology in American attitudes and policies is not generally recognized, yet it stood at the very core of American nationalism.[3] The American national myth saw the United States as destined to play the role of redeemer to the rest of humanity, guiding the peoples of the world to liberal democracy and modernity, and protecting them from the selfish ambitions of the other great powers. America's selflessness and affinity with the peoples of the world (as opposed to the governments that ruled them), and the universal relevance of American values and institutions, were the central assumptions of an ideology that shaped Americans' understanding of the Cold War. Thus Eisenhower regarded the US Cold War effort as one "conducted in the belief that if there is no war, if two systems of government are allowed to live side by side, that ours, because of its greater appeal to men everywhere, to mankind, in the long run will win out."[4] In the same vein Senator John F. Kennedy, speaking in 1957 on the problem of winning the support of Arab, African, and Asian peoples for the United States, insisted that "the strength of our appeal to these key populations – and it is rightfully our appeal, and not that of the Communists – lies in our traditional and deeply felt philosophy of freedom for all peoples everywhere."[5]

The central role of communication followed from this view of the Cold War as a psychological contest. Both sides gave a high priority to the use of media for persuasion: to mobilize their domestic populations, and to win the support of public opinion internationally. As a result the Cold War had a major impact on media content, while at the same time the media significantly affected development of the conflict. This chapter first examines the nature and effectiveness of Soviet propaganda during the Cold War, then the role of privately owned commercial media in the United States. For a number of reasons the US media gave wholehearted support to anti-Soviet and anti-communist positions. The far-reaching impact of the Cold War on the American press, and especially on film and broadcasting, was reflected in the blacklisting of alleged communist sympathizers and in media content. Finally, the chapter examines the West's international propaganda – in the form of both psychological warfare and cultural diplomacy – and assesses its role in the Cold War.

The Soviet Union: Media as Servants of the State

The story of communication in the Soviet Union during the Cold War was one of media in the service of government. The propaganda apparatus developed in the early years of the Soviet regime was adapted to Cold War purposes. The Soviet leadership, untroubled by the negative connotations evoked by the word "propaganda" in liberal democratic societies, viewed the role of the media primarily as mobilizing public support for the regime. The Department of Agitation and Propaganda (Agitprop) of the Central Committee of the Communist Party fed government propaganda to media and other organizations. Government control over the appointment and training of media personnel, close scrutiny by the censors, and habits of self-censorship that were a consequence of the severe punishment meted out to "deviationists" under Stalin's rule, helped ensure that the media served the regime's purposes and that political content in newspapers and magazines, film, radio, and television closely followed official policy.

Outside the Soviet Union, Stalin's creation of the Communist Information Bureau (Cominform) in September 1947 marked the start of a systematic campaign, masterminded by Agitprop, to marshal international support for Moscow against the Western powers. A network of "front" organizations was established, including the World Peace Council, the World Federation of Trade Unions, and the International Union of Students, that followed Moscow's positions on international issues, while giving the appearance of independence from Soviet control and influence. Sympathetic Western journalists and academics were encouraged to act as Soviet "agents of influence," gaining privileged access to Soviet sources of information and financial rewards in return for their willingness to advocate the communist cause. Various agencies of the Soviet government and Communist Party, including the state-owned newsagency Tass and the Ministry of Foreign Affairs, provided information to media throughout the world. The Cominform itself, from the late 1940s, published in many languages a weekly magazine, *For a Lasting Peace, For a People's Democracy!*, and similar magazines were produced subsequently. These overt forms of propaganda were supplemented by covert "black" propaganda – based on falsehoods and deception – orchestrated by the Committee for State Security (KGB).

The purpose of this vast propaganda effort was to win domestic and international support both for Moscow's stance on particular Cold War issues and for the general Soviet worldview. Simple juxtapositions of good and evil – worker and capitalist, revolutionary and counter-revolutionary, communist and fascist – had always been central to the Soviet mentality. Now the West, especially the United States, was given the demonic role in Soviet imagery that had recently been reserved for Nazi Germany. In Soviet rhetoric the United States was portrayed as "imperialist" and war-minded, while the Soviet Union championed "peace," "disarmament," "democracy," "liberation," and the world's "progressive" forces.[6]

Crude abuse of the Western powers followed logically from this emotionally charged view of the world. Violent anti-Western language reached its peak during the late 1940s and early 1950s, but for many years after Stalin's death such epithets as "criminal regime" and "racist government" were commonplace in Soviet news broadcasts.[7] Images of American society emphasized capitalist exploitation of the workers, extremes of wealth and poverty, high unemployment, persecution of unions, racism, and the trashiness of popular culture. The fat banker with cigar and the Ku Klux Klansman were common cartoon stereotypes. By contrast the Soviet Union was portrayed in positive, often utopian, fashion as a model society in which the Soviet people should take pride and which the rest of the world should emulate. At their most critical, the Soviet media dealt with those social problems – such as alcoholism, poor workmanship, corruption, a high divorce rate – on which the regime tolerated public discussion. Yet for the most part emphasis was given to the alleged prosperity of domestic life, to scientific, technological, and cultural achievement, and to the might of the Soviet armed forces.[8]

Even taking into account the difficulties of assessing the influence of propaganda on public attitudes in a closed society, some conclusions can be drawn on the effectiveness of Soviet propaganda during the Cold War. These offer no support for alarmist fears held in the West about the communists' skill as propagandists. The belief that totalitarian regimes had found the key to manipulation of the human mind, and that the populations of communist countries were held in slavery partly by terror, partly by "brainwashing," was encouraged by a commonly held but mistaken belief that Chinese techniques of indoctrination had persuaded large numbers of American and British prisoners of war to collaborate with the enemy during the Korean War.[9] Yet the very characteristics that many in the West regarded as the keys to the alleged success of communist propaganda – monotonous stress on a few simple ideas, exaggeration and distortion, crude abuse of opponents – were its weakest points, for they strained credibility, especially among audiences of any sophistication.[10] The Soviet regime, despite its control of the media, never succeeded in winning an uncritical acceptance of communist ideology or of the communist system among the Soviet population. Large-scale jamming of Western radio broadcasts was symptomatic of the weakness of Moscow's position: the regime itself was convinced that it could not afford to expose the public to alternative views on international affairs.[11] Public indifference or hostility to government propaganda was all the more common when it challenged deep-seated convictions and customs. Religious beliefs and practices survived seven decades of communist rule despite systematic persecution and antireligious propaganda.[12] The extent of prosperity and progress in Soviet society also affected public trust in government. By the 1980s problems of economic decay, low living standards, and official corruption and incompetence were so pervasive that the shrewdest propaganda could not overcome Soviet citizens' alienation from the regime.

It would, however, be wrong to conclude that propaganda had no significant impact on public attitudes and beliefs. In the 1950s and to a lesser extent the 1960s, with invasion and victory over Nazi Germany a recent memory, with an impressive performance in some areas of industry, and with the launch in 1957 of Sputnik, the first man-made satellite, propaganda enjoyed a fertile field in which to work by appealing to the public's patriotism and expectations of economic growth. Interviews with Soviet emigrés in the 1950s found acceptance of "many of the regime's values" even among these opponents of the communist government.[13] The first scholarly surveys of public opinion in the Soviet Union, conducted in the late 1960s, showed that the great majority of respondents accepted the regime's critical views of the United States and its international behavior.[14]

The achievement of Soviet propaganda inside the USSR seems all the more impressive in the light of the fact that throughout the Cold War era the Soviet population included millions of victims of the Soviet regime. They included the survivors of collectivization, the man-made Ukrainian famine of 1932–3, and mass deportations. They also included millions of survivors of the labor camps. Since the regime admitted to no wrong-doing, these people were given no compensation for their suffering. They "received no victim counseling, no psychoanalysis, no cures for post-traumatic stress syndrome."[15] Millions of others were related to labor-camp survivors or in other ways – for example, as factory workers or soldiers – had witnessed the cruelties and failings of Stalinism. Yet the evidence suggests that most of these people, both victims and witnesses, not only failed to develop any sense of rebellion against the regime but escaped lasting psychological damage. Indeed, they reconciled themselves to the Soviet state, finding a sense of purpose by identifying with the collective struggle for human liberation that was central to the Party's ideology.[16] These attitudes cannot be accounted for entirely as the product of propaganda, but the images and interpretations of inter-national events that the Soviet media disseminated in support of Moscow's Cold War policies were bound to have an impact on public attitudes, all the more so because alternative views were not presented.

Outside the Soviet Union a similarly complex picture emerged – one that supports the observation that propaganda's effectiveness usually depends on its success in tapping into people's existing beliefs or direct experience. In the Soviet client states of Eastern Europe a propaganda barrage as thorough as that experienced by the citizens of the Soviet Union made little headway in overcoming popular resentment that stemmed from Moscow's imposition of communist regimes on these countries between 1945 and 1948. The Soviet Union's failure to create any viable basis for its East European empire other than coercion was high-lighted by the Red Army's brutal suppression of reformist movements in Hungary in 1956 and Czechoslovakia in 1968 and by the eventual unrav-eling of Soviet power in the 1980s. By contrast, Soviet denunciation of "American imperialism" found a receptive audience in much of Asia, Africa, and Latin America, in countries where a history of colonization and exploitation at the hands of Western powers lent plausibility to the Soviet Union's claim to be the champion of anti-imperialist forces. Even so, Third World governments were wary of Moscow's embrace, and most were determined to remain apart from both the Soviet and Western camps. Many were happy to accept economic or military aid from the Soviets. The main inducement, however, was not ideological sympathy for Moscow but a rational desire to exploit the Cold War for their own purposes, and to play off the Soviet Union against the United States, later the Soviets against China, accepting assistance from the highest bidder. In the Third World, Soviet propaganda succeeded in promoting and reinforcing negative images of the United States but failed to win a long-term victory in the contest for hearts and minds.

In the West such success as Soviet propaganda enjoyed outside the ranks of communist parties depended on its alignment with causes – "peace," nuclear disarmament, opposition to American military intervention in Vietnam – that had widespread appeal for reasons more deep-rooted than the effects of communist propaganda. Few of the many people who supported these causes between the 1950s and 1980s looked upon the Soviet Union with loyalty or admiration. In the 1930s and 1940s many Western intellectuals had embraced communism as an attractive alternative to the evils of capitalism. After the late 1940s it enjoyed little such support: too much was known about the realities of Stalinism and the stagnant, repressive system that survived Stalin's death.

The United States: Commercial Media as Instruments of Propaganda

If government control of the Soviet media ensured their uncritical support for Moscow's policies, the media of major Western powers, while not usually subject to direct political control, for the most part cooperated with their governments and voiced support for their international policies during the Cold War. Contrary to the view commonly held in the West that only totalitarian regimes engaged in propaganda, Western media, including privately owned media organizations, played their part in the Cold War struggle. Nowhere in liberal democratic societies was enlistment of the media in the global contest with communism more important than in the United States – the country in which government controls over the media were weakest.

From 1947 the American media disseminated images of communism and the Soviet Union, and interpretations of international events, that derived from Cold War ideology. The central assumptions were that communism was a monolithic movement with its headquarters in Moscow, and that a messianic ideology compelled international communism to embark on a virtually limitless drive for world domination. The Cold War, therefore, as the authors of the important US government policy statement NSC 68 declared in the months before the outbreak of the Korean War, was "a basic conflict between the idea of freedom under a government of laws, and the idea of slavery under the grim oligarchy of the Kremlin." At stake was no less than "the fulfillment or destruction not only of this Republic but of civilization itself."[17] Only firm action by the United States against communism in all parts of the world could save the "free world" from the relentless ambitions of this sinister form of totalitarianism. A strategy of "containment" of Soviet power followed from these beliefs.

The media were central to the mobilization of public support for the foreign and defense policies of the US government. Newspapers, radio, and television provided presidents, secretaries of state, and other officials with the means of communicating directly to the public, by giving generous coverage to their speeches, statements, and press conferences and their "off-the-record" background briefings. Journalists relied heavily on official sources of information, giving government agencies considerable influence over media coverage of the news. From 1947 dissenting views of the Cold War were rarely given exposure in news coverage and political commentary. The national television networks even collaborated with federal government information agencies in the production of news and public affairs programs. Until the mid-1950s many of these were produced or scripted by the Department of Defense and other government agencies.[18]

The international realities of this period were more complex than the US government and Cold War orthodoxy allowed. US policymakers were justified in concerning themselves with the possible political and military consequences of a failure to contain Russian power on the European continent. Large-scale economic aid to Western Europe through the Marshall Plan of 1947, and American leadership of the North Atlantic Treaty Organization (NATO) from 1949, were constructive responses to the circumstances of the time. But some of the assumptions underlying American policy were questionable, as the disastrous experience of US military intervention in Vietnam in the 1960s would make clear. The Cold War framework within which American policymakers operated underestimated the importance of tensions between

Soviet and Chinese communism and the nationalist character of non-European communist parties, overstated the extent of Moscow's and Beijing's influence over Asian communism, greatly exaggerated the role of ideologically driven expansionism in Chinese and Vietnamese communism, and overestimated the Western powers' ability to influence events in the Third World. At the height of the Cold War a small number of officials, academics, journalists, and others made these criticisms, but it was rare to find them expressed in mainstream media. Journalists and commentators who expressed unconventional views were edged aside or restricted to uncontroversial subjects.

Yet the American media were no mere mouthpiece for government propaganda. Often they followed a more extreme version of Cold War orthodoxy than the White House would have liked. Between 1948 and 1950 much of media and public opinion started to run ahead of government policy, demanding extreme and simplistic approaches to international problems. Demands for increased US intervention in the Chinese civil war on behalf of Chiang Kai-shek's Nationalist forces in 1948–9, intense hostility to the new communist regime in Beijing from 1949, demands for extreme solutions to the Korean War (including the use of nuclear weapons), and a refusal to contemplate any form of rapprochement with Russia through the 1950s and 1960s all severely limited the US government's freedom of action in foreign policy.[19]

The fact that media responses to the Cold War were not identical to those of the executive arm of the US government is a reflection of the range of influences at work in the American media. These included pressures from Congress, which was a major center of anti-communist sentiment and maintained constant surveillance of perceived communist influence in the media, as in other areas of American life. Commercial pressures were also important. Withdrawal of advertising, and in the case of the film industry withdrawal of financial support from Wall Street, were effective sanctions for business and the banks to employ against media organizations that failed to measure up to the test of political correctness; fear of such penalties gave media organizations every incentive to assert their anti-communist loyalties. Also important were the beliefs of media proprietors and personnel, who often had firm convictions on how to deal with the communist threat. Nor should the role of the public be discounted. It is impossible to say with certainty to what extent the media created, rather than simply reflected, simplistic and inflexible public attitudes to the Soviet Union and communism. It is likely that at times the media were driven to adopt extreme anti-communist positions by fear of adverse public reaction to any suggestion of moderation in dealings with communists.[20] The origins of these attitudes lay ultimately in a deep-rooted American antipathy to communism and radicalism that predated the Cold War and stemmed from a nationalist preoccupation with "Americanism" (and rejection of "un-American" ideologies). However, elements of the media played a major role in lending credibility to these extreme views and in extending their influence among the American public.

This generalization holds true even more for the domestic Cold War than in matters of foreign and defense policy. The most extreme forms of American anti-communism were manifest less in ideas on external policy than in the paranoid approach to internal affairs associated with Senator Joseph McCarthy of Wisconsin: in the deeply felt conviction that American society was riddled with spies and traitors, many holding positions of influence in the US government and other institutions, and in the belief that radical measures were required to root out these subversives. The Soviet Union did have considerable success in the 1930s and 1940s in penetrating the US government with its agents, but the victims of McCarthy's witch-hunts were seldom the real witches. Few Soviet spies were ever caught. McCarthy's targets were the strongly anti-communist Democratic Party administration of President Truman and hundreds of other people who were innocent of any connection with Soviet espionage.[21]

Sections of the media played a major part in the growth of domestic anti-communist extremism. Not only did the effectiveness of McCarthy and other red-baiters depend on adept use of television and the press to attract maximum publicity. The broadcasting media and many newspapers (including those of the Hearst organization and Robert McCormick's *Chicago Tribune*) also connived in the witch-hunts of the period. This was partly because their owners, executives, and editors supported McCarthy's views, partly because of a cynical refusal to let the facts stand in the way of newsworthy stories, and partly because of a misplaced sense of "objectivity," which counselled against close examination of the veracity of politicians' assertions. Some major newspapers and magazines (including the *New York Times* and the *New York Post*) and leading columnists (including the popular Drew Pearson and the eminent Walter Lippmann) consistently opposed McCarthy. Nonetheless, the overall record of the media in their handling of anti-communist demagoguery was a sorry one.[22]

The United States: Film, Broadcasting, and the Cold War

The impact of the Cold War was especially far-reaching in American film and broadcasting. In the context of global ideological conflict, the film industry was widely perceived to have a central role. Any suggestion that Hollywood's output might be tainted by ideological impurity demanded close scrutiny. In 1947 the House Committee on Un-American Activities (HUAC), a committee of the US House of Representatives, opened an investigation into allegations of communism in Hollywood. It did so at the urging of conservative elements within the industry, organized in the Motion Picture Alliance for the Preservation of American Ideals, in the aftermath of bitter labor disputes that had affected the major studios and led to charges of "red" infiltration. In closed hearings in Los Angeles in May, "friendly" witnesses testified to the prevalence of communist activity, especially in the Screen Writers' Guild and the Screen Actors' Guild. In Washington in October the allegations were repeated at public hearings by studio heads Walt Disney and Jack Warner and by such celebrities as Gary Cooper, Robert Taylor, Robert Montgomery, Lela Rogers (the mother of Ginger), Ronald Reagan, and Adolphe Menjou. Nineteen "unfriendly" witnesses – those suspected of communist subversive activity or at least of communist sympathies – were subpoenaed to appear before the Washington hearings. Ten (seven writers, two directors, and one producer) agreed among themselves to plead their constitutional right to free speech and refused to answer the question, "Are you now or have you ever been a member of the Communist Party?" For their refusal, the "Hollywood Ten" were indicted for contempt of Congress and sent to prison for up to one year. HUAC conducted further investigations of communist influence in the film industry in 1951–2.

The HUAC investigations occurred at a time when the film industry was especially vulnerable to outside pressure. A longstanding anti-trust action by the federal government against the major firms (resolved against the studios in 1948), and the prospect of intense competition from the new medium of television, undermined the industry's capacity to ward off political intervention. Although industry leaders declared their determination not to "accept dictation on hiring or editorial policies," their actions belied their words. At a meeting at the

Waldorf-Astoria Hotel in New York on November 24, 1947, film executives agreed to "suspend without pay," in effect to fire, the Hollywood Ten. They declared that the industry would no longer "knowingly employ a Communist or member of any party or group which advocates the overthrow of the government of the United States by force or illegal constitutional methods."[23] The studios moved immediately to deny employment to writers, directors, producers, and actors whose political affiliations were deemed unacceptable. Expanded after the second round of HUAC investigations in 1951–2, the Hollywood blacklist affected around 300 people in the film industry and remained in operation until the early 1960s. A ritual of humiliation and conversion, by which HUAC demanded that former communists give up the names of party comrades as proof that they had renounced their past sins and embraced the secular faith of Americanism, awaited many of those who tried to avoid blacklisting.

Less well known than the Hollywood blacklist was the blacklisting of alleged communist sympathizers in the radio and television industries. Broadcasting was the main target of *Counterattack: The Newsletter of Facts on Communism*, a weekly newsletter started in 1947 by three ex-FBI agents with the assistance of Alfred Kohlberg, a businessman prominent in anti-communist causes. *Counterattack*, which set out to expose communist front organizations and demanded that action be taken against individuals associated with them, quickly built up a profitable subscription list among business firms and government offices. American Business Consultants, the publishers of *Counterattack*, also did loyalty investigations, for a fee, for broadcasting executives wishing to check the anti-communist bona fides of entertainers, writers, directors, announcers, producers, and other employees. The company had already acquired considerable influence over the hiring policies of radio and television companies when, in June 1950, it published *Red Channels: The Report of Communist Influence in Radio and Television*. Claiming that "the Cominform and the Communist Party USA now rely more on radio and TV than on the press and motion pictures as 'belts' to transmit pro-Sovietism to the American public," the book listed 151 people – mostly writers, directors, and performers – as alleged subversives within the broadcasting industry. *Red Channels*, soon followed by other lists, was the starting point for a broadcasting blacklist comparable in its impact to the film industry's blacklist.[24]

The blacklists ruined the careers of hundreds of people. Many victims, including the Hollywood Ten, were or had been communists in the formal sense of membership of the Communist Party. But in their communist allegiances they had committed no crimes: the Communist Party was not an illegal organization, and there was no suggestion that any of them had plotted violent revolution or engaged in espionage for Soviet Russia. They were Stalinists, but not in the sense that they approved of Stalin's crimes; rather they denied that these had taken place.[25] Their greatest sins were those of naivety or stupidity, not treason. Their political views have to be understood against the background of the 1930s, when the Depression, the rise of fascism, and the sorry record of the Western powers in contending with Hitler's expansionism had encouraged a highly idealized view of the USSR and an interest in communism as an alternative to capitalism. Moreover, many of the blacklists' victims had never been communists even in this sense but were targeted simply because of a past association with liberal causes: support for the New Deal, condemnation of lynching of blacks in the South, opposition to General Franco's reactionary forces in the Spanish Civil War, support for cooperation between America and Russia.

The political and commercial pressures reflected in the introduction of blacklists also shaped film and broadcasting content. In their efforts to find evidence of communist influence in the film industry, HUAC's investigators could identify at most three films that might be described as pro-communist or pro-Soviet, all products of Hollywood's wartime effort to marshal public support for America's Soviet ally: *Mission to Moscow* (1943), *The North Star* (1943), and *Song of Russia* (1944). That there were so few is not surprising: whatever the political sympathies of writers and directors, the industry's entrenched policy of refusing to touch politically or socially controversial subjects virtually guaranteed that radical points of view would seldom be aired in feature films. By the end of the decade, with the industry under close scrutiny from HUAC and its supporters, the major firms had adopted an even more restrictive definition of what was controversial. In the late 1930s and early 1940s the films of Frank Capra (*Meet John Doe, Mr Deeds Goes to Town, Mr Smith Goes to Washington*) and John Ford (*The Grapes of Wrath, Tobacco Road*) had shown that it was possible to make successful films that criticized businessmen, politicians, and injustices in American society. In 1946 the head of the Motion Picture Producers' Association, Eric Johnston, heralded the start of a less tolerant era, telling screenwriters: "We'll have no more *Grapes of Wrath*, we'll have no more *Tobacco Roads*, we'll have no more films that deal with the seamy side of American life. We'll have no more films that treat the banker as a villain."[26] The late 1940s did see a spate of Hollywood movies with a social or political message, but Johnston's remarks highlighted the dangers faced by filmmakers involved in these productions. In 1947 widespread condemnation of Universal's *The Senator Was Indiscreet*, a satire about a corrupt senator, demonstrated that such themes were now taboo. Controversy surrounding Edward Dmytryk's *Crossfire*, in which a Jew is murdered by an anti-Semitic war veteran, suggested that an inclination to examine the darker side of American life could give rise to charges of communist subversion. Dmytryk was one of the Hollywood Ten, and it is likely that *Crossfire* fuelled his accusers' antagonism to him.[27]

From the end of the 1940s Hollywood usually steered clear of such themes and concentrated on the production of musicals, Westerns, and other uncontroversial genres. Criticism of the political status quo did not disappear from the screen, but subtlety was now essential. *High Noon* (1952) presented such an oblique attack on anti-communist conformity that the film's star, Gary Cooper – one of HUAC's "friendly" witnesses of 1947 – probably did not grasp the message.[28] Subtlety was not a feature of Hollywood's anti-communist propaganda films, which included *The Iron Curtain* (1948), *The Woman on Pier 13* (originally *I Married a Communist*) (1949), *The Red Menace* (1949), *I Was a Communist for the FBI* (1951), *My Son John* (1952), and *Big Jim McClain* (1952). Giving full expression to McCarthyite obsessions, these films portrayed a world in which ruthless, corrupt, and cynical communist bosses, virtually indistinguishable from the central characters of gangster movies, plotted the overthrow of American democracy and exploited the gullibility of teachers, intellectuals, trade unionists, and blacks to gain recruits to their cause. If any doubts remained about the film industry's willingness to play its part in the Cold War, the studios cooperated with the State Department and other federal government agencies to ensure that unsuitable films were not exported. They took advice on film content from representatives of the Joint Chiefs of Staff and from agents of the Central Intelligence Agency (CIA) placed in Hollywood for that purpose.[29] Cold War politics also exerted a major influence on television entertainment, with images of East–West conflict and warnings of communism's menace to the United States frequently conveyed in a number of television genres.[30]

The Cold War's influence on the US media took its most extreme forms in the 1950s. In the early 1960s, and especially after the Cuban missile crisis of October 1962, a relaxation of Cold War tensions occurred and was matched by a tempering of domestic anti-communism. The media were affected by this change. The blacklists in film and broadcasting ceased to operate, while the release of such films as *The Manchurian Candidate* (1962) and *Dr Strangelove* (1964) showed that it was possible to criticize or ridicule American institutions, leaders, and policies in an overt way that had been out of the question ten years earlier.

Yet the most important effects of media involvement in the Cold War were more long-lasting. Even taking into account the limitations to media influence on public opinion, it remains a persuasive argument that, by failing for so long to examine critically US government policies, and by denying the public access to unorthodox views of international affairs, the media helped lay the groundwork for the foreign-policy disaster of American military involvement in Vietnam (see Chapter 10).[31] Moreover, as late as the 1980s Cold War imagery still prevailed in American film and television depictions of the Soviet Union, with the Soviets portrayed "as inhumane, vicious torturers who enjoy inflicting pain and murdering children."[32] The effects of decades of anti-Soviet propaganda could still be seen in an opinion poll that suggested that 25 percent of US college students believed the Soviets had invented the atomic bomb; while 28 percent of respondents to a *New York Times* survey in November 1985 believed that in the Second World War the Soviet Union had fought against the United States.[33] While it would be wrong to attribute such ignorance wholly to the effects of media manipulation, the media nonetheless had contributed greatly, over four decades, to the dissemination of the attitudes and images from which these flawed impressions were derived.

International Propaganda: Psychological Warfare and Cultural Diplomacy

While the US government relied on commercially based media organizations to mobilize domestic support for the Cold War, the conduct of international propaganda required direct state involvement. Washington created its own agencies to influence international opinion, including public opinion inside the Soviet Union and the satellite states of Eastern

Europe. From 1947 the United States invested heavily in "psychological warfare" and "cultural diplomacy." The latter refers to the dissemination of cultural products – such as films, magazines, radio and television programs, art exhibitions – to enhance the nation's image among the populations of other countries, with a view to influencing the policies of their governments through pressure of public opinion. "Psychological warfare" is more difficult to define. After 1945, US officials usually employed the term to refer to strategies that linked the use of communications systems for propaganda to the selective use of violence in, for example, sabotage, assassinations, and counter-insurgency operations. Among communications scholars no clear consensus emerged on the meaning of "psychological warfare," and often it was used simply as a synonym for "propaganda." Generally it implied propaganda of a particularly aggressive kind; and in this respect it reflects the purpose of US propaganda operations against countries behind the Iron Curtain.[34]

An intensive effort to shape world opinion had bipartisan support within the United States. Despite rhetorical differences between Democrats who favored containment policies and Republicans who insisted that the free world must not simply contain but "roll back" communism and deliver "liberation" to the captive peoples behind the Iron Curtain, both Democrat and Republican administrations worked to bring about the collapse of communist regimes in Eastern Europe and the Soviet Union. Propaganda was a means to this end.

By 1948 alarm at the seeming effectiveness of Soviet propaganda had created support for the Smith–Mundt Act, which created the legal framework for a permanent overseas information program, using the media, exchange programs, and exhibitions to combat the Soviets' "campaign of vilification and misrepresentation" against the United States.[35] The responsibility for clandestine psychological warfare and "black" propaganda – as well as such other covert tasks as sabotage, subversion, and assassinations – was given to a lavishly funded, secret branch of the newly formed CIA: the Office of Policy Coordination. By the spring of 1950 the stage was set for what Edward Barrett, the *Newsweek* editor appointed assistant secretary of state for public affairs, called "an all-out effort to penetrate the Iron Curtain with our ideas." With NSC 68 warning of a grave deterioration in the world situation and recommending a vast increase in defense expenditure and other measures to protect US security, Truman launched an aggressive international propaganda campaign, the "Campaign of Truth." Calling for a "sustained, intensified program to promote the cause of freedom against the propaganda of slavery," Truman declared that the Cold War was "a struggle, above all else, for the minds of men," one that the forces of "imperialistic communism" were currently winning.[36] Responding to the president's appeal, Congress increased by $80 million the normal appropriation of $32 million for the overseas information program. To coordinate the government's psychological warfare strategy, the Truman administration in 1951 created the Psychological Strategy Board (PSB). In 1953 the Eisenhower administration replaced the PSB with the Operations Coordinating Board and separated government information activities from the State Department, creating an independent United States Information Agency (USIA) with a director who reported to the president and the National Security Council (NSC). Eisenhower "planned to elevate psychological warfare to the center of Cold War strategy."[37]

Although the United States led the free world's campaign of psychological warfare against the communist regimes, the propaganda and intelligence agencies of other Western governments also played a part. The most influential was the Information Research Department (IRD), a secret branch of the British Foreign Office that fed non-attributable anti-communist propaganda to the BBC, the film industry, and the press, as well as to politicians, academics, trade-union leaders, and British diplomatic missions throughout the world.[38]

By the early 1950s, therefore, the Western powers attached high priority to psychological warfare and were employing propaganda measures to win international opinion to support the free world and, ultimately, to bring about the disintegration of communist regimes. US overseas information centers and libraries, documentary films and newsreels, and material fed to newspapers and magazines by a US press service and Britain's IRD all played a part in this campaign.

As a means of disseminating propaganda within the Soviet Union and its East European empire, radio was the most effective weapon available to the West's psychological warriors. With powerful radio transmitters in Central Europe and the Mediterranean, it proved possible to penetrate the Iron Curtain, despite Moscow's systematic jamming of Western broadcasts. In the vanguard of this campaign was the Voice of America (VOA). Established in 1942 as a wartime expedient, the VOA was quickly adapted in the postwar years to the purposes of

US international propaganda. State-funded, operated first by the State Department then by the USIA from 1953, it has "always been used and recognised as an instrument of US foreign policy."[39] By 1953 it broadcast in forty-six languages, with more than half its budget devoted to programming behind the Iron Curtain. Its broadcasts featured aggressive, often crude, anti-communist propaganda. Making heavy use of the words of refugees from communist regimes and of US and other Western leaders, VOA programming, according to a State Department internal study of 1950, contrasted "the virtues of democracies with the vices of communist regimes," emphasized "the inevitability of our ultimate triumph," and depicted the USSR as "the scheming villain," the United States as the country that "stands up against the powers of evil." For fear of inducing "propaganda fatigue" among listeners, the propaganda message was softened by other programs – straight news, features, and music.[40]

The VOA's development as an effective broadcasting arm of US propaganda was far from trouble-free. In 1953 Senator McCarthy turned his attention to the organization. In an episode that underlined the irrationality of the period's anti-communist extremism, McCarthy's brutal interrogation of VOA staff uncovered no evidence of communist influence but destroyed the careers of several employees, undermined morale within the organization, and probably affected its funding. In that year "Song of India" was temporarily removed from the VOA's music library, on the grounds that "it's by Rimsky-Korsakov, and we're not supposed to use anything by Russians."[41] The VOA also suffered from its status as the voice of the US government, and comparisons with the BBC brought into question internationally its journalistic independence.

The BBC, formally independent of the British government although state funded, continued during the Cold War to enjoy its wartime reputation for objectivity, accuracy, and trustworthiness. A 1953 study of English-language radio services observed that the BBC "sounded like a news service almost self-consciously trying to make everything come out 50 percent on each side," in contrast to Radio Moscow, which "sounded like a propaganda agency using news to illustrate themes," and the VOA, which "sounded like the news service of one of the great protagonists of the Cold War … neither as neutral as the BBC nor as carefully propagandistic as Radio Moscow."[42] Nonetheless, the BBC functioned as an instrument of international propaganda, its effectiveness enhanced by its credibility as an independent broadcasting service. Like the VOA, its overseas broadcasting reflected government priorities, established not by direct government control but by formal and informal ties with the British Foreign Office. The BBC's external services were legally obliged to broadcast in languages determined by the Foreign Office, to accept information from it, and to seek its advice on countries to which to broadcast. Both BBC executives and Foreign Office officials shared the common outlook on world affairs of the British establishment.[43]

The external operations of the BBC and the VOA were supplemented by broadcasts of the West German service Deutsche Welle and by two German-based US radio stations, ostensibly private but covertly funded by the CIA: Radio Free Europe (RFE) began broadcasting in 1950, Radio Liberation (from 1964 Radio Liberty (RL)) in 1953. Staffed largely by anti-Soviet émigrés, RFE broadcast anti-communist propaganda to the populations of the East European satellite states, RL to the Soviet Union.

The evidence suggests that the VOA, the BBC, RFE, RL, and Deutsche Welle developed a large audience behind the Iron Curtain. The success of their broadcasts as an influence on public attitudes is more difficult to gauge. Interviews with Soviet and East European defectors – by definition an unrepresentative group – form the main part of rudimentary audience research, suggesting that Western radio propaganda was successful. What is clear is that both the Western powers and the Soviet regime believed radio propaganda to be effective: the former demonstrated this by large-scale investment in broadcasting behind the Iron Curtain, the latter by its desperate attempts to counter the broadcasts, through jamming and vehement criticism of Western programs in the Soviet media. Two conclusions seem persuasive. One is that Soviet leaders were less concerned by propaganda attacks on communism than by images of Western affluence that invited comparison with the low living standards of communist countries. Another is that Soviet leaders were more anxious about Western broadcasts in the East European satellite states than in the Soviet Union itself. In the former the impact of foreign propaganda was not to create disaffection with communism – such attitudes were already inherent in the relationship between Moscow and the peoples of Eastern Europe – but to sustain hopes for eventual liberation and a determination to work toward that end.[44]

Events in Hungary in 1956 encouraged charges that in this last respect the Western broadcasts were too successful. When an uprising against Soviet domination was brutally suppressed by the Red Army, international radio propaganda was widely accused of raising false expectations of Western intervention, thus encouraging the revolt and contributing to the Hungarians' suffering. Such charges had most substance in the case of RFE, least with the BBC, which emerged from the crisis with its credibility intact.[45] For the VOA, criticisms arising from the Hungarian episode encouraged a shift away from the use of strident anti-communist propaganda toward an attempt to emulate the BBC's "objective" approach. This change reflected the declining importance of psychological warfare in American Cold War propaganda from the mid-1950s and an increasing emphasis on cultural infiltration of the communist bloc. Radio remained an important weapon in the West's Cold War arsenal, and the Cuban missile crisis of October 1962 underlined the medium's value as a tool of superpower diplomacy, as well as a means of disseminating propaganda. During the crisis both Washington and Moscow used radio to communicate with each other, supplementing traditional diplomatic channels.[46] But, increasingly, broadcasting was seen less as the chief medium for waging psychological warfare against the Soviets and more as one of a range of means by which the United States might win hearts and minds throughout the world through the gradualist approach of cultural diplomacy.[47]

The universal appeal of American mass culture had been clear as early as the 1920s, with the enormous success of American movies, music, and other mass-produced goods. The Cold War, widely perceived as a conflict between opposing ways of life, gave this attraction added political significance. From the mid-1950s US policymakers believed that cultural diplomacy would complement psychological warfare and that in the long term it might prove more effective. Between the 1950s and the 1980s the export of American culture was heavily subsidized by the US government and coordinated by the USIA. Cultural-exchange programs, international trade fairs and exhibitions, and the distribution of Hollywood movies, documentary films, books, magazines, and music were all means by which the United States extracted propaganda value from the appeal of America's way of life, especially its popular culture and material prosperity.

The promotion of international jazz tours typified this approach. From 1956 to the late 1970s the State Department sponsored concert tours of the Middle East, South Asia, Africa, Latin America, Europe, and the Soviet Union by America's leading jazz musicians, including Dizzy Gillespie, Louis Armstrong, Duke Ellington, Dave Brubeck, and

Benny Goodman. These highly successful tours both exploited the universal appeal of an American art form and – because of the prominent role of black musicians – countered Soviet propaganda's emphasis on American racism. From the mid-1950s, too, VOA programmers exploited the popularity of jazz and later rock 'n' roll among audiences behind the Iron Curtain, using music programs to boost the image of the United States. Before the end of the Cold War, the worldwide popularity of such symbols of "Americanization" as blue jeans, Coca Cola, and McDonald's testified to the success of this approach to the confrontation with America's ideological rival.[48]

Also central to the cultural Cold War was the mobilization of Western intellectuals in the anti-communist cause. While CIA agents in Hollywood sought to exploit media influence on mass opinion, much of the organization's propaganda activity was aimed not at the general public but at "opinion leaders." From the late 1940s the CIA developed an extensive network of cultural front organizations, the most important of which was the Congress for Cultural Freedom (CCF). Founded in 1950 and based in Paris, the CCF's aims were to combat communist and neutralist sentiment among the intelligentsia, especially in Western Europe, and to advocate the virtues of the American way of life. The CCF sponsored liberal, anti-communist magazines throughout the world, including *Encounter* (Britain), *Preuves* (France), *Der Monat* (Germany), *Quest* (India), and *Quadrant* (Australia). It sponsored the publication of hundreds of books and organized conferences, concerts, and art exhibitions. The CIA covertly funded these activities on a generous scale, with private foundations used to disguise the source of the money. Many writers and artists collaborated, unwittingly or otherwise, in the US government's Cold War propaganda campaign. They included eminent intellectuals of the period: Arthur Koestler, Raymond Aron, Sidney Hook, Bertrand Russell, Isaiah Berlin, Daniel Bell, Julian Huxley, W. H. Auden, Robert Penn Warren.[49] Britain's IRD also made a major contribution to the cultural Cold War, paying trusted academics and journalists to write articles and books with anti-communist content and covertly subsidizing the publication and worldwide distribution of works by approved authors.[50]

The exposure from the late 1960s of CIA backing of the CCF led to a varied response. Some of the beneficiaries of CIA largesse saw no harm in an intelligence organization's underwriting of culture. Like Yehudi Menuhin, they thought "much more of the CIA" for associating with "people like us."[51] According to this defense, the very fact that writers and artists were unaware of the CIA's involvement in funding proves that no political strings were attached to the process. Yet, if the CIA had operated merely as a generous facilitator of independent intellectual and artistic activity, there would have been no need for secrecy about its involvement. CIA support did, of course, come at a price, even if the ties that bound it to such organizations as the CCF were more subtle and complex than those at work in Moscow's control of its many fronts. The purpose of CIA subsidies for cultural activity was to inculcate favorable attitudes to American culture and society and to US policies. The result was interference in and corruption of the process of intellectual enquiry. The publisher Jason Epstein summed up the problem well:

> What most irritated us was that the government seemed to be running an underground gravy train whose first-class compartments were not always occupied by first-class passengers: the CIA and the Ford Foundation, among other agencies, had set up and were financing an apparatus of intellectuals selected for their correct Cold War positions, as an alternative to what one might call a free intellectual market where ideology was presumed to count for less than individual talent and achievement, and where doubts about established othodoxies were taken to be the beginning of all inquiry.[52]

The ability of the CIA and IRD to disguise their sponsorship of cultural activity for many years – until the late 1960s for the former, the late 1970s for the latter – highlights the key to the success of Western propaganda: so much of it was not generally recognized as propaganda. The IRD, like the BBC, gained credibility from an emphasis on a factual, balanced approach to its material. Similarly, American political messages were often presented in the form of information and entertainment. The CIA encouraged its front organizations to preserve their appearance of independence from the US government by not slavishly following every aspect of US policy. In this respect they contrasted markedly with their Soviet counterparts. Moreover, particular care was taken to cultivate intellectuals of the non-communist left; it was reasoned that anti-communist messages would be all the more credible when voiced by left-wing figures.

The complicity of intellectuals in the West's propaganda campaigns also affected some academic disciplines, especially in the United States. Thus US government psychological warfare programs funded the growth of mass communications research as a scholarly field in American universities between 1945 and 1960. The financial support came at a price, ensuring that priority was given to development of the discipline as the study of techniques by which elites could persuade, manipulate, and dominate target groups. Similar patterns were evident in social psychology and sociology.[53]

The most far-reaching claim for the effectiveness of the West's propaganda is that psychological warfare and cultural infiltration, by exposing populations behind the Iron Curtain to a highly attractive alternative way of life, played "a major, perhaps decisive, role in the collapse of the Soviet and East European regimes."[54] Yet the circumstances of this collapse suggest the need for a more cautious assessment. The main causes of Soviet decline are to be found in deep-seated economic and social problems, the causes of which lay not in the impact of US foreign policy or Western propaganda but in the inherent weaknesses of the Soviet political and economic system. Nonetheless, in the context of a deteriorating economy and social decay, the West's propaganda campaigns highlighted the deficiencies of the Soviet system and therefore exacerbated the crisis facing the regime. In the East European satellite countries the effects of the West's psychological warfare and cultural diplomacy were to reinforce existing antagonism toward the Soviet Union, to help sustain hopes of eventual liberation, and to encourage resistance to Moscow's domination. Beyond the Soviet bloc, American mass culture and material abundance had a universal appeal that the Soviets could not match. The US government's exploitation of that appeal was the most successful aspect of the West's Cold War propaganda.

8

Television and Consumer Societies

Television, a 1962 report on broadcasting in Britain claimed, was "one of the major long-term factors that would shape the moral and mental attitudes, and the values of our society." With this assertion the Pilkington Committee both gave expression to a view of television's influence that has remained widespread and highlighted the importance of understanding the medium's role in society.[1] In the second half of the twentieth century the rise of television transformed the media. The popularity of cinema, newspapers, magazines, and radio declined, while television became the dominant medium. Television was central to the rise of "consumer societies."

After a brief discussion of the origins of television, this chapter examines the postwar growth of the medium in the United States and Britain and the development of contrasting organizational arrangements – commercial and public service – in those countries. Further expansion from the 1970s, the proliferation of channels, and increasing commercialization of television are then discussed, along with the implications of those developments for programming. The chapter also examines US domination of international television markets, developments in public-affairs programming, the influence of television on politics, and television's role as an agency of socialization.

Origins

The invention of television was based on "a complex of inventions and developments in electricity, telegraphy, photography and motion pictures, and radio," many of them not specifically aimed at television development.[2] By the 1920s the work of a number of individuals had demonstrated the feasibility of using radio waves to carry visual images. In Germany, Paul Nipkow had developed a mechanical scanning dish in the 1880s. Others, such as Boris Rosing in Russia and A. A. Campbell Swinton in Britain, had experimented with a cathode-ray tube to scan objects electronically. A key figure in early television development in Britain was John Logie Baird, who energetically promoted experiments based on a mechanical scanning device. In experimental transmissions Baird televised objects in outline in 1924, recognizable human faces in 1925, and moving objects in 1926. He even, quite remarkably, demonstrated a rudimentary form of color television in 1928. But his system proved inferior to electronic scanning.

In the 1920s and 1930s the work of Manfred von Ardenne in Germany and the Russian-born Vladimir Zworykin in the United States led to further technical progress on the problem of electronic scanning. In 1929 Zworykin joined Radio Corporation of America (RCA), which put resources into research and development and the purchase of relevant patents. In 1931 RCA acquired part ownership of Electric and Musical Industries (EMI), which itself had resulted from the merger of two British companies involved in the music recording industry. EMI, with direct access to American research, adopted the sophisticated electronic scanning system based on Zworykin's work and pressed for its use by the British Broadcasting Corporation (BBC). Although Baird secured a short-term agreement with the BBC for test transmissions using his mechanical device between 1932 and 1934, it was the RCA system that formed the basis for the beginning of television broadcasting in both the United States and Britain.

Limited television services began in Germany in March 1935, in Britain in November 1936, and in the United States in April 1939. In Nazi Germany television was used entirely for propagandist purposes, and reception was restricted to special halls in Berlin. The British service was closed from the outbreak of war in September 1939; the war also delayed development of television in the United States. In each of these countries the major expansion would take place in the more favorable conditions of the postwar years. Television's development would be shaped in part by technology but also by political and social systems and by the institutional arrangements already established for radio broadcasting. The influence of existing forms of entertainment was also important. Like radio, television was a parasitical medium: it borrowed much of its content from existing events – sport, royal weddings, and political conventions, for example – and developed genres that owed much to vaudeville, theatre, radio, and cinema.

Eventually the medium would be organized almost universally on the basis of television sets in individual homes. This development was not determined by the technology of television. In some cases – including Nazi Germany, China before the 1970s, and Italy in the early years of television – receivers were placed not in homes but in public places. Indeed, before the 1950s some observers believed that television was most likely to develop in cinemas, in direct competition with the movies, rather than on a domestic basis.[3] These examples remind us that aspects of television often assumed to be inherent in the medium are instead the product of interaction between technology and society.[4]

Postwar Growth: Television from the 1940s to the 1960s

The United States and Commercial Television

In the United States the prosperity of the 1950s encouraged a rapid growth in television. The number of households with television sets jumped from under four million in 1950 to forty-four million in 1959, an increase from 9 percent to 86 percent of total households. The number of stations on air increased from 69 in 1949 to 609 in 1959.[5] That US television would develop along the lines of the distinctive American system of broadcasting pioneered by radio in the 1920s was scarcely questioned. The main features of that system – privately owned broadcasting companies funded by the sale of advertising, with limited government regulation through the Federal Communications Commission (FCC) – were established at the outset of the new medium's development. By the mid-1950s the structure of US commercial television had been consolidated. The two original broadcasting networks, the National Broadcasting Company (NBC) and the Columbia Broadcasting System (CBS), along with the younger and weaker American Broadcasting Company (ABC), formed an oligopoly that owed its privileged economic position to the FCC's decision to restrict television services initially to the Very High Frequency (VHF) portion of the electromagnetic spectrum, severely limiting the number of channels in each population center and therefore the possibility of competition. A fourth network, DuMont, struggled and went out of business in 1955.

In the 1950s and 1960s almost all local television stations were affiliated with one of the networks and devoted over 60 percent of their air time, including evenings, to national programming.[6] Despite the high costs of television production, a rapid growth in advertising revenue from the early 1950s ensured high profits for station owners.[7] The decade from 1945 saw a vast increase in the availability of consumer goods in the United States, and in the early 1950s advertisers quickly appreciated the advantages of national television for mass marketing. Television's share of advertising agencies' business expanded enormously as they established new departments to exploit the qualities of the medium. Combining the visual appeal of magazines with the sound and intrusiveness of radio, television seemed to many advertisers to offer special powers of persuasion.[8]

Television advertising at first took the form of sponsorship. As in radio, program development was controlled not by a broadcasting network but by an advertising agency, usually working for a single sponsor. Sponsorship came at a price. In paying to sponsor entire programs, companies felt entitled to have the last word on content, as when the agency representing Camel cigarettes, the sponsor of the *Man Against Crime* series, instructed that scripts were not to "have the heavy or any disreputable person smoking a cigarette."[9] More pervasive than interference with program details was pressure on producers to avoid controversy, for fear of jeopardizing the sponsor's image. Sponsors' concerns and Cold War political pressures had the same effect: television's early growth coincided with the implementation of the blacklist, and the inclination to tread warily with political and social matters influenced television entertainment as well as its coverage of news and public affairs (see Chapter 7).

Yet the early 1950s is often called the "golden age" of American television. Ideological conservatism did not stand in the way of programs, which were sometimes of a quality that would later be considered rare in US network television. Interference by sponsors was not the rule; some valued the prestige to be gained from association with programs of high quality and for this reason allowed producers considerable creative freedom.[10] One result was an exploration of the possibilities of television drama. Sponsored anthology series such as Kraft Television

Theatre, Philco Playhouse, and General Electric Theater presented live plays from New York each week and launched the careers of many distinguished dramatists and actors. Raymond Williams has pointed to the value of such television plays as *Marty* (1953), *Twelve Angry Men* (1954), and *Days of Wine and Roses* (1958): "In substance and in method – the exploring 'eye of the camera', the feel for every-day ordinary life, the newly respected rhythms of the speech of work and the streets and of authentic privacy … this new television drama stimulated similar work elsewhere …"[11]

The golden age lasted no longer than the mid-1950s. The rapid growth of television in working-class households in itself encouraged a shift from studio drama to lighter entertainment. Moreover, the heyday of anthology drama was a period of network dependence on live broadcasts. It ended with the introduction of videotape and the forging of a new collaborative arrangement with the Hollywood film studios. From the mid-1950s the Hollywood majors began to make their feature-film libraries available to television. In the next decade movies became a staple of prime-time programming. At this time, too, the major film studios became convinced of the profits to be made from telefilm production. The way had been shown by the ratings success in 1952 of *I Love Lucy* and *Dragnet*, weekly series produced in independent Hollywood studios. In 1954 ABC's negotiations with Walt Disney, then with Warner Bros., led to the production of two highly successful weekly filmed series, *Disneyland* and the Western *Cheyenne*. The other majors followed. By the late 1950s, with live drama all but extinct, prime-time television was dominated by filmed series produced in Hollywood. Westerns were most common (including *Have Gun Will Travel, Rawhide, Gunsmoke*, and *Bonanza*). Other successful genres of the late 1950s and early 1960s were private detective series (such as *77 Sunset Strip, Surfside 6*, and *Hawaiian Eye*), and drama series about doctors (*Ben Casey, Dr Kildare*) and lawyers (*Perry Mason*). For the networks, filmed series offered the advantages of being both popular and, by comparison with live drama, cheaper to produce. Advertisers also saw advantages in these programs. Their glamorous settings, attractive stars, and happy endings promised to put viewers in the right mood for the sales pitch of the commercials; while the series form, by creating viewer attachment to particular stars, characters, and situations, allowed advertisers more easily to predict the size and nature of a program's audience.[12]

A fundamental change in the role of advertisers accompanied the shift from live to filmed production. As production costs rose, and as demand for airtime increased advertising charges, it became difficult for one company to sponsor an entire program. Single sponsorship gave way to joint sponsorship and, increasingly, advertising in the form of short "spot" commercials inserted within and between programs. The networks acquired the control over production that had previously been the preserve of sponsors, licensing independent production companies to make programs and selling spots to advertisers. A rigid preoccupation with ratings was the consequence. With advertising spots priced according to the number of people watching a program, networks aimed to maximize profits by attracting the largest possible audience. In the early 1950s a program's viability had depended on the availability of a sponsor. By the end of the decade this was no longer sufficient. Networks cancelled sponsored programs that were well regarded but had a low rating, fearing that they would adversely affect audience "flow" to the next program. The search for high ratings accentuated the conservative bias of network television. Fear of offending or excluding any significant part of the potential audience reinforced an unwillingness to touch controversial themes and bred a creative caution that was reflected in slavish reliance on proven formulas.

By the end of the decade it was a common view that the networks had betrayed the promise of television's early years. The public interest, critics charged, had been sacrificed to commercial interests, a view fueled by the 1959 revelation of "fixing" in the popular prime-time quiz programs. In 1961 Newton Minow, President J. F. Kennedy's appointment as chairman of the FCC, spoke for these critics when he condemned network television as "a vast wasteland:"

> You will see a procession of game shows, violence, audience participation shows, formula comedies about totally unbelievable families, blood and thunder, mayhem, violence, sadism, murder, western badmen, western good men, private eyes, gangsters, more violence, and cartoons. And endlessly, commercials – many screaming, cajoling, and offending.[13]

In the early 1960s the networks sought to appease such high-placed critics and assert their public-service bona fides with increased prime-time programming of documentaries and news. The concession was enough to suppress calls for greater government regulation. For all the critics' concerns, there was little evidence of public dissatisfaction with the status quo.[14] News programs aside, the networks defended their programs by appealing to a view of the public interest expressed by CBS president Frank Stanton: "a program in which a large part of the audience is interested is by that very fact ... in the public interest."[15] In the 1960s the networks provided a steady diet of formulaic situation comedies ("sitcoms") and drama series and increasingly large doses of sports programming.[16]

The contention of the networks' critics that American television should provide for a different view of the public interest found expression in the Public Broadcasting Act of 1967, which established the Public Broadcasting Service (PBS). The country's many non-profit "educational" television stations, permitted on the Ultra High Frequency (UHF) band since 1952, were brought together in a system that was to be partly funded by the federal government. Supporters of the new service hoped that it would provide a successful alternative to commercial television.

Great Britain and Public Service Television

In Britain, too, television grew rapidly in the context of a consumer boom in the 1950s. The proportion of the adult population who owned a television set increased from 4 percent in 1950 to 40 percent in 1955 and 80 percent in 1960. In Britain, indeed, unlike the United States, ownership of television sets outstripped refrigerator ownership: 78 percent of respondents to a British survey in 1960 owned a television, only 24 percent a refrigerator.[17] As in the United States, British television developed within an organizational framework inherited from radio. The BBC was at first granted a national monopoly over television. Forbidden to advertise, it was funded by the sale of annual licenses for television and radio receivers. Though state funded and state regulated, the BBC was not subject to direct government control. This independence, however, was qualified by the government's power to appoint the Corporation's Board of Governors, which in turn appointed the Director General and senior staff. It also owed much to an expectation that the BBC would not depart from the orthodoxies of the British establishment. The difficulty of defining the public interest clearly in a way that distinguished it from the state interest, and the tendency for political leaders to assume that the two were synonymous,[18] were highlighted by tensions between the Corporation and both major political parties when in power.

The BBC's approach to television programming was heavily influenced by Sir John Reith's definition of broadcasting as a public service – by the idea that broadcasting has a cultural and educative role and is not merely a means of entertainment. In the first postwar decade the Corporation's critics blamed the Reithian ethos for television programs that were often cautious, conservative, and, they claimed, dull. The limitations were typified by an avoidance of domestic political discussion, for fear of upsetting the political parties, and by news bulletins that relied heavily on still photographs and, until 1955, did not show the faces of newsreaders. These criticisms were often misplaced. The BBC needed to maintain a broad audience to justify its funding by annual license fee. Even before the start of its postwar television operations, it had moved beyond the narrow interpretation of broadcasting's role that had prevailed in the early years of radio (see Chapter 4). The BBC's public-service mission and its broadcasting monopoly did contribute to conservative programming, but just as important were a bias toward radio, in a period when the Corporation's senior managers were men whose careers had developed in the older medium, and, especially, the austerity of the early postwar years, which limited both the ownership of television sets and the BBC's scope for expenditure on television production.[19]

The advent of general prosperity was bound to bring changes to programming, but widespread dissatisfaction with the BBC's monopoly led to more far-reaching reforms to British television. In 1951 a committee of inquiry on broadcasting chaired by Lord Beveridge criticized the BBC for "the four scandals of monopoly: bureaucracy, complacency, favouritism and inefficiency."[20] Beveridge, nonetheless, recommended that the BBC's monopoly and funding by license fee should continue, on the grounds that commercial television, to judge by the American experience, would be worse. A dissenting report by one of the committee members, Conservative parliamentarian Selwyn Lloyd, urged the establishment of a commercial alternative to the BBC and was welcomed by commercial interests, centered on the entertainment and advertising industries. These groups waged a campaign for the introduction of commercial television, against the opposition of the Labour Party and a large part of the British establishment, including the churches and universities. Although the opposition included prominent members of the Conservative Party – and despite the fact that there were "far more Conservative voters who object to commercial television than Labour voters" – a Conservative government accepted the case for a commercial alternative to the BBC.[21] The Television Act of 1954 established a commercial television service, Independent Television (ITV), administered by an Independent Television Authority (ITA) that owned transmission facilities and granted licenses to fourteen companies based in different regions, a provision that responded to the Beveridge Report's criticism of centralization under the BBC. The companies were funded by sales of advertising spots, limited to six minutes per hour, with sponsorship ruled out on the grounds that it would give advertisers too much influence on programs.

Such restrictions underlined a determination to avoid the worst abuses of American network television. Indeed, the British version of commercial television, far from emulating the US model, represented a distinctively British application of "public-service" principles to a commercial broadcasting service. Members of the ITA – and from 1972 its successor, the Independent Broadcasting Authority (IBA) – were government appointed, like the BBC Board of Governors. The ITA enjoyed extensive regulatory powers, designed to ensure that ITV companies maintained "balance," "impartiality," and high programming standards. Thus the state-funded BBC and the "independent" commercial companies existed side by side as separate arms of a public-service television system.[22]

Nonetheless, to attract large audiences – the key to advertising revenue and profitability – ITV did introduce new kinds of programs to British television, including soap operas, variety shows, quiz programs produced according to American formats, imported American series, and an innovative news service. Inevitably, these programs made inroads into the BBC's audience. The extent to which they did so is difficult to measure and was probably exaggerated both by ITV and within the BBC.[23] But the rise of commercial television did generate criticism of what was perceived to be a lowering of cultural standards and an excessive reliance on imported American programs. These anxieties informed the report of the Pilkington Committee of inquiry into broadcasting in 1962. Pilkington criticized ITV for crass commercialism and the alleged triviality and sensationalism of its programs. His report insisted that "winning the largest number of viewers … is not the only, and by no means the most important, test of good broadcasting."[24] In the tradition of Reith, the Pilkington Report insisted that programs of a high cultural standard should be presented to the broad population rather than confined to an educated minority. As a result of its recommendations, the powers of the ITA were strengthened and a second BBC channel, BBC 2, was established in 1964.

Encouraged by the Pilkington Report, the BBC in the 1960s adopted a more innovative approach to programming. Competition between the BBC and ITV proved beneficial for British television. The prosperity of the 1960s provided economic security for both systems and allowed greater investment in production. ITV attracted high levels of advertising revenue, while the BBC's income benefited from an increase in license fees with the introduction of color on BBC 2 in 1967. The existence of a rival television system prevented the BBC from becoming dull or complacent and compelled it to aim at "establishing a relationship with a diverse audience which enlightened, informed, amused, but did not patronize."[25] The ITA's regulatory powers kept ITV aware of its public-service responsibilities and deterred it from seeking to satisfy the lowest common denominator in public taste. Both systems enjoyed about half the viewing audience. British television was responsible for outstanding programs of various kinds: drama, comedy, documentaries, and public-affairs programs. If the early 1950s were the golden age of American television, the 1960s were Britain's equivalent.

State Television

Television broadcasting started in different years, and ownership of sets grew at different rates from country to country. The contrast between two cases was typical of this diversity. In France, where postwar transmission began as early as 1947, television ownership by 1960 was only one-fifth that of the United Kingdom. Yet in Sweden, where transmission commenced relatively late – in 1956 – the expansion of ownership was so rapid that within three years there were more television sets per 1,000 inhabitants than in any country except the United States, Canada and Britain.[26] By the end of the 1960s, however, television ownership was widespread throughout the West, as well as in parts of the communist bloc in Eastern Europe. Television's expansion was influenced in part by American and British organizational models: the American system was influential especially in Latin America, the British in the Federal Republic of Germany, Sweden, and those

Commonwealth countries – Canada, Australia, New Zealand – where public broadcasters modeled on the BBC coexisted with commercial networks influenced by the US example. Yet before the 1970s neither the British nor the American system was typical of television's institutional arrangements in other countries: direct state control of television services was more common than either. This was true not only of authoritarian regimes such as the Soviet Union and China but also of West European democracies. In these cases public-service objectives were paramount, but, by comparison with Britain, the public interest was less insulated from the interests of government and consequently political interference was more direct and pervasive. State monopoly created obstacles to the medium's development. Without the commercial competition that discouraged the BBC from taking its audience for granted, state channels limited broadcasts usually to a few hours each day, while strict government regulation of political and moral content imposed limits on what viewers were permitted to see and encouraged conventional, often dull, programming.[27] The next three decades would see continuing tension between commercial and public-service objectives and significant changes in the role of government in the world's television systems.

The Triumph of Commercialism: Television since the 1970s

The United States

The 1970s saw the American networks at the height of their power and profitability. At the end of that decade they enjoyed a 90 percent share of the television audience. Their total revenues increased from $1 billion to $3 billion despite apparent setbacks in the early 1970s. A Congressional ban on cigarette advertising on television from January 1971 cost the networks a lucrative source of revenue. The FCC's Prime Time Access Rule, designed to assist local stations, limited the networks to three hours of prime time nightly from October 1971. The restriction had the unintended effect of increasing demand for limited network advertising time, and this, as well as the new interest in network advertising of such major companies as McDonald's and Coca-Cola, allowed CBS, NBC, and ABC to increase advertising rates steadily through the decade.[28] A preoccupation with ratings continued to govern program-ming, with the networks' news services the one remaining concession to the idea of broadcasting as public service.

By now, however, the search for high ratings was complicated by a concern for the demographic characteristics of viewers. Research into television audiences taught advertisers to value not large audiences in themselves but large numbers of those viewers most likely to buy the advertised product. For this reason CBS canceled such high rating prime-time programs as *The Beverly Hillbillies* and *The Andy Griffith Show*: their popularity was based too much on an appeal to elderly, low-income, and rural viewers, rather than the young, affluent urban-dwellers most prized by advertisers.[29]

This preoccupation with "demographics" combined with broader cultural change to shape programming in the 1970s. Beginning with CBS, the networks sought to exploit the changing attitudes and values that resulted from the Vietnam War, the black civil-rights movement, women's liberation, and the 1960s sexual revolution. The largely mono-racial world of network programs gradually disappeared, as black characters and images of ethnic togetherness became common.[30] Sitcoms of the early 1970s reflected the new willingness of CBS to deal with controversial subjects – race, bigotry, abortion, the role of women in society – in order to shift its audience appeal from rural and small-town America, perceived as culturally conservative, to liberal urban and sub-urban audiences. Such series as *All in the Family, Maude, The Mary Tyler Moore Show, M*A*S*H*, and *Rhoda* won critical acclaim as well as enjoy-ing high ratings. Less sophisticated, and more based on a simple appeal to voyeurism, were the programs that in the second half of the decade lifted ABC from its perennial status as third network to ratings leader. The highly successful sitcoms *Three's Company* and *Soap* relied heavily on sexual situations and dialogue. The action-adventure series *Charlie's Angels*, the mini-series *Roots*, and the movies featured on ABC also owed much of their popularity to sexual content. Such programs were intended to attract a younger audience; their success in doing so could not be ignored by CBS and NBC.[31]

Concerns about trends in US television had led to the establishment of a public broadcasting alternative to the networks in 1967, but the weakness of PBS soon became apparent. From the outset PBS proved vulnerable to political influence. Members of the Corporation for Public Broadcasting (CPB), which distributes federal funds through the system, were presidential appointees, and all too often appointments were made purely on the basis of political allegiance or ideological commitment. The Nixon, Reagan, and second Bush administrations, in particular, were out of sympathy with public broadcasting, regarding PBS as a hotbed of left-wing ideology. Republican control of Congress in the late 1990s and from 2003 to 2007 posed another threat: federal funds for PBS were cut from $312 million in 1996 to $250 million in 1998; and again in 2005–6 PBS struggled to keep its funding intact in the face of Congressional threats of cuts.[32]

Funding of PBS has always been precarious. Thus in 1993, while Britain spent US$38.99 per citizen on public television and Canada $31.05, the United States spent $6.83 per citizen; and of that amount a mere $1.09 came from the federal government.[33] For the balance of its revenues PBS had to look to a number of sources, including state and local governments, corporate sponsors, and subscribers. The fund-raising appeals that have formed a frequent and tedious part of PBS programming underline the extent of the problem. Moreover, revenues are diluted by the decentralized structure of public broadcasting. PBS is a loose federation of many local stations throughout the United States – 355 in 2007 – each with its own transmission equipment, studios, offices, and bureaucracy. Whatever its responsiveness to local needs, the inefficiency of such a system has severely limited the amount of money available for making programs.

PBS has presented some very successful programs. They include the Ken Burns documentary series *The Civil War*, *The MacNeil–Lehrer NewsHour* (later *The NewsHour with Jim Lehrer*), and some children's programs, notably *Sesame Street*. But not surprisingly, in view of the chronic shortage of money, many of PBS's best programs have been imported British products, especially from the BBC. In the 1990s that source, too, began to dry up, as the BBC increasingly favored cable channels at the expense of PBS. A chronic fear of antagonizing corporate sponsors, the White House, Congressmen, and anyone else whose displeasure might threaten PBS stations' funding, encouraged bland, cautious programming, reflected in a paucity of good documentaries and of original drama and comedy, and in programs that were often indistinguishable from the content of commercial television (they often included reruns of old network programs).[34] Yet these concessions to commercialism did not win PBS popularity: its ratings remained consistently at around 2 percent of the total viewing audience. PBS, therefore, suffered the worst of both worlds, failing as both a public-service and a commercial broadcaster.

While PBS posed no threat to the oligopoly of CBS, NBC, and ABC, the rapid rise of cable television from the late 1970s, made possible by the use of satellite technology, followed by growth in the number of independent stations in the 1980s and the creation of Rupert Murdoch's Fox network in 1986, caused the established networks far greater concern. These new forms of competition greatly eroded the three networks' audience share, from around 90 percent in prime time in the late 1970s, to 60 percent in 1990, to around 50 percent in 2000. A boom in video cassette recorder (VCR) ownership and video rentals during the 1980s further undermined the networks' dominance. The use of VCRs for "time shifting," and the growing popularity of remote control devices, interfered with careful calculations of audience flow and, by allowing viewers more easily to avoid commercials, further reduced the attraction of network television to advertisers (see Chapter 11).[35]

In the fiercely competitive market of the 1980s and 1990s, all three networks were taken over by conglomerates: NBC by General Electric (1986), ABC by Disney (1995), CBS by Westinghouse (1995) and Viacom (1999). In their insistence that every division be profitable, these vertically integrated organizations heightened the commercial networks' preoccupation with ratings and their desperation to please advertisers. The scope to do so was extended by the triumph of an ideology of "deregulation" in the FCC in the 1980s – the body's chairman during the Reagan administration defined the public interest simply as "that which interests the public"[36] – effectively eliminating public-service concerns as an obstacle to commercial interests in broadcasting.

In three ways television played a central role in the collapse of those barriers that, until the 1980s (though with diminishing effectiveness throughout the television age), had protected "home, school and church" from "the intrusion of the market."[37] First, the removal of FCC restrictions led to an increase in the amount of advertising time on television. By the mid-1990s around fifteen minutes of commercials were screened per hour – a 50 percent increase from ten years earlier.[38] Second, the lines between commercials and programs were blurred. Since the 1950s television programs had served "to naturalize the world of consumer goods by turning even domestic dramas into de facto fashion shows and shopping catalogues."[39] From the mid-1980s the commercial purpose of programs was even more blatant, with product placement, long a feature of movies, becoming increasingly common in television entertainment.[40] Third, a desire to maximize advertising revenues and profits encouraged network complicity in the growth of "trash television" – programs characterized by tabloid journalism of a particularly sensationalist kind, by a frequent blurring of the lines between reality and fiction, and by a preoccupation with sleaze. The term embraces a number of kinds of programs, including daytime "talk shows," "news magazine" programs such as *Hard Copy* and *A Current Affair*, and "reality" shows that purport to examine the lives of real people – all programs that were both popular and cheap to produce.[41] Meanwhile the quality of television news and public-affairs programming – as measured by willingness to allow journalistic values to prevail over the conventions of television entertainment – declined. In the last years of the century, therefore, competitive pressures and the end of regulation led to programming trends that seemed to vindicate the worst fears of commercial television's critics.[42]

There was, however, another side to the story. The 1990s and early years of the new century also saw the production of television entertainment of such a high standard that the period has been described as the new "golden age" of American television. This view was not universally accepted: many of these programs attracted criticism for violence and sexual content and for what seemed to some to be the gratuitous use of obscene language and the celebration of dysfunctional families.[43] Nonetheless, it was a common view that such programs represented the pinnacle of achievement in television entertainment. They included sitcoms (*Cheers, Frasier, Seinfeld, Sex and the City*) and satirical cartoons (*The Simpsons, South Park*). Most prominent, however, were contemporary drama series, which, while commercially successful, also attracted critical acclaim for their fully drawn characters and the complexity of their narrative structure and subject matter.[44] Some of these series were broadcast by the networks, including *The West Wing* and *ER* (NBC), *Desperate Housewives* and *Lost* (ABC), and *24* (Fox). Significantly, however, some of the most outstanding drama series were broadcast by Home Box Office (HBO), the "premium cable" subsidiary of Time Warner (premium cable channels are those for which viewers must pay a premium on top of their standard cable subscription). HBO series included *The Sopranos* (widely regarded as the greatest American television drama), *The Wire, Six Feet Under, Oz*, and *Deadwood*. HBO enjoyed two advantages over the networks. As a cable channel it was not subject to a law that prevents free-to-air channels from broadcasting "indecent" images or language between 6 a.m. and 11 p.m. It was free of advertising, and therefore unhampered by the preoccupation with ratings that stems from commercial television's dependence on the whim of advertisers. In both respects HBO's freedom from constraint formed a basis for the production of successful entertainment – so much so that the networks were compelled by commercial pressures to try to emulate HBO's programs.

The "golden age" of American television in the early twenty-first century, therefore, unlike its short-lived equivalent of fifty years earlier, was based on an acceptance of the fragmentation of audience. Successful programs still commanded huge audiences by international standards, ranging from thirteen million to twenty-six million prime-time viewers each week for the most popular network drama programs. The proliferation of channels, however, meant that their share of the overall audience was significantly reduced. While the most popular program of the 1960s, *I Love Lucy*, was watched by two-thirds of all viewers, its 1990s equivalent, *Seinfeld*, attracted only one-third of the prime-time audience. The key to commercial success now lay in programs that appealed to a substantial segment of the population – not in programs intended for a broad mass audience. Restructured in this way, American television proved remarkably durable, with Americans in 2006 still devoting more time to watching television (four hours a day on average, or sixty-four days a year) than to any other leisure activity.[45]

Great Britain

Commercial considerations became more important in British television from the 1970s. The period did see one significant development in Britain's public-service broadcasting system with the creation of Channel 4, which began transmission in 1982. A commercial channel but heavily regulated by the IBA, it was intended to cater for minority audiences, who were thought not to be well served by ITV. It was funded by an annual levy imposed on the ITV companies, which were allowed to sell advertising on the new channel. It also differed from the existing ITV stations in that it did not produce programs, taking them instead from independent production companies. Channel 4 was generally greeted as a valuable addition to Britain's television system. However, other forms of public broadcasting faced new difficulties.

Starting in the 1970s, the BBC encountered increasing financial difficulties when revenue from the license fee failed to keep pace with rising production costs. ITV, for its part, responded to the growing costs of programming by raising the price of advertising, a solution that led advertisers to be more critical of restrictions on the nature and amount of advertising on ITV and to press for the creation of new channels. The rise of cable, satellite, and VCR technology in the 1980s increased pressure on both ITV and the BBC: on the former by creating competition for advertisers' expenditure on television, on the latter by threatening the BBC's audience share and therefore its case for an increase in the license fee.[46]

Growing ideological opposition to public-service broadcasting, one aspect of the neo-liberal economic ideas that gained influence after the 1960s, found a powerful political voice in Margaret Thatcher, prime minister from 1979 to 1990. Thatcher's government showed scant respect for the conventions of BBC independence from the state, filling the Board of Governors with government sympathizers who tended to view the Corporation as a center of left-wing bias, unpatriotic attitudes, and loose morals. It did not hesitate to interfere in the management of the public broadcaster. The BBC's revenues were severely cut by the simple expedient of not increasing the license fee in a period of inflation. Staff numbers were reduced, the powers of the Board of Governors were increased, the Corporation was required after 1990 to draw more of its programs from independent production houses, and morale was further eroded by a restructuring that reflected some of the excesses of late-twentieth-century "managerialism."[47] These circumstances threatened the public-service ethos of BBC programmers. In the name of accountability program-makers were directed to produce dramas that responded specifically to supposed audience tastes, instead of following their creative impulses.[48] Documentaries were increasingly entertainment-driven. BBC 1 came to be (according to a member of its current-affairs unit) "a no-go area for serious current affairs programmes."[49] The Corporation stood accused of abandoning "its commitment to enlighten and inform" by presenting "a distinctively English mix of gardening, cooking, quiz shows, home improvement, and low-end comedy, interspersed with nostalgic recollections from its better days."[50]

The 1990 Broadcasting Act, which reorganized ITV, also highlighted the threat to public-service broadcasting. Franchises for television companies were to be auctioned, and the IBA was replaced by the weaker

Independent Television Commission (ITC), with reduced powers to control program quality. In 2003, in turn, the "New Labour" government of Tony Blair replaced the ITC with another regulator, the Office of Communications (Ofcom), which saw its regulatory role as almost entirely involving economic matters, not content. Deregulation and the pressures of a competitive television market led to reduced spending on production, a greater reliance on imports, and increased emphasis on the pursuit of ratings and, therefore, the lowest common denominator in popular taste. News and information programs were removed from prime time. A steady diet of "pop, chat, soap, and sport," on ITV as well as cable and satellite stations, was the result.[51]

For supporters of Britain's public-service television system, these developments were a cause for pessimism. Even so, there remained some encouraging signs. One was the fact that "people went on watching television in far greater numbers and for far more of the time" than had been predicted through the 1990s; the vast majority of them, moreover, continued to watch terrestrial channels.[52] Another was the resilience of the BBC. Despite the trials faced by the Corporation during the last two decades of the century, it resisted political pressure to introduce advertising, retained an audience share of 44 percent, and continued to make programs of high quality. Internationally, BBC World and the BBC website proved enormously successful. The BBC remained the world's pre-eminent public-service broadcaster.[53] Moreover, its position was reinforced in 2005 when the Blair government decided to renew the Corporation's charter and license fee for another ten-year period, beginning in 2007. Supporters of the public-service broadcasting ethos could also take heart from the fact that the government accompanied its decision with a warning to the BBC that it "should not play copycat" or "chase ratings for ratings' sake." Yet the tensions inherent in the position of a public-service broadcaster in the early twenty-first century were evident in the fact that this injunction was accompanied by an insistence that all decisions made by a newly created BBC Trust – intended to replace the Board of Governors – must be "clearly grounded in viewer and listener opinion" as determined by constant market research.[54] The BBC's announcement in 2007 of its intention to make substantial job cuts, in order to meet the government's demand for a 3 percent annual "efficiency saving" as a condition of the new license fee agreement, also highlighted the vulnerability of a public broadcaster. The pressures facing public-service broadcasters in the new century were even more evident outside Britain. Internationally, the idea of the viewer as consumer has had a pervasive influence.

International Developments

The 1970s saw the start of a vast expansion of the television audience outside its initial strongholds in the developed world. In the last three decades of the twentieth century there took place a huge increase in the number of television sets in the Soviet Union, China, and developing countries. By the 1990s the majority of the world's television audience lived in the Third World, with the largest audience in China.[55] During the same period major institutional and technological changes occurred. From the 1980s commercial interests took on a greater importance in television throughout the world. The growth of consumer societies, the ready availability of advertising revenue, financial pressures on state-funded television systems, growing ideological support for deregulation, and the undermining of political regulations by a vast proliferation of cable and satellite stations, often transmitting programs that could be received by viewers in more than one country, weakened state television monopolies in many countries, especially in Western Europe and Asia. The creation of new commercial stations, the privatization of some state-owned channels, and an easing of restrictions on advertising on state networks were the results. In Western Europe, where state television monopolies were the rule in the 1970s, the effect of the growing commercialization of the medium was to increase the number of terrestrial stations from 38 in 1980 to 125 in 1991, while by the early 1990s there were more than 140 satellite channels. The expansion continued more rapidly during the next decade, to the point where by 2002 an estimated 1,500 channels were operating in Western Europe alone. The extent of change is also underlined by the growing importance of advertising even in the television system of the world's one remaining major communist power, China.[56]

In the 1990s, therefore, public broadcasters in many countries came under pressure. To maintain audience share in the face of new forms of competition, and to justify continuation of their public funding, they increasingly resorted to programs that were indistinguishable from those shown on commercial television; and in this way they brought into question the very reason for their existence. The new technologies lent plausibility to the argument that minority audiences, formerly dependent on public broadcasting, could be catered for by cable television rather than subsidized by the taxpayer. By the early years of the new century the future of public broadcasting systems, and of the public-service ethos that had supported them, was uncertain. The triumph of commercial television, meanwhile, presented a fundamental paradox. While the twenty years from 1980 saw a huge increase in the number of television stations globally, and in this sense a far more competitive medium, real program choice had been greatly circumscribed. Competition for advertising revenue had created a universal trend to follow the path pioneered by US commercial television: to emphasize formulaic entertainment at the expense of alternative program forms.[57]

Global Television and "American Cultural Imperialism"

During the 1950s the American networks built upon their domestic ascendancy and achieved an international influence that became a continuing feature of global television. There are two aspects to the international role of the United States. One has already been noted: the expansion of the American commercial model of television. The other concerns the sale of programs abroad, on such a scale that US companies have dominated international television markets. American programs have enjoyed a prominent place in prime-time television throughout the world, accounting for almost half of all imported programs worldwide, far more in Canada and Latin America. In 2001 the United States was estimated to account for 75 per cent of the value of world trade in television programs, as well as between two-thirds and three-quarters of the trade in television fiction by volume.[58]

The causes of American dominance of international markets lay in the expense of television production, which gave other countries a strong economic incentive to import programs, and in the American industry's capacity to respond to international demand for popular and relatively cheap entertainment. The international advantages of US television were the same as those of the US film industry; and, of course, the lines between the two were blurred when Hollywood involved itself in telefilm production. Control of a large domestic market permitted high levels of investment in production, while American filmmakers proved adept at creating entertainment – including television sitcoms, drama series, Westerns, soap operas, and cartoons – that enjoyed worldwide appeal. The real measure of that appeal was the popularity of American imports among programmers and audiences even in non-English-speaking countries, where, because of the need for subtitling or dubbing, American exporters faced an obstacle that did not exist in the English-language markets of Britain, Canada, and Australasia.

By contrast, the success of other major television export industries was largely limited by region, language, and cultural ties: this was the case with program exports from Brazil, Mexico, Egypt, India, Hong Kong, Taiwan, Canada, and Australia. Japan was a major exporter, globally as well as within East Asia, but predominantly of a limited range of programs: animation constituted the majority of Japanese exports. In the case of Britain (often regarded as the world's second-largest exporter of television programs), success in global markets was limited by the public-service ethos of British television – a result of which is that British programs find a ready market among public broadcasters in Commonwealth countries, Western Europe, Japan, and the United States, and with some specialty pay-TV channels, but less so in commercial systems.[59] From the 1980s the proliferation of cable, satellite, and terrestrial television channels throughout the world and consequent shortage of programming, pressure to cut costs in a new competitive market, growing dependence on advertising revenue, and increased pressure on state media systems to be responsive to audience tastes all increased international demand for American programs.[60]

From the 1950s American preeminence in global television contributed to a renewal of the widespread fears of "Americanization" that exports of American movies and consumer goods had generated since the early twentieth century. In the second half of the century such fears were expressed in a number of ways. In the 1970s communications scholars – both Americans and others – warned of the impact of American (or Western) "cultural imperialism," especially on what they regarded as the vulnerable societies of the "Third World." European politicians and intellectuals lamented the supposed consequences of American influence in their own countries: for the Left, this was the triumph of "capitalism;" for others, it was the loss of "national identity." There was, of course, more to such fears than the perceived influence of television: Hollywood movies, jazz, rock 'n' roll, chain stores, supermarkets, shopping malls, Coca-Cola and fast food, theme parks, blue jeans, T-shirts, baseball caps, and the *Reader's Digest* were all criticized as vehicles for imposing the American way of life on the rest of the world.[61] But television held a special place in the anxieties of opponents of American mass culture and "cultural imperialism" – a significance that derived in part from the medium's ubiquity, in part from the widely held belief that visual entertainment profoundly affects culture. The French minister of culture, Jack Lang, gave expression to this belief when in 1983 he denounced the melodrama *Dallas* as the "symbol of American cultural imperialism."[62] In response to these fears the European Community imposed quotas on non-European programs permitted into Western Europe, restrictions that became an issue in trade negotiations with the United States.[63]

Warnings of American cultural imperialism gained plausibility from the political, economic, and military preeminence of the United States in the postwar period, from the pervasiveness of American popular culture, and, in the case of television, from US dominance in international markets. For the same reasons the belief that the United States behaves as an imperialist power in the cultural sphere continues to form part of popular anti-Americanism in many countries (and is widely held in the United States itself). Since the 1980s, however, an important body of scholarship has identified serious weaknesses in the concept of cultural imperialism. Studies from a number of disciplines have argued that "cultural imperialism" should be replaced by a concept described variously as "cultural transfer," "cultural transmission," and "cultural interaction." Viewed in this light, national, regional, and local cultures are not replaced by a homogeneous global culture imposed by the United States. Instead, recipients in Europe, Asia, and elsewhere select from American cultural exports: they reject some, accept others, and adapt them to their own purposes. As a result, it is argued, the impact of American mass culture "is superficial and more limited than most people assume;" American movies, fashions, and fast food have not "substantially changed the political institutions and social mores of other countries." Moreover, the process of cultural transmission works both ways: America's own culture is a hybrid, for "the United States has been as much a recipient as a creator and exporter of modern culture."[64]

These arguments are examined in Chapter 12, but of particular significance for an understanding of global television are the ability of audiences to enjoy programs as mere entertainment, rather than passively absorbing foreign cultural values; the importance of exported programming from countries other than the United States; and above all the national character of television. For all the importance of the international market in programs, the world's television systems continued to reflect heavily their national origins. Most television programs are locally made and are not distributed internationally. There is strong evidence that audiences in all parts of the world prefer home-grown content when good locally made programs are available. A heavy reliance on imported content is usually not a reflection of public demand for foreign programs but an indication that the national television system is not sufficiently wealthy to produce its own programs. As television markets become wealthier, they tend to rely more heavily on locally produced material.[65] Thus since the mid-1990s free-to-air channels across Western Europe – even in small markets such as the Netherlands and Sweden – have reduced their levels of imported programming (including American programs) in prime time, with US series increasingly restricted to daytime and late-night slots.[66] Japan provides an even more striking example. In the 1950s Japanese television relied heavily on imported American programs; but by 1980, as a result of Japan's postwar economic miracle, the local television industry had grown to the point where only 5 percent of all programs were imported, and American imports were less popular than Japanese television entertainment.[67]

The American case itself illustrates the same phenomenon. The US television market is unusual in that from the beginning it has been largely self-sufficient. Its tiny percentage of imported programs, mainly from Britain, has in recent decades been limited to PBS and cable. The commercial networks have preferred to remake foreign series for American audiences (thus *Sanford and Son, All in the Family, Three's Company, Men Behaving Badly,* and *The Office* were based on the British sitcoms *Steptoe and Son, Till Death Us Do Part, Man about the House, Men Behaving Badly,* and *The Office* respectively).[68] American resistance to imported programming is not the result of a peculiar American parochialism (though it may well reinforce American insularity) but one example of a universal phenomenon: the tendency of television channels to try to cater to perceived viewer demand for locally made entertainment. The peculiar aspect of American television is that it has always been sufficiently "mature" – or wealthy – to avoid major reliance on imported content.

In factual programming national differences were even more salient than in entertainment. National and local news and current-affairs programs continued to reach the vast majority of viewers; only small audiences relied on global organizations for their television news. And from the late twentieth century it became a general trend to reduce foreign news coverage (one of the central paradoxes of media in a globalized world).[69] Those factual programs that succeeded in export markets were science, wildlife, and natural-history programs, which unlike most news and current affairs were not culturally specific. Thus *Walking with Dinosaurs* and *The Blue Planet* were highly successful British export series in part because their UK origins were not obvious to foreign audiences.[70]

International trade in television formats (the sale of program concepts that have proved successful in one market for adaptation in another) also raises questions about the relative importance of the local and the global in audience tastes and the role of American influence on global television. Television entertainment is very similar throughout the world. The same genres tend to appear everywhere: police and medical dramas, soap operas, sitcoms, quiz shows, "reality" shows, gardening, cooking and home-improvement shows, nature programs, movies, sport, and news. A major expansion in the global trade in formats since 1980 has reinforced that similarity. While it is more expensive to purchase a format and produce a series locally than it is to import ready-made programs, the former does have the advantage of obviating the cost and risk associated with the development of domestic programs from scratch. The sale of formats began in the 1950s and was long dominated by the United States, with quiz shows such as *The Price Is Right* and *Wheel of Fortune* proving particularly attractive in Europe and elsewhere. But since the 1990s non-American companies have come to play a prominent part in the format trade, and the United States has become a major export market.

A few examples illustrate the range of this trade. In the 1990s it included the sale of Australian soap operas to Europe: *Sons and Daughters, Prisoner, The Restless Years* (the basis for the popular and enduring series *Goede Tijden Slechte Tijden* in the Netherlands, and *Gute Zeiten Schlechte Zeiten* in Germany). The Dutch company Endemol, the creator of the reality game show *Big Brother*, established itself as a dominant agency in the global format trade, selling that program's format in over eighteen countries and developing a format catalogue of over 400 titles. Japan is also an important exporter of program formats, not only to East Asia but to Europe, the United States, and other parts of the world with formats such as *Iron Chef, Happy Family Plan, Wakuwaku Animal Land,* and a variety-show segment that became the basis of *America's Funniest Home Videos,* the format of which was purchased by the US ABC network in 1989 and subsequently sold to more than eighty countries. The export of formats was also an important source of revenue for the British television industry. Successful British formats included quiz shows (*Who Wants to Be a Millionaire?*, *The Weakest Link*), the reality game show *Survivor,* talent shows (*Popstars, Pop Idol*), and factual programs.[71] One conclusion to be drawn from the active trade in formats is that, like the widespread international appeal of American programs, it points to a broad global similarity of taste in television entertainment. But it also highlights the resistance of national markets to imported programming: it reflects recognition of the need to adapt content to local viewers' expectations, which are in turn a result of local traditions and values.

Moreover, content is only one aspect of the differences between national television cultures: television was also presented to the public in different ways. Approaches to scheduling, the mix of programming, preferences for dubbing or subtitling of imported programs, and the *style* of television varied widely even in Europe, where, under the European Union, economic and political barriers between states were reduced to a historically low level. At the end of the twentieth century, Tony Judt has observed, European television "served very effectively to reinforce national distinctions and a high level of mutual ignorance."[72] Although, therefore, the period from the 1980s saw the rise of transnational media corporations with near-global reach (most of them based in the United States), made possible by the development of satellite delivery platforms (see Chapter 12), their success depended on an accommodation to national markets. The failure of attempts to establish pan-European and pan-Asian television in the 1980s and 1990s underlined the continuing importance of the national and the local in television.[73]

Yet, if evidence of the national character of television undermines the concept of cultural imperialism, there is nonetheless a danger that recent attempts to show the complexity of America's cultural impact may underestimate the extent of US global influence in the twentieth century. As Richard Kuisel has written, cultural transfer "may be a two-way street, but most of the traffic has been heavily in one direction – from the United States."[74] While the limits to American cultural influence are more significant than has often been recognized, Americanization has nonetheless been a central feature of cultural transfer. And from the 1950s television, because of American influence on the world's commercial television systems, was even more powerful than film as an agency of Americanization.

Most straightforward was the medium's impact on language: the television age hastened greatly the adoption of American usage, although the process had been evident since at least the late nineteenth century. Its influence on vocabulary, idiom, accent, and pronunciation affected not only the English-speaking populations of the United Kingdom, Ireland, Canada, Australia, and New Zealand but that large proportion of the world's population for whom English is a second or third language (many of whom speak English with a local approximation of an American accent); at the same time Americanisms increasingly found their way into languages other than English. Also important was the influence of American television entertainment on fashion – especially clothing, and above all styles of dress among young people – and on the marketing of consumer goods and the dissemination of popular culture, especially music, of American origin.

American television programs depicted varied images of the United States. They included images of crime, violence, poverty, and urban decay – one reason why the global preeminence of American popular culture does not inevitably translate into the "soft power" by which the attractions of a country's culture can supplement the hard power of military or economic might.[75] Yet American programs (as well as non-American versions of US genres and formats) have typically presented a view of the good life that extols an "aggressive contemporaneity"[76] and the accumulation of wealth; and the advertising that forms an integral part of programming in the American commercial model of television has preached the same message. Ross McKibbin's observation that Hollywood movies of the 1930s "made inequality acceptable by making it glamorous"[77] can be applied with equal merit to much exported American television programming. We need not assume that audiences passively absorb everything they see on television, or that there are not also other historical forces at work, to conclude that content of this kind is likely to have affected values and behavior.

Yet it is also true that the effects of Americanization are difficult to disentangle from the related (but more fundamental and more long-term) processes of modernization and globalization. The latter, including the apparent emergence of a global mass culture, is in one view the culmination of America's push to impose its own values and institutions on the rest of the world; but in another perspective it is the product of international trends that are not the creation of any one country and that governments, including the US government, are powerless to control (see Chapter 12).

Public-Affairs Programming

Since the 1960s a majority of respondents to opinion polls, at least in the United States and Britain, have claimed to rely mainly on television for news and to find television more trustworthy than newspapers, radio, and other sources of news.[78] Whether this apparent trust is justified is a question of central importance to an understanding of the role of television in society.

In the United States the networks' news divisions enjoyed a special status for two decades from the early 1960s. In September 1963 CBS and NBC extended their evening news bulletins from fifteen to thirty minutes (followed by ABC in 1967) and freed their news divisions from the commercial considerations that governed other programs. By respecting the professional autonomy of good journalists, the networks sought to regain prestige and protect themselves from government regulators such as FCC chairman Minow.[79] In Britain, meanwhile, the development of strong news services was one of the benefits of competition between the BBC and ITV. Raymond Williams, writing during the early 1970s after systematically watching both British and American television news bulletins, commented on the high journalistic standards of television, noting that "the selection and relative priority of news items" were similar to those of quality newspapers and far removed from those of the tabloid press.[80] Moreover, the advantages of the visual element in television news have often been made clear – for example, in reporting on the civil-rights marches and demonstrations in the United States in the early 1960s, the student demonstrations and massacre in Beijing's Tiananmen Square in 1989, the downfall of East European communist regimes in the same year, the terrorist attacks on New York and Washington on September 11, 2001, and the Asian tsunami of December 2004.

Televised public proceedings also demonstrated the medium's value as a source of information; especially important were coverage of national political party conventions and Congressional hearings in the United States, and of parliamentary sessions in Britain and other countries. As early as 1951 Edward R. Murrow's weekly public affairs program *See It Now*, on the CBS network, underlined the potential of the medium for investigative journalism. In Britain the golden age of the 1960s and early 1970s included the production of outstanding documentaries and public-affairs discussion and interview programs. With these in mind Williams observed, "broadcasting as a whole, and television especially, has markedly broadened the forms of public argument and discussion."[81]

Often, however, television news and public-affairs programming have been marked by superficiality; a temptation to emphasize the visual at all costs, placing the demands of entertainment above journalistic criteria, has accentuated this.[82] Political timidity and an unthinking conservatism, arising from television's relationship with society and the state, have also been apparent. This characteristic was most obvious in state-controlled media, especially in closed societies such as the Soviet Union and China, but it has also been evident in democracies, such as France, where political interference was a feature of television's development. Even the BBC, although not subject to direct government control, limited its news service and domestic political discussion during its period of television monopoly in the early 1950s, partly out of fear of offending the political parties.

On commercial television, too, news and public-affairs programming has proved vulnerable to political pressures. The example of television in Russia after 1991 highlights the potential abuse of privately owned television outside the framework of a stable democracy: in the 1996 presidential election television was used as a weapon to attack opponents of the incumbent, Boris Yeltsin. In the United States television's postwar development was shaped by the Cold War and the blacklisting of alleged communist sympathizers in broadcasting. In the 1950s television news and political commentary reflected the industry's collaboration with the US government and whole-hearted engagement in the anti-communist cause (see Chapter 7).

It is often pointed out that television contributed to Senator Joseph McCarthy's downfall. A series of documentaries by Edward Murrow on *See It Now* in 1953–4 exposed McCarthy as an unscrupulous bully.

Televised Senate hearings between McCarthy and the army in 1954 further undermined his credibility and helped bring about his censure by the Senate. Yet it is significant not only that the Murrow exposé was late in coming (four years after McCarthy's rise to national prominence) but that it received only minimal support from CBS and *See It Now*'s sponsor, Alcoa. In the aftermath of McCarthy's downfall neither CBS nor the other networks showed any enthusiasm for the investigative journalism with which Murrow was identified. *See It Now* was axed in 1958, after several years of difficulty in maintaining adequate sponsorship, and was not replaced by anything similar. Its decline was symptomatic of the priorities of American television, as was the fact that the Army–McCarthy hearings were televised only on the weaker ABC and DuMont networks, with CBS and NBC preferring to fill their daytime schedules with entertainment.[83]

Even in the 1960s, when the American networks elevated public affairs to a more prestigious role in their programming, news and documentaries still reflected an uncritical view of US government policy.[84] A more critical approach did develop in the late 1960s and early 1970s in the context of the failure of US military intervention in Vietnam and the Watergate scandal involving the administration of President Richard Nixon. Tensions emerged between the media and political leaders, with Vice-President Spiro Agnew attacking network television for alleged ideological bias and excessive power. Yet a new willingness to interrogate or criticize politicians – especially unpopular politicians – did not alter the fundamental tendency of the networks to avoid programs that were likely to alienate any significant part of the mass audience that is crucial to the medium's appeal to advertisers. The need to remain in step with majority opinion discouraged critical examination of the policies of political leaders who, like President Ronald Reagan in the 1980s, were skilled in exploiting popular sentiment. In the last years of the Cold War, as in the 1950s, network news and public-affairs programs aligned themselves with the strident American nationalism that flourished in that period.[85]

The pattern was repeated after the terrorist attacks of September 2001 (now commonly referred to as "9/11"). While Fox News and stations owned by the Sinclair Broadcasting Group played the unambiguous role of cheerleader for the US invasions of Afghanistan and Iraq, and for the policies of the administration of President George W. Bush in general, coverage of these events by the three broadcasting networks and the Cable News Network (CNN) was also characterized by timidity and deference toward the White House: by uncritical acceptance of Bush's rationale for the invasion of Iraq, obsequious treatment of administration officials, heavy reliance on guests and commentators with conventional views, and a reluctance to consider evidence that the progress of American interventions in the Middle East and Central Asia was far less successful than the administration and its supporters asserted.[86] The veteran CBS news "anchor" Dan Rather gave an insight into the conformist pressures that confronted American journalists after 9/11 when he told a BBC interviewer in May 2002 that "patriotism run amok," a fear of finding oneself out of step with the rest of the country, was preventing journalists "from asking the toughest of the tough questions."[87]

Television's deference toward the Bush administration reflected influences similar to those responsible for media complicity with the more hysterical forms of anti-communism during the Cold War (see Chapter 7). One was that many television executives, producers, and journalists shared the nationalist values that underlay Bush's determination to respond to 9/11 with a "war" on "terror" or "terrorism," and themselves supported the administration's policies. As Rather put it, the temptation to self-censor "starts with a feeling of patriotism within oneself."[88] Some of the professional practices and attitudes of American journalists also played a part: excessive reliance on official sources, and a tendency to assume that such sources provide the basis for balance and objectivity. Also important was pressure – or anticipation of pressure – from the White House (or the wish to curry favor with the administration) and intimidation from conservative groups, not least from vocal critics of "liberal bias" and "the elite media" at Fox News, in talk radio, and among the ranks of Internet "bloggers." And important once more was the commercial imperative that ruled out any program content that might jeopardize audience share and support from advertisers.[89]

On local television news – the main source of news for most Americans[90] – the tendency to repeat uncritically the administration's version of events was often less complicated than in the national networks, with increasingly heavy use made of prepackaged news reports produced by federal government agencies. The Government Accountability Office's condemnation of the practice as "covert propaganda" – the origin of these reports was not revealed to the audience – did not stop it. The FCC showed no interest in penalizing the stations concerned, while the commercial benefits of using free prepackaged segments, rather than employing staff to produce original news reports, were obvious.[91]

Commercial pressures, indeed, played a more fundamental role than political interference in the decline of American television journalism. Deregulation and fierce competition in the 1980s had a major impact. The networks were no longer willing to quarantine their news divisions from commercial considerations. The importance of network news bulletins for nightly audience flow exposed them to pressure to be more conscious of ratings. So too did the success of a new form of competition in the provision of national news with the rise of cable news: CNN began in 1980, Fox News in 1996. From as early as the 1970s, too, the profitability of local news services, in which journalistic content was minimal, demonstrated to network executives the benefits to be gained from redefining the news as entertainment. The same lessons were learned from the success of "news-magazine" programs – which defined the news as "what's got good pictures, what's got sex appeal"[92] – beginning with such programs as *60 Minutes* and *48 Hours* and culminating in the popularity of *A Current Affair*, *Hard Copy*, *20/20*, and similar tabloid programs. As a result, the journalistic standards once important in network news were eroded. The consequences were a greater emphasis on visual imagery, ten-second soundbites, and "human-interest" stories, and the substitution of talk, commentary, and the clash of strong opinions for news. Reporting on national politics was reduced and increasingly trivialized. International affairs received little attention at all, except in cases where Americans were directly affected, as in the war in Iraq from 2003.[93]

Nor did the rise of twenty-four-hour news channels compensate for the growing superficiality of network news. Fox News, consistently the ratings leader of US cable news networks from 2002, was characterized by its highly opinionated approach to the news; in pandering to conservative prejudices it made a mockery of its own marketing slogans ("Fair and balanced", "We report, you decide"). Its chief rival, CNN, was as guilty as the broadcast networks of reducing news to entertainment, all the more so as it lost ground to Fox.[94]

The short history of cable news channels has highlighted a deep-seated problem: the daily challenge of filling twenty-four hours of television, along with the need to appear to report the news as it happens, has had a number of detrimental consequences. The careful checking of sources is discouraged (there is too little time), while heavy reliance on unconfirmed reports and mere conjecture, usually by non-specialist reporters with little knowledge of the context of their news stories, are encouraged. Talking heads, in the form both of talk shows and of interviews with newsmakers, observers, and reporters, made up a proportion of program time that would be hard to justify on purely journalistic grounds. The practice of crossing "live" to reporters with nothing meaningful to say – for no better reason than that a satellite, once booked, has to be used – became a feature of cable news. Lastly, distinctions between the important and the inconsequential have become blurred: war in Iraq and terrorist attacks on New York, Washington, Madrid, and London were given exhaustive coverage, but so too were the trial of O. J. Simpson and the death of Princess Diana, as well as the fortunes of countless other celebrities and reports on floods, fires, storms, droughts, and airplane crashes, the newsworthiness of which was usually determined on no better basis than the availability of pictures. The very existence of twenty-four-hour news channels intensified the competitiveness of television news and therefore promoted adoption of the same practices by the news departments of terrestrial television.[95]

Equally disturbing as the decline of television journalism was the erosion of the news audience. Whereas in 1980 the evening network newscasts were viewed by 75 percent of the television audience, their share had fallen to 60 percent by the early 1990s and 34 percent by 2004. Nor did this decline indicate that viewers had migrated to CNN, MSNBC, and Fox News: the cable news audience remained far smaller than that for network news. With the rise of cable television, an increasing proportion of American viewers either avoided news programs altogether or received their "news" in the distorted forms of tabloid television journalism.[96] The trend was most prominent among young people – and not much less so among viewers in their thirties and forties.[97] With newspaper circulations in decline, the prospect that the audience for serious coverage of public affairs would be restricted to an educated minority has disturbing implications for democratic politics.

The question whether these developments are peculiar to the United States, or are instead part of a global trend that is likely to be confirmed as the 21st century proceeds, is controversial.[98] It is, however, clear that television coverage of foreign news has been reduced in many countries since the late twentieth century, even in the public-service system of the United Kingdom. Moreover, even public broadcasters, concerned to justify their public funding in an increasingly hostile environment, have often succumbed to pressure to "dumb down" the news. Yet in some countries the percentage of total programming devoted to information remained high – as high as 30 percent on some European public broadcasting channels in the late 1990s.[99]

Three conclusions can be drawn about public-affairs programming globally in the early twenty-first century. One is that, in those countries where publicly funded broadcasters were well established, audiences were often still well served by news and public-affairs programs, despite pressure to blur the lines between information, entertainment, and propaganda. Even American audiences continued to have access to good public-affairs television on PBS channels with *The NewsHour with Jim Lehrer* and the investigative reporting of *Frontline*, as well as on cable with BBC World News and ITN *World News for Public Television*. Moreover, in those countries where commercial television channels were required by government regulation to respect public-service principles (as in Britain, Sweden, Norway, Denmark, and Finland), these stations produced information programs of a similar quality to those of public broadcasters. Lastly, where commercial considerations prevailed, unrestrained by public-service objectives, the effects were highly detrimental for television public-affairs programming. In these cases the trends highlighted by the US experience were all too evident.[100]

Television and Politics

Television's role in politics has been the focus of much of the discussion of the medium's influence. From the 1950s television increasingly played a central role in the conduct of political campaigns. It enabled political candidates to reach large audiences quickly, without the time-consuming travel that had previously characterized campaigning. Also attractive to politicians and their advisers were the opportunities that television provided to "package" a candidate's presentation to the public without the mediation of journalists. As early as the 1952 US presidential election campaign an advertising agency prepared a series of short television commercials for the Republican candidate, Dwight D. Eisenhower. Vice-presidential candidate Richard Nixon used his

Checkers speech, an emotional television appeal to the public, to defend himself from charges of financial impropriety.

Of course, television sometimes played a more constructive role than facilitating politicians' manipulation of voters. Where public-affairs programming was well developed, as in Britain in the 1960s and 1970s, political leaders submitted themselves to "more open and public questioning of their policies than has ever been the case in any comparable communications system."[101] Nonetheless, the idea that the key to political success lay in the skillful use of television to create a politician's image came increasingly to be taken for granted. It received a major boost from the political career of the telegenic John F. Kennedy. A televised "debate" between Kennedy and Nixon in the 1960 presidential election campaign soon became the centerpiece in a store of commonly accepted wisdom on the crucial role of television image in politics. Kennedy appeared fit, tanned, and well groomed; Nixon, showing the effects of a recent illness, was pale, underweight, and haggard. Polls indicated that a majority of viewers believed Kennedy had won, while among the radio audience most thought Nixon the winner. Two decades later, the political success of President Ronald Reagan was widely believed to stem from clever management of image, especially through television. In such cases the effects of media manipulation were too readily assumed rather than subjected to analysis; it is questionable whether voters were so easily swayed by slick media presentation of politicians and their policies.[102] Yet the belief that this was the case acquired the status of a truism among political parties and their public-relations consultants, not only in the United States. In Britain a preoccupation with political leaders' television image began with Conservative prime minister Harold Macmillan in the late 1950s and culminated in the tightly controlled television appearances of Margaret Thatcher between 1979 and 1990.[103] The trend was virtually universal.

In the United States, politicians' fondness for media packaging converged with television's blurring of the lines between public affairs and entertainment. The result was television treatment of politics as a kind of sporting contest, preoccupied with who is winning, who is losing, and with image and personality at the expense of issues and policies. Since the 1980s the central role of journalism in television reporting on presidential campaigns has more and more been superseded by "infotainment" programs. In 1992 Democrat candidate Bill Clinton set the tone for this approach, making forty-seven appearances on television talk shows.[104] In 2000 and 2004 coverage of the national party conventions by the three broadcasting networks, once a normal part of presidential elections, was greatly reduced, but the Republican candidate George W. Bush and Democratic candidates Al Gore and John Kerry made frequent appearances on a range of entertainment programs, including *Dr Phil*, *The Oprah Winfrey Show*, *Live with Regis and Kelly*, and the comedy talk shows of Jay Leno, David Letterman, and Jon Stewart (Kerry, who was widely regarded as too patrician and too wooden to succeed in a presidential contest, attempted to correct his image by arriving on the set of Leno's program wearing a leather jacket and riding a Harley Davidson – an act that, unlike Clinton's appearance with saxophone and dark glasses on Arsenio Hall's late-night comedy show twelve years earlier, failed to convince many of the candidate's affinity with ordinary people). An almost complete absence of discussion of issues was the hallmark of television coverage of the 2000 and 2004 US elections.[105] The huge cost of television advertising, the main means by which political candidates get their message across to voters, also gave an enormous advantage to those candidates who were either personally wealthy or received "campaign contributions" from the wealthy.[106] It is hard to avoid the conclusion that, on balance, television has played a deleterious role in politics in recent years, especially in the United States.

Television and Socialization

The global impact of television in the second half of the twentieth century was far-reaching. Its influence on political campaigning has already been examined. Another illustration of the medium's impact is provided by changes in the world of sport. Television afforded the possibility of huge national and international audiences for sporting events, as well as enormous advertising potential through sports sponsorship. Links between television, sport, and sponsorship progressively tightened. Television stimulated greater professionalization of sport. It led to new game formats, rule changes, and game modifications, in some cases specifically to allow advertising breaks during games to satisfy sponsors. Sports sponsorship grew exponentially. The interrelationship between television and sport is illustrated in the enormous amounts now paid by television networks for rights to televise major international events such as the Olympic Games and the soccer World Cup.[107]

Apart from its institutional impact, television's importance as an agency of socialization is indisputable, even though the precise nature of its influence has long been contentious. There is now little scholarly support for claims that television has the power easily to manipulate popular attitudes and values. Such views exaggerate the passivity of audiences and, by attributing too central a role to television, underestimate the complexity of cultural change. Yet, while the more far-reaching claims for the medium's influence may be rejected, it is clear that images and ideas conveyed by television can help shape and reinforce popular attitudes. Its influence on behavior, ideas, language, and fashion derived from the power to suggest what is normal, desirable, and important. In three respects its impact may have been fundamental.

First, television did much to diminish cultural isolation. It not only exposed the inhabitants of different cities, towns, and regions to the same programs – as national radio systems had also done – but afforded them the same visual experience. Television's integrative role depended on widespread ownership of sets – the case in the United States and United Kingdom by 1960, most of Europe and the West by 1970, and most of the world by 1990. It was also most salient where there were few channels to choose from; and most of all where, as was true of much of Europe and Asia until the 1970s, a state monopoly existed, so that on any evening a very large proportion of a national population watched the same programs. One of the central problems concerning the role of media in society in the early twenty-first century is the extent of the challenge posed to television's community-building role by the end of state monopolies, by the rise of cable and satellite stations, and by the general growth in the number of channels since the 1970s.

The United States best illustrates this development. Beginning in the mid-1970s, driven by the rise of cable television, advertisers developed a vision of America as a fragmented population of selfish, suspicious individuals whose ties extended no further than people who share the same "lifestyle." Target markets, in which advertisers and media companies divide the population into narrow segments according to such distinctions as age, income, ethnicity, gender, marital status, and sexuality, replaced the mass marketing of the past.[108] To some, the likely consequences for social cohesion seemed alarming. Yet the United States may be an exceptional case. As James Curran has observed, the proliferation of channels can give a misleading impression of audience fragmentation. In 2000 it remained the case in all major West European countries that a handful of channels – only three in most cases – accounted for over 60 percent of the prime-time audience. These channels remained "the principal meeting places where people in the nations of Western Europe still gather together, not for special events but routinely, night after night."[109] Even in the United States, where by 2000 television households had access to an average of sixty-three channels, the three established national networks still attracted 50 percent of the prime-time audience, and audiences for network programs were far bigger than those for cable programs.[110]

The US case also presented a paradox. It was the country where media fragmentation was most pronounced, where people were now less connected to each other by the fact of watching the same television programs, and where therefore a weakening of national identity might have most been expected. But it was also one of few Western countries in which a nationalist myth – in this case one that asserts America's special relationship to liberty and its redemptive mission to spread democracy and freedom to the rest of the world – has proved most enduring, continuing to exercise a crucial influence on public life beyond the 1960s.[111] Public and Congressional support for the Bush administration's response to the 9/11 terrorist attacks – a response that took the form not of policies designed to combat a specific threat to the United States but of a crusade against a global evil ("terrorism") – highlights this influence.[112] The American example serves as a reminder that the relationship between media, national identity, and cultural change is more complex than is commonly supposed.

Less complicated were the consequences of television's development as a commercial medium, with advertising and the celebration of consumption at the center of its programming. Television was, as Jürgen Kronig has written, the most effective instrument in the creation of "a world in which a global taste for images and goods is created around logos, advertising slogans, sponsorship, brand names, trademarks and jingles; a world in which global markets seek to shape people so that they join the universal tribe of consumers."[113] In the affluent West the growth of commercial television strengthened those tendencies, promoted by American advertising since the 1920s, to view society as prosperous and classless – with the only significant differences those of freely chosen "lifestyle." The rise of television consolidated the tendency in commercial popular culture to distract attention from economic and social inequalities and to undermine support for political measures to deal with them.[114] In poor countries, meanwhile, it seemed likely that television had created new levels of dissatisfaction among people whose own living standards were far removed from those depicted on screen. The Turkish novelist Orhan Pamuk, writing shortly after 9/11 and trying to understand the anger toward America and the West of many people in Third World and Islamic countries, pointed to the "crushing humiliation" felt by a large part of the world's population, resulting from the huge gap between rich and poor and from the fact that "at no time in history have the lives of the rich been so forcefully brought to the attention of the poor through television and Hollywood films."[115]

Finally, television played a central role in the shaping and transmission of collective memory. Both factual programs and entertainment contributed to this role. One of the striking features of the history of television, especially since the 1990s, has been a large growth in the number of programs on historical subjects. In these years all Britain's terrestrial channels gave history programs a prominent place in prime time. In the United States the rapid growth of cable from the 1980s – and in particular the creation of the Discovery Channel and the History Channel – gave American audiences unprecedented exposure to history on television. Historical documentaries intended for British and American audiences were also sold in global markets; and the most successful of these programs – once sold internationally, shown and repeated on both terrestrial and cable stations, and reproduced on video and DVD – reached worldwide audiences in the tens of millions.

Television history programs took a range of forms. They included lectures directly to camera – an approach pioneered with considerable success by the English historian A. J. P. Taylor in 1957, but later judged to be not viable in mainstream television. More common was the detached documentary, consisting of narrated scenes and "talking heads" (edited interviews with experts and eyewitnesses). The BBC series *The Great War* (1964) and Thames Television's *The World at War* (1974) were two early examples of this approach that were to serve as models for much subsequent history programming. The other common format was the presenter-led series, of which notable examples were Kenneth Clark's *Civilisation* (1969), Alistair Cooke's *America* (1972), Jacob Bronowski's *Ascent of Man* (1973), and the more recent series of

Simon Schama (*A History of Britain*), David Starkey (*Elizabeth, Monarchy*), and Niall Ferguson (*Empire – How Britain Made the Modern World, American Colossus*). Archival film footage was a staple of programs dealing with twentieth-century topics. An influential approach to the problem of how factual programs might deal successfully with earlier historical subjects – or deal with twentieth-century topics for which little or no archival footage is available – was American filmmaker Ken Burns's PBS series *The Civil War* (1990), which made impressive use of archival still images, readings from letters and diaries, and atmospheric location shooting.

Other approaches developed since the 1990s – the use of actors in reconstructions and computer-generated imagery – were more contentious. Also controversial were program formats designed to make history more palatable to a mass audience: historical "reality" shows (*The 1900 House, The 1940s House, The Edwardian Country House, The Frontier House, The Ship*) and, even closer to the boundary between information and entertainment, historical drama documentaries (programs that purport to reconstruct dramatically real events and the lives of real people).

At its best, television history played an educative role, bringing history to many more people than had ever occurred through books and education systems. The immediacy and power of visual imagery gave television a considerable advantage as a medium for historical reconstruction. Yet it was also claimed, especially by professional historians but even by some program-makers, that history programs far too often failed to make good use of the medium's potential, and that there are limitations to what can be expected of television as a vehicle for historical understanding: that television history gave disproportionate attention to a limited range of topics (especially the world wars, the Nazis, and kings and queens of England); that it is better at narrative than analysis or context, and seldom engaged with historical controversies or problems involved in the interpretation of historical evidence; that it failed to acknowledge the limitations of oral testimony; that too often it did not make good use of its main asset, visual evidence; that it sometimes succeeded in re-creating the material conditions of the past but not the ways people felt and thought; and that historians usually had too little influence over the making of these programs. By the early twenty-first century these specific criticisms fed into a growing suspicion that the makers of factual programs were more heavily influenced by the needs of the marketplace than by the value of their programs as history (or science, natural history, or archeology); and that even the BBC, through its co-productions with the Discovery Channel, had yielded to the entertainment-driven priorities of American cable.[116]

Television history as entertainment was a vehicle for collective memory, not historical awareness. Memory, unconstrained by the historian's emphasis on the careful scrutiny of evidence and respect for the autonomy of the past, and susceptible to the distortions of tradition and nostalgia, is a poor guide to the past.[117] Moreover, its influence was more overt in television drama – in programs that, because of the scale of their audiences and their emotional appeal, played an even bigger role than factual programs in reinforcing, and sometimes altering, popular versions of history.

The potential of television entertainment to shape popular views of the past was demonstrated with particular force by the impact of the NBC miniseries *Holocaust*. Watched by almost 100 million Americans in April 1978, it was "the most important moment in the entry of the Holocaust into general American consciousness;" and its influence was confirmed by the reception of subsequent television programs as well as Steven Spielberg's 1993 film *Schindler's List*.[118] In Germany the miniseries had an even greater impact. Broadcast on West German television in January 1979, it confronted German audiences with aspects of their history that many of them had not known or thought about, prompting the journalist Heinz Hohne to write:

> An American television series, made in a trivial style, produced more for commercial than moral reasons, more for entertainment than for enlightenment, accomplished what hundreds of books, plays, films, and television programs, thousands of documents, and all the concentration camp trials have failed to do in the more than three decades since the end of the war: to inform Germans about crimes against Jews committed in their name so that millions were emotionally touched and moved.[119]

These comments were a reminder that television versions of history, while often presenting a view of the past that is shaped by the distortions of collective memory and the priorities of mass entertainment, could also have positive effects. In this respect, history programming reflected the range of cultural possibilities that are highlighted by an examination of television in historical and comparative perspective.

The commercial organization of television and an emphasis on popular entertainment programs, though often assumed to be a natural outgrowth of the technology, are in reality a product of political and economic arrangements in particular societies. The prominence of public-service television in some countries, and the attention given to cultural and journalistic criteria in some broadcasting systems, serve as a reminder that the technology itself is neutral, and that the uses to which it can be put are varied. "What are the effects of television?" is a useful question only when the role of television is viewed in historical context, with full regard to the interests and ideas that have shaped the uses of the medium.[120]

9

Media, Information, and Entertainment

The impact of television on older media was difficult to foresee in the early postwar years. Samuel Goldwyn was more prescient than most when he suggested that Hollywood was about to enter a new stage in its development – after the silent period and the sound era, the film industry now faced the "Television Age."[1] The same might have been said of the print media and radio. At the end of the Second World War there was, as James L. Baughman has written, "a rough equality among the mass media."[2] Television upset this equilibrium and established its dominance to such an extent that fears were held for the survival of cinema, newspapers, magazines, and radio. Yet, by coming to terms with television's supremacy and accepting a secondary role in the provision of information and entertainment, these media adjusted well to the altered circumstances of the second half of the century and the first decade of the twenty-first century. In each case the adjustment involved major changes in the medium's structure and content. It also raised questions about the balance between information and entertainment in media content and, in the case of the press, the medium's success in continuing to play the public-service role that had often been regarded as its most important function. In considering the development of these media, this chapter looks first at changes in the US film industry and its relationship with cinema in other countries. In examining the experience of the press and radio, the chapter continues the American and British case studies begun in Chapters 2 and 4.

American Cinema and the Rise of the Entertainment Conglomerate

The world's dominant film industry prospered from its wartime collaboration with the US government's propaganda campaigns (see Chapter 6). At the end of the war, with the oligopoly of eight major firms still intact, Hollywood appeared to be at the height of its success. In 1946 average weekly movie attendances in the United States reached ninety million, a level not seen since 1930. At the same time pent-up demand for American films in postwar Europe provided a rich source of profits for the US industry. Yet such signs of health were misleading. There followed a rapid decline both in the fortunes of the major film companies and in the status of cinema as a mass-entertainment medium. By 1956 American weekly movie attendances had fallen to around half their level of a decade earlier, while weekly attendance per household declined rapidly from a postwar peak of 2.35 in 1946 to 1.38 in 1950 and 0.76 in 1960. One of the Big Five, RKO, went out of business in 1955, while the other majors suffered a steady decline in box-office receipts and profits.[3]

Competition from television, which grew rapidly from 1948, provides a large part of the explanation for film's decline, but other factors also contributed. As a result of the postwar growth of suburbs – with theaters still concentrated in downtown areas – and of the financial commitments of young families with the start of the "baby boom," cinema-going became less convenient and less affordable. More difficult to assess is the long-term impact on the US film industry of the HUAC investigations and the blacklisting that followed (see Chapter 7). But it is clear that this episode both encouraged extreme caution toward movie content and deprived the industry of a large pool of talented actors, directors, writers, and technicians at a time when it could least afford to lose them.

Another cause of the US industry's problems is also clear. In 1948 the majors were dealt a severe blow when the Supreme Court ruled on *United States* v. *Paramount*, the federal government's longstanding anti-trust case against the film industry. Accepting the Justice Department's argument that vertical integration constituted an illegal restraint of trade, the court ordered the Big Five to divest themselves of their theater chains. They therefore relinquished the most profitable part of their activities – exhibition – and became chiefly production and distribution companies. Moreover, all eight majors were affected by the court's prohibition of the practice of "block booking," which had obliged exhibitors to rent films in blocks rather than individually and had guaranteed the film companies a return on every film made. With the loss of their control over exhibition and with profits less certain, the majors cut production, concentrated on making films that seemed most likely to succeed at the box office, and relied more on distribution as a source of revenue. The films they distributed were increasingly made by independent production companies: unburdened by high studio overheads, independents received a boost from the Supreme Court ruling. The decline of the Hollywood studio system – by which stars, producers, directors, writers, and all the technical staff involved in film production were employed on long-term contracts by the studios, each run by a powerful "movie mogul" – was hastened by the *Paramount* decision. By 1960 that system had collapsed. Film production was now based on deals negotiated by freelance producers, directors, or stars; the majors acted chiefly as distributors and financiers.

While seeking to adjust to these fundamental structural changes, the film industry adopted two main strategies to meet the challenge of television. One involved forging a cooperative relationship with the television networks. During the 1950s the majors recognized that in some respects the success of the new medium could be turned to their advantage. Production of television programs, the sale of old movies to television, and, by the late 1960s, the production of movies for television, became important sources of revenue for the major film companies. The other strategy was to exploit film's relative advantages. With television viewing confined mainly to small, black-and-white sets, technological innovation offered such a possibility. An experiment with three-dimensionality was short lived, but a move from black-and-white to color films (with color the norm by the 1960s) and development of stereophonic sound and widescreen projection had a more lasting impact.

In the 1950s the majors looked to exploit these innovations with big-budget, prestige films, relying on lavish production values and spectacular visual appeal to entice audiences away from their television sets. Westerns, musicals, and especially epics like *Quo Vadis* (1951), *The Robe* (1953), *The Ten Commandments* (1956), and *Ben Hur* (1959) lent themselves especially well to this approach and were also politically uncontroversial, an important consideration at the height of the Cold War. At the same time, drive-in theaters appealed to suburban and teenage audiences: the number of drive-ins in the United States increased from 820 in 1948 to over 4,000 ten years later.[4]

These strategies enabled the US film industry to survive the immediate challenge from television but did not provide a long-term solution to the problem of Hollywood's decline. In 1962 box-office receipts fell to a postwar low of $903 million.[5] The studios continued to look to the production of big-budget prestige films as the surest road to profitability. Vindication of this approach seemed to come with the commercial success of *Lawrence of Arabia* (1962), *Doctor Zhivago* (1965), and a number of musicals: *West Side Story* (1962), *Mary Poppins* (1964), *My Fair Lady* (1964), and the highly successful *The Sound of Music* (1965). But the huge risks of this "blockbuster" approach were highlighted by the failure of *Cleopatra* (1963) – the film that almost bankrupted 20th Century Fox – and of a string of musicals with which the studios attempted to emulate the success of *The Sound of Music*. In 1969 most of the major firms incurred losses, and big-budget musicals were thought to be largely to blame.[6] A series of takeovers between 1967 and 1969 highlighted the majors' financial vulnerability. Paramount was purchased by Gulf and Western, a conglomerate chiefly involved in steel and mining; Warner Bros. by Kinney National Services, a funeral home, car rental, and parking lot company; United Artists by TransAmerica, a banking and insurance company; and MGM by Kirk Kerkorian, a Las Vegas hotel magnate.

The limited success of the prestige films of the 1960s emphasized the costs of Hollywood's persistence in trying to produce movies with universal appeal. Such an approach had worked well in the 1930s and 1940s but was far less appropriate when television became the dominant medium of mass entertainment. Above all, it ignored the cinemagoing potential of two demographic groups: teenagers and young college-educated adults. Neither group had much interest in musicals, regardless of their lavish production values. Hollywood began to appeal to teenage audiences in the 1950s with the production of "teenpics," but it was not until the late 1970s that the industry began to exploit fully the market potential of this age group.[7] As for 18–25-year-olds, their patronage of foreign "art house" and independent films suggested an interest in movies that contained more adult content – particularly movies that demonstrated a more open attitude to sex – than could be found in most Hollywood products. The majors' capacity to take advantage of this market was hamstrung by their attempt to make movies suitable for all age groups and, related to that, by their insistence on retaining the 1930 Production Code, even though it lived on in an increasingly watered-down form in the 1950s and 1960s and was challenged by adventurous filmmakers such as Otto Preminger in *The Moon Is Blue* (1953), *The Man with the Golden Arm* (1955), and *Advise and Consent* (1962), Elia Kazan in *Baby Doll* (1956), and Stanley Kubrick in *Lolita* (1962). In contrast to the 1920s, when Hollywood had reflected and helped define changing cultural values, the US film industry was slow to respond to the changes of the 1960s.[8]

The box-office success of two films produced in 1967, Arthur Penn's *Bonnie and Clyde* and Mike Nichols's *The Graduate*, the former characterized by graphic depiction of violence and the latter by its direct approach to sex, marked the end of this approach. The Code, now regarded as untenable, was abolished in 1968 and replaced by a ratings system. Freed from the Code's constraints, the studios in 1969 released films that proved popular with the "baby-boom" generation: *Easy Rider*, *Midnight Cowboy*, *The Wild Bunch*, *Alice's Restaurant*, and *Goodbye, Columbus*. A new generation of American directors demonstrated that it was possible to make low-budget films that were both commercially and artistically successful. The first half of the 1970s saw the release of movies generally regarded as representing one of the most impressive periods of American filmmaking. They included Martin Scorsese's *Mean Streets* (1973), *Alice Doesn't Live Here Any More* (1975), and *Taxi Driver* (1976), Peter Bogdanovich's *The Last Picture Show* (1971), Robert Altman's *M*A*S*H* (1970), *McCabe and Mrs Miller* (1971), and *Nashville* (1975), Francis Ford Coppola's *The Godfather* (1972), and *The Conversation* (1974), George Lucas's *American Graffiti* (1973), and Roman Polanski's *Chinatown* (1974).

Changes in the commercial environment of film affected Hollywood's willingness to continue its support for movies of this caliber beyond the 1970s. Of particular importance was a significant change in the ownership structure of the US film industry. In the 1980s and 1990s all the major film companies were absorbed into huge vertically integrated entertainment conglomerates that sought to take advantage of "synergies" between movies and other media products (see Chapter 12). The Australian newspaper magnate Rupert Murdoch's News Corporation purchased 20th Century Fox in 1985. Warner Bros. merged with

Time Inc. in 1989 to form Time Warner Inc. In the same year Columbia was acquired by the Japanese electronics firm Sony. MCA-Universal was purchased by another Japanese electronics corporation, Matsushita, in 1990, and subsequently (in 1995) by the Canadian liquor company Seagram, which in 2000 was bought by the French corporation Vivendi, creating the media conglomerate Vivendi Universal. Paramount was acquired by Viacom in 1993. Disney, the only major firm not to change hands, itself became a conglomerate through diversification.

These organizations had interests not only in film and television production and distribution but in cable and satellite television networks, free-to-air television stations and networks, video stores, movie theaters, recorded music, newspaper, magazine, and book publishing, theme parks, hotels, professional sport, and merchandising. This concentration of economic power was made possible by US governments' ideological commitment to deregulation in the 1980s and 1990s and by their unwillingness to view the mergers of the period as cause for anti-trust action. Even a partial reversal of the *Paramount* decision of 1948 was viewed favorably: Columbia, Paramount, Warner Bros., and Universal were all permitted to acquire chains of theaters and again play a significant role in domestic film exhibition. The conglomerates achieved an unprecedented degree of market control, as a result of which the film industry became far more profitable than it had been even during Hollywood's golden age of the 1930s and 1940s. In the changed circumstances of the late twentieth century, however, theatrical exhibition was no longer the main source of profits. By the 1990s video (and later DVD) sales and rentals accounted for over half the revenues earned by films released by the majors, while sales of rights for cable and network television and other "ancillaries" were also significant revenue sources.[9]

The film industry's new ownership structure encouraged the revival of a blockbuster mentality. The enormous commercial success of *The Towering Inferno* (1974), *Jaws* (1975), and *Star Wars* (1976) convinced studio heads that their best course was to make fewer films and concentrate on "megahits." These lavishly produced movies fully exploited the appeal of superstars and the technology of special effects. They were supported by expensive publicity campaigns that typically accounted for more than 30 percent of the cost of making and marketing a film. Payments to stars escalated. The majors' production costs jumped from less than $10 million for the average film in the early 1970s to over $40 million by the late 1990s and $106 million by 2007.[10]

"Conglomeratization" provided a clear financial logic for these huge investments. At worst, losses at the box office would be offset by profits made from video, DVD, television, and the parent company's other ancillary operations. At best, a successful movie would create enormous profits, generated not only by the film in its various forms of release – cinema, video/DVD, pay television, network television – but by product placement, which from the early 1980s became more important than ever, and by "cross-promotional" deals. These movies did not stand alone but formed part of marketing packages that included film-related toys, games, books, stationery, clothing, soundtrack albums, and fast food.[11] The blockbuster strategy was aimed especially at the two segments of the population regarded as the most frequent movie attenders: the 10–24 age group, and "families" (children, parents, and grandparents).[12]

The trend was firmly established in the late 1970s and 1980s. Especially popular were action-adventure and science-fiction fantasy films, including *Close Encounters of the Third Kind* (1977), *Superman* (1978), *Star Trek* (1979), *ET* (1982), two *Star Wars* sequels (1980 and 1983), *Back to the Future* (1985), *Batman* (1989), Steven Spielberg's Indiana Jones trilogy (1981–9), and the films of Arnold Schwarzenegger and Sylvester Stallone. Comedy and pop-musicals were other successful genres: box-office successes included *Saturday Night Fever* (1977), *Fame* (1980), *Beverly Hills Cop* (1984), *Ghostbusters* (1984), and *Dirty Dancing* (1987). The blockbuster trend continued in the 1990s with *Jurassic Park* (1993), *The Lion King* (1994), *Independence Day* (1996), and *Titanic* (1997), and in the next decade with *Pearl Harbor* (2001), *Troy* (2004), *The Da Vinci Code* (2006), and a number of big-budget series: *Harry Potter* (2001–8), *The Lord of the Rings* (2001–3), *Spider-Man* (2002–7), *Pirates of the Caribbean* (2005–8), and *The Chronicles of Narnia* (2005–8).

Hollywood's preoccupation with megahits prompted widespread criticism of American cinema, typified by *New Yorker* film critic Pauline Kael's 1980 essay "Why Are Movies So Bad?;" by film historian David Parkinson's 1995 observation that the US film industry's "main preoccupation seems to be making money rather than movies;" and by actor George Clooney's 2008 lament that Hollywood had stopped making masterpieces in the 1970s.[13] Yet blockbusters, while accounting for the greater part of investment in production and distribution, remained a minority of films made by the US industry. The rise of home video and cable television in the 1980s increased demand for film product. Production grew from 350 movies a year in 1983 to almost 600 in 1988.[14] Even the highly capitalized majors did not have the financial resources to meet this demand; many films were released by independent companies.

The majors, however, did not ignore the profit-making potential of low-budget films or of non-teenage and non-family audiences. Nor was their control of the North American market ever threatened by the rise of independents. They formed alliances with independent producers, who depended on the majors for domestic distribution of their films. At the end of the 1980s many independent production companies went bankrupt; during the next decade other independents were purchased by the majors. By the end of the century most "independent" American films were released by subsidiaries of the majors: Miramax, New Line, Warner Independent, Fox Searchlight, Paramount Vantage, Focus Features, Sony Classics, and others.

The creation of these "boutique" or "specialty" companies reflected recognition of the "cost-to-earnings" potential, and the limited financial risk, of low-budget and mid-range films. The gross revenues earned by films such as *Fargo* (1996), *Capote* (2005), and *Good Night, and Good Luck* (2005) – $60 million, $49 million, and $54 million respectively – were dwarfed by the earnings of successful blockbusters. *Pirates of the Caribbean: Dead Man's Chest* (2006), for example, grossed $1,066,179,725; but that film's production budget was $225 million, compared to a mere $7 million for each of the other three movies. Often the exhibition of small-to-mid budget films in North America was limited to "art houses;" nonetheless, such films, released either by the majors or by their subsidiaries, sometimes succeeded with mainstream audiences. In 2005, for instance, *Walk the Line*, with a production budget of $28 million, earned gross revenues of $119 million in North America, $186 million worldwide. *Brokeback Mountain*, which cost $14 million to make, earned $83 million in North America, $178 million worldwide.[15] Even in the age of the blockbuster, films that dealt intelligently with social and political concerns and contained insights into the human condition were still made. A number of acclaimed American directors flourished, including Sidney Lumet, Robert Altman, Clint Eastwood, Martin Scorsese, David Lynch, Gus Van Sant, Joel and Ethan Coen, Spike Lee, and Steven Soderbergh. In contrast to the frequent lamentations about Hollywood's decline, some observers pointed to the richness of American cinema in the first decade of the twenty-first century.[16]

Such assessments were part of a general willingness to acknowledge cinema's achievement as an art form. The Australian novelist Christopher Koch made this very point when he compared film favorably to the contemporary novel, pointing to the German director Florian Henckel von Donnersmarck's 2006 film *Das Leben der Anderen* (*The Lives of Others*) as an example:

> That incredible German film called *The Lives of Others* – that film is a serious great work of art. It delivers most of what good novels used to deliver. There is an absolutely gripping plot, deeply felt characters, a sort of crisis in it that puts you on the edge of your seat, and it has things to say that really matter. I don't think the contemporary novel delivers these things.[17]

Distributed in the United States by Sony Classics, *The Lives of Others* attracted international attention partly because of its US commercial success. In this respect its reception underlined the importance of the US film industry in international cinema.

International Cinema

Following the disruption of the Second World War, the US film industry was quick to re-establish its main export markets. It did so with support from US government agencies, which regarded Hollywood as vital to their Cold War cultural diplomacy. With the decline in domestic box-office takings, foreign sales became more important than ever to the major US firms. By the 1960s more than half Hollywood's income came from exports, especially to Western Europe.[18] Dependence on overseas markets declined in the 1970s and 1980s, as the US industry concentrated on opportunities offered within North America by the rise of cable television and home video. Export revenues fell to a low of 33 percent in 1984.[19] But from that year two developments ensured that US film companies would rely increasingly on foreign sales. First, production costs rose to a point where the domestic market alone was not sufficient to sustain acceptable profit levels. Ultra-high budget movies were made on the assumption that they would attract large international audiences. Moreover, from the 1980s worldwide demand for American films increased as a result of the growth of home video, the end of state broadcasting monopolies in Western Europe, the rise of satellite and cable television, and the proliferation of commercial terrestrial stations. Home video replaced theatrical exhibition as the main source of foreign revenue, but the cinema remained important and was boosted by the upgrading of theaters in Western Europe, especially by the building of new multiplex cinemas. By the early twenty-first century it was common for the most successful films at the North American box office to generate even larger box-office revenues abroad. In some cases the "foreign" share of worldwide earnings was as high as 80 percent.[20]

The American industry's international dominance was not affected by its post-1945 domestic problems. The Italian, French, and British film industries each enjoyed a brief postwar "golden age," but Hollywood's competitive advantage was as clear as it had been in the interwar years. Moreover, that advantage increased in the last two decades of the century when the US majors achieved levels of investment in production and advertising that were far out of the reach of foreign competitors. With few exceptions – Japan, India, Hong Kong, the protected markets of communist countries before 1990 – film industries outside the United States struggled to maintain economic viability.[21]

Nonetheless, the postwar period saw significant changes in the relationship between the United States and cinema in the rest of the world. Although few national film industries could compete with Hollywood, even in their home markets, the US industry's postwar cuts in production allowed a larger number of imported foreign films to be shown in American theaters, to the point where in the 1960s imports accounted for a substantial proportion of films screened in the United States.[22] Above all, the postwar rise of "art-house" cinemas in the United States and Europe, and the establishment of international film festivals at Venice and Cannes, enabled many European and Asian directors to achieve international success, especially among young, middle-class, educated film-goers who saw cinema as an art form as well as entertainment. Filmmakers who rose to international prominence between the 1940s and the 1970s – not least in the United States – included Akira Kurosawa (Japan), Satyajit Ray (India), Carol Reed (Britain), Ingmar Bergman (Sweden), Luis Buñuel (Spain), and Miloš Forman (Czechoslovakia). They included also the main figures of late-1940s Italian Neo-Realism (Roberto Rossellini, Vittorio De Sica, Luchino Visconti, Giuseppe De Santis) and subsequent cinematic revivals in Italy (Federico Fellini, Michelangelo Antonioni, Bernardo Bertolucci),

France (the New Wave of François Truffaut, Jean-Luc Godard, Claude Chabrol, Jacques Rivette, Eric Rohmer, Alain Resnais, Louis Malle), Britain (the New Cinema of Tony Richardson and John Schlesinger), and Germany (the New German Cinema of Rainer Werner Fassbinder and Wim Wenders). Similarly, many European actors – including Brigitte Bardot, Sophia Loren, Jeanne Moreau, Marcello Mastroianni, Yves Montand – achieved international stardom without the need to emigrate to Hollywood or star in American films.

From the 1960s the lines between Hollywood and foreign cinema became increasingly blurred. This was partly because foreign cinema, especially the films of the French New Wave, influenced the new generation of American directors who came to prominence in the late 1960s and early 1970s (these French filmmakers, in turn, acknowledged a debt to such Hollywood directors as Alfred Hitchcock, John Ford, Howard Hawks, and Nicholas Ray). Production also became increasingly internationalized as Hollywood discovered the advantages of making films in Europe. At a time of economic pressure on the film industry at home, European government subsidies, cheap labor, and lower production costs offered a powerful incentive to make movies abroad. Hollywood's increased dependence on exports afforded an additional motive: foreign locations and European casts could enhance a movie's appeal to international audiences. Foreign funding was another advantage; by the 1960s the US studios drew on overseas financial sources for a substantial part of the costs of production abroad. This "runaway" production reached a peak in that decade: in 1969 183 films, 60 percent of Hollywood's output, were made abroad.[23] As a shorthand name for the US film industry, the term "Hollywood" has always been misleading. In relation to the period from the 1920s to the late 1940s it had failed to reflect the central roles of distribution and exhibition for film companies that were directed not from Los Angeles but from New York. From the 1950s the term ceased to convey accurately even the nature of US film production, which was increasingly carried out not in Hollywood but on location, and more and more outside the United States.

Starting in the 1950s, also, US companies took advantage of American exhibitors' growing demand for foreign movies by investing heavily in European cinema. Some of Europe's leading directors benefited from American funding as well as the support of US distributors. United Artists financed both Truffaut and Bergman for some of their films. Two British directors were involved in highly successful co-productions: David

Lean in *The Bridge on the River Kwai* (1957), *Lawrence of Arabia* (1962), and *Doctor Zhivago* (1965); Tony Richardson in *Tom Jones* (1963) and *Far from the Madding Crowd* (1967). In the following years Italian directors figured prominently in co-productions: Michelangelo Antonioni in *Blow-Up* (1968), *Zabriskie Point* (1970), and *The Passenger* (1975); and Bernardo Bertolucci in *Last Tango in Paris* (1972), and *The Last Emperor* (1987). American investment played a crucial part in European film production in this period.[24]

Co-production has continued to be central to international cinema. For filmmakers outside the United States it constituted one of two main ways (the other is collaboration with television) to compensate for the absence of self-sufficient national film industries. It maximized the prospects of a movie gaining international appeal and facilitated entry to the all-important US market. Since 1980 many foreign films have been successful at the US box office, even beyond the art-house circuit. They included (in the 1980s) *Chariots of Fire, Gandhi, The Killing Fields, Mad Max beyond Thunderdome,* and *Crocodile Dundee;* (in the 1990s) *Cinema Paradiso, The Crying Game, Howard's End, The Remains of the Day, The Piano, Like Water for Chocolate, Four Weddings and a Funeral, Shine, The English Patient, Life Is Beautiful, Elizabeth,* and *Notting Hill;* and (in the 2000s) *Crouching Tiger, Hidden Dragon, Amélie, Whale Rider, Finding Neverland, Pride and Prejudice, The Constant Gardener, The Queen,* and *Atonement.* American companies were involved in the financing and distribution of most of these films, and many involved American actors.

Such films were typically made with an eye to international markets and, in particular, to the tastes of US audiences; their content was influenced by this consideration. This influence did not make them "American" films, but nor can a film that results from international co-production easily be described as, say, British, French, or Italian. Identification of such films with particular national cultures has become increasingly problematic. Baz Luhrmann, the Australian director of the 2001 blockbuster *Moulin Rouge* – a film made in Sydney with a largely Australian cast but a Scottish male lead, set in Paris, and financed by 20th Century Fox – insisted on the film's Australian character by claiming that his own "artistic sensibility" is "particularly Australian." Such comments are interesting as a director's perception of his work, but they say little about the realities of international filmmaking.[25]

If the independence of Australian, British, and Italian film industries was threatened by the internationalization of film production, developments in the 1980s and 1990s also raised questions about the extent to which Hollywood's products could still be regarded as "American." In the round of mergers that occurred in the 1980s and 1990s three of the six major Hollywood firms – 20th Century Fox, Columbia, MCA-Universal – were acquired by non-American owners. Foreign ownership was not reflected in the content of Hollywood movies. The newly acquired studios did not proceed to produce and distribute films that were in any meaningful sense Australian, Japanese, or French; the strength of the domestic US market prevented such a radical change in cultural content. Yet, although the heterogeneous character of American society has always compelled Hollywood film-makers to cater for a wide range of audiences, and the studios have long employed directors, actors, and technical staff drawn from many countries, in the late twentieth century it was arguably less common for the most popular US-produced films, regardless of studio owner-ship, to present a distinctively American cultural outlook. Some movies did reflect American nationalist values; this was true of films as diverse as *Rambo* (1985), *Independence Day* (1996), *Saving Private Ryan* (1998), and *The Patriot* (2000). Far more pervasive, however, was the influence of commercial values that demanded that Hollywood movies be easily understood by audiences around the globe.

Cinema therefore defied the predictions of those who, at various times since the advent of the television age, had questioned its chances of survival. Yet as a medium and as an industry it changed greatly in the second half of the twentieth century. Two fundamental features remained constant, with an oligopoly of firms controlling the US film industry and these companies also dominating international film mar-kets. But the nature of that oligopoly was altered. The "Hollywood stu-dios" of the 1930s and 1940s had been, as the name suggested, film companies: they produced, distributed, and exhibited movies. By the 1990s most of those companies still existed but under new – and not always American – ownership. As production/distribution companies they were now but one part, and not necessarily the most important part, of huge multinational media conglomerates.

These organizations aimed to build synergies between film and their other media and entertainment interests. Theatrical exhibition remained important: success at the box office was still crucial to a film's commer-cial success. But, as sources of revenue, home video, DVD, and televi-sion had surpassed the cinema. These realities reflected the leisure patterns of the populations of affluent countries at the turn of the century. Most people spent considerably more time watching videos and DVDs than movies at the cinema, and far more time watching television than videos/DVDs.[26]

How well were audiences, and the public interest, served by these developments in film history? Hollywood's late-twentieth-century blockbuster strategy would not have succeeded if the US majors had failed to provide films that large international audiences wanted to see. These films, however, were designed to appeal to particular segments of the population: children, teenagers, adults with juvenile tastes, adults accompanying children. Other tastes were often catered for by "independent" US filmmakers and by film industries outside the United States. But films for these groups were more readily available in video and DVD format and on television rather than in movie theaters. Moreover, while it was sometimes suggested that the megahits that filled the majority of the world's cinema screens provided value-free entertainment, these films did have an ideological dimension. Both the movies and the marketing packages that accompanied them were a celebration of consumerism: they promoted the idea that the only significant differences within society are those of lifestyle and individual choice. Like television programs, Hollywood's films influenced language, fashion, and consumer behavior.[27]

The Press: Decline and Concentration

Newspapers, like cinema, experienced a marked audience decline after the Second World War. In the United States circulation fell steadily from 1.25 newspapers per household in 1953 to 0.97 in 1973, 0.84 in 1977, and 0.68 in 1990. Total daily newspaper circulation in 1995 was no greater than it had been in 1960 – around 59 million – although the population had grown from 180 million to 260 million in that period. In 1967 73 percent of American adults reported reading a newspaper every day; by 1991 the proportion had fallen to 51 percent. The trend was most pronounced among young people, despite the postwar expansion of both high-school and college education. In 1990 a mere 24 percent of those under 35 years reported reading a newspaper on the previous day, compared to 52 percent in a similar survey in 1965.[28]

These trends accelerated after 1990. Newspaper circulation fell by 11 percent in the period 1991–2004, then by 2 percent or more in each six-month period in 2005–6. According to surveys conducted by the Pew Research Center, the percentage of Americans who reported reading a newspaper on the previous day fell from 49 percent in 1994 to 42 percent in 2004. The young, in particular, relied increasingly on the Internet as a news source or avoided news altogether: a mere 19 percent of respondents to a 2004 survey of Americans between the ages of 18 and 34 said that newspapers were their main source of news. Equally striking was the decline in public trust in the press. The Pew Center's surveys showed that the percentage of Americans who "said they could believe little or nothing of what they read in their daily paper" rose from 16 percent in 1985 to 45 percent in 2004 (for the news magazines *Newsweek* and *Time* the 2004 figure was a less extreme but hardly reassuring 37 percent).[29]

Not surprisingly, many papers did not survive the television age. Many closed in the 1960s and 1970s, leaving large cities with just one or two daily newspapers. New York, a city with seven dailies in 1960, lost four of them by 1966, including the *Herald Tribune*, once the main rival of the *New York Times*, and the *New York Mirror*, despite sales of almost a million copies a day when it closed in 1963. Boston, a city with seven newspapers and a total circulation of 1,552,000 in 1950, had only two newspapers with a combined circulation of 857,876 by 1987 (despite a 67 percent growth in the city's population in the same period). By the end of the twentieth century, few American cities still had competing daily papers.[30]

The rise of television helps explain the post-1945 decline of the press, but as in the case of cinema other factors were also involved. One of these was increased production costs, caused by rising newsprint expenses, the wage demands of unionized printers, and the disruption that arose from industrial disputes. Publishers faced a choice between higher newspaper prices – with the likely loss of readers – and reduced profits. This problem remained until the introduction of new technology in the 1970s and 1980s transformed the press from a labor- to a capital-intensive industry. The postwar expansion of suburbs also undermined the economic viability of many publications, especially afternoon city newspapers: delivery problems were exacerbated by traffic congestion around the major population centers. The related growth in car ownership and the decline of public transport reduced opportunities for newspaper reading: commuters could not read a daily paper while driving, as they could on a train, bus, or streetcar. Finally, the rapid growth of the Internet from the 1990s confronted newspapers with a major new form of competition.

Yet, of those papers that survived, most did well. Newspapers remained the most popular vehicle for local advertising; those that did not suffer the problems of the big-city dailies, particularly papers that established a monopoly and exploited new technology, often made spectacular profits. Prominent among these were suburban and small-city newspapers, especially those owned by chains. The degree of concentration in the American press increased after 1960, as companies such as Gannett, Knight-Ridder, Times Mirror, and Newhouse, possessing the capital essential for exploitation of new technology, extended their ownership of the more profitable publications. By 2002 ownership chains accounted for 80 percent of American newspapers.[31]

If the effects of television largely account for postwar changes in the US newspaper industry, television's impact on magazines was even more direct. Because the United States did not possess national newspapers, magazines and network radio had been the main forums for national advertising. The efficiency of network television as a means of reaching audiences across the country therefore posed a direct threat to the advertising revenue of general-interest magazines. The country's great weekly mass-circulation magazines did not survive this threat; competition from television undermined both their attractiveness to advertisers and their sense of immediacy and visual appeal to readers. *Collier's* collapsed as early as 1956. The *Saturday Evening Post*, *Look*, and *Life* ceased publication between 1969 and 1972. They were revived as monthlies in the 1970s, but only *Life* lasted for long, and after 2000 it was published only on a limited basis, mainly as a free weekly supplement to various US newspapers between 2004 and 2007. The fate of these periodicals demonstrated that, in order to prosper in the television age, magazines had to specialize – to "help specialized advertisers reach specialized audiences." On this basis many magazines were successful, with *TV Guide* the most profitable. Meanwhile those magazines that most resembled newspapers in their content – *Time*, *Newsweek*, and *US News & World Report* – retained large circulations. Assisted by the high proportion of tertiary-educated readers in the US population, these middle-brow publications had no equivalent in other English-speaking countries. Their survival, however, depended on significant changes in content. With daily newspapers increasingly providing news analysis of the kind once characteristic of the news magazines, and with the *Washington Post*, the *New York Times*, and the *Wall Street Journal* publishing national editions, the magazines gave less attention to public affairs and more to show business, celebrities, and lifestyle features.[32]

The experience of the press in Britain in the second half of the century in many ways resembled that of the United States, with newspapers experiencing a steady decline in circulations and readership. Until 1956 the press was insulated from competition by the extension of wartime rationing of newsprint. With a consequent shortage of advertising space, even papers with weaker circulations had no trouble attracting sufficient advertising to remain profitable. The removal of this protection exposed the press to commercial television's threat to advertising revenue and to the same problem of rising production costs that troubled US newspapers. A number of famous national dailies, including the *News Chronicle* and the *Daily Herald*, did not survive. Medium-circulation dailies, unable to deliver advertisers either the affluent readership of the broadsheet "quality" press or the mass circulation of the tabloids, were prominent among those papers that closed between 1960 and the early 1970s.[33]

The British press, like its American counterpart, was marked by increasing economic concentration. A series of takeovers and mergers left nearly 60 percent of the national daily and Sunday newspapers in the hands of three chains by 1988. The introduction of new technology, inaugurated by Rupert Murdoch's removal of his printing operations from Fleet Street to Wapping in East London in 1986, consolidated the position of the leading chains. While the British newspaper market in 2000 gave the appearance of being competitive, with twenty national daily and Sunday papers, just five companies controlled over 80 percent of national newspaper circulation. A similar level of concentration prevailed in the regional and local press.[34] Concentration of ownership in the British and US press was typical of a worldwide phenomenon.[35]

The Press, the State, and Society

In much of the world in the early twenty-first century, press activity was still severely limited by political controls. In the unreconstructed totalitarianism of North Korea, for instance, newspapers remained organs of state propaganda. In the modified form of communism that emerged in China, newspapers were still state owned and controlled by the Communist Party's Propaganda Department but in some cases were allowed sufficient flexibility to publish non-political information and entertainment and even editorial criticism of local officials.[36] Elsewhere, private ownership of newspapers was permitted but did not in itself guarantee press freedom. The 2006 murder of the prominent Russian journalist Anna Politkouskaya – a writer for the small circulation paper *Novaya Gazeta* and a prominent critic of the Kremlin – and the contract-style murders of at least twelve other Russian journalists between 2000 and 2006 (more than in any country except Iraq and Algeria) highlighted how dangerous a journalist's work could be outside the context of a stable democracy. Meanwhile state-owned Russian newspapers – along with other media outlets – were increasingly subject to heavy censorship.[37] A different problem was evident in Indonesia, as it made an uneasy transition to political democracy after the collapse of the military despotism of President Suharto in 1998. The common practice of "envelope journalism," where reporters accepted bribes to influence what they wrote, underscored the long-term deleterious effects on journalism of an authoritarian political culture.[38]

In Western Europe, North America, Japan, and Australasia, privately owned newspapers and magazines were the norm, political murders of journalists were unknown, and the craft of journalism was well established. In these countries a complicated relationship developed between the press and the state. A longstanding liberal view of the role of the press was expressed in Thomas Jefferson's 1787 declaration that the "basis of our governments being the opinion of the people, the very first object should be to keep that right; and were it left to me to decide whether we should have a government without newspapers, or newspapers without a government, I should not hesitate a moment to prefer the latter."[39] Jefferson regarded the press as crucial to an informed citizenry, and therefore to the health of democracy. This belief, and the related idea of the press as a watchdog – the job of which is to scrutinize the actions of politicians and government officials and expose failures and abuses – continued to have widespread support, not least among journalists. Sometimes the press did play this role, but there were pressures that worked against it, as an examination of the post-1945 history of the press in the United States and Britain will show.

In the United States institutional developments encouraged changes in newspaper content. In the first half of the twentieth century it was common for proprietors to regard their papers as forums for their own political views. William Randolph Hearst and Colonel Robert McCormick, publisher of the *Chicago Tribune,* are two notable examples of highly opinionated owners who used their publications in this way. Gradually this approach gave way to an acceptance of the separation of ownership and the editorial function, a change that was accompanied by the professionalization of journalism. It was increasingly believed that journalists should be guided by a professional ethos of objectivity; in this way they would serve the public interest rather than the political or commercial interests of their employers. A symbolic milestone occurred when the *Los Angeles Times,* traditionally a strongly pro-Republican paper, adopted a neutral stance in the 1960 presidential elections.

"Objective journalism" represented an advance on the partisan newspaper content of the early twentieth century, but it did not always serve the public well. Characterized by a heavy dependence on official sources of information, respect for political authority, and often an uncritical acceptance of the statements of government officials, it restricted analysis to questions of strategy and tactics – whether a policy was politically successful rather than whether it was right or wrong. The consequences of this approach included an avoidance of the problems of entrenched poverty and racial inequality in American society, a neutral stance toward the activities of Joseph McCarthy, and unquestioning support for US foreign policy during the Cold War and military intervention in Vietnam.[40]

The ethos of objective newspaper journalism, along with the related view that newspapers should present "hard" news as it happened, was eroded during the 1960s and 1970s. The first challenge came from the television network news bulletins, which increasingly took over the role of "breaking" the news; simply reporting on events could no longer be the newspaper's role. Another challenge came from political and cultural change – from the breakdown of political consensus during the years of the Vietnam War, the Watergate affair, and conflict over black civil rights and women's rights. This more critical and partisan approach to the "powers that be" was evident in both the decision of the *New York Times* in June 1971 to defy the federal government and publish the Pentagon Papers, a top-secret Defense Department study of the history of US involvement in Vietnam, and in the prominent role played by the *Washington Post* in investigating the Nixon administration's involvement in the June 1972 break-in at the Democratic Party's offices in the Watergate building. As a result of the changes of the 1960s and 1970s an emphasis on presentation of the news increasingly gave way to analysis, interpretation, and "investigative journalism," with the journalist's subjective judgment given far greater scope. Opinionated columnists increasingly became a feature of print journalism.[41]

Nonetheless, the extent of change in journalistic practice should not be exaggerated. The American press did not, as is commonly supposed, become an institutional adversary of government as a result of the Vietnam War and the Watergate affair. Indeed, press relations with the administration of George W. Bush from 2001 – and press coverage of the administration's policies – showed how little had changed since the 1960s. The pattern of the Vietnam War was repeated in newspaper coverage of the invasions of Afghanistan and Iraq and of the domestic front in the "war on terror": largely uncritical support for the administration at the outset slowly gave way, as policy failures became harder to ignore and as public opinion changed, to a less deferential and more questioning attitude (on the press and the Vietnam War, see Chapter 10). The initial uncritical attitude reflected, however, the same values, pressures, and professional practices that shaped American television's treatment of Bush and his policies in 2001–4 (see Chapter 8): the influence of American nationalism, fear of the White House, intimidation from vocal conservative groups, fear of alienating public opinion, and a heavy dependence on government officials as supposedly "objective" sources of information.

Not that the record of the US press in this period was as consistently bleak as that of American television. In the months before the invasion of Iraq in March 2003 journalists at the *New York Times* and the *Washington Post* and at Knight Ridder's Washington bureau subjected the administration's case for war to close scrutiny and wrote skeptically about White House claims to have hard evidence of Saddam Hussein's possession of "weapons of mass destruction" (WMD) and close links with the al-Qaeda terrorist organization. But *The Times* and the *Post* usually printed these reports on inside pages, and their impact was therefore minimized; while the fact that Knight Ridder had no New York or Washington paper limited its reporters' influence on opinion-makers. Front-page coverage, by the *New York Times* and the *Washington Post* as well as other American papers, for the most part accepted uncritically the administration's claims. After the invasion began, they were similarly lacking in skepticism in their coverage of the progress of the war and occupation.[42] In May and August 2004, when it was clear that Saddam's supposed WMD stockpiles did not exist, the editors of the *New York Times* and the *Washington Post* printed apologies for their papers' reporting of the issue. *The Times's* coverage, its editors admitted, "was not as rigorous as it should have been." Too much trust had been placed in information provided by Iraqi defectors, as a result of which articles "based on dire claims about Iraq tended to get prominent display, while follow-up articles that called the original ones into question were sometimes buried." The *Post's* editors similarly admitted to the mistake of being "so focused on trying to figure out what the administration was doing that we were not giving the same play to people who said it wouldn't be a good idea to go to war and were questioning the administration's rationale."[43]

After the fall of Saddam Hussein, the press adopted a more questioning approach to the Bush administration's "war on terror." Newspapers reported on the failure to find WMD in Iraq, the intelligence failures evident in the period 2001–3 (and the cynical misuse and abuse of intelligence for political purposes), and the lack of adequate planning for the occupation and postwar reconstruction of Iraq. Eventually the press reported critically on the torture of prisoners held by the United States at Guantanamo Bay in Cuba and in Iraq and Afghanistan, and on the CIA's use of secret prisons in Eastern Europe. The change to a less deferential position followed the failure of the war, the unraveling of the previous political consensus on the war, and the erosion of Bush's popularity. In these altered circumstances editors and journalists were emboldened to emphasize the costs of war, including the cost in American lives, and to adopt a more independent stance generally toward the administration. Its ineffective response to Hurricane Katrina in August–September 2005 was given close attention. In December 2005 the *New York Times*, in an action that would have been unthinkable in the first years of the Bush presidency, defied the administration by reporting on a National Security Agency domestic surveillance program operating in apparent violation of the law. In June 2006 the *New York Times* and the *Los Angeles Times* published a front-page report giving details of a secret government program to track terrorist financing by monitoring international banking transactions.

In mid-2007 the *New York Times* for the first time took a strong editorial stance in support of withdrawal from Iraq.[44]

Even so, the habit of deference to government policy died slowly. Until 2005, when American newspapers reported on growing casualties in Iraq and Afghanistan they did so unobtrusively, on their inside pages. With some exceptions, the American press was slow to give the Abu Ghraib scandal of 2004 – when photographs taken at the Abu Ghraib prison near Baghdad revealed torture of Iraqi prisoners by American soldiers – the attention it deserved, and was reluctant to use the word "torture" to describe the acts depicted in the photographs (they were more commonly described as "abuses"). Even after 2004 there remained strict limits on American press reporting from Iraq. The huge human cost of the invasion and its prolonged aftermath, and in particular Iraqi civilian deaths resulting from US military action, were badly underreported. There were a number of reasons for this failing. They included physical limitations on journalists' access in a highly dangerous environment and their lack of Arabic language and cultural expertise. But they also included the journalists' tendency to share the military's mental outlook on the conflict – a tendency reinforced by the practice of "embedding" (see Chapter 10) – and "the deep-seated fear that many US journalists have of being accused of being anti-American, of not supporting the troops in the field."[45]

Though limited resources were not the main reason for the poor coverage of the American invasion of Iraq and its aftermath, nonetheless cuts in staff and in newspaper space devoted to news did limit the ability of the press to cover adequately the Iraq conflict and the "war on terror." And they contributed significantly to what informed critics regarded as the poverty of investigative journalism in the early years of the twenty-first century.[46] In part this failure of the press to inform and question was a consequence of the decline of the family-run companies that had owned most American newspapers until the 1970s. These companies, based in the cities and towns where their papers were published, regarded profits as only one measure of a successful newspaper. Generally they protected journalists from the priorities of the stock market and the shareholders. In the 1970s and 1980s, however, most American papers were sold to corporations. For these publicly traded stock companies, profit margins were the overriding concern. The result, as John S. Carroll, formerly editor of the *Los Angeles Times*, put it, was the loss of "the notion that a newspaper should lead, that it has an obligation to its community, that it is beholden to the public."[47] In the first years of the new century, as circulations declined, competition from the Internet increased, advertising revenue fell, and newsprint prices rose, and, as control of corporations shifted to Wall Street investment funds, the organizations that owned newspapers sought to retain and increase profit margins by sacking staff and reducing the news content of their publications.

This change to corporate control also intensified an emphasis on marketing at the expense of journalistic values. In the 1980s, in an effort to attract younger readers (the "demographic" that was at once highly valued by advertisers and most resistant to reading newspapers) and to reduce costs while increasing profits, American papers increasingly followed the model of Gannett's daily *USA Today*, which began national publication in 1982 and, its critics claimed, did for the news what McDonald's had done for food. Short and simple stories, heavy use of color and graphics, and much attention to celebrities, sport, fashion, and "lifestyle" characterized the "McPaper" approach to newspaper publication. At the other end of the scale, the prestige American dailies continued to provide serious coverage of domestic and international public affairs, but even they made concessions to readers whose expectations had been conditioned by the television age. Entertainment and lifestyle feature sections were expanded. In the 1990s the *New York Times* embraced color, graphics, and bigger headlines and extended its coverage of local news and sport. "The trick," a senior editor commented, "is how to do [all] this and still be the *New York Times*."[48]

The *New York Times* was far from a typical American newspaper. "Anyone who travels around America knows how mediocre most of its daily papers are," wrote Leonard Downie Jr and Robert G. Kaiser in 2002.[49] Unlike the vast majority of papers, the *New York Times*, the *Washington Post*, and (until 2007) the *Wall Street Journal* remained under the control of family-run companies and were therefore cushioned from Wall Street's demands for ruthless cost-cutting. The Sulzberger family, publishers of the *New York Times*, began selling stock on the New York Stock Exchange in 1967, the Graham family at the *Washington Post* in 1971; but both used a two-tier stock structure to preserve family control of the business (in 2006 the *New York Times* survived an attempt by the Morgan Stanley Company to dismantle the paper's ownership structure and wrest control from the Sulzbergers). Despite their sometimes less than creditable record in reporting the policies of the Bush administration, both the *New York Times* and the *Washington Post* remained in the front ranks of the world's leading newspapers. Other papers were less fortunate: the *Los Angeles Times*, the *Chicago Tribune*, the *Baltimore Sun*, the *Philadelphia Inquirer*, and the *Des Moines Register*, as well as many less prestigious publications, suffered badly from the loss of jobs and reduced news coverage forced on them in the first years of the new century. They became less successful as newspapers, and therefore less valuable to readers, even while they remained highly profitable businesses.[50] In 2007, too, the decision of the Bancroft family, which controlled the *Wall Street Journal*, to sell the paper to Rupert Murdoch's News Corporation served as a reminder that continuing family control of America's other leading newspapers could not be taken for granted.

Murdoch's approach to newspaper management had been demonstrated by his ownership of papers in the United States and other countries but above all in the United Kingdom. Murdoch extended his Australian newspaper empire to acquire the UK publication *News of the World* in 1968 and subsequently the *Sun*, *The Times*, and the *Sunday Times*. He was the most controversial of a new generation of press barons who came to dominate the British press after the 1960s. As in the United States, the postwar years saw a decline in political partisanship in British newspapers, with proprietors less willing to impose their own political views on their publications and more prepared to accept the professional autonomy of editors and journalists. But to a far greater extent than in the American press, this trend was reversed with the arrival of powerful owners – Murdoch, Victor Matthews, Robert Maxwell, Conrad Black – who did not hesitate to use their newspapers to promote their own conservative political views and to further their business interests. "I did not come all this way," Murdoch declared at the *News of the World*, "not to interfere." These proprietors selected their senior staff according to political criteria, gave detailed instructions on the content of editorials, and did not hesitate to express strong approval or disapproval of particular articles, columns, and headlines.[51]

Unlike the press magnates of the interwar period, proprietors such as Murdoch were not concerned primarily with newspapers; they were instead the heads of global corporations with other media and commercial interests. They were also not wedded to political parties in the fashion of the previous generation of interventionist proprietors. Thus Murdoch in the mid-1990s withdrew his support from the Conservative Party and threw the weight of his newspaper empire behind the Labour Party of Tony Blair, having first satisfied himself that a Blair government would be well disposed toward the interests of Murdoch's News Corporation.[52]

With the press dominated by proprietors who treated their publications as tools for their own commercial and political interests, the fundamental conflict that characterized the recent history of the American press – between the demands of the marketplace and the idea of journalism as public service – was also evident in Britain. As in the United States, corporate ownership, along with declining circulations, the rise of the Internet, and fierce competition for advertising revenue led to a decline in news and in coverage of political, social, and economic issues and a greater emphasis on entertainment, sport, human interest, and lifestyle features aimed at particular markets (and especially at young readers). The trend was apparent even in the quality press. In the popular press it began as early as 1969, when Murdoch acquired the *Sun* and recast the paper in a way that was soon emulated by other popular newspapers. The result was a triumph of forms of tabloid journalism more extreme than could usually be found in other countries. As Kevin Williams has written: "The amount of news and information in the popular press has as a result declined, to be replaced by an endless spewing out of sex, nudity, exposés of the private lives of people (and not only those in the public eye) and countless stories about the comings and goings of the Royal Family and the characters of soap operas."[53]

The US and UK cases illustrated the external and internal pressures that affected the press in Western countries in the early twenty-first century. The most immediate external challenge came from the Internet, which, like television before it, ate into newspaper and magazine circulations and advertising revenue. In some respects the Internet proved to be an asset. Journalists found it an invaluable tool that speeded up the process of gathering information and checking facts. The loss of readership from declining circulations was offset by a growing online audience. The Internet, indeed, expanded the readership for quality news, with the world's leading newspapers' websites attracting large global audiences. Because it provided an inexpensive means of transmitting newspapers, the Internet even offered the promise of a basis for ensuring the long-term viability of the press. It was not clear, however, to what extent those younger readers whose failure to purchase newspapers had contributed greatly to the industry's economic problems were more likely to read news online. Above all, it was unclear whether the online editions of newspapers would retain large audiences if they were no longer free, as most still were by 2008.

The main internal challenge to the press arose from its growing alignment with big business, the consequence of which was to erode further newspapers' capacity to perform a public-service role. The results included the increasingly frequent sacrifice of journalistic standards to the demands of commerce, the decline of investigative journalism, reduced spaced for news, and a greater emphasis on popular culture, celebrity, fashion, and lifestyle. A narrowing of ideological range was also part of this change: the development of the press in both the United States and Britain from the 1980s was marked by a shift to the political right. British newspapers adopted editorial positions that were frequently to the right of public opinion. In the United States even the liberal *New York Times* gave little attention to problems of class and poverty in American society. The increased emphasis on popular culture and lifestyle promoted the view that social and economic inequalities do not exist, that all problems should be understood in individual terms, and that individuals can find solutions to their problems in consumerism. In both countries the press gave favorable treatment to the beliefs of those political and economic elites who had succeeded in redefining the "center" of politics to incorporate uncritical acceptance of the chief tenets of neo-liberal economics and its ideological offshoot, market managerialism. In these circumstances the press, rather than being an independent watchdog, sometimes formed an alliance with the state, one based on common interest and ideology.[54]

These developments prompted the question of whether corporate ownership was compatible with a public-service role for the press. Two solutions to this perceived problem received widespread support. In Western Europe from the late 1960s many countries introduced state subsidies for newspapers. Their purpose was to try to ensure that the press gave expression to a diversity of views. Whether these subsidy schemes were an effective and efficient antidote to the effects of market forces was a controversial question at the end of the century.[55] In the United States there were increasingly calls for a return to local ownership of newspapers, with wealthy individuals indicating their interest in purchasing papers from the corporations and promising to make community service a higher priority than profit.[56] It remained to be seen whether these good intentions would lead to a significant changes in newspaper ownership, management, and content.

From the perspective of the public interest, there was much at stake in the efforts of the press to deal with its internal and external challenges. As a source of news and information the press was still unequalled by other media. Newspapers and magazines continued to employ the vast majority of journalists and were still responsible for most original reporting. Good newspapers contained up to 100,000 words daily, compared to less than 4,000 words in a typical half-hour television news program. They could, therefore, provide a range, depth, and quality of news coverage that television could not match. As a watch on the powerful, no other medium promised to be as effective.[57]

Radio: Decline and Adjustment

The postwar growth of television immediately affected American radio broadcasting. Large radio receivers were replaced by television sets, and leading radio stars were lured to the new medium. Even Bob Hope, the most popular radio performer, saw his rating drop from 23.9 in 1949 to 5.4 in 1954.[58] Network radio declined rapidly: local stations took less and less network programming, and hundreds disaffiliated from the networks. Yet radio continued to thrive in a greatly altered form. The development of transistor radios and car radios, both of which became enormously popular in the 1950s and 1960s, sustained the medium; typically people now listened to their radio receivers individually, in the bedroom, kitchen, or car, rather than with the family. Public demand for radio remained high, but local stations, not the networks, now dominated the medium. The number of stations increased from 996 in 1945 to 2,819 in 1950, 4,086 in 1960, and 6,745 in 1970.[59] Most of them filled their airtime relatively cheaply by playing recorded music. Instead of trying to reach a mass audience, as the networks had done, they specialized in particular formats – country and western, rhythm and blues, mainstream popular, and "easy listening" were common – and attracted advertising on the basis of their appeal to niche audiences, distinguished by characteristics of age, region, class, gender, or religious preference. Especially lucrative, as the postwar baby-boom generation grew into adolescence, was the teenage market. Its expansion persuaded many stations from the mid-1950s to adopt a Top 40 rock 'n' roll format, presenting a steady diet of rock music accompanied by the patter of a disk jockey. Format radio encouraged rigid and cautious programming: fear of alienating listeners, and therefore advertisers, discouraged any departure from tried-and tested-formulas. A willingness to experiment and greater openness to diversity in music programming marked the beginnings of a boom in FM radio in the late 1960s and early 1970s; but there, too, commercial pressures eventually prevailed. "By the 1980s," Susan Douglas has written, "much of FM, once so vibrant and experimental, had been sliced up into predictable, homogenized formats that offered little surprise and no interaction."[60]

As in other media, deregulation and growing economic concentration shaped the development of American radio in the last two decades of the twentieth century. In the 1980s the Federal Communications Commission (FCC) began to lift restrictions on ownership of radio stations, in a process that culminated in the Telecommunications Act of 1996. New national radio companies were formed. By 1997 a number of companies owned between 200 and 300 stations each. One, Chancellor Media Corporation, controlled 463 stations by 1998, with an estimated audience of sixty-five million. At the same time satellite technology, by allowing instant and inexpensive transmission of syndicated programs, led to the re-networking of radio, but with many more networks than in the pre-television age, and with many of those dedicated to a single format, such as talk, "beautiful music," or "music from the eighties and nineties." Unlike the old networks, the corporations that now dominated American radio did not distribute uniform programming for a national audience. Rather they took advantage of their ownership of multiple stations in major markets to broadcast a range of formats, each designed to appeal to a "demographic" highly prized by advertisers. In this sense each of the major companies controlled a number of different networks. Thus the new forms of networking and concentration, while undermining localism, did not reverse that fragmentation of the national radio audience that had characterized radio broadcasting since the advent of television.[61]

Deregulation encompassed content as well as ownership and control. In radio as in television, during the 1980s the FCC abolished the public-service regulations that had previously applied to American broadcasting. Station licensing periods were extended from three to seven years, restrictions on advertising time were relaxed, and requirements that stations provide a balance of views and devote a proportion of their programming to news and public affairs were removed. Freed of political regulation, the radio corporations recognized no responsibility other than that of maximizing their profits. As in the case of television, public-affairs programs were the main casualty: on all but a small minority of stations, such programs gave way to even larger doses of music, selected to comply with rigid formats, and to even more commercials.

Douglas has argued that the growing popularity in the 1980s and 1990s of talk radio and National Public Radio (NPR) – the radio arm of public broadcasting – stemmed from public discontent with these developments. By the mid-1990s talk radio was second only to country music as a popular format. Combined with the re-networking of radio, it made national figures of such "shock jocks" as Don Imus, Howard Stern, and Rush Limbaugh. The rise of NPR was surprisingly successful, especially by comparison with its ailing television cousin, PBS. By 1995 NPR's morning and evening news programs, *Morning Edition* and *All Things Considered*, commanded an audience of between ten and eleven million in a typical week. Large numbers of Americans also tuned into NPR's documentaries and public-interest programs and its live coverage of congressional hearings and debates, as well as its drama programs and Garrison Keillor's affectionate send-up of small-town America and old-time radio, *A Prairie Home Companion*. Talk radio and NPR appealed to very different listeners. The former was politically right-wing and its audience predominantly working-class and lower-middle-class males who looked to the shock jocks for emotional reinforcement of their prejudices. NPR was more liberal, and its listeners tended to be more highly educated, though it also provided a wider range of information and opinions than could be found on talk radio. But they had in common a more detailed coverage of public affairs than could be found elsewhere on radio or in some other sections of the media. They both spoke to "a profound sense of public exclusion from and increasing disgust with the mainstream media in general and TV news in particular."[62]

The post-1945 development of radio in Britain in some ways paralleled the American experience, though there were also significant differences. The central role of a public-service broadcaster, not dependent on advertising revenue, worked against the degree of fragmentation of the radio audience that occurred in the United States. But even the BBC, in seeking to retain its audience in the face of a challenge from offshore "pirate" stations, expanded to four networks by 1967 and began local radio operations. Moreover, the Sound Broadcasting Act of 1972 created additional radio services in the form of independent commercial radio. The Independent Broadcasting Authority required each of these stations to provide a range of programs, including news services. In this way the public interest was protected, but the regulatory framework undermined the ability of these stations to appeal to specialized audiences and provide advertisers with niche markets. The lifting of most of these restrictions by the Broadcasting Act of 1990 allowed independent radio to become more profitable and led to the creation of additional stations. But the promise that audience needs would be better served through greater diversity in programming has not been vindicated. In Britain, as in the United States, radio companies have embraced rigid formats as the surest way to attract advertising revenue.[63] In both countries a balance between commercial interests and public-service considerations proved elusive.

Radio, the press, and cinema remained major media in the post-Second World War decades by taking on secondary roles within a new media environment. A common feature of their adjustment to the television age was the attempt to capture specialized audiences, having relinquished to television the role of providing entertainment and information to a mass audience. Before the Second World War the media – movies, mass-circulation newspapers and magazines, national radio – had been forces for cultural integration. Now this was much less the case, with different population groups receiving different kinds of media content. Some groups were better served than others by these media. The fragmentation of audience was closely linked with the predominance of commercial forces at the expense of public-service values, and with an increasing tendency to favor entertainment over information. Some elements in the media still provided serious reporting on and investigation of political, social, and economic matters; but it was now taken for granted that substantial sections of the population would opt out of receiving this content, and that if these groups were to become consumers of news it could be done only by blurring the lines between information and entertainment. Finally, increased concentration of media power was a central feature of the history of radio, the press, and film in this period. In the middle of the twentieth century it was already the case that a small number of companies owned the mainstream media. But in the last decades of the century sympathetic governments allowed the development of a more extreme degree of concentration. In these years the US film and television industries – as well as other media and entertainment interests within the United States and to a large extent film and television internationally – came to be dominated by a handful of transnational conglomerates. The nature and role of this global oligopoly will be further examined in Chapter 12.

10

Media, War, and International Relations

Since the development of a mass press in the late nineteenth century, through the twentieth century, with the growth of other mass and communications media (radio, film, television, the Internet), and into the twenty-first century the media have played a controversial role during war. Attention was given to mass media, particularly television, during the Vietnam War in the 1960s and 1970s, as efforts were made to explain the American defeat in that southeast Asian conflict. The BBC broadcaster Robin Day expressed a particularly influential view when he observed: "One wonders if in future a democracy which has uninhibited television coverage in every home will ever be able to fight a war, however just…. The full brutality of the combat will be there in close up and colour, and blood looks very red on the colour television screen."[1] In subsequent "limited" and "asymmetric" wars, in peacekeeping operations, and in the "war on terror" after the September 2001 attacks in the United States, the relationship between the military and the media has attracted much attention, with media increasingly considered as powerful "instruments of warfare."

In recent conflicts the term "media war" has been used. This partly reflects a longstanding interest among historians in the role of media coverage of war. It is perhaps also due to more overt discussion of the strategic importance of "soft power" – information operations, "psychological operations" ("psyops"), public diplomacy – and appropriation by the military of public-relations and strategic-communications approaches. The first few weeks of the US-led war against Iraq in 2003 have been referred to as the "media war," as distinct from the subsequent long-running military occupation.[2] During this brief period embedded journalists provided a wealth of reports, and the invasion was covered extensively by global media. While "media war" focuses attention on the importance attributed to media in twenty-first-century conflicts, it is important to consider whether there have been fundamental changes in military–media relations.

As indicated above (see Chapters 2 and 6), during the "total wars" of the twentieth century (1914–18, 1939–45) media were used for political purposes, to disseminate official information, to sustain home-front morale, to persuade and spread propagandist messages. During the Second World War both totalitarian regimes and democracies imposed wartime controls over information and used the media for their own purposes in a war of competing ideologies. Journalists and news agencies in both the First and Second World Wars tended to cooperate willingly with governments, acceding to censorship requirements and collaborating in the war effort. War correspondents largely supported nationalist and patriotic causes, there was a broad consensus based on shared values and beliefs, and there was little conflict between the mass media and political and military leaderships. In these circumstances war reporting was often less concerned with accuracy than with impact. Phillip Knightley's frequently cited work on war and the media uses the phrase derived from Hiram Johnson's statement to the United States Senate in 1917, "the first casualty when war comes is truth," specifically to describe war reporting.[3]

While war reporters and media organizations had largely accepted censorship and restrictions as part of the impositions of wartime up to that time, such cooperation broke down during the Vietnam War in the 1960s. As a result, many began to consider the media as adversarial. Lessons were drawn from the Vietnam experience, and in the limited wars of the 1980s, in the 1991 Gulf War and wars in Afghanistan and Iraq following the 2001 terrorist attacks in the United States, military management of the media became a recurrent theme. During the "war on terror" the global mediascape has continued to change, technological developments have continued to provide apparently novel means of war reporting, and different approaches to managing military–media relations have been employed. However, basic questions about the role of media during war remain, particularly their significance relative to other factors, the extent of their use for propagandist purposes, and whether they lead or merely reflect public opinion.

The Media and War in Korea and Vietnam

The spread of television as a mass medium after the Second World War made it possible for civilian populations to be more exposed to the "realities" of war. Television broadcasting was becoming established in the 1950s just as the United States engaged in a Cold War conflict in Korea in 1950–3. However, television was not sufficiently widespread to be considered a mass medium; it had not achieved saturation coverage of American homes, and it was not technically or professionally sophisticated enough to report the war thoroughly, or to exploit the possibilities of integrating sound and moving images. Television news was still modeled on radio, and the networks relied on the established newsreels for footage or on film supplied by the US Army Signal Corps. Thus Korea was not a television war. It was a war in which the military imposed formal censorship, and in which war journalists, typical of media cooperation with government during the Cold War (see Chapter 7), tended to be complicit with governments and the military in not posing fundamental questions about war aims and objectives, in not questioning Western interventionist foreign policies in what were essentially civil wars.[4]

In the following two decades the relationship between the media and the state during wartime (especially in the United States) changed considerably. The high level of nationalist and patriotic support that prevailed during the Korean War was eroded; in the 1960s older values of uncritical loyalty to the state were questioned, and there was greater willingness to consider "victims" of US foreign policy (see Chapters 8 and 9 on changing cultural values in the United States). The Vietnam War of the 1960s and 1970s ended in defeat for the United States and its allies, and, in searching for explanations, conservatives drew attention to the importance of the mass media, particularly television. The lack of formal censorship was considered to have been important: the United States did not impose censorship because there was a gradual build-up first of military advisers and then of military units without any declaration of war; because it claimed to be in South Vietnam, a sovereign state, by invitation; and because limiting media freedom would have been inconsistent with the aim of restoring a democratic Vietnam. It followed that uncensored coverage provided a realistic picture of the brutality of the war. Influential politicians and others credited the media with exerting great influence on public opinion, leading to a withdrawal of support for American foreign policy in southeast Asia. This traditional view, put concisely, was that "the media lost the war." Television brought images of war into American living rooms, turned the American public against the war, and made continuing US military involvement in Vietnam impossible.

Such conclusions about the war were possible because of techno-logical changes, the establishment of television broadcasting on a large scale, and the absence of formal restrictions on media coverage of the war. By the 1960s, when American and allied forces became involved in Vietnam, almost all American homes had a television set. It became easier for reporters and cameramen to cover the war because of techni-cal improvements in lightweight sound cameras, improved transport and communications. Moreover, the extension of network evening news bulletins from fifteen minutes to half an hour in 1963 allowed more detailed coverage of American military operations. It was argued that the American people, tuning into nightly television news in their living rooms, saw the full horrors of the war. Because this was the first war in which the United States suffered a decisive defeat, the simple cause-and-effect argument developed: this was "the first television war," this was America's first defeat; therefore the first "caused" the second. In other words, the outcome of the war in Vietnam was deter-mined on the television screen rather than on the battlefield.

President Lyndon Johnson shared this view. He maintained that America was defeated because the war was televised; regular public exposure to the awful realities of war turned the public against the war, forced the withdrawal of US troops, and left the way open for a communist victory in Vietnam. Similarly, President Nixon maintained that the American news media came to dominate domestic opinion about the purpose and conduct of the Vietnam War. They showed images of suffering and sacrifice and caused serious demoralization on the home front; this resulted in withdrawal of American support from the South Vietnamese and the final victory of the communist North. American generals expressed similar views, as did others out-side the political and military establishment. Robert Elegant, himself a correspondent in Vietnam, blamed the media for American defeat, referring to the collective policy of the news media to seek "the victory of the enemies of the correspondents' own side" by "graphic and unre-mitting distortion" of the facts.[5] Such views formed the basis of what came to be referred to, in scholarly and journalistic writing on the war, as "the oppositional media thesis."

It was easy to move from this interpretation to a view that no televised war can long retain political support at home. According to this, the media – especially television – exercise a profound influence on the conduct of foreign policy during war. Television viewers nightly see images of the brutality of war; the immediacy and horror of these images cannot fail to have an impact; the public, alerted to the costs of war, will not tolerate continued hostilities.

This widely accepted view of television and war led to considerable debate among scholars. By the 1980s media historians were challenging the "oppositional media thesis." Broadly, their argument was that the United States failed in Vietnam for a number of reasons, especially the costs of prosecuting the war, and the media merely mirrored pre-existing attitudes, following rather than leading public opinion. Daniel C. Hallin concluded:

> The collapse of America's "will" to fight in Vietnam resulted from a political process of which the media were only one part. And that process was deeply rooted in the nature and course of the war – the fact that it was a limited war, not only in its tactics but in its relevance to vital American interests; and also the fact that it was an unsuccessful limited war …[6]

These critics – or "revisionists" – examined the arguments about media impact. They pointed out that it was not clear what proportion of the population actually watched television news at the time it was supposedly influencing public opinion against the war. They also referred to lack of evidence about the proportion of those watching who actually paid attention or remembered items from nightly broadcasts. They cited polls and surveys that showed less television viewing and lower recall than the orthodox view implied. They argued that battle scenes on television lost any sense of reality or danger: real battles in Vietnam were seen as "just another Hollywood drama," and this induced apathy or rendered the war trivial. Very little of the combat footage broadcast on American television showed heavy fighting in detail. More common were images of helicopters landing and American soldiers engaged against an invisible enemy in apparently successful but unspecified battles. This conveyed a misleading impression of the war, creating unfounded optimism rather than stimulating opposition to the war – and barely hinting at the effect of the war on the Vietnamese.

One much cited statistic was that American acceptance of the conflict, as measured by public opinion polls, consistently declined in step with the rise in American casualties, falling some 15 percentage points each time the total number of Americans killed and wounded rose by a factor of ten. Thus, when total casualties from all causes went from 1,000 to 10,000 or from 10,000 to 100,000, public regret grew by about 15 percent. This reaction occurred regardless of whether the war appeared to be going well or poorly, and in spite of favorable or unfavorable press or television coverage. A similar parallel between casualties and public opinion occurred during the Korean War, when television news was still in its infancy.[7]

As well as arguing that American losses in Vietnam were more important than media coverage, revisionists questioned the links between television and public attitudes. For example, television coverage may have merely reinforced existing attitudes rather than changing them; television may have encouraged support rather than opposition by stirring viewers' patriotism and backing for the American soldiers they saw fighting on the screen. Furthermore, there was deep-seated anti-war sentiment in the United States before television and before Vietnam (as evidenced, for example, by the strength of isolationism and late US involvement in both the First and Second World Wars), and, although this was the first televised war, it was not the first unpopular war.

Accounts of media coverage of the war have emphasized the importance of television reporting of the Tet offensive. Until late 1967, notwithstanding the "oppositional media" view, mainstream American media had largely supported the war, with journalists voluntarily cooperating with the US military in Vietnam. However, during the Tet offensive of early 1968, when a strong communist offensive was launched, the city of Hue was occupied, and a Vietcong commando squad entered the US Embassy compound in Saigon, television coverage showed the contradiction between political and military optimism at home (and claims that the United States was winning the war) and the "real happenings" in South Vietnam. However, as Hallin points out:

> The conventional wisdom is that the Tet coverage, and television pictures of the battles of Khe Sanh that followed, were the last straw for

214 Media, War, and International Relations

the American public. There is little doubt that these actions played an important part in strengthening opposition to the war, but it is apparent that the tide of public opinion had already turned. All the media did was confirm the widespread public view held well before Tet, that the people had been the victims of a massive deception.... Tet was less a turning point than a crossover point, a moment where trends that have been in motion for some time reach balance and began to tip the other way.[8]

Subsequent media revelations in the United States, such as the breaking of the story of the My Lai massacre (when American soldiers, reportedly under orders from their platoon commander, massacred 504 Vietnamese civilians – including women and children – in March 1968, an event not reported until late 1969), confirmed the impression of adversarial media. However, the My Lai story broke at a time when American public opinion was prepared to believe it, partly because of the shock caused by news of the Tet offensive and the blow to the credibility of the Johnson administration, partly because of growing frustration regarding the war. By the early 1970s media opposition was even more apparent when the *New York Times*, in defiance of the government, supported publication of the Pentagon Papers, the classified history of the war. By this time President Nixon and his administration were facing war weariness and disillusionment; and the media were one among other factors contributing to opposition to the war. It should be noted, moreover, that there were limits to the adversarial role of the media. At this time media editors and producers, apparently judging that the war in Vietnam was almost over and that public interest was declining, began to give it less attention despite public disillusionment and questioning of foreign policy. Moreover, American journalists tended to continue to identify with "their side," to revert to "consensus journalism," and to privilege the administration rather than the antiwar movement in relation to news. According to Hallin, the "constraints of ideology and of journalistic routines tying news coverage to Washington perspectives" excluded basic questions from the news agenda (including the wisdom of US intervention in Vietnam and the outcomes of the war for the people of Indochina), containing the extent to which the media could be genuinely oppositional.[9]

The debate over the role of media in the Vietnam War is important in media history in focusing attention on links between public opinion and media, and in raising the fundamental question about the extent of television's influence. In the case of the Vietnam War, it is important to acknowledge the complexities of that conflict: the enormous problems facing successive US administrations in their prosecution of the war, the impact on American society of continuing losses in a prolonged conflict, and the complex reasons for the emergence of the anti-war movement. No single-cause explanation of the war's outcome can be satisfactory, and certainly not an explanation in terms of media influence that singles out one mass medium – television – for blame. While media may have served as communications channels for the growing anti-war movement and facilitated heightened awareness of the war, they did not "lose the war."

The Media and Limited Conflicts in the 1980s

Scholarly debate on the role of media in the US defeat in Vietnam had little effect on military and political leaders in the United States and elsewhere. In post-Vietnam conflicts they acted as if television – or the media more generally – had indeed lost the war. One legacy of American involvement in southeast Asia in the 1960s and early 1970s (an aspect of the so-called Vietnam syndrome) was the desire to avoid any protracted military involvement abroad, and, in the event of any US engagement, to keep it short and to control media reporting so that public opinion at home did not have time – or the basis for informed decision-making afforded by detailed media coverage – to become disenchanted and to withdraw support from American foreign policy.

A key issue in post-Vietnam conflicts has been the extent of official control over war correspondents. In the Vietnam War there had been no formal censorship, large numbers of reporters had gone to Vietnam, and they had moved around conflict zones (the US military provided journalists, so long as they obtained a press card, with free ground and air transport, meals, shelter, and access to field commanders). In limited wars of the 1980s governments acted to curtail such media freedom.

Britain took account of the perceived lessons of Vietnam during the war with Argentina in 1982, the Falklands War. This was Britain's "first taste of a campaign fought in the full glare of modern media attention."[10] The remoteness of this war in the south Atlantic facilitated media management. Places on Royal Navy taskforce ships were limited, and the government and military leadership decided which organizations should be allowed to report the war at first hand, excluded non-British correspondents, and controlled communications from the war zone. Correspondents relied on the Navy to transmit copy, and reports were subject to delays and censorship.

The Falklands War highlighted the conflict between, on the one hand, the perceived public right in any democratic system to be informed and, on the other, government and military needs to withhold information for reasons of operational security. The British government and military leadership practiced a policy of "deception, misinformation, disinformation and media manipulation through denial of access, control of communications and politically based censorship."[11] Because this was a short and limited war in a remote area, it was relatively easy for the government and military to employ these restrictive tactics.

British media management during the Falklands War provided a model for American military–media relations during other limited conflicts. When US forces went into Grenada in 1983 (in a commando-raid operation to rescue Americans supposedly held by a government friendly with Cuba), the US Defense Secretary excluded journalists during the initial landing. Media reports were largely accounts after the event, based on officially released information. Following this operation, and at the request of the chairman of the Joint Chiefs of Staff, General Vessy Jr, a commission was set up to make recommendations on press–military relations in any future operations. The Sidle Commission Report provided for public-affairs planning alongside operational planning. It recommended that media compliance with military guidelines should be voluntary, and that sufficient military personnel should be available to assist correspondents to cover operations adequately.

In another limited American operation in Panama in 1989 (against General Noriega), the media were again excluded initially. Once journalists were allowed access, they depended on the military for transport and access to transmission facilities, and the military censored their reports. A "pool" system was used in Grenada, with reporters assigned to military units and accompanied by military escorts. Those journalists who were not part of the pool could operate only on the fringe of the war without access to the action. Despite the Sidle Commission Report, the "Vietnam lesson to keep the press out was too well established in the culture and the routines of the military" for any change to occur.[12]

Media historians see the experiences of Grenada and Panama as stages in a process of increasingly rigid military management of the media. They "reinforced the post-Vietnam model of military operations: use overwhelming force, do the job quickly, keep casualties to a minimum ... and attempt to control what the public sees."[13] Military–media relations in these limited conflicts of the 1980s were based on the traditional view, derived from the experience of the Vietnam War, that attributed power to the media during war, and they became a model for further restrictive military management of the media.

Media Management during the 1991 Gulf War

During the 1991 Gulf War (sometimes referred to as the First Gulf War, with the 2003 war against Iraq the Second Gulf War) the US military had taken to heart the lessons of Vietnam and subsequent experiences of tight media management in Grenada and Panama. The Gulf War provided an even more striking example of military restraint of media.

After the Iraqi invasion of Kuwait in 1990 and unsuccessful United Nations (UN) attempts to bring about a solution through sanctions and an embargo, a US-led coalition began Operation Desert Storm against Iraq on February 24, 1991. The war lasted forty-two days and included a heavy allied bombardment and a brief ground offensive. It resulted in the defeat of Iraq and the liberation of Kuwait, although Saddam Hussein remained in power in Iraq.

The official approach to the media in the Gulf War was largely determined by the idea that the United States would, by means of a short, sharp, victorious war, put the Vietnam War behind it. President George Bush stated, "we've kicked the Vietnam syndrome once and for all," depicting the Gulf War as a surrogate for wars the United States could not win in Southeast Asia. Americans needed a victory, and the supposed "mistakes" of Vietnam could not be allowed to recur. The media had to serve the interests of the state and the military once war began (as indeed they had during earlier conflicts such as the two world wars).[14]

Technological change (enabling real-time television broadcasting), and the advent of the twenty-four-hour global television news service, Cable News Network (CNN), made the 1991 Gulf War a media event on a grand scale with extensive and virtually instantaneous coverage.

American, Iraqi, and other leaders used CNN to send messages to one another, bypassing traditional diplomatic routes via embassies and foreign ministries. Television coverage of the conflict was extensive in terms of airtime devoted to it. Yet analysts depict the war as one of the worst reported because of military management of the media. To a large extent this view reflected journalists' and media organizations' expectations rather than reality: it could be argued that in some respects the Gulf War was more comprehensively reported than previous conflicts (several high-profile television correspondents from CNN, the BBC, and ITN ignored attempts to regiment Western media, went to Baghdad, and filed vivid reports "from the other side," showing the results – including civilian casualties – of allied bombing of Iraq).

However, the majority of journalists found themselves subject to restrictions. The pool system, used earlier in the limited conflict in Grenada, was again used to limit media "intrusion," and the military issued specific guidelines on reporting. Journalists were not permitted into the war zone except as part of a designated pool and could not move freely in combat areas; non-pool reporters were forbidden access to forward areas. Military escorts were provided for journalists, and all copy was subject to military security review. US Defense Department rules banned publication or broadcast of specific information such as numbers of troops, aircraft, weapons, equipment and supplies, future plans and operations, locations of forces, and tactics. In addition, military briefings set out the official viewpoint for reporters, and official footage filmed from US combat aircraft was supplied to television broadcasters.

Such restrictions resulted in "sanitized coverage" of a "clean war" in which images of "smart," high-tech weaponry dominated. There was little footage of casualties (and certainly none of casualties from "friendly fire"). There was overwhelming emphasis on the air war rather than the ground war. Much of the television coverage consisted of interviews, reporters talking to cameras, still photographs, graphics, and maps. The military press conference was the most frequently portrayed single event in the Gulf War.

Many reporters chaffed at the restrictions imposed on them, seeing themselves as merely "hotel warriors," reporting the war from hotel rooms, relying on information from televised briefings, pool reports, and CNN coverage rather than on first-hand experience of the conflict on the ground or in the air.[15] At a time when sophisticated technologies offered the possibility of immediate and extensive reporting to a global audience from the war zone in the Middle East, the military policy of containment constrained media coverage of the 1991 conflict. More fundamentally, historians of this and other recent wars have argued that the very nature of television as a medium impedes reflection and interpretation, instead valuing speed over judgment and accuracy (see Chapter 8).[16]

The experience of the First Gulf War raised concerns about journalistic independence and the degree of freedom of contemporary media – both the press and broadcasting media – even in democratic societies. There was criticism of high levels of political influence over the media, and of the power of the US military to dictate to American media how wars should be covered. There was a widely shared view that governments and the military had realized the importance of public opinion during war and developed policies of containment and control to harness the media and enlist and maintain public support.[17] Yet a review of the relationship of the media and government during other wars of the twentieth century serves as a reminder that in most cases media cooperated with governments, complied with measures such as censorship, implemented to protect the national interest in wartime, or indeed acted in such a way that regulation was unnecessary (see Chapters 2, 4, 6, and 7). From this perspective, the adversarial stance of some media during the late 1960s and 1970s was an aberration rather than the norm.

Global Media, Peacekeeping, and Humanitarian Interventions

In the final decade of the twentieth century media attracted attention not only for their role in war but also for their significance in peacekeeping and humanitarian operations. Various developments seemed to increase the potential for influence of global media: the extension of satellite broadcasting, the rapid growth of the Internet, and the emergence of new means of communications such as blogs, swiftly changing and converging technologies (particularly based on mobile/cell phones – see Chapter 11).

The term "the CNN factor" was used to refer to the power of the media, particularly global television broadcasting across national boundaries, to influence public opinion and have an impact on policy.

It was argued that certain global crises were constituted by global media and the responses that media coverage evoked. Taken to an extreme, the "CNN effect" described a situation in which government officials supposedly lost control, and media and public opinion became the key players in foreign policy-making.[18]

It was suggested that pervasive media images of famine-ravaged populations could stimulate public support for multinational humanitarian efforts coordinated through UN agencies; or that images of the impact of civil war could boost popular demand for peacekeeping operations in parts of the world that had negligible strategic interest for the peacekeepers. Various events seemed to illustrate the CNN factor at work, when global media portrayals of crisis situations led to international action: sending US and then UN troops to establish security for humanitarian relief efforts in Somalia between 1991 and 1995; peace operations following the civil wars in the former Yugoslavia between 1991 and 1995; US and then UN intervention in Haiti in 1994 to restore the elected government of President Jean-Bertrand Aristide; international intervention in Rwanda in 1993–4 following ethnic strife, mass slaughter, and a refugee crisis; NATO intervention in Kosovo and Serbia in 1999 in another Balkan War.

However, in each of these instances a detailed analysis of factors influencing decision-making would be necessary to determine the relative importance of media. In some of them a crisis situation had developed and many lives been lost before international intervention occurred. Perhaps the timing of media focus might have been influential, but this needs to be considered alongside other considerations (geopolitical, national security, and so on). Samantha Power, in a study of American responses to genocide (including the genocide of Serbs against Muslims in Bosnia in 1992 and of Hutu against Tutsi in Rwanda in 1994), has pointed out how difficult it is to disentangle the effects of public inertia and government indifference. She concludes that US policymakers have avoided engagement in conflicts posing little threat to American interests, and there has not been any pressure from American public opinion to change their lack of will. She has highlighted the lack of attention given by major Western media to crises such as that in Rwanda and linked this to the absence of public or elite pressure in the United States for military intervention.[19] Detailed studies such as this illustrate how complex are the interactions of media, public opinion, and policymaking.

More generally, it has been argued that in the late twentieth century there was little popular interest in war. Audiences in the United States, Britain, and Western Europe, for example, did not feel at risk and some watched war on television as a "spectator sport" (hence the notion of "virtual war"). However, this has not led to media being ignored in conflict situations. On the contrary, many continue to consider media as integral to wartime strategy. The 1999 war in Kosovo illustrated trends that continued in twenty-first-century wars. In that conflict Slobodan Milosevic used "media power" as a weapon, attempting through propaganda to impose limitations on the United States and its NATO allies in prosecuting the war. While propagandist use of media during war has a long history, what emerged in the new century were more sophisticated and integrated approaches to information operations, "psyops," military public affairs, public diplomacy, and political news management (pejoratively referred to as "spin").[20] The interesting question for media historians is whether these approaches – using the range of communications technologies available in the twenty-first century – resulted in substantially different use of media as instruments of policy during war.

Media and the "War on Terror"

On September 11, 2001 ("9/11") terrorist attacks occurred in New York and Washington. The role of global media during crises was highlighted in the days and weeks following the attacks. Stunning images of the hijacked planes hitting the twin towers of the World Trade Center in New York and the Pentagon in Washington were disseminated with hitherto unparalleled speed to global audiences. In the subsequent American-led "war on terror", initially directed at the man assumed responsible for the attacks, Osama bin Laden, and the al-Qaeda network, supposedly based in Afghanistan, conventional and new media played an important role.

After 9/11 most US mainstream media complied unquestioningly with government requests. They stressed American outrage and supported military intervention in Afghanistan. US television broadcasters in particular have been criticized for uncritically accepting the decisions to wage war against Afghanistan and later against Iraq, for being nothing more than "agents of state propaganda." The networks agreed to a Bush administration request to stop live broadcasting of Osama bin Laden's words and to omit his more inflammatory oratory. Commercial networks also self-censored programming, removing advertisements and content (such as movies with a terrorist theme) that might have been offensive.[21]

One novelty of media coverage of this crisis was the extent to which information on the Internet supplemented traditional broadcasting and print. Within ten minutes of the first plane striking the World Trade Center, traffic to major Internet news sites increased exponentially, with millions of hits (for example, nine million page views per hour of CNN.com on the morning of 9/11, with a total of 162 million that day). As sites such as MSNBC.com, ABCNews.com, CBSnews.com, and FoxNews.com rapidly published information, Internet traffic became so heavy that many sites became inaccessible because of congestion. Efforts were made to cope: image-intensive graphics were removed, available bandwidth was expanded, user registration processes and traffic-tracking software were suspended, but use of the Internet as an alternative site for breaking news in 2001 was not without problems. However, users appeared not to have been deterred: Allan argues that not only did significant numbers of US users turn to websites for updates, but many in the United States also sought information from international sites (including the BBC and Al-Jazeera news sites). Such sources were important in offering alternative viewpoints, including Muslim perspectives.[22]

In 2001 non-Western media played an important role globally, particularly the Qatar-based, twenty-four-hour satellite news channel Al-Jazeera. Founded in 1996, Al-Jazeera gained a reputation for "bringing independent journalism to a region where much of the media are state-run or controlled," for offering alternative perspectives on Middle Eastern affairs and on wars in that region, for establishing Arab media "as a viable alternative to Western news organizations and … attracting global recognition of Arab media voices." During the "war on terror" other Arabic broadcasters such as Al-Arabiya, established in Dubai in February 2003, emerged. Later in the decade Al-Jazeera expanded its global reach by introducing English-language as well as Arabic services from centers in Doha, London, Washington, and Kuala Lumpur in 2006. (CNN also launched an Arabic website in 2002, and BBC World and Voice of America delivered services in Arabic.)[23]

Al-Jazeera attracted global attention with its coverage of the US-led war against Afghanistan. In October 2001 the United States launched military operations ("Operation Enduring Freedom") against Afghanistan to destroy al-Qaeda sanctuaries and remove the Taliban regime, which was considered sympathetic to terrorists. Al-Jazeera reporters documented the effects of US bombing on Afghan civilians, presenting very different footage from the "sanitized" US media coverage, which avoided showing civilian casualties. When a US bomb fell on Al-Jazeera's offices in Kabul, it was suggested that this was deliberate rather than accidental. (Another incident during the Iraq War in 2003, when Al-Jazeera attempted unsuccessfully to safeguard its office in Baghdad by providing the US military with details of its location, led Hoskins to conclude: "it appears that media organizations and their personnel can do little to protect themselves if reporting from outside of the systems laid down by the Pentagon."[24]) Given the subsequent policy of "embedding" during the 2003 war against Iraq, it is interesting to note that, although media were excluded during early operations in Afghanistan, a small number of selected journalists were "embedded" with US forces there in late 2001.

As the "war on terror" continued beyond 2001, media offered various interpretations. Some saw it as a "clash of civilizations" (Samuel Huntington's term), Western versus Muslim, with the rise in Islamic fundamentalism an important feature. Others considered particular wars – in Afghanistan and Iraq – as attempts by the United States to impose superpower dominance in the post-Cold War era. In January 2002 US President George W. Bush spoke of an "axis of evil," identifying Iran, North Korea, and Iraq as states supporting terrorism and developing "weapons of mass destruction" (WMDs). When the Bush administration decided on war against Saddam Hussein's regime in Iraq in 2003, it claimed that a major objective was to destroy WMDs. For the media, the "war on terror" presented challenges in terms of explanation and contextualization: difficulties in identifying "the enemy", the potential global scope but lack of geographical specificity compared with earlier wars that were defined in relation to nation states and their boundaries. Media – and decision-makers – were criticized for failing to subject the US claim about WMDs to close scrutiny, especially as no such weapons were located in Iraq.

When the US-led coalition launched "Operation Iraqi Freedom" against Iraq in March 2003, global media – both Western and Arabic – provided extensive coverage, making the war the most heavily televised to that time. Much of the discussion of media in the Iraq War has focused on the US decision (also applied by British forces) to implement a policy of "embedding" journalists. Over 700 reporters were "embedded" with coalition troops, each assigned to a particular unit by the military for the duration of operations. In addition, the US military gave regular briefings both in Washington and at Central Command Headquarters in Doha, Qatar (where a Hollywood-style backdrop was created for the briefings). As well as the embedded reporters there were others who covered the Iraq War independently, the "unilaterals," without assistance from coalition forces.[25]

While the term "embedding" gained prominence in 2003, this was not dissimilar from practices during earlier wars. However, critics of embedding saw it as a further step in more rigorous media management that imperiled good war reporting. The danger was that reporters would come to identify with their military colleagues, making objectivity difficult. They were still limited in what they could report because they depended on the military for transport and means of subsistence, even if new technologies (particularly portable satellite phones) meant they relied less on military-controlled means of communications. Embedded journalists necessarily witnessed only "slices" ("mosaic chips") of the action and were not in a position to provide "the big picture." They contributed a "soda-straw view, rich in human and tactical detail but poor in abstract and strategic oversight."[26] They were under pressure to satisfy the voracious appetite of global media and constantly provide news items, but it was difficult to gain a sense of distance and perspective, to offer critical analyses that went beyond everyday preoccupations.

Justin Lewis has argued persuasively that embedding was one element of an increasingly sophisticated approach by the military that integrated media management, psychological operations, and information war into overall strategy, incorporating public-relations practices into military planning. (The US Assistant Secretary of Defense for Public Affairs, Victoria Clarke, who had previously worked for the public-relations firm Hill and Knowlton, was a key figure in developing these aspects of military public affairs.) Embedding contributed to overall strategic objectives by putting a human face on combat operations and by providing such a volume of frontline footage that there was no room for Iraqi views or "disinformation." The integrated political and military strategy focused attention on the progress of the short (three-week) "media war" at the expense of broader issues of politics or ideology. The "media war" ended with the symbolic toppling of Saddam Hussein's statue on April 9, 2003. Lewis has also argued that, even though there was no formal military censorship, and embedded journalists could report freely as long as their reports would not endanger operational security, they appear to have exercised a degree of self-censorship, presenting "sanitized" coverage that avoided gruesome scenes, offering a view of the war that was no less sympathetic to the military than reporting under tightly managed situations.[27]

Apart from the mainstream media, which took content from embedded reporters and to a lesser extent from media briefings and independent ("unilateral") reporters, another significant source of information was the Internet. The Internet "came of age" as a news medium during the Iraq War. While traffic to Internet sites had increased enormously after "9/11," technical problems caused by congestion had meant that the Internet could not be considered entirely reliable as a source of news during the 2001 events. In the period after 2001 established media had continued to develop an online presence, and in 2003 expanded high-speed broadband access and enhancements meant that more users could access news sites that offered regularly updated news and features such as live audio and video reports, multimedia presentations, and interactive maps. Traffic to Internet sites increased dramatically with the beginning of the war on March 19, 2003. US media sites experienced greatly increased use – 9 million visitors to CNN.com in one day, 6.8 million to MSNBC; traffic to the UK *Guardian* newspaper's website increased by approximately 30 percent on 19 March to around 4.5 million impressions; the percentage rise for the BBC news site was similar.[28]

While established media used their websites to provide breaking news and to supplement print and broadcast coverage, the proliferation of blogs (see Chapter 11) – and specifically "warblogs" – meant that Internet users could access information that supplemented mainstream media coverage. Blogs written in Baghdad during the war, such as those of "Salam Pax," a 29-year-old architect who wanted to send news to a student friend in Jordan, and of "Riverbend," a 24-year-old Iraqi woman who began "Baghdad Burning: Girl Blog from Iraq" in 2003, became the focus of international attention. They offered vivid eyewitness accounts from an Iraqi perspective (and were considered sufficiently important by Western publishers later to be produced in book form[29]). Such civilian accounts and the products of "citizen journalism," which can be distributed easily and instantaneously via the Internet, have emerged as important sources additional to established media. In some cases they range beyond "the narrow ideological parameters of much Western news coverage;" importantly, they "have the capacity to bring to bear alternative perspectives, contexts and ideological diversity to war reporting, providing users with the means to connect with distant voices" that might otherwise be marginalized.[30]

Overall, assessments of media coverage of the 2003 Iraq War have been both positive and negative. On the positive side, embedding has been commended for improving the relations between media and military, for providing better access for war correspondents, and for doing away with the military security review (censorship) of copy that had applied in 1991. Reports from embedded reporters have been praised for their authenticity and immediacy. Contributions from "citizen journalists," easily accessible via the Internet, have been seen as useful supplements to mainstream media (although selecting from, and assessing the authenticity of, the volume of material can be a problem).

On the negative side are the criticisms of narrow coverage of only specific "slices" of the military action and of journalistic standards being compromised because embedded reporters found it difficult to be objective and maintain professional "distance." Mirzoeff, borrowing from Hannah Arendt, referred to the "banality of images" from the Iraq War; and Aday concluded that, despite embedding and access to advanced technology, coverage did not provide a more "realistic portrait" of war – there were few images of casualties, "a lot of action, but no consequences." US media, particularly Fox News, were labeled "weapons of mass deception" because they functioned as conduits for Bush administration and Pentagon propaganda and presented the war as a great military spectacle. The reporting of incidents such as the US Special Forces "rescue" of Private Lynch on April 1, 2003 has been likened to reality television, exemplifying "the constructed nature of the Iraq media spectacle." Furthermore, while journalists tended still to view the media–military relationship through the lens of censorship, the military had embraced a public-relations model that had less to do with preventing negative coverage than with creating positive coverage.[31]

Although the "media war" concluded swiftly in April 2003, and although US forces captured Saddam Hussein in December that year (he was convicted by the Iraqi interim government and executed on December 30, 2006), military occupation continued despite the transfer of sovereignty to Iraq. In the following years media attention tended to focus on specific incidents. In April 2004 evidence of prisoner abuse was reported by print and broadcast media after photographs had been circulated on the Internet. The photographs, taken at Abu Ghraib prison in Iraq by American soldiers, showed US military personnel, prison guards, and dogs torturing, terrorizing, and humiliating Iraqi prisoners (the images included sexually exploitative acts described as "porno-torture"). They were especially shocking, not only because they pointed to breaches of the Geneva Convention and US war crimes legislation, but also because of the apparent lack of any sense of wrongdoing on the part of those involved. Shortly after these photographs were made public, a video purporting to show the beheading of an American civilian in Iraq, Nick Berg, was released on the Internet by an Islamic organization. It was claimed that Berg's death was in revenge for the Abu Ghraib prison abuse. There was debate about the authenticity of the beheading video (including a suggestion that it might have been the product of US psychological warfare specialists "to provide the media with a moral relativity argument to counter the adverse publicity over torture at Abu Ghraib"[32]), and mainstream media were hesitant about publishing the Abu Ghraib photographs and the video. However, the important point is the ease with which war images can be circulated globally and the potential for such content to have an impact. (The Abu Ghraib photographs gave added impetus to investigations of prisoner abuse, which led in 2004–5 to a number of US military personnel receiving prison sentences, demotions, or being removed from duty, and to moves to close the Abu Ghraib facility.) While earlier wars had generated shocking images, the difference in the twenty-first century was the speed and ease with which testimony to the horror of war could be disseminated globally.

Terrorist attacks in other parts of the world have illustrated the potential of new media and scope for "citizen journalists" when traditional means of reporting are difficult. In central London on July 7, 2005 four suicide bombers detonated explosive devices on three Underground trains and a bus, killing themselves and 52 others, and injuring more than 700 people. The Secret Organization Group of Al-Qaeda of the Jihad Organization in Europe claimed responsibility. Because three of the bombings occurred in the Underground and media access was impossible, members of the public using mobile phones and digital cameras at the scenes of the bombings provided images and information during this terrorist incident. As in 2003, mainstream media used websites to provide breaking news, drawing on this "citizen journalist" material. They included content posted to personal blogs and invited eyewitnesses to contribute materials (photographs, amateur video, text messages, emails).[33]

Media coverage of the 2005 London bombings illustrates how technological change continues to affect news-gathering during times of crisis and the potential for greater "democratization of news coverage." However, such richness – and Allan has estimated that there were sixty times more blogs in 2006 than there had been three years previously, with some 75,000 new blogs being created every day – creates its own problems: how to filter/select, verify, deal with issues of intellectual property and with ethical aspects such as using photographs of victims.[34]

In conclusion, in media coverage of wars (and peacekeeping operations) of the second half of the twentieth and early twenty-first centuries noticeable changes due to evolving technologies were apparent: Vietnam as the "first television war," the 1991 Gulf War as the "first real-time war" with CNN delivering twenty-four-hour news to global audiences; the 1999 NATO air war against Serbia over the expulsion of Kosovar Albanians as the "first Web war;" the 2001 war in Afghanistan as the "first videophone war;" while the 2003 Iraq War saw warblogs on the Internet give global voice to the victims of war. However, the technological means of reporting war is only one of a range of important aspects to be considered in relation to media and war. Media–military relations became a major concern for media historians, particularly after the Vietnam War, the emergence in the United States of the "oppositional media" view, and subsequent efforts by the military to manage or control the media. Despite new approaches and different terminology ("embedding"), tensions are likely to continue to characterize the relationship between war reporters and the military and policymakers so long as the former remain committed to traditional journalistic values. In recent years other considerations have become a focus of attention, including the extent to which media are adequately covering a different kind of conflict, the "war on terror." Conclusions have tended to be critical: much mainstream coverage has presented a "sanitized" view in the case of specific war zones, and more generally the media have not significantly advanced public understanding by scrutinizing the bases for foreign-policy decisions or explaining broader ideological issues. Such criticisms, however, raise questions about what the public expects from media during war. For example, surveys in the United States have indicated nationalist and patriotic fervor at the time of crises such as 9/11 but low levels of public interest in international affairs at other times. Also, there is high public demand for infotainment rather than traditional genres such as current affairs, and programming based on the reality TV genre has enjoyed enormous popularity. Furthermore, increasing numbers of people are turning to the Internet as a source of information, with implications for the extent to which any form of "gatekeeping" or filtering role can be exercised by mainstream media organizations (or by states). Trends such as these suggest that developments in media coverage of war and international affairs are aligned with broader social trends and audience preferences.

11

The Rise of New Media

The mass media that developed between the late nineteenth century and the 1970s – the newspaper and magazine press, radio broadcasting, the film industry, television broadcasting – are now often referred to as "traditional media" (or "mainstream media"). As each developed on a mass scale, initial competition and uncertainty about the extent to which older media might survive gave way not only to accommodation but in many instances to mutually beneficial relationships. From the 1970s technological change made possible, and socio-economic, political, and ideological contexts provided opportunities for, the emergence of "new media." While new media potentially threatened established media, again accommodations proved possible, and in the complex global "mediascape" of the late twentieth century there seemed to be scope for both traditional and new media. Indeed, some traditional media owners embraced, and made extravagant claims for, new media. Rupert Murdoch in the 1990s hailed advances in telecommunications technologies, particularly satellite broadcasting, as "an unambiguous threat to totalitarian regimes everywhere."[1] The "dotcom" crash of 2000 cast some doubts on future developments, but its impact was short-lived, and during the first decade of the twenty-first century expansion of the Internet has been fundamental to many new media (and the concept "Web 2.0" suggests a second generation of the World Wide Web).

Ongoing, rapid technological change (made possible by digitization and manifest in "convergence") has produced a second wave of new media that may have the potential to change quite radically the relationship between "audiences" or "consumers" and media. Phenomena such as (online) social networking and large-scale projects built on participation and user-generated content (Wikipedia is the outstanding example) highlight the importance of examining the social uses of emerging media. The rapid rise of search media, particularly the global "giant" Google, is also part of new media history and draws attention to issues of access and to relationships between commercial interests and media. The contemporary media world in all its complexity includes adaptation by old media, the establishment of strategic alliances between old and new media, and more flexible modes of delivery; but there is an ever-present need for innovation, and there are particular challenges in meeting younger audience needs and establishing viable business models for the future.

There are different views on the overall political, social, and cultural significance of developments in new media. On the one hand, enthusiasts have claimed transformative impacts: new media are seen as liberating and democratizing, empowering citizens, promoting egalitarianism and tolerance, global understanding, and a global civil society. Critics, on the other hand, argue that the extent of change has been overstated, that their impact on politics has been slight, that they have merely reinforced the dominant role of big business, and that access to new media diverges so widely, because of continuing inequalities between rich and poor, that claims of global effects are simply not true. Aspects of these debates are considered here and in Chapter 12.

New Media and Convergence

The concept of convergence runs through the literature on new media, but there are differences of opinion about definitions of both "convergence" and "new media." Early definitions of "convergence" drew attention to technology, foreseeing the development of a single device through which diverse media content would be delivered. For example, in 2000 Peter Forman and Robert W. Saint John described convergence as "the union of audio, video and data communications into a single source, received on a single device, delivered by a single connection.... We will be able to enjoy movies, TV shows, Internet video, and music on our home theater, computer or wristwatch wherever we are, whenever we want." However, they recognized that convergence was more complicated than this, noting "three subsidiary convergences: content (audio, video and data); platforms (PC, TV, Internet appliance, and game machine); and distribution (how the content gets to your platform)."[2]

Current approaches place less emphasis on devices (which have continued to proliferate, despite earlier predictions) and more on consumer behavior. Henry Jenkins provides the following definition:

> Convergence: A word that describes technological, industrial, cultural, and social changes in the ways media circulates within our culture. Some common ideas referenced by the term include the flow of content across multiple media platforms, the cooperation between multiple media industries, the search for new structures of media financing that fall at the interstices between old and new media, and the migratory behavior of media audiences who would go almost anywhere in search of the kind of entertainment experiences they want. Perhaps most broadly, media convergence refers to a situation in which multiple media systems coexist and where media content flows fluidly across them. Convergence is ... an ongoing process or series of intersections between different media systems, not a fixed relationship.[3]

This affords a useful framework for considering new media, because it implicitly acknowledges the importance of context, it captures the important fact that media ("old" and "new") content can be accessed in many ways, that audience behavior is significant, that media industries are finding ways to navigate this changed world, and that change is ongoing.

In attempting to find a satisfactory definition of "new media," it is useful to think of two waves. The term became popular in the 1990s to describe changes dating from the 1980s, and the first wave included video, new ways of delivering television (via cable, satellite, direct broadcasting by satellite/DBS) on a subscription basis (pay television), CD-ROMs, various forms of multimedia, advanced facsimile machines, handheld databanks, electronic books, and videotext networks.[4] The second wave has been dominated by the extraordinary growth of the Internet and the World Wide Web. Continuing digitization, the development of wireless access, and ongoing technological developments have added various devices – DVDs, palmtop computers and personal digital assistants (PDAs), MP3 music players. Some efforts to define "new media" include software and features of the Web environment such as email, blogs, wikis, podcasting, and web application hybrids ("mashups"), or they adopt an all-embracing approach covering things that can be seen, "graphics, moving images, sounds, shapes, spaces, and texts that have become computable ... simply another set of computer data," as well as things that cannot be seen, such as WiFi (wireless networking) connections.[5] Relevant to the approach taken here are definitions that attend to use rather than underlying technologies. Martin Lister et al., for example, see new media as "those methods and social practices of communication, representation, and expression that have developed using the digital, multimedia, networked computer" and point to key characteristics – digitality, interactivity, hypertextuality, dispersal, virtuality. Terry Flew is sympathetic to such an approach, while noting core characteristics of new media: convergence of information and communications technologies, communications networks and media content; digitization of content so that it can be delivered speedily and stored in small physical spaces; networked distribution on a global scale through open, flexible, adaptable infrastructures; reduced access barriers to being a producer as well as a consumer of content; interactivity between producers and users; and the scope for multiple modes of communication not subject to traditional "gatekeeping" functions. He sees the critical questions about new media being their impact on social arrangements and organizational forms and how they are organized and governed.[6]

One important development during this second wave has been the "metamorphosis into media" of the mobile phone.[7] The rate of take-up of mobile phones has been extraordinary: it took about ten years to get to the first billion mobile subscribers globally, then some three and a half years to get to the second billion, but a mere eighteen months to get to the third. It is predicted that in 2008 "half of humanity will own a mobile handset. In a decade's time we'll have gone from half the world never having made a telephone call to half the world owning their own phone."[8] Because of digitization and convergence, mobile phones can be far more than devices for person-to-person communication. With wireless access to the Internet, they have the capacity to link to content that originates with traditional media but is made available via that platform; because they are "hybrid devices that articulate with other new technologies such as digital cameras, portable digital assistants, or location technologies," they are "of intense economic and political interest because they are at the centre of the vast transformation in communication and media summed up by the rubric of 'convergence', or 'digital technology' or 'new media'."[9] Already development of third- and fourth-generation mobile technology is underway, and the importance of such "mobile media" for the social uses of media is significant. Nonetheless, while the rise of the mobile phone has been rapid and its capacity to exploit convergence is considerable, it should not be forgotten that – if the estimate above is accurate – half of the world's population does not own a mobile phone and is not participating in the "vast transformation in communication and media."

In addition to appreciating ways in which the terms "convergence" and "new media" are used, it is worth noting that terms such as "digital media" are also current; that media in general are sometimes subsumed under the term "information and communications technologies" (ICTs); and that there is some support for abandoning distinctions between "old" and "new" media altogether and simply using the term "media." Some writers are being creative with terminology to emphasize their focus on social uses of media. Christina Spurgeon, in a work on advertising and the new media, refers to the "shift from mass media to the new media of mass conversation;" and Manuel Castells refers to the rise of "mass self-communication" to describe horizontal networks of interactive communications via the Internet, mobile communications, digital media, and social software to distinguish them from the top-down, one-way message distribution associated with mass media.[10]

The rise of new media must also be seen in the context of globalization not only because former boundaries (geographical, political, social) have lost much of their relevance but also because of evolving institutional frameworks and changes in media ownership, including strategic alliances that cross earlier media "borders" (see Chapter 12).

Early New Media, the Internet, and the World Wide Web

Media that were considered new in the 1980s have now merged into the complex "mediascape" of the twenty-first century. However, as they were being taken up on a mass scale, their likely impact on traditional media appeared threatening. For example, video recordings, home videotape players, and video rentals initially had a negative effect on the film industry, as cinema attendance and box-office revenue declined. However, the advent of video also opened up opportunities for existing media interests. In the early years of video there was considerable delay between box-office and video release of new films, but, when it became apparent how lucrative and popular the home video rental business was in the 1990s, film studios began almost simultaneous release of new films in cinemas and on video. While the film industry had suffered from declining ticket sales at cinemas, it benefited from increasing video sales, and established film studios became major providers for the home video entertainment industry. Corporations with large stakes in the American entertainment industry and links to the Hollywood studios – Fox, Warner, CIC, Columbia-Tristar – were prominent in video production and distribution. There were other spin-offs: the popularity of video helped to revive interest in cinema, and new multiplexes of numerous cinemas were built in major centers of population, cinema admissions increased, and public and media interest in film-related events such as festivals revived. While there would be ongoing problems (such as financial losses to the industry because of video piracy), the way in which the film industry came to accommodate, and reaped significant financial benefit from, the spread of home video illustrated not only the adaptability of traditional media but also the way in which an oligopoly of large corporations could establish dominance in new as well as old media.

Another potential threat to existing media emerged in the form of subscription television services (pay TV) delivered by cable or satellite. There had been experiments in Britain in the 1930s and then delivery of television signals to subscribers' homes via coaxial cable in the 1950s, but large-scale use of the technology followed the development of fiber-optic cables and the possibility of combining cable with satellite delivery. In the United States media interests began to use satellite services in conjunction with cable in the 1970s, transmitting to a particular locality by satellite, then by cable to individual households. Ted Turner bought a failing television station in Atlanta, Georgia, and transformed it into the first "superstation," WTBS, transmitting low-cost sports and entertainment programs via satellite to cable systems throughout the country. Gerald Levin of Time Inc. also did much to spread cable services, with Home Box Office disseminating film as home entertainment via cable services.[11] Other big names in the entertainment industries became involved: the Movie Channel, the Disney Channel, MTV for music entertainment, and Nickelodeon for children's television. US cable companies enjoyed growing profits in the 1980s and 1990s, challenging the free-to-air national networks by offering multi-channel services, catering to particular audience tastes, and providing greater choice than network programming. (Cable services have been less successful in other markets such as Britain, Western Europe, and Australia.)

The great cable television success story of the 1990s was Ted Turner's Cable News Network (CNN), founded in 1980 as an advertising-supported, twenty-four-hour service devoted entirely to news. It offered live coverage of events as well as regular programming devoted to international news, business and sports news, health issues, and enter-tainment news. CNN sprang into prominence as an influential global news provider during the Gulf War of 1991. By 1992 it was reaching a global audience of some fifty-three million viewers in 138 nations and sixty million in the United States. It remained important as a source of information for global audiences, as an influential news provider for other media, politicians, and policymakers, and as a model for other such services (see Chapters 8, 10 and 12).

While these services competed for viewers with the established free-to-air networks, they also drew the attention of advertisers, who began to shift advertising dollars from network to cable television in the 1980s. The national networks felt the combined impact of home video and cable/pay TV, and to a lesser extent of direct broadcasting by satellite (DBS). DBS broadcasts directly to viewers' homes, using receiving dishes purchased by individual households. It became available in the United States in the 1970s, in Europe in the 1980s, and in other parts of the world in the 1990s, but (with some exceptions such as News Corporation's BSkyB in Britain and Europe) has been less successful than cable services because of inadequate technology, weak financing, and poor marketing strategies.[12] By the end of the twentieth century, although network television in the United States had faced significant competition from new media such as video and pay TV, losing audi-ences and advertising revenue as a result, it was still the most pervasive of the mass media (see Chapters 8 and 9).[13] The second wave of new media – particularly developments in the Internet – would provide both threats and opportunities in the twenty-first century.

Expansion of the Internet has been one of the most significant devel-opments for media in the twenty-first century. This builds on a history that goes back to the 1950s and has depended on a range of technologi-cal advances. In 1957, against the Cold War background of heightened tension between the United States and the Soviet Union, especially

Soviet success in the space race with the launch of Sputnik, the first satellite, the US Department of Defense established the Advanced Research Projects Agency. The project involved designing a communications system capable of surviving nuclear attack. The intention was to create a decentralized system of linked computers so that information could be rerouted if any part of the network was damaged or ceased to function. The first network was named the Advanced Research Program Agency Network (ARPANET) and was used by computer experts in research centers associated with the US Department of Defense. Thus the origins of the Internet lay in a national security project based on military and strategic concerns. This can be considered the first phase of Internet development.[14]

Over the following decades the Internet emerged as a means of linking research centers and academic institutions, its growing use linked closely with the spread of computers. Electronic mail – email – developed for communications purposes, and mail lists were created to disseminate information. Use expanded considerably as more host computers were linked to the network. In 1969 only four host computers were connected; by 1980 there were 213.

In the 1980s the network moved into a second phase of development and further away from its original military strategic purpose. In the United States the National Science Foundation took over the Department of Defense role, established five supercomputing centers around the country, linked them with its own high-speed network, NSFNet, and encouraged research institutions to form regional networks, producing the basic structure of the Internet with its multiple layers of networks. As use of the network expanded, it became necessary to introduce various organizational principles and practices. In 1986 domain names were introduced ("edu." for educational institutions, "com." for commercial enterprises, "mil." for military forces).

Arrangements to extend and provide reliable access to the Internet were important in the 1980s and 1990s. Academic networks negotiated with telecommunications companies, prompting the emergence of Internet service providers (ISPs). Commercially based companies began to provide Internet services, and what was originally a tax-funded enterprise was handed over to the private sector. CompuServe started in 1979 and by the mid-1980s claimed 3.2 million users in 120 countries. America Online also emerged, with commercial relationships with the German group Bertelsmann and the French group Hachette. The

National Science Foundation in 1995 handed over the backbone of the system and its management to private telecommunications companies, Sprint, Ameritech, and Pacific Bell.

Use grew rapidly, particularly as personal-computer ownership increased: in the late 1980s some 90,000 computers were linked to the Internet, and the numbers expanded from 1.3 million in 1993 to 9.5 million (estimated to be linking some forty million people) in 1996, to 19.5 million host computers with registered IP addresses in 1997. By 1998 more than 100 million email messages were being sent daily. Dramatic growth continued, so that by 1999 there were approximately 153 million users worldwide; by the end of 2007 this had risen to 1,262 million.

While Internet use rose very rapidly, considerable inequalities in access persisted. Most African countries lagged behind the world in Internet use. In July 2000 Somalia had approximately 200 Internet users; South Africa had almost 60 percent (1.8 million) of all African Internet users; and less than 0.2 percent of the 760 million people in the rest of Africa had access. Internet use in Africa did grow by almost 880 percent between 2000 and 2007, but Internet penetration in 2007 was still only 4.7 percent of the total population (compared with 71 percent for North America). In the Middle East, despite rapid growth (920 percent between 2000 and 2007), only 17.4 percent of the population had access to the Internet in 2007; and, despite considerable expansion in China, for Asia as a whole Internet penetration was to only 12.4 percent of the population. Extension of broadband is critical to further significant growth. In 2007 China had the second highest number of Internet broadband subscribers (48.5 million) after the United States (66 million), but that number represented only 3.7 percent of the Chinese population (for India the figure was only 0.2 percent).

In addition to access, other aspects illustrated distortions or inequalities: for example, a high proportion of computer hosts located in the United States and Europe, the bulk of online content generated in those regions. English has remained the "top Internet language" (accounting for some 380 million users in late 2007, or 30 percent of all Internet users). However, between 2000 and 2007 the use of Chinese grew rapidly (approximately 185 million or 15 percent of all users), and, while starting from a low base, the rate of growth for Arabic between 2000 and 2007 was 1,576 percent (to some 46.3 million, or 4 percent of all users), indicating some change in the extent of English-language dominance on the Internet. It is also important to note that, although it is not easy to impose censorship in the decentralized Internet, governments can – and do – censor content and impose controls on media organizations, thus limiting users' access to certain types of content (see Chapter 12).[15]

During its early development phase the Internet not only provided a means of communicating and transferring information; it also offered new and alternative modes of expression. New terms such as "cyberspace" gained currency – from William Gibson's 1989 novel, *Neuromancer*. Users established new conventions – for example, the use of symbols and punctuation to convey "emotion" in text messages and the descriptive term "emoticons" in 1979. Groups used electronic news groups and bulletin boards to share information and exchange ideas. The notion of "virtual communities" emerged, implying that geographical distance had become irrelevant. (Debate continues in the twenty-first century about the importance of "virtual worlds." One view is that their importance has been exaggerated and that they merely extend real-world structures and processes rather than reconfiguring society.[16] Social networking has led to concerns about various aspects of "virtual worlds" – see below.) Throughout the 1990s regional and international organizations, including the European Commission and the World Trade Organization, supported growth of the Internet as a vehicle for mass communications.

The work of Tim Berners Lee at the European Laboratory for Particle Physics (CERN) led to the introduction in 1991–2 of the World Wide Web. Berners Lee developed Hypertext Markup Language (HTML), software (the WorldWideWeb) to view HTML documents, and the Hypertext Transfer Protocol (HTTP), a new protocol for distributing information via the Internet. New ways of accessing information were created: the Mosaic web browser, developed at the University of Illinois and made freely available to universities and colleges in 1993, followed in 1994 by the first commercial browser, Netscape.

With increased use of the World Wide Web, growth was rapid, and the Internet entered a third phase of development in the mid-1990s. There was greater commercialization, a shift from educational to commercial use, from e-communication to e-commerce. As mass use of the Internet developed, it became obvious to advertisers that this was a new vehicle for marketing products and a potentially important player in consumer societies. Web-based advertising became attractive, new features such as banner advertisements were included on websites, and businesses began to develop their own websites. By 1996 Internet advertising revenue was estimated at $300 million, compared with advertising revenue going to traditional broadcast television of some $38 billion.[17]

Powerful corporations became involved in commercial exploitation of the Internet, with Microsoft an outstanding example. Established by Bill Gates in the 1970s, Microsoft developed computer languages such as BASIC, FORTRAN, COBOL, and Pascal, and in 1980 entered into an agreement with IBM to supply software for IBM's first personal computer, as well as developing the disk operating system (DOS). In the 1980s Microsoft went on to develop software that became virtually the universal standard (Microsoft Word for word processing, Excel for spreadsheets) and the Windows operating system. The company went public in 1986, and by the 1990s it was showing massive profits. Its business practices – considered by some to be excessively aggressive – and its success in having its software included as "part of the package" with personal computers attracted attention in the 1990s. Legal suits were brought against Microsoft for monopolistic practices, and for stifling competition. Given the ubiquity of Microsoft products on computers worldwide and its global reach and power, it was questionable whether penalties would achieve any diminution in the influence of the giant corporation. Microsoft remained important into the twenty-first century as a global provider of computer software. With Bill Gates withdrawing from day-to-day management of Microsoft, and with the rise of Google, it was suggested that Microsoft had ceded its place to Google, although a Microsoft bid for Yahoo! in 2008 indicated the company's interest in expanding into the area of search (see below).[18]

By the end of the twentieth century, with the withdrawal of the US government and with greater private company involvement, the nature of the Internet had changed substantially since its beginnings. Internet service providers such as America Online, Yahoo!, and Microsoft Network had become important players, managing or renting physical assets and enabling subscriber access to the system. ISPs exercised a degree of control by setting charging policies and playing a "gatekeeper" role, using portals to structure or customize content, categorize web pages, and direct users to particular resources. While a range of interests had taken advantage of the Internet, including small businesses and non-government organizations, mass-media conglomerates had played an important role in its development, in the process reinforcing their corporate dominance.

In the late 1990s great optimism about the future of the Internet fostered speculation on a grand scale, with millions of dollars being invested in "dotcom" ventures. The stock exchange established to deal with high-technology stocks and shares, the Nasdaq, reflected both the buoyancy and volatility of the e-world market. Following dramatic rises, the Nasdaq began falling from March 2000, venture capitalists became wary of investment in Internet start-up companies, and there were casualties of the "dotcom" crash, which ushered in a period of greater caution about the e-environment.

In spite of the events linked with the stock market, the Internet had wrought significant changes in global communications by the year 2000. Services such as email facilitated instantaneous and easy contact between individuals; listservs, synchronous chat services, and asynchronous online forums linked users in inexpensive and user-friendly ways. Electronic networking encouraged some advocates of the e-world to make large claims for the Internet. It was suggested that Marshall McLuhan's idea (from the 1960s) of a "global village" was achievable: the Internet removed the limitations of time and place, enabling global interaction; it potentially empowered groups and individuals on the socio-economic and geographical margins because of interactivity and independence of existing power structures. Its decentralization would, it was argued, have a democratizing impact. Against these claims, especially with increasing commercialization, others argued that use of the Internet was determined by the economics of production and distribution, and arguments about empowerment and its democratizing potential ignored enormous inequalities of access. Such debates have continued through the most recent phase of Internet development.

"Web 2.0," Blogging, Social Networking, User-Generated Content, and Search Media

The term "Web 2.0" came into use after a 2004 conference. Although it suggests a second generation of technologies, Tim Berners Lee, who pioneered the first World Wide Web ("Web 1.0"), has argued, among others, that it does not refer to an update in technical specifications but rather to changes in the ways the Web is used. Important to Web 2.0 are ideas of participation and interactivity, the sharing of data, content, and platforms, encouragement of innovation through such sharing and networking, with software to support these activities. Examples include blogging, podcasting, forums, wikis, various open source initiatives, as well as the release of source code of Application Programming Interfaces/APIs to facilitate user innovation of web application hybrids or "mashups."

These developments constitute what might be considered the fourth phase of Internet development, characterized by the growing importance of user-generated content, the rapidly expanding phenomenon of online social networking through websites such as MySpace, Facebook, and Bebo, and easy ways of customizing or individualizing content accessed on the Internet (for example, through Really Simple Syndication/RSS feeds). A simple comparison is to see Web 1.0 as an information source and Web 2.0 as a participatory environment. However, as with an earlier phase of Internet evolution, its importance in commercial terms should not be underestimated. Another way of considering Web 2.0 is to see it as differentiating "those internet businesses that survived and prospered following the collapse in the market value of technology stocks in 2000, from those that did not.... Where Web 1.0 firms view the internet as a platform for publishing and selling, Web 2.0 firms, such as Amazon.com and Google, use it as a services interface ... to facilitate advertiser and consumer participation and interaction."[19]

Rapid and widespread take-up of blogging and social networking illustrate social uses of the Web 2.0 environment. Such development has been possible because of the expansion of infrastructure, which allows speedy Internet access as well as the continuing spread of personal computers and other devices such as mobile phones and PDAs that support easy connections. "Blogs" emerged in the late 1990s. The term is a shortened form of "weblog," an individual's online diary or journal, regularly updated, with most recent entries at the top (reverse chronological order). (The term "weblog" is attributed to Jorn Barger, who, in 1997, was keeping a daily net journal, "Robot Wisdom," and the shorter version, "blog," to Peter Merholz in 1999.) Early blogs specialized in providing links to other websites on matters that were of interest to the "blogger," that is, a "log" of relevant sites, and they required a degree of technical expertise, including mastery of HTML. Software was developed to facilitate the production and maintenance of blogs, and the online form has evolved to include other formats as well as text – photoblogs, vlogs (of videos), moblogs (written from a mobile phone or PDA), MP3 blogs (of music), and micro-blogs (very short postings). Another feature is that many foster interaction (with opportunities to comment) and a sense of community (encouraging repeat visits for those with shared interests).

Blogs attracted widespread attention during times of crisis, in 2001 after "9/11" and in 2003 during the Iraq War. In September 2001 bloggers provided links to content on relevant sites for citizens anxious for updated information after the terrorist attacks. Similarly, in the early phase of the Iraq War in 2003 blogs became a source of information supplementing mainstream media coverage with different views of the war. Notable examples were the blogs by "Salam Pax" and "Riverbend," eyewitness accounts from an Iraqi perspective in Baghdad.[20]

In 2003 the word "blog" was included in the *Oxford English Dictionary*. During the five years 2002–7 the number of blogs worldwide (tracked by the blog search engine Technorati, established in 2002) grew at an extraordinary rate: whereas 20,000 were identified in 2002, by 2006 the "blogosphere" was sixty times bigger than three years previously, and by the end of 2007 there were 112 million (although how many were active is another question – one estimate was about fifteen million; some analysts were suggesting that the novelty value of blogs was wearing off and that many former bloggers had ceased posting to their online diaries, creating much unwanted "dotsam" and "netsam" on the Web).[21]

While early weblogs were the preserve of a few online enthusiasts, blogs can now be seen as just another component of the twenty-first-century "mediascape." They have come to play a role in politics alongside traditional media, used successfully by some political candidates and with negative results for others. In some instances blogs have been the first to break news subsequently picked up by mainstream media. In 2004 bloggers were responsible for what is referred to as "Rathergate," when they questioned the authenticity of documents concerning US President George Bush's National Guard service presented on CBS's *60 Minutes* program by the veteran television journalist Dan Rather. CBS issued an apology, and Rather announced he would retire in 2005, a year earlier than planned.

Alliances and crossovers with mainstream media have become commonplace. Long-established organizations such as the BBC support blogs; news agencies source content from blogs; bloggers who have gained a reputation in the online world have gone on to publish books or work for traditional media. The world of advertising has entered the "blogosphere," with personal bloggers writing sponsored posts for advertisers. Individuals select the products they want on their sites and are paid according to number of clicks on the relevant image (which may link to another site about the product). Blogs have been "absorbed" into the media world.

Social networking, like blogging, has experienced a dramatic rise as Internet users – especially "digital natives," the younger generation – have flocked to join social networking websites. In January 2008 Wikipedia listed 97 such sites, citing extraordinary numbers of registered users for the most popular. They include MySpace, popular in the USA, UK, and Australia with 217 million registered users; orkut, popular in Brazil and India with 67 million users; Facebook 58 million; Friendster 50 million; hi5 50 million; and Bebo 40 million.[22]

These sites are based on users providing personal information and using the network to develop their circle of friends. For example, MySpace users post their personal profile (which they can customize) and can submit other content (photographs, music, videos), engage in a group, and maintain a blog. With their profiles, musicians can upload a number of MP3 songs, and music sharing has become a popular feature of the site. Access via mobile phone (through carriers such as AT&T and Vodafone) and instant messaging features are available, as well as a news service with RSS feeds.

MySpace is an example of traditional media incorporating online activities: established by eUniverse (later Intermix) in 1999, it was purchased by Rupert Murdoch's News Corporation in July 2005 for $580 million. It has continued to expand, establishing a number of regional sites in 2006–7. (The Chinese version, launched in April 2007, has been contentious. In order to operate in China, restrictions had to be observed, with filtering of content on matters such as Taiwan, the Dalai Lama, and Falun Gong, and users able to report others for offences including "endangering national security, leaking state secrets, subverting the government, undermining national unity, and spreading rumors or disturbing the social order."[23]) MySpace illustrates how novel uses of media are incorporated into mainstream activities: it has been used by political candidates, as in Australia when Labor Party candidates used the MySpace Impact channel, launched in July 2007 prior to that year's federal election. MySpace has also become a major advertising platform as a result of an agreement between News Corporation and Google. This $900 million deal gave Google rights to sell advertising on Fox Interactive Media properties including MySpace. Spurgeon notes that a social network such as MySpace has commercial value not only as a channel for communicating advertising messages but also because it can be used as a market research platform "where advertisers would be invited into the quasi-private worlds of young consumers ... MySpace opens up unprecedented opportunities for News Corporation to capture market intelligence that will be highly valuable for cross-platform marketing of News Corporation content brands, as well as those of other advertisers." Significantly as far as media are concerned, she points to the enhancement of News Corporation's "specialist knowledge in media targeted to youth demographics. In future, News Corporation could more closely resemble a specialist youth marketing company than a media and content company."[24]

Another popular social networking site is Facebook. Developed at Harvard College and named after the facebooks issued to incoming college students and staff, it was launched in February 2004. It was initially restricted to Harvard College students but was soon made available to other universities and high schools, and from September 2006 was opened to anyone aged 13 or older. It is similar to MySpace in that users maintain their personal profile, share photos, plan events, and seek people they know, send gifts (icons of novelty items), but it has less scope for customization of individuals' sites. The corporate world has become involved in Facebook too: millions of dollars have been invested by venture capital companies; Microsoft purchased a 1.6 percent share for $240 million in October 2007, and in November 2007 it was announced that twelve global brands (including Coca-Cola, Blockbuster, Sony Pictures) would participate through Facebook Ads. The site offers considerable scope for advertising: businesses can host pages for brands, products, and services; "Facebook Social Ads" is a targeted advertising program based on users' profiles and activity data; and "Facebook Insights" provides advertisers with analytic data. One critic describes Facebook as a "heavily funded program to create an arid global virtual republic, where your own self and your relationships with your friends are converted into commodities on sale to giant global brands."[25]

Bebo, another social networking site established in 2005 and popular in Europe, North America, Australia, and New Zealand, encourages bands and solo performers through "Bebo Music" (begun in mid-2006, enabling musicians to create a profile showcasing their music and upload music) and writers through "Bebo Authors" (begun in early 2007, for authors to upload chapters and have them reviewed). It offers a mobile service allowing users to receive text alerts and update their profile using their mobile phone. Bebo has also created the opportunity for collaboration between traditional and new media with the "Bebo Open Media Platform." In late 2007 organizations such as CBS, Sky, and the BBC were reported to have reached agreements with Bebo to make video content available via this platform, allowing "the media companies to take their content to where people are spending their time online."[26]

Other social networking sites are popular in particular geographical areas: Friendster, a privately owned service established in 2002, is most used in Asia and available in Chinese, Hindi, Japanese, Korean, Spanish, Indonesian. Hi5, also founded in 2002, is popular in Central and South America and parts of Asia. The social networking site run by Google, orkut, launched in January 2004, is most used in Brazil, followed by India. Others dominate in particular countries: Cyworld in South Korea, LunarStorm in Sweden, LiveJournal in Russia, Mixi in Japan, Skyblog in France, and Arto in Denmark. Slightly different but also promoting social networking and global communications is Twittervision.com, a site that combines the online equivalents of private text messages (postings – or "tweets" – are limited to 140 characters) with Google maps to provide a continuous scrolling of new "tweets" from around the globe. Users create a brief profile, and their postings usually focus on what they are doing at the time.

While social networking sites offer unprecedented opportunities for easy communication at the global level and for extending circles of acquaintances and developing friendships, during the short time they have existed they have become controversial. One of the most serious concerns relates to privacy and the extent to which (especially young) people are readily divulging personal information. Associated with this are questions not only about privacy but about identity and the extent to which details of everyday lives are being recorded and are ever more readily accessible through mobile devices. The enormous quantities of personal data can be misused (identity theft), exploited (users have become victims of pedophiles or sex offenders in the real world as a result of contact in the virtual world), used as "intelligence" or for surveillance purposes by authorities or prospective employers. Other concerns relate to the time young people spend in online communities, the apparent superficiality of many online "relationships," and the impact of virtual engagement on "real" social relationships. Lister et al. summarize a moderate view on these issues: the real world is not left behind, but new media do have an impact on everyday life in that technology, media, performance, play, consumption, family, and gender relationships are intertwined.[27] The dangers of cyberbullying in social networking sites have also drawn attention (following reports of death threats, derogatory comments about students and teachers on social networking sites, and youth suicide allegedly because of online cruelty and harassment). While bullying is not new, the online environment can embolden persecutors (not coming face-to-face with their victim, feeling protected by anonymity), provide access to previously private activities (photographs taken on mobile phones in a school sports change room can quickly be uploaded to a website and distributed widely), and exacerbate the effects of bullying (victims are unable to escape – cyberbullying knows no boundaries and transcends the schoolyard – and demeaning or humiliating information can be spread to a global audience in a short time).[28]

Finally, as indicated above, some social networking sites have become closely linked to commercial concerns and advertising. This raises an important question about the extent to which their purpose as platforms for social networking has been subverted, turning them into marketing platforms and in some cases implicating users themselves as advocates of particular brands or advertising content generators. As a result of such concerns some schools and public libraries (in countries including the United States, the United Kingdom, Australia, Malaysia) have restricted access to social networking sites.

Although not classified as a social networking website, another significant venture based on user-generated content is the video-sharing, participatory online site YouTube. It was created in February 2005 and grew rapidly: by July 2006 some 65,000 videos were being added daily, localized versions in the relevant languages were launched in many countries in 2007; and by January 2008 it was said to host more than sixty million videos, with an average 800,000 being added daily.[29] Like MySpace, YouTube was purchased by a global corporation, Google, in

October 2006 (for $1.65 billion). Also like some of the social networking sites, its content is accessible not only via computer but on mobile phones, MP3 players, and via YouTubeTV. YouTube too has a business model dependent on advertising, even though its content is provided by users; in 2007 some users were invited to become YouTube partners and earn revenue from advertisements placed next to their videos. Like other online sites, YouTube has created celebrities, some of whom have "crossed over" to work with established media or whose work has been picked up by the mainstream. (The most popular YouTube video of 2007, "Obama Girl," achieved extraordinary circulation, being viewed more than four million times as well as featured on television news and talk shows; another 2007 video of a battle between water buffaloes, lions, and a crocodile in South Africa's Kruger National Park was viewed more than twenty-one million times, featured on television news and in *Time* magazine, and will be the basis for a documentary for National Geographic Channel.[30])

Of all the recent online services YouTube has become most prominent in politics, being used by political candidates in countries including the United States, France, Italy, and Australia. It has joined with mainstream media to provide new forms of political engagement: in the run-up to the 2008 US presidential elections YouTube invited users to submit questions for a debate among Democratic Party political candidates that was aired by CNN. (This inspired references to "the YouTube election.") While YouTube can be seen as a democratizing influence, encouraging greater citizen engagement in politics – particularly among young people, who are seen as having become disengaged from politics in many countries – use of YouTube for political purposes has its problems. Viewers can be very unforgiving of politicians unaccustomed to operating in the online environment; hoaxes can be perpetrated and inauthentic materials circulated in an environment where party organizations, politicians, and their media offices have little control; and viral video campaigning, using computers and mobile devices, can be swift and widespread, characteristic of a far less filtered world than the one dominated by old media. As to whether YouTube and the Internet more generally represent a force for political emancipation, while they may have encouraged some citizens to engage in politics in new ways, it remains the case that " 'real world' activism and political engagement are still needed to bring about real change."[31]

YouTube illustrates another set of challenges in the online environment: how to deal with issues of copyright and how to manage site content to ensure that materials are not published that are pornographic, defamatory, or encourage criminal conduct. With the enormous volume of video content uploaded to the site, there have been many breaches of copyright (film clips, music videos, television shows, and so on). Google has used anti-piracy software, agreements with media companies (since October 2007 they can block their copyrighted video content loaded onto YouTube without seeking prior permission), and ongoing work on content filtering in an attempt to deal with the problem. In addition to copyright, other issues include videos posted showing violence, sexual content, racist abuse, and animal abuse. Because of controversial content on the site, parts or all of YouTube have been blocked in some countries (including Morocco, Iran, Turkey, and the United Arab Emirates).

Another site that deserves attention is Second Life, which is not a social networking site but an Internet-based virtual world. Developed by Linden Research, Inc. and launched in 2003, it offers "virtual immersion" in a fantasy world where the slogan is "your world, your imagination." Users create an avatar (which allows anonymity) to negotiate Second Life, where the avatar can interact with others in a three-dimensional environment (walking, flying, teleporting to engage in activities such as shopping or visiting museums and galleries). While Second Life has experienced rapid growth and claimed twenty million registered accounts in 2007, there are no reliable figures on long-term, consistent use.

As well as offering a "virtual world," another distinguishing feature of Second Life is that users ("residents") can create products, trade them (using the virtual currency, Linden dollars), and exchange virtual for real-world currencies in a marketplace of Linden Lab and Second Life residents. Second Life earns revenue through sales of virtual land and regular maintenance fees paid by residents with land and premium accounts. It has been estimated that over a twenty-four-hour period in 2007 the equivalent of approximately US$1.3 million was spent in Second Life.[32] As use of Second Life expanded, some large companies established a virtual presence. For media and communications companies Second Life offered opportunities to gain brand recognition and to link virtual and real worlds. The Australian Broadcasting Corporation, for example, became a resident, enabling it to provide program content via podcasts to other Second Life residents. (Some countries have established virtual embassies in Second Life; universities and colleges have opened virtual campuses; politicians have established a presence.) Problems associated with Second Life include "grey areas" about the applicability of taxation legislation, digital rights management, and codes of behavior, conduct, and social communication.

The social networking sites YouTube and Second Life exemplify new uses of media that are generating vast quantities of content. The term "user-generated content" (describing web publishing and new-media content production) became current in the first decade of the twenty-first century, and in 2006 *Time* magazine asserted its importance by announcing that the person of the year was "You." Such media production obviously depends on easily accessible technologies and software supporting blogging, digital video, podcasting, mobile-phone photography, wikis, and open-source collaboration.

Any account of user-generated content would be incomplete without consideration of Wikipedia. Founded by Jimmy Wales in 2001, the encyclopedia (named from the Hawaiian expression "wiki, wiki," meaning "quick") is based on wiki software that allows collaborative writing and editing, with anyone able to contribute. The intention is to develop free, open content in an ideologically neutral manner, using collaborative information-gathering, and not deferring to experts. It illustrates a shift in media production, with content creation in the hands of users (seen as creative and participatory) rather than established media organizations. From a modest beginning – 20,000 entries in its first year – Wikipedia grew rapidly to about two million entries in early 2006, and by 2007 it had become the largest and most extensive encyclopedia in human history, with more than seven million articles in more than 200 languages. Comparisons have been drawn between the venerable *Encyclopaedia Britannica*, which first appeared in the eighteenth century, and Wikipedia, which has, in a short time, outstripped it in total number of entries. (A survey by *Nature* in 2005 compared forty-two entries on scientific topics and found that Wikipedia had four errors for every three in the *Encyclopaedia Britannica*.)[33]

While its growth has been extraordinary, demonstrating the potential for user-generated content to create "products" that were previously unimaginable, there are great differences of opinion about the accuracy and reliability of entries, and there is discontent about lack of recourse regarding false claims or defamatory statements (Wikimedia

Foundation is only a hosting company, not a publisher, and therefore cannot be sued). There are also uncertainties about the future of Wikipedia – the extent to which it will be able to remain true to the original vision and not "succumb" to bureaucratic structures, powerful administrators, and arbitrators (tension between "deletionists" and "inclusionists" has been reported); whether the flood of contributions will dry up; whether focus on the encyclopedia will be diluted by the addition of other services (Wikinews, drawing on citizen journalism, was added in 2004). Some of the debate is about fundamental questions such as what constitutes knowledge – does Wikipedia offer knowledge that is useful as opposed to knowledge that is reliable; has it shifted what counts as knowledge away from topics sanctioned by traditional encyclopedias to "a much broader range of topics of interest to specialized interest groups and subcultures"? – and what counts as expertise (recognized academic authorities or "collective intelligence"?). Others see Wikipedia as symbolic: "Wikipedia is a combination of manifesto and reference work. Peer review, the mainstream media and government agencies have landed us in a ditch. We are impatient with the authorities and in a mood to talk back. Wikipedia offers endless opportunities for self-expression." However, contributors gain no financial reward for that self-expression (their intellectual property). As one critic notes: "Many Wikipedia entries are excellent but many others are inaccurate, stupid or vandalized beyond repair. In the wiki world everyone is an expert whether they are trained or not. The unifying factor is that no one is paid a cent."[34]

User-generated content has positive connotations in allowing for participation and peer collaboration, and claims are made that it may "pose a challenge to mainstream media's monopoly role in the production, packaging and distribution of cultural content." Nonetheless, from the comments above it is apparent that there are advantages and disadvantages. Although user-generated content may challenge mainstream media, it is also a source of (often free) content. Large organizations actively encourage non-media professionals' involvement both to provide new content and to use existing content in new ways (the BBC set up a user-generated content team in 2005; CNN launched iReport in 2006 to bring user-generated news content to CNN; Fox News Channel has uReport, Sky News solicits photographs and videos from viewers).[35] Furthermore, there are issues concerning intellectual property and the extent to which content-creators in online environments are protected. There are also questions about users in some online contexts becoming tools for advertisers, both endorsing products and in some cases freely creating advertisements (there is now a view that people tend to trust user-generated advertisements more than company-generated advertisements).

In the context of these "new media of mass conversation" and of the enormous volume of content available via the Internet – including content from traditional media as well as (citizen) user-generated content – search media have become very influential. Search engines have established the Internet as an advertising medium and platform for commercial activities as well as a means of purveying information and entertainment. Battelle points to the considerable power of a search engine such as Google, claiming that search will "rewire the relation-ship" between citizens and their governments.[36] At least of equal impor-tance is the extent to which search is delivering Internet users to powerful commercial interests through online advertising.

Google, like earlier search engines such as WebCrawler, Lycos, and Altavista, was designed to help users locate information on the Internet. It began as the research project of students Larry Page and Sergey Brin at Stanford University in 1996. (The name originated from the misspell-ing of "googol," the number 1 followed by 100 zeros.) They registered Google.com in 1997; and Google Inc. was incorporated as a privately held company in 1998. It escaped the worst effects of the "dotcom" crash of 2000, and by 2000 had grown into the world's largest search engine, with over one billion pages in its index of websites. In the following year AOL/America Online adopted Google as its search engine, adding millions of users. In August 2004 Google became a public corporation, its initial public offering of stock raised $1.67 billion, and by that year it was indexing eight billion web pages. By 2006 it had become so much part of contemporary culture that the verb "to google", meaning to use the Google search engine to obtain information on the Internet, was added to the *Oxford English Dictionary*. The company began with an idealistic mission of making the world's information freely accessible and useful, and its slogan continues to be "Don't be evil." It has retained a reputation for having a relaxed corporate culture that fosters strong loyalty and innovation and for being a good corpo-rate citizen (emphasizing sustainable environmental practices, sup-porting global public health) even while it has become a vast global corporation deriving its income from advertising.[37]

Its success has derived particularly from the original page ranking search strategy developed by Page and Brin; its relatively economical infrastructure (servers and low-cost computers in data centers around the world); and the exploitation of advertising opportunities linked to search. A system was developed to sell advertisements associated with search keywords; the small text ads appear to the right of the free search results (it has been suggested that many Google users do not realize these "Sponsored Links" are in fact advertisements); and advertisers are charged on the basis of price bids or the number of clicks on ads. The Google system is the reverse of mass marketing via mainstream media; rather, advertisements are triggered by consumer preferences identified through search. Google has profited from the expansion of the Internet, the desire of advertisers to access online consumers, and the resultant move of advertising expenditure away from traditional media to the Internet (in 2006 the company's reported advertising revenue was $10.5 billion). Google's pricing strategy also made it attractive for small and medium-sized businesses, because no large financial outlay was required, and the advertising was more targeted than mass-media advertising.

Initially specializing in text-based Internet searching, Google expanded its services to include image searching, web-based email, online mapping, video sharing (it acquired YouTube in 2006 – see above), news delivery (based on access to thousands of news sites, regular updates, and scope for users to customize, filter, and personalize stories according to region, language, user interests), text messaging, and services aimed at the academic community (Google Scholar searches peer-reviewed papers, theses, books, abstracts, articles, preprint repositories, universities, and other scholarly organizations).

Google has entered partnerships with established media interests such as Time Warner AOL, News Corporation, the *New York Times*, and various news agencies such as Associated Press, Agence France-Presse, the UK Press Association; it has ventured into other advertising markets with traditional media, newspapers, and radio; it has made Google services available via mobile devices; in 2007 there were reports that Google might invest in infrastructure (a trans-Pacific undersea cable to facilitate high-speed communications, with implications for Internet access in the Asia–Pacific region) and that it was involved in a business alliance to develop a mobile phone that would include Google software to support social networking, video sharing, and other services. Google

Earth, the interactive mapping program linked with satellite and imaging, has revolutionized access to maps on a global scale (provoking fears about national security in some quarters). One of Google's most ambitious projects, announced in late 2004, is the digitization of some fifteen million books, a collaborative venture with major university libraries such as Oxford, Harvard, Michigan, New York, and Stanford. This too has provoked debate about copyright, cultural integrity, and the different motivations behind the unilateral, monocultural, commercial Google concept (with Google as "chief cultural broker") compared with a multilateral European Union digital library project based on collaboration among European libraries and governments. A bleak cultural view of this and other Google projects sees them as symptomatic of an obsession with "seeing everything in the universe as 'information' to be linked and ranked," foreshadowing the possibility that culture will be reduced to "machine-generated lists of what everyone else is looking at." Furthermore, "there is a catch. Google bears the costs of producing high quality, fully searchable, digital archives in return for the right to direct users to appropriate sales sites."[38]

Google has been remarkably successful in developing global brand awareness without itself spending heavily on advertising and marketing. It has succeeded partly because Internet searching has become embedded in everyday practice (at least in those parts of the world with Internet access); but Google has also taken advantage of its affiliations with established global corporations – the Google search box, name, and logo feature on sites of partners such as AOL.[39] Google has become a giant with complex entanglements with traditional and new media. David Vise indicates its relative "worth" against other twenty-first-century companies: during the first year after going public Google was worth more than the world's biggest media company, Time Warner; and by 2006 its stock-market value was greater than Amazon, eBay, and Yahoo! combined, and greater than Disney, Ford, and General Motors combined.[40]

Google certainly offers users many advantages as an Internet search tool: it is free, simple, accessible, and indexes vast quantities of data. However, it is criticized on various counts. One relates to the basic search methodology: because it is based on page ranking and numbers of links, much of the web is seldom accessed, and the sites that "rise to the top" do so because of popularity and use. There are problems about establishing the authority of the information delivered through a Google search, and there can be problems about lack of context. There are criticisms of the insidiousness of advertising, as many users apparently do not distinguish between the free search results and advertisements (the "sponsored links"). Google is leading the way in delivering select audiences to advertisers through "behavioral targeting, social networking algorithms, predictive economics and other mathematical strategies."[41] Advertisers themselves have been critical of the inability to combat click fraud (resulting in charges generated by clicks by people or automated scripts with no real interest in their products). Underlying the criticisms of information collection practices that benefit advertisers are concerns about user privacy. Google not only has information based on individuals' search patterns, but it may have other data supplied for its email, blogging, mapping, or advertising services (including users' bank account details). In the case of Google, as with other search engines and social networking sites, the Internet affords power to infiltrate privacy.

How long Google will retain its pre-eminence remains to be seen. In 2008 Microsoft showed interest in acquiring Yahoo! and thereby some search market share. Other competition for Google may emerge – from specialist sites for particular products, from search engines that rely on contributions from people rather than algorithms, from semantic search engines for which authors decide keywords, from demographic engines that enable searches based on geographic and personal preferences – "as new, and deeper, ways of search unfold, particularly for the estimated 75% of the potential internet not yet mined."[42]

In summary, new media, Web 2.0, and the expanded uses of twenty-first media have introduced additional complexity to the role of media in society. While some concerns predate the expansion of new media but have been sharpened by their development, new problems have also emerged. The trend to increasing commercialization, resulting in the Internet becoming a "commodified medium," is an example of the former, matters of privacy and identity in the online environment of the latter. It is also important to reiterate that matters relating to new media and the online environment still have no meaning for millions of people, because large segments of the world's population do not have Internet access. The "digital divide" has not disappeared.

Contemporary Media

In the light of this examination of new media and their uses, and of various manifestations of convergence, what conclusions can be drawn about contemporary media? As indicated above, much analysis of new media focuses on how users access media content and how they use new technologies and media opportunities that allow interactivity and participation. There is an emphasis on activism, access, participation, on the desire for flexibility in how, where, and when media and information are consumed.[43] Whereas twentieth-century mass media could be seen as "pushing" content to mass audiences, now media users are being described in ways that capture the notion of interaction and social participation, "the creative agency of consumers": as citizen consumers, "participatory DIY media cultures," "prosumers," "viewsers," "co-creators," "produsers." However, as argued in other chapters, mass-media audiences were not as passive as "mass-society" theories maintained; and with respect to new media it is important to test large claims about participation, interactivity, and their effects against the extent to which new media users' "real-world" experiences have been substantially altered.[44]

It is apparent that the media world of the twenty-first century is complex, but "old" media have not died. Newspapers, radio and television broadcasting, and the film industry all remain integral to contemporary societies; but the traditional media industries have had to adapt, to forge new alliances, to be innovative in content development and delivery. Several examples illustrate what has been achieved as well as future possibilities.

Long-established organizations such as the British Broadcasting Corporation have been leaders in reshaping public-service broadcasting, initially supplementing traditional broadcasting by providing content on the Internet (podcasts, streamed audio and video) and increasingly commissioning programs for use across multiple platforms, incorporating citizen-generated content in news coverage, and through the Action Network encouraging citizens to exchange information and contribute content (providing free online training modules to develop skills in video-making and photography).

Newspapers have been under pressure to develop online outlets and new revenue streams because readerships have declined (particularly younger age groups) as readers access news and information elsewhere (television, the Internet). The threat of losing classified advertising compelled many newspapers to develop their own online classified advertising services. Newspapers moved into the online environment, with the most successful using online news delivery to add value to their traditional product. Such sites provide opportunities for interactivity, continuous updating, easy access via electronic archives to related stories, and customization or targeted news delivery. Some traditional news providers have formed alliances that offer new ways of providing news and information. An example is the agreement between the Washington Post company (owner of the *Washington Post* newspaper and of *Newsweek* magazine), MSNBC, and NBC News, with the newspaper company providing enhanced content for the MSNBC.com online news site.

At the other end of the spectrum from mainstream media adjusting to new opportunities are "bottom-up" ventures. Independent media, IndyMedia, for example, emerged after 1999 protests in Seattle against the World Trade Organization meeting. By 2006 there were about 150 independent media centers in 45 countries, offering alternatives to mainstream media supplied by volunteers and non-professionals. Another example of "citizen participatory journalism" is OhmyNews, the South Korean people's news service that relies for the bulk of its content on citizens as reporters and editors. After its establishment in February 2000 it rapidly built up a large following (with millions of daily page views), achieved financial profitability based on advertising and voluntary donations, and went on to launch an English-language version in 2004. As indicated in the section on blogging and in Chapter 10, during times of crisis established media have drawn on citizen-generated content to supplement information provided by professionals.

There is lively debate about the potential of such developments to effect significant change with respect to media, news, and information. On the one hand, there are those who see the "blogosphere" as a means of fostering "popular deliberative democracy," taking back power from corporations and "returning conversation to the people." This is in a context of perceived popular discontent with commercialism, too great an emphasis on entertainment, celebrities, and frivolous subjects, and the lack of a genuine public sphere with room for debate and popular participation in political life. Some present an optimistic scenario that a public-service ethos (exemplified by the BBC) might combine with citizen activism to redefine news and create expanded opportunities for investigative journalism. Others are more negative, arguing that, while Web 2.0 is a threat to newspapers, record companies, movie studios, and conventional publishers, what it offers – amateur content – is an inadequate replacement for mainstream media, and that faith in the integrity of amateurs, citizen journalists, or mash-up musicians is misplaced. Others predict that new methods of news delivery by mobile devices will become dominant, based on commercially driven models developed for the online environment rather than the old media industries.[45]

The comments above focus on news and information, but similar developments have affected the media and entertainment. A wealth of content is readily available because of the diversification of media platforms, devices, and activities. For traditional media such as network television this has meant significantly increased competition. However, it too has adapted, making programs accessible via the Internet, and changing program formats, with "digital add-ons" to engage audiences through websites, blogs, and phone polling (examples include the *Big Brother* series, *Dancing with the Stars*, *American Idol*, and other national versions of that program). Established media organizations have invested in online ventures (for example, ITV, the British commercial broadcaster, purchased the social networking site Friends Reunited, and NBC Universal acquired the iVillage network) as means of surviving in the changed environment.[46] New forms of program creation and delivery have emerged. Current TV is an example of interactivity and participation. It was established in 2005, the brainchild of former US Vice-President Al Gore, to create a platform for citizen journalism and for young people to tell their stories. Delivered by cable and satellite, a year after its creation Current TV was being watched in thirty million American homes, and about one-third of content was viewer created. Like the BBC, it provides training in production techniques and storytelling; it also involves audiences in program selection.

As far as the film industry is concerned, audiences can still experience blockbuster movies on the big screen in multiplex cinemas, but they can also enjoy them in increasingly sophisticated home-entertainment settings (while the trend for most hardware/devices has been to smaller, lighter, and more portable – computers, mobile phones, music players – the opposite has been the case with television screens, which were around 50 centimeters wide in the 1950s and are now about

380 centimeters, with ever larger screens for home projection of DVDs). In promoting films, Hollywood studios include digital campaigns via the Internet (advertisements on social networking sites, studio-sponsored blogs, free online games related to particular films, downloadable trailers). Such promotion can be relatively cheap compared with mainstream media; it has the advantage of global reach; and online advertising can target niche markets identified by their activities in social networking sites (Sony Pictures publicity for *Spider-Man 3*, for example, was tailored in line with blog and message-board content).[47] It seems that whole industries have burgeoned around the promotion of movies or movie characters as "brands," with a wealth of products to attract consumers.

Even the music industry, whose history has been closely entwined with mass media, has weathered the challenges and found new opportunities through new media. Legal action against the online venture Napster, which enabled the free exchange of music files among Internet users in breach of copyright, led to Napster's closure in 2001. Subsequently fee-based music downloading developed so that listeners could continue to enjoy music on radio and television (music video has remained popular) but also with downloads from the Internet to devices – MP3 players, including Apple's iPod, which, since its launch in 2001, has succeeded the Walkman in popular culture. (Newer versions provide access not only to music but also to news, radio, movies; the video iPod user can view TV shows on the iPod after they have been broadcast. The iPod has even inspired a building project in Dubai: a twenty-three-storey tower, the "iPad," based on the shape and angle of an iPod in its cradle/docking station.[48]) New opportunities for musicians have also emerged on social networking sites (see above). While issues of copyright and music piracy remain of concern to the industry, for the consumer there is considerable choice, flexibility, and opportunity for "customization."

Opportunities to access not only music but also television and movies have increased with the development of pay services and associated technology. By early 2007 the largest fee-for-song downloading service, the Apple Computer iTunes Music Store, had 4 million songs, 250 movies, 350 television shows, and more than 100,000 podcasts in its catalog, and by that date had sold more than 2 billion songs, 50 million television episodes, 1.3 million feature films. Established industries have made more media content available; for example, Paramount

Pictures joined Disney to offer movie downloads over the iTunes service.[49] Apple launched its iPhone in 2007 to enhance access to such content. It combines mobile phone, camera, iPod, wireless Internet connectivity, simple access to services such as Google maps and route directions, and has a virtual keyboard on its small screen.

New media have also created new ways of accessing books and new opportunities for the book publishing industry. Readers can access e-books on handheld devices (Amazon.com offers an electronic book reader called the Kindle, Sony the Reader Digital Book); some social networking sites encourage aspiring authors; the work of some bloggers has been published by mainstream publishers; and digitization projects such as Google's Book Search promise enhanced accessed to published works. A recent publishing phenomenon in Japan is works of fiction composed entirely on mobile phone handsets, some of them attracting very sizable readerships. As for the music industry, with opportunities have come threats, particularly regarding intellectual property and protection of copyright.

These examples illustrate how traditional media are adapting to new opportunities presented by the online environment and by evolving technology, how new alliances are being formed, and how consumer demand for greater flexibility and choice is being met. There are, nonetheless, two areas of uncertainty that will be important in determining the future of media. One relates to the "digital natives" and how their media use patterns will evolve; the other is the large question of financial viability in a changing "mediascape."

Considerable research would be required to support sound global generalizations, but media analysts have pointed to declining use of traditional media (newspapers, magazines, radio, cinema, television) and increasing use of the Internet by the younger generation, the "digital natives" (Rupert Murdoch used this term in 2005 to contrast them with older generation/s of "digital immigrants"). In Australia, Lifelounge Urban Market Research has published the following high figures for young people's new media ownership and use: between 2002 and 2007 14–25-year-olds doubled their Internet use; in 2007, for the 16–30 age group, 81.5 percent owned an MP3 player, 89.3 percent a computer, 98.6 percent a mobile phone, 98.5 percent used the Internet regularly (up to six hours a day) (and, sadly for the music industry, 32.4 percent downloaded music illegally over a four-week period).[50] Presumably the Internet use included substantial amounts of time on social networking sites (based on the statistics cited above on numbers of registered users of these sites). Key questions for media in the future include the extent to which they will be able to satisfy the demands of the digital natives as they grow older and as their preferences as media consumers develop.

Another important question for contemporary media is whether they can develop business models that will sustain operations as traditional and online contexts evolve. Competition for advertising revenue has become critical, with media markets fragmenting and pressure on mass-media advertising revenues growing. Emerging search media such as Google have devised new and profitable approaches to accessing advertising revenue, but traditional media have lost out as advertising expenditure has moved to the online environment (in 2006 there was a 17 percent increase to $9.8 billion in online ad spending) and new ways of developing and delivering advertising content have emerged (advertising videos delivered to mobile phones, advertisements in online fantasy worlds such as Second Life, viral ads spread via email and blogs, "webisodes" – short sitcoms with a branded message, consumer-generated advertising). There is debate about the extent to which media users will tolerate new advertising approaches. One view is that media-literate consumers are resistant to marketing ploys: "Television programs infused with selling pitches; social networking sites corrupted by advertising: neither will wash in this emerging culture."[51] Perhaps this view is too sanguine about the discriminating power of audiences. As the discussion above of social networking sites, user-generated content, consumers' engagement as creators of advertising copy, and Google's combination of "sponsored links" and free search implies, it is often not easy to detect where advertising begins and ends, and some users have, wittingly or unwittingly, become enmeshed in the advertising world. Some established media have positioned themselves to take advantage of new opportunities (as noted above, News Corporation's acquisition of MySpace positions it well as a youth marketing as well as a media company), but many have not yet made a successful transition. Spurgeon notes that, as "new commercial media mature, they are compelled to embark on programmes of perpetual innovation in order to remain competitive in conversational media."[52]

Overall, traditional media have been resilient, and in one sense the question of business models only carries over into the new media world what had always been a feature of the world of mass media – that is, competition for advertising revenues as the foundation of commercial media. As for the quality and variety of content available to consumers in the complex media world of the twenty-first century, it is likely that profit-making imperatives will continue to carry great weight. Developments in new media have certainly enhanced users' access to content, but the tendency has been for media organizations to use the same content across a range of platforms rather than develop richer and more diverse content.

Chapter 12 takes up questions about the broader significance of new media in a globalized world, but, to conclude this discussion of the rise of new media, it is important to draw attention to continuities as well as change. In 2003 Curran and Seaton noted, referring to the Internet in particular:

> The wide-eyed, internetphiliac approach is deeply flawed. The net has changed out of all recognition from its pioneering days when the vision of the net as the redeemer of social ills was first promulgated. The civic discourse and subcultural experiment that so excited early net commentators has given way to an increased emphasis on entertainment, business and electronic mail. The second defect of this approach is more fundamental than merely being out of date. It failed to grasp that inequalities in the real world distort cyberspace, and limit its potential for improving society.[53]

Five years on, and, taking into account the second wave of new media, Web 2.0, and phenomena such as blogging and social networking, such a conclusion does not require significant modification. Certainly there are enhanced opportunities for horizontal networks of interactive communications (Castells's "mass self-communication", Spurgeon's "new media of mass conversation"). If blogging and social networking site statistics have any reliability, large numbers of users of new media are engaging in different ways (with higher levels of interactivity and participation) than mass audiences engaged with traditional media. However, "social ills" have not disappeared with the extension of new technologies; "real-world" politics have not been transformed by the advent of YouTube; global inequalities continue to exclude a sizable portion of the world's population from access to the Internet and all that it offers. Many players from the "old-media" world continue to provide information and entertainment to new media users, even if they have harnessed new potential (for example, citizen journalists' contributions to mainstream media). Certainly new and powerful players (such as Google) have emerged alongside established corporations, but there are strong continuities in that advertising and commercial imperatives are integral to their success in the same way that they were for traditional commercial media (although globalization has had an impact on scale and levels of profitability). As argued elsewhere, media must be seen in relation to the contexts in which they originate; whether "old" or "new," they cannot be divorced from "real-world" structures and processes. Issue considered in the next chapter include the extent to which globalizing influences, particularly exercised through new media, have eroded loyalty to local and regional communities, and to the nation state, as well as the impact of global media on politics.

12

Globalization and Media

"Globalization" is now a frequently used term, yet it came into common usage only in the 1990s, when, with the end of the Cold War, the relationship between the United States and the Soviet Union no longer dominated international affairs. It refers to changes in international relationships, particularly in economics and international trade, but also social and cultural changes, for which media and international communications are especially important. This chapter outlines the main features of globalization and then focuses on changes in global communications networks and the media. It analyzes the evolution and importance of global media institutions, the apparently ever-expanding "mega-media corporations", and the problems they pose in relation to traditional conceptions of the role of media in society. It extends the debate about media or cultural imperialism to the contemporary context of globalization. Finally, it summarizes the nature of media in the early twenty-first century and highlights contemporary expectations and assumptions about their role in society.

Definitions of Globalization

Definitions of "globalization" abound – some are general, others specific; some attempt to capture the history, others the contemporary situation; some focus on processes, others on outcomes. At a general level "globalization" can be seen as "an inexact expression for a wide array of worldwide changes in politics, communications, business and trade, life styles, and culture," or it can be understood as "a multidimensional set of social processes that create, multiply, stretch, and intensify worldwide social interdependencies and exchanges while at the same time fostering in people a growing awareness of deepening connections between the local and the distant." A number of writers have empha- sized that, as the constraints of geography decline, social processes are especially important. That is, if globalization is to be meaningful, people need not only to be aware of change but also to act accordingly.[1]

Terry Flew has provided a comprehensive list of components of the process of "globalization", various "interrelated trends ... which have accelerated in scale, impact and significance since the 1980s." They include (among others):

- the internationalization of production, trade, and finance, the rise of multinational corporations, reductions in cross-border tariffs upon flows of goods and services, the deregulation of financial markets, and the rise of Internet-based electronic commerce;
- the international movements of people ... the development of diasporic and emigrant communities, and the increasingly multicul- tural nature of national societies;
- international communications flows, delivered through telecommu- nications, information and media technologies such as broadband, cable, satellite and the Internet, which facilitate transnational circulation of cultural commodities, texts, images, and artifacts;
- the global circulation of ideas, ideologies, and 'keywords', such as the so-called export of 'Western values', democracy, the 'War on Terror', 'fundamentalism', feminism, environmentalism;
- the establishment of international regimes in intellectual property ...;
- the development of international organizations, including regional trading blocs ...;
- the globalization of war and conflict ...;
- the use of overt programmes of public relations or 'spin' by govern- ments, corporations and NGOs [non-government organizations] aimed at shaping opinion at international, national and local levels.[2]

In the "globalized world" of the twenty-first century, information is of crucial importance, as are vast computer networks; and English remains the dominant language of business and popular culture (but see Chapter 11 on language shares on the Internet).[3]

Insofar as media are concerned, the developments in communi- cations technologies and infrastructure (including satellite broadcast- ing and the Internet) have been fundamental to globalization, as they have made previous "boundaries" irrelevant. Developments in media organizations, particularly the growth of global corporations, have also been crucial, rendering national borders increasingly less important.[4] With respect to the content transmitted by media, the key questions relate to the impact of globalization on diversity and cultural distinctiveness.

In considering the nature of a "globalized world," it is also important to note the debate about the relative importance of the nation state. It has been suggested that, as national economies and societies become integrated into a more unified political, economic, and cultural order, the power of nation states is diminished, especially relative to global corporations and international agencies such as the United Nations, the World Bank, and the European Community. However, the converse argument also has supporters: that is, that the nation state remains significant.[5] Furthermore, globalization itself has both supporters and opponents. There is debate not only about the extent to which processes described as "globalization" are having an impact but also about the desirability of such changes.

Global Communications and the Media

Technological developments and the rise of new media (see Chapter 11) have been fundamental to changes in global communications. The extension of fiber-optic cable systems, of satellite links, of Internet communications networks, as well as the deregulation of telecommunications systems, have made it possible to bypass the borders of nation states that traditionally exercised regulatory powers over media institutions.

Recent developments have not occurred in isolation, and late nineteenth- and early twentieth-century innovations were important for the emergence of global communications networks. One such development was the extension of underwater cable systems by the European great powers beginning in the 1850s. A global system of communications emerged, capable of transmitting messages separately from slower means of physical transportation. Another was the establishment of international news agencies. Charles Havas established the first in Paris in 1835; this was followed by Paul Julius Reuter's agency in London and by the Berlin agency of Bernard Wolff in the 1840s. International news agencies, particularly Reuters, Associated Press and United Press International (both American), and Agence France-Presse (which succeeded Havas as the French international news agency), retained an important global role in collecting and distributing news. At the international level the formation of organizations (such as the International Telecommunication Union in 1865) to introduce order into the allocation of the electromagnetic spectrum (and later radio spectrum) was important for global communications.[6]

Twentieth-century technological developments facilitated global communications and the global spread of media. Telecommunications satellites provided greater geographical reach and distribution, enabling virtually instantaneous global communications without microwave relays and coaxial cable, and serving as distribution points for both traditional network systems and cable television systems nationally and internationally. Satellites in turn became integrated into wider telecommunications networks (for telephone, fax, electronic mail, and so on). The global spread of media services has also been driven by the large corporations (such as General Electric or Time Warner – see below) that emerged as key players in the global system of communications and information diffusion. The reduction or elimination of traditional institutional and legal barriers – or the capability simply to bypass them – facilitated the spread of global media. In the late twentieth century, support, among Western governments in particular, for free market policies resulted in minimal government intervention in many areas, the reduction or elimination of barriers to free trade, deregulation, and the privatization of previously public services. New technologies and laissez-faire policies opened up media markets to highly integrated global corporations.

As an example of deregulation, policy changes in the United States in the 1980s and 1990s stimulated greater competition in telecommunications, produced a less-regulated broadcasting environment, and enabled greater consolidation in media industries, and greater integration into global media markets. AT&T lost its monopoly over telephone services but diversified into other areas, buying a cable television company and an Internet company, extending its international operations, contributing to greater convergence and global expansion. There was also lighter regulation in American broadcasting with the relaxation of limits on advertising time. Rules that had restricted cross-media ownership were eased, opening the way to greater concentration. It was possible for a single global corporation (such as News Corporation – see below) to accumulate extensive interests in newspapers, the film industry, and network and cable television. In the United Kingdom similarly the privatization of British Telecom and the deregulation of telecommunications industries led British Telecom to seek new global partners and to enter other markets such as cable television.[7]

While changes in national policies have contributed to globalization, international organizations, too, have encouraged commercial media at the global level. In a world where information exchange is vital, the media are central to the world economy. Organizations such as the International Monetary Fund (IMF) and the World Trade Organization (WTO) have supported global media in the service of the market economy. One implication is that national governments face difficulties in retaining control over vital areas of communication. Furthermore, global media operate increasingly in a world where commercialization has triumphed (see Chapters 8 and 9).

Some analysts consider that such changes in global communications have profoundly altered international interaction. Hachten and Scotton, for example, propose that history is "speeded up" as nations and people react more quickly to important events because of the wide and rapid dissemination of information; diplomacy has changed, given the impact of public opinion (influenced by global communications) on foreign relations. Gilboa claims that the "video-clip pace" of global television has accelerated the pace of diplomatic communications, creating pressures on foreign-affairs bureaucracies and policymakers.[8]

While it is true that changes in global communications mean that audiences have rapid access to international news – the term "CNN effect" was used in the 1990s to describe the supposedly simple cause-and-effect relationship of media coverage, public opinion, and policy-making – other factors (geopolitical, economic, national interest) cannot be ignored. Gowing concludes categorically that "real-time television coverage … will create emotions but ultimately make no difference to the fundamental calculations in foreign policy-making." In relation to the impact of new media such as the Internet, caution is also advisable, as the relationship between media and decision-making is always complex, and foreign-policy decisions are affected by many variables.[9]

Giant Media Corporations

In the 1990s giant media corporations expanded, exploiting the possibilities of multiple media ownership and unconstrained by national boundaries. Media companies, responding to the market situation, moved toward being larger, global, and vertically integrated, so that they could achieve cost savings and take advantage of cross-selling and cross-promotion opportunities. Many media businesses became part of global conglomerates producing entertainment and media products, and computing software, with global distribution networks. Some large media concerns in turn became part of even larger corporations whose interests extended far beyond media. In the twenty-first century new terms were used to capture the scale of these global players: Hachten and Scotton, for example, refer to "media behemoths."[10] By 2004 the top ten media and entertainment corporations (in descending market value) were General Electric (with extensive non-media interests but also a major stake in NBC Universal), Microsoft (primarily computing and software but also digital media and games), Time Warner, Comcast, News Corporation, Walt Disney (these first six all US-based), Sony (electronic goods and media/entertainment, based in Japan), Vivendi Universal (France), Viacom (USA), and Thomson Corporation (Canada).[11] Bertelsmann was also important as a very large, European-based corporation with interests in television, radio, newspapers, books and magazines, music, and Internet websites. The reach of such corporations can be illustrated by data for News Corporation, which, by the late 1990s, reached approximately 75 percent of the world's population; Time Warner (AOL-Time Warner between 2000 and 2003), which was in 212 countries through its CNN subsidiary alone in 2002; and Disney, which estimated that at least 1.2 billion people in the world's primary markets used at least one of its products in 2002.[12]

Giant media corporations enjoyed advantages of scale and integration; and they exploited opportunities for cross-promotion (see Chapter 9). For example, a Disney film could be shown on pay cable and commercial network television, with the company creating spin-off television series, establishing related amusement-park events, producing CD-ROMs and DVDs, books, comics, and merchandise to be sold in Disney retail stores, and promoting the film and related material across its media properties. With increasing media convergence, opportunities for broader distribution via the Internet and personalized devices have expanded.

The development of giant media corporations has raised questions about the role and responsibilities of media in contemporary societies. The Italian media magnate and politician Silvio Berlusconi, and his company, Fininvest, provide a case study of the concentration of media ownership, the intersection of media power and politics, and the potential conflict of interest. In the Italian election of 1994 Berlusconi, having established a new political party, Forza Italia, exploited the control he exercised over Italian media through his company, Fininvest, won the election and became prime minister for a brief period (until December 1994). Berlusconi was criticized at the time for having turned the Italian political system into a "videocracy."[13] He was again successful in the 2001 elections and was prime minister for two terms until he lost the May 2006 elections and resigned. In 2008 he staged a comeback, being elected for a third term.

Berlusconi was both political leader and media magnate. He and his family owned 96 percent of Fininvest, with extensive media and other interests, including a large stake in three television networks in Italy – Canale 5, Italia 1, Retequattro – through the company Mediaset. These networks carried 60 percent of Italian television advertising. Berlusconi had a stake in Mondadore, Italy's largest publishing group and publisher of the leading newspaper, *Il giornale*, and of the influential weekly magazine, *Panorama*, Pubitalia, the leading Italian advertizing agency, Medusa Video, a film production and distribution company, and the video rental chain Blockbuster Italia (as well as owning the football club A. C. Milan, and having business interests in other sectors such as insurance and banking). Berlusconi's dominant role in Italy's communications industries provided the means to exercise considerable influence over public opinion. While prime minister, he also extended his influence over the state television network, RAI, bringing the total audience share of enterprises in which he had an interest (state television and his private commercial channels) to more than 90 percent. This period in Italy saw "unparalleled concentration of the political and media power in a single person's hands."[14] In such a situation it is likely that media independence and opportunities for free expression via the press and broadcasting will be severely curtailed. By 2006 Berlusconi, Italy's richest person and named thirty-seventh by *Forbes* magazine in its list of the world's richest people, was facing legal inquiries into his business dealings, following allegations of financial irregularities and corruption; nonetheless, as indicated above, in elections in 2008 Berlusconi was returned to power.

While this Italian example focuses on a national context, at the global level a giant media corporation that has attracted constant attention in relation to the power and influence of transnational media – and of a media magnate, Rupert Murdoch – is News Corporation. This is the example *par excellence* of a global media enterprise: its investments span five continents, and its interests include newspapers, magazines, film, broadcast, cable and satellite television, music, publishing, Internet sites, and sports.[15]

Murdoch had been a dominant figure in News Corporation since the 1950s, as it expanded from a local Australian company involved only in newspaper publication to a giant global corporation with diverse media and other interests. Murdoch inherited an Australian newspaper, the *Adelaide News*, from his father in 1954. In the 1960s he acquired papers in other Australian state capital cities, and he established a national newspaper, the *Australian*, in 1964. He bought into the British press in the late 1960s with *News of the World* and the *Sun*, and then in the 1980s the prestigious broadsheets, *The Times* and the *Sunday Times*. He modernized British newspaper publishing practices, in the process taking on the powerful print unions and breaking with tradition by moving his newspaper offices away from Fleet Street.

In the 1980s Murdoch expanded his media interests in the United States. He had acquired newspapers there in the 1970s, including the *New York Post* in 1976. In 1985 he renounced his Australian nationality and became an American citizen so that he could purchase US television stations, avoiding laws that restricted foreign ownership of television assets. News Corporation acquired the Metromedia chain of television stations, and in 1985 purchased a 50 percent share of 20th Century Fox and launched Fox Broadcasting Company as a fourth network, competing against the three longstanding national networks, CBS, NBC, and ABC. In 1996 Fox News, a twenty-four-hour cable television service, was established. Fox News provided direct competition for CNN, and over the following years (when it was noted for its strong support of the Bush administration and the war in Iraq) it seriously eroded CNN's market share.

In addition to substantial media holdings in the United States and the United Kingdom, News Corporation retained ownership of newspapers in Australia and New Zealand. It also expanded in the United Kingdom, launching Sky Television in 1989. Sky merged with British Satellite Broadcasting to form BSkyB in 1990, providing involvement in digital television services via satellite. In Asia News Corporation gained a controlling interest in Star Television, based in Hong Kong, in 1993, and in 2000 it gained limited broadcasting rights in China through the Phoenix television service. News Corporation took advantage of technological change and media convergence, exploiting the opportunities of the digital age. In 2005 it moved into the online environment with the purchase of Intermix Media, which included the social networking website MySpace.com. This provided a means of engaging a younger generation of media users (see Chapter 11). News Corporation interests continued to expand: in 2006 a Turkish television channel was added; in late 2007 Dow Jones and Company, owners of the prestigious *Wall Street Journal* (which dates back to 1889), was acquired after lengthy negotiations. This provided an opportunity for News Corporation to revitalize the *Journal's* editions in Europe and Asia, where globalization was seen as offering important opportunities (in India and China in particular).

News Corporation's diversified global operations include the production and distribution of motion pictures and television programs; television, satellite, cable, and digital broadcasting; the publication of newspapers, magazines, and books; the production and distribution of promotional and advertising products and services; the creation and distribution of online programming; and the facilitation of online social networking.

As a large global media corporation, News Corporation has continued to attract attention, particularly because of Rupert Murdoch's interventionist style (see Chapter 9). Critics maintain that it represents an enormous concentration of power in the hands of one man. This undermines the capacity for media within this giant corporation to fulfill traditional expectations about objectivity in news and information delivery, and for untrammeled journalistic independence. Furthermore, the extent of News Corporation control over certain media markets has reduced diversity and limited the variety of information available to the public. Policy decisions about media content have been based on commercial or political considerations (as in the case of News Corporation activities in China), raising questions about the extent to which traditional expectations of media retain relevance in the face of strong commercial, profit-making considerations or of pressure from political authorities.

News Corporation is only one example of traditional media moving into new media environments. Such convergence of old and new media has expanded the power and influence of global corporations. At the same time traditional media functions have been absorbed into very large corporations with multiple interests and driven primarily by the profit motive. In these circumstances questions arise about the extent to which media can exercise any real independence. In relation to their information-providing function, as news becomes just another product sold by big media companies, it is regarded simply as a commodity. It tends to be more entertainment-based, and traditional values such as objectivity and regard for accuracy are lost. Another problem for traditional media, facing pressures to make content available via the Internet in order to retain audiences – and to appeal to younger audiences – is that viable business models for traditional media operating in the "virtual environment" have remained elusive. Finally, another set of concerns focuses on the impact on culture of the decline of nationally based media. This calls for re-examination of earlier debates about media or cultural imperialism.

Global Media and Imperialism

The impact of globalization on the media has revived interest in the notion of cultural or media imperialism. The expansion of corporate ownership of media and related industries and the strong global influence of American programming suggest that globalized media are subject to predominantly American influences in the same way that national film and television industries in earlier periods were subject to US ascendancy in international markets. However, some analysts also see the need to couch discussions about media within a more current framework, informed by recent theoretical analysis of the phenomenon of globalization.

Resentment and concern at US domination of media content were recurring themes in the twentieth century, provoked initially by the powerful international position of the US film industry in the 1920s. In the post-colonial era such concern was expressed in ideas of cultural or media imperialism. Theories of dependence emerged in the 1960s, especially in Latin America; these were applied not only to political and economic relations between the former colonial powers and the newly independent, developing nations but also to culture. Newly independent countries saw themselves as victims of cultural colonialism, with the media playing an important role in transmitting and imposing ideas and values.

In 1973 representatives of non-aligned countries at a summit in Algiers called for a "new international economic order." This was endorsed by the United Nations General Assembly in 1974, and at a meeting in Tunis in 1976 a similar resolution called specifically for a "new information and communication order," with a free and balanced flow of information among all countries. In 1976 UNESCO appointed an International Commission for the Study of Communications Problems. The commission issued an influential report entitled *Many Voices, One World*, referred to as the MacBride Report (Sean MacBride chaired the commission).[16]

The MacBride report – and other critics of media imperialism – criticized Western news agencies for their monopoly of news and the one-way news flow between industrialized and developing countries. Agencies such as Associated Press, Reuters, United Press International, and Agence France-Presse tended to transmit information to developing countries while bringing back relatively little. Moreover, much of what little Western coverage there was of events in developing countries presented stereotyped views and emphasized dramatic events such as war, natural disasters, and political instability.

In the 1980s US domination of the film and television industries continued to provoke dismay at the lack of balance in distribution and programming flow, but not only with respect to Third World countries. In Europe, too, there was concern about the harmful effect on national, regional, and local cultures of US media exports and American mass culture (see Chapter 8). The power of the US film industry and broadcasting networks was such that it was difficult for others to compete. The result was that production elsewhere was limited, and imported values dominated what local cultural product there was.

Advertising exemplified striking inequities, particularly with respect to developing countries. There was a predominantly one-way flow in advertising that emphasized Western consumer culture, and encouraged people elsewhere to respond to, and conform with, the requirements of predominantly US-based transnational consumer-goods manufacturers. The success of global brands such as Coca-Cola, Levi, and McDonald's seemed to confirm the power and influence of transnational corporations and of capitalist values. The advent of new technologies that enabled transborder, global data flows created challenges to states attempting to regulate or control media and content.

New terms for inequalities supplemented older approaches to media imperialism. "North–South" relations described the relationship between the predominantly highly industrialized and developed countries of the northern hemisphere and the less developed countries of the south. The "core"/"periphery" thesis depicted industrialized countries as the core or center of the global system, with less developed countries marginalized in the "periphery." This idea of "peripheral players" was applied to non-US media industries in the 1990s.[17]

In the 1980s UNESCO continued to support the idea of a new information and communication order, but unity among the non-aligned nations declined, and attention shifted to the increasing trends to deregulation of media and privatization of public-sector enterprises. Problems about international information flows remained, particularly given the significance of information and communication in contemporary societies, but there was little prospect that these would be priority concerns of Western governments supportive of free-market ideologies or of giant media corporations operating globally.

Yet, while global corporations expanded and inequalities persisted, the real impact of cultural or media imperialism at national and local levels was questioned in the 1990s. It was suggested that there were limits to US dominance and that the spread of American influences had been uneven. Nor could it be assumed that all American programs simply conveyed the values of Western capitalism; not all exported US media content supported capitalist society or consumer culture. Audiences interpreted American content in their own contexts, and they understood film and television programs in diverse ways. Moreover, various non-American media industries were flourishing, confirming that it was unwise to overemphasize American influence or the importance of imported products.

In the complex "international mediascapes" of the 1990s new conceptions of media relationships suggested that any simple model of media imperialism was inadequate to capture the many factors that influenced cultural exchange. These included leisure traditions and viewers' attitudes and perceptions, decisions by "gatekeepers" about what should or should not be imported, when programs should be scheduled, and what the balance between local and imported programming should be; the regulatory frameworks of particular countries; and perceptions of difference between national and imported programs. Audiences received global media products and interpreted them in many and varied ways; and different cultures were resilient in transforming and absorbing foreign influences and putting "mass culture" to local use (terms such as "hybridization" and "indigenization" were used to describe the appropriation of Western cultural imports). Rather than global mass culture being seen as replacing local culture, it was more appropriate to consider the two as coexisting. Work on globalization accepted cultural and political differences, seeing global culture as embracing people's or nations' particularity or distinctiveness.[18]

Successful film and television industries in countries such as Australia, Canada, India, Mexico, Brazil, and Egypt demonstrated that the concept of US media imperialism was inadequate to describe relationships in regional and global markets in the 1990s. In the Indian subcontinent, for instance, Bombay became a center of media production and trade for the Hindi film industry, exporting film on video to the UK, Singapore, Hong Kong, the United Arab Emirates, and elsewhere where large Indian minority populations ensured strong demand for Hindi films. Hong Kong and Taiwan exported film and television programs to Chinese-speaking populations in other Asian countries, as did Egypt to other Arabic speakers. In Mexico and Brazil local media entrepreneurs reversed earlier trends. Using videotapes, Mexican producers developed programs for export, and, with the advent of satellite, Mexican Televisa broadcast Spanish-language programs to some fifteen million Hispanic households in the United States from the late 1980s. Brazil's TV Globo built up a thriving export industry, marketing its telenovelas or soap operas in Portugal and in more than 100 other countries. Other examples of "contra-flow," reversing the directions in which media content had historically moved, were the successful film and television exports from Australia and Canada to the United States and the United Kingdom. In the European Union there was a shift in policy from support for free trade in film and television programs to a culturally led approach designed to stimulate production, afford adequate protection against US imports, and foster an industry that could compete with the United States. The 1991 and 1996 MEDIA I and II programs, for example, promoted co-production, distribution, and financing of projects within the European Union.[19]

However, as McChesney pointed out, "second-tier media firms" (Televisa in Mexico, Globo in Brazil, Clarin in Argentina, the Cisneros Group in Venezuela, for instance) did not retain an oppositional stance within the global system. They joined the world's sixty or seventy largest media corporations; they came to dominate their own national and regional media markets; and they developed ties to, and joint ventures with, the largest media transnational corporations and US investment banks.[20] Such instances illustrate a process whereby countervailing trends to globalization were absorbed into it.

The broad impact of globalization led to new conceptualizations. The media imperialism thesis was considered deficient as a means of describing global media and providing a more nuanced view of US influence. One approach was to see globalization as a process transforming both developing and developed countries alike, heightening feelings of interconnectedness or cosmopolitanism, and refocusing attention on Marshall McLuhan's idea of a "global village." Terms such as "disembedding" (lifting social relations out of local contexts) and "deterritorialization" (weakening links between identity and place) were used, linked to optimistic predictions about new cultural energy and a new kind of international politics (especially on environmental issues and peace movements). John Tomlinson, rather than seeing cultural imperialism as a negative force, argued that "globalization has been perhaps the most significant force in creating and proliferating cultural identity."[21]

A theory from the 1990s that Flew labeled "strong globalization" is relevant to media. This maintained that there had been a qualitative shift in economic, social, political, and cultural relations within and between states and societies, rendering older analytical tools inadequate to explain the resulting social processes. Manuel Castells's work has been influential, proposing the emergence of a new economy that is global, networked, and informational. Castells claimed that the global proliferation of new forms of entertainment and information through digitally networked information and communications technologies meant the end of mass media and the association of nationally based media with the development of national culture. However, this approach was controversial. Flew, for example, noted that "arguments that we are at the end of the age of mass media may both overstate the success of broadcast television in aggregating populations around particular media consumption patterns, and ... underestimate the continued pull of media that can reach large segments of the population simultaneously and therefore act as a magnet for associated advertising revenues."[22]

By the end of the 1990s views of globalization could be categorized broadly into optimistic and pessimistic. The positive view, particularly influenced by cultural theorists, was that globalization was promoting global consciousness, increasing international dialogue, empowering minorities, and creating new alliances and solidarities that supported a progressive politics. The negative, especially from a radical political–economic perspective, was that globalization represented a victory of undesirable features of capitalism, dispossessing democracy, imposing pro-market policies, weakening organized labor, and undermining the political Left. With respect to media, it was argued that there was growing concentration of media ownership and ever more homogeneous media content, with a small number of mostly US-based conglomerates globally dominant.[23]

From a twenty-first-century perspective, elements of these debates remain current. There is not agreement on the impact of globalization on the nation state (and its importance with respect to culture); nor is there consensus about the relative importance of US culture and, by implication, the legacies of the twentieth-century argument about media/cultural imperialism.

With respect to the nation state, Curran's conclusion is persuasive: we should not overstate the decline of the nation state, as "national governments are still key sites of power." They can determine communications policy (licensing broadcasters, defining media laws, regulating media content), and they can subsidize media and stimulate local film and television production through quotas and other means. As Curran notes, different languages, political systems, power structures, cultural traditions, economies, international links, and histories "find continuing expression in the media of different nation states." Steger, also cautious about "pronouncements of the impending demise" of the nation state, nonetheless draws attention to the growing difficulties states face in performing some traditional functions.[24]

On the continuing relevance of US cultural imperialism, while this remains a concern in many parts of the world, the idea that corporate media firms are no more than purveyors of US culture "is ever less plausible as the media system becomes increasingly concentrated, commercialized and globalized. The global media system is better understood as one that advances corporate and commercial interests and values and denigrates or ignores that which cannot be incorporated into its mission."[25] The extent to which such commercialism has particular implications for political activity or civic values is an important matter for consideration.

Global Media and Politics

As indicated above, one of the optimistic claims made for global media – especially television and the Internet – is that they have the potential to spread democratic values, empower and encourage participation by marginalized groups, and challenge governments whose power and authority have depended on the control of information. This is related to the view that globalization and developments in global media have lessened the power of nation states.

The People's Republic of China provides an interesting case study. Coverage of the Chinese government clampdown on the pro-democracy movement in Tiananmen Square in 1989 appeared to exemplify the potential of global media. International satellite television showed Chinese authorities' use of force against pro-democracy demonstrators to a global audience, stimulating widespread condemnation of Chinese government and military actions. Chinese students successfully used Western media to further their cause, bearing banners with American symbols and written in English for the wider television audience. The scope of global television seemed to have been redefined, showing its power to affect political events within national boundaries and to influence world diplomacy and international public opinion.[26]

However, relations between Chinese governments and Western media have not been one-sided. Tension between News Corporation and the Chinese government four years after the Tiananmen Square incidents led to a backdown by the media corporation. In 1993 Rupert Murdoch, in a widely publicized speech, claimed: "Advances in the technology of telecommunications have proved an unambiguous threat to totalitarian regimes everywhere.... Satellite broadcasting makes it possible for information-hungry residents of many closed societies to bypass state-controlled television." Chinese authorities had earlier objected to foreign coverage of the events of 1989, and, reacting to this statement, threatened to block access to the Chinese market for News Corporation, in particular its StarTV service. Murdoch took steps to placate China, and News Corporation removed the BBC World Television Service from its Asian satellite service. In another incident in 1997 Murdoch appeared to take heed of pressure from China when the News Corporation publishing company, HarperCollins, repudiated an agreement to publish a controversial book by the former governor of Hong Kong, Chris Patten, to whom the Chinese government was hostile.[27] More recently, MySpace, owned by News Corporation, has observed locally imposed restrictions on its operations in China.

Growth of new media, and particularly the expansion of Internet take-up in China, created a dilemma for Chinese authorities. Chinese Internet use had surged from just over two million households in December 1998 to twenty-six million by mid-2001; by 2007 there were approximately 48.5 million broadband subscribers in China. While access to information and participation in the commercial opportunities offered by the Internet were considered important to China's economic development, freedom of information threatened Chinese Communist Party authority and posed a challenge in a society where tight political control over information had been the norm.

Unwilling to allow free access to global information and entertainment sources, Chinese authorities developed complex legislation, regulations, and sophisticated Internet filtering systems. Content transmitted via email, web pages, blogs, online discussion forums, and social networking sites was censored; access to materials including pornography, political dissent, and religious matters was subject to blocking (specific examples included content on the Tiananmen Square events of 1989, Taiwanese and Tibetan independence, the Dalai Lama, and the Falun Gong movement).[28] Internet sites of Western news sources (including BBC News) were blocked. Despite efforts to regulate access, it has been difficult for Chinese authorities to enforce restrictions. Some Internet users in China have been able to use secure connections to computers outside the mainland and use proxy servers, circumventing firewalls on Internet content; in addition, other media have been used to disseminate content, with text messaging via mobile phones being especially difficult to regulate.

Assuming that popular pressure to have unrestricted access to Internet content will continue, it remains to be seen what will be more

influential in effecting change in China – possibly political liberaliza-
tion, possibly increasing difficulty of "policing" communications technologies. Both in China and elsewhere, the Internet challenges efforts at
political censorship, but even more noteworthy has been its capacity
globally to subvert moral censorship, providing easy access to pornographic and similar websites. The very nature of the medium continues
to make censorship or regulatory measures difficult to implement (see
Chapter 11).

These examples illustrate difficulties for nation states in regulating
or controlling media, given technological and institutional change.
Globalization and the communications revolution have posed new
challenges, because interest groups can ignore earlier constraints of
time and place. Emerging transnational "communities," unsympathetic
to globalization or other issues, see global media as providing new
avenues to exert pressure. Groups organized around human rights,
environmental, consumer, and other issues have used the Internet to
coordinate rapid responses to international events and to bring pressure to bear on governments, corporations, and international organizations. Actions by these new coalitions have been labeled "netwars",
"smart mobbing," or "virtual demonstrations." Their targets have
included world trade talks and issues such as world debt and geneti-
cally modified foods.[29] It has been suggested that such actions may pose
a threat to capitalism and neoliberal economies, but such claims should
not be accepted at face value. As argued above, there is insufficient
evidence to support a move from discussion of the potential of new
communications technologies and global media to the assertion that
globalization has "killed the nation state" and supplanted it with "virtual
communities."

In relation to global media and politics, it is important to remember
that, even in the twenty-first century, access to communications technologies remains unequal. The continuing discrepancies between rich
and poor countries are a reminder of the limitations on arguments
about the democratizing potential of global media (see Chapter 11).

Finally, an important new feature of global media, with implications
for politics and international relations at a global level, has been the
emergence of non-Western media with global reach. Al-Jazeera, now
with English-language bureaux in Doha, Kuala Lumpur, London, and
Washington, as well as its Arabic-broadcasting base in Qatar, has not
only transformed the media environment in the Arab world since its

foundation but also established an Arab broadcaster as a viable alternative to Western news organizations (see Chapter 10). The period of the Iraq War marked the end of the monopoly of American/Western media in global news. Just as the term "CNN effect" was used to describe the impact of the American twenty-four-hour global news broadcaster in the 1990s, so has the "Al-Jazeera effect" been used in relation to the transformation of the media environment since 2003. The longer-term influence of Arab media such as Al-Jazeera in nurturing a pan-Arab consciousness, helping to develop a sense of community among the Arab diaspora, remains to be seen. However, during its relatively short existence it has already emerged as an alternative agenda-setter, challenging the Western-media-dominated status quo and, importantly, providing an Arab perspective to global audiences.[30]

Media and Society in the Twenty-First Century

The rise of global media conglomerates has highlighted a central paradox in the history of communications. The advocates of global communications forecast the breakdown of national and ethnic differences and the growth of international understanding, all to be achieved through the influence of media operating on a global scale. The promise is hard to reconcile with the realities of media development since the 1980s. Far from creating a unified world, commercial media organizations have increasingly fostered a fragmentation of audiences and stronger social barriers. Where big-city newspapers and national radio and television programs once reached mass audiences, the tastes of specialized groups, distinguished by different "lifestyles" and perceived as niche markets for advertising revenue, shape media content to an unprecedented degree. Far from fostering international understanding, the same organizations have presided over a marked reduction in serious coverage of public affairs in both broadcasting and print media, not least in treatment of international affairs. Analysis of major US network coverage of international affairs in their main evening television news broadcasts has revealed a persistent decline (apart from periods of crisis such as "9/11"), and the networks support fewer foreign bureaux than in the past. This has been accompanied by declining public interest in international news and a perceived loss of public trust in the news media.[31]

There are several other trends that support a pessimistic view of contemporary media in relation to traditional expectations of their role in society. These include the general decline in news and public-affairs programming, with entertainment and "infotainment" far outweighing news and current affairs, the decline of the public-service ethos, the triumph of commercial/market-driven concerns, with much greater emphasis on lifestyle programs (and the rise and rise of "reality television"), with several of these fueling the tendency for media to give exaggerated attention to certain events. Several writers refer to the "symbiotic link" between terrorism and media, to "mass-mediated terrorism," and, indeed, to the pervasiveness and influence of media in conflict situations. Nacos accuses media organizations of seeming to be increasingly inclined to exploit terrorism as infotainment for their own imperatives (ratings, circulation).[32] There is another paradox: the great diversity of media outlets contrasts with the reality of circumscribed content. Increasingly, productions seem to adhere to rigid formulas, calculated to maximize advertising revenue, supporting a global trend to rely on similar forms of entertainment as the basis for profitability.

These trends highlight a central question about what it is reasonable for citizens to expect of media. One argument, favored by media corporations, is to point to the vast audiences commanded by modern media as a source of legitimacy. In this view the very popularity of programs and publications demonstrates that they serve the public interest. Thus media products are treated as commodities; their success or failure determined by the market. This view is now so deeply ingrained that it has come to be regarded by many as common sense. It attributes no political or cultural importance to the media. Yet the study of the history of media in a number of societies demonstrates that there are other possibilities for media organization and content. Admittedly there are considerable challenges; for news media, for example, there is "an international community that is more amorphous than in the past ... evolving communities of interest, such as the European Union ... which make coverage of transnational entities important ... giant corporations [that] transcend nationality and are governed through cyberspace ... [and] terrorists [who] compensate for their small numbers by being able to disregard borders and use media to enhance the impact of their actions."[33] Nonetheless, it is important not to lose sight of the cultural and political importance of media, or of the fact that there are models other than those that have come to dominate early twenty-first-century media.

13

Conclusion

Writing at the start of the 1960s, Raymond Williams argued that the interaction of two processes lay at the heart of the history of modern communications. One was the vast expansion of audiences created by the emergence of the mass-circulation press, cinema, radio, and television. This phenomenon, which Williams regarded as part of the extension of democracy, was, he believed, so significant as to have "the effect of a cultural revolution." The other process was a narrowing of ownership and control, which "has passed or is passing, in large part, to a kind of financial organization unknown in earlier periods, and with important resemblances to the major forms of ownership in general industrial production." He suggested that media dependence on advertising revenue had ensured that the main purpose of communication – "the sharing of human experience" – had been subordinated to an emphasis on profits and "the selling of things." There was, therefore, a contradiction at the center of the history of twentieth-century media, "between democracy and limited ownership: between genuine extension and the drive to sell."[1]

Developments in the following decade confirmed Williams's analysis: in 1975 he still regarded the interaction between these two processes as central to an understanding of media. In much of the popular culture of the 1960s, and in such developments as the rise of alternative newspapers and magazines and the growth of community and street theater, he saw signs of a healthy democratic culture. But he also found ample evidence of a continuing contraction of ownership and the triumph of commercial forces: in the commercial exploitation of popular culture, the dwindling number of major newspapers, the growing influence of commercial interests in radio and television, and "the subordination of a general communications process to an increasingly powerful system of advertising and public relations."[2] He also recognized the conflicting possibilities raised by the emergence in the 1970s of the first wave of "new media." There would be opportunities, for example, for new kinds of community broadcasting and independent production made possible by cable television; but there could also be "new kinds of commercial exploitation." In satellite television he even saw the prospect of "an international system beyond the control of any democratic authority."[3]

Though changes in media technology since the 1970s have been so extensive as to warrant the description "communications revolution," viewed from another perspective there was a large degree of continuity between the history of mass communications in the first eight decades of the twentieth century and subsequent developments. The more recent history of media and society has been characterized by the continued playing-out of the interaction, and the contradiction, identified by Williams – between expansion and contraction, between "democracy" and commerce. Thus the new media that developed from the 1970s vastly expanded the range of content, allowed levels of interactivity and audience participation that had not been possible in traditional media, and enabled new voices to be heard. For these reasons they have often been lauded as empowering, liberating, and democratizing. Yet new media technologies were rapidly developed for commercial uses, and important sectors – including the most popular Internet news and entertainment sites as well as cable and satellite television networks – are owned by major corporations, including established media organizations.

New media were therefore not immune to the broader trends toward oligopoly and commercialism, which, by the early twenty-first century, had advanced far beyond the levels that concerned Williams in the early 1960s. Increased concentration of ownership characterized all the mainstream media. The late-twentieth-century history of the press in the United States and Britain – where most major newspapers came to be owned by a handful of chains – typified this development. Moreover, acceptance by governments of increased levels of cross-media ownership led to an even greater concentration of economic power, which, in the form of the great media conglomerates that emerged in the 1980s and 1990s, was global in reach. A growing emphasis on commercial priorities – on "the drive to sell" – was part of this trend. The erosion of those barriers that quarantined journalists and journalistic values from the demands of commerce – especially in the quality press but even in the US television networks until the 1970s – undermined commercial television's role as a provider of news and information and threatened the role of the press as an independent source of information and a check on government. In radio and television, state-owned systems continued to provide an alternative to commercial broadcasting, but their role has been challenged and often diminished (to varying degrees in different countries) by the end of state broadcasting monopolies in Europe and Asia, increased competition from commercial stations, loss of audience share, funding cuts, ideological opposition to public broadcasting (often reflected in the policies of national governments), and political pressure to chase ratings and accept advertising as a revenue source.

The great expansion in the range of media content from the 1980s (especially because of the growth of cable and satellite television), and the increasing ability of media organizations to cater to niche markets, were often pointed to as evidence of the benefits of growing media diversity. But the majority of people continued to rely mainly on traditional media as sources of information and entertainment; and watching television, especially free-to-air terrestrial television, was still the main leisure activity in Western countries by the early twenty-first century. It was questionable whether the advantages of a wider range of content were sufficient to offset the costs of a weakened regulatory framework, cuts in state funding for public broadcasters, reduced advertising revenue for commercial broadcasters, and the decline of news and journalistic standards in broadcasting and the press.

A central theme of *Media and Society into the 21st Century* concerns the question of media influence: do media shape society, or are they products of society? The book argues that the more far-reaching claims for media influence are not warranted. A number of episodes in the history of media and society since the 1890s suggest the limitations to that influence. For example, the effectiveness of media as instruments of political and commercial persuasion usually depends, in the former case, on the success of propaganda in appealing to and reinforcing existing beliefs, attitudes, and values, and, in the latter case, on advertising's interaction with broader cultural influences as well as on the intrinsic merits of the consumer goods advertised. In neither case is there evidence of the power of media fundamentally to change beliefs or to create attitudes out of thin air. Similarly, in post-1945 international conflicts, including the Cold War, the Vietnam War of the 1960s, the Gulf War of 1991, and the early twenty-first-century conflicts in Iraq and Afghanistan (and the wider "war on terror"), the extent to which media coverage reflected orthodox opinion, and was influenced by political and societal pressures, is striking. In none of these cases did media win or lose the war, though it sometimes proved convenient for political leaders and others to suggest that media did have that power.

The same limitations applied to the influence of mass entertainment. Tabloid newspapers and magazines, movies, and television entertainment all helped define personal and social behavior. But, in a more fundamental sense, trends in popular entertainment responded to prevailing cultural values – an observation illustrated by the changing treatment of race, gender, and sexual morality in US television programs from the 1950s to the 1970s, then to the new "golden age" at the end of the century. Mass media, and especially the visual media, have from the beginning been the object of criticism from moral reformers, alarmed by what they assumed to be the harmful influence on youth of sex and violence in movies and television programs. Insofar as these critics assumed the power of media to create values and alter behavior independent of other factors, they greatly exaggerated the media's role. The Hollywood majors' implementation of the Production Code in the 1930s, a concession to the demands of pro-censorship groups, was a clear reminder that the actions even of powerful media organizations cannot be understood outside a social context.

In broadcasting, too, the emergence of different models of ownership and control – both privately owned commercial and state-owned publicly funded systems – highlighted the importance of social context. The British broadcasting system, unique in the degree of independence from the state afforded a publicly funded broadcaster and in the BBC's mission of cultural uplift, was well suited to Britain's hierarchical society. By contrast, it was never likely that a strong state broadcasting system would emerge in the United States, where a more limited view of the role of government in society and the economy prevailed.

By the end of the twentieth century it seemed to many that the creation of global media conglomerates had fundamentally changed the longstanding relationship between media and society, and that these organizations were so powerful as to override the authority of national governments and impose a globalized culture on all countries.

Yet government policy was crucial to the rise of these companies: they were the product not of irresistible forces of globalization but of the actions of sympathetic governments, motivated by an ideological commitment to deregulation. The experience of News Corporation and Google in China – where major concessions were made to the Chinese government in return for being allowed to do business in that country – demonstrated that it was still within the power of national governments to regulate the conglomerates' activities if they chose to do so. The continuing strength of national television cultures, the failure of attempts to establish pan-European and pan-Asian television in the 1980s and 1990s, and the need for transnational organizations to accommodate themselves to national television markets, further illustrate the fact that there are limits to the power even of these global media companies.

The correct analysis, therefore, is that media influence is the product of interaction with broader cultural factors. Media have helped shape attitudes, values, and behavior in a number of ways discussed in this book. Two of these influences may be regarded as fundamental. First, newspapers, cinema, radio, and television, because of their command of mass audiences, played a crucial role of cultural and national integration. By exposing the inhabitants of different cities, towns, and regions to the same publications and programs, they encouraged them to identify with people they could not know and would never meet, in what Benedict Anderson has called "the imagined community" of the nation.[4] They made "what were in effect national symbols part of the life of every individual," and thus broke down "the divisions between the private and local spheres in which most citizens normally lived, and the public and national one."[5] The fragmentation of audiences that resulted first from post-Second World War attempts by the press, film, and radio to capture specialized audiences as their main strategy in adjusting to the television age, and even more so from the rise of new media technologies from the 1970s, raised questions about the extent to which media would continue to promote national integration. But the continued dominant role of free-to-air television services in most Western countries is a reminder that the degree of fragmentation should not be exaggerated; and, while the decline of nationalism was a general phenomenon in the West in the second half of the twentieth century, its main causes are not to be found in the history of media.

Second, mass media were vehicles for the promotion of consumerism and the extension of US global influence. To be sure, this process was a complicated one, and it has often not been well understood. Weaknesses in the concept of cultural imperialism are examined in Chapters 9 and 12. As the experience of the US-based global media conglomerates suggests, these flaws include an exaggerated view of the tendency of audiences to absorb passively foreign cultural values. Claims that the global reach of US media fostered an uncritical acceptance of the American way of life or sympathy for US political interests are hard to reconcile with, for example, the largely negative views of the United States revealed by opinion polls in most parts of the world in the first years of the twenty-first century.[6] Nonetheless, both the global expansion of the US commercial model of television and the dominant place of American movies and television programs in international markets exerted a powerful influence on language, the spread of American popular culture, the marketing of consumer goods, and the promotion of consumption as a value.

Media and communications in the first decade of the twenty-first century have continued to be shaped by tensions, competition, and contradictions: between democratic expansion and oligopoly, between public service and commerce, between information and entertainment, between information and manipulation, between the national and the global. The interaction between different, and sometimes contradictory, processes remains central to an understanding of media; and history provides the key to understanding that interaction. Media history reminds us that practices and institutions that are often regarded as unavoidable or as the result of common sense are instead the product of particular historical circumstances or ideologies; that prevailing approaches to media organization and content are not the only possibilities; and that, even in a commercialized, globalized era, it is possible to envisage alternatives.

Notes

Chapter 1.   Introduction

1   John Tosh, *The Pursuit of History: Aims, Methods and New Directions in the Study of Modern History*, 2nd edn. (London: Longman, 1991), pp. 16, 18.
2   Kevin Williams, *Get Me a Murder a Day! A History of Mass Communication in Britain* (London: Arnold, 1998), p. vii.
3   The book that is closest to the present study in scope and purpose is now twenty years old: see Ken Ward, *Mass Communications and the Modern World* (Basingstoke: Macmillan, 1989). Two recent works are concerned with a larger historical period and are consequently less detailed than this book in their coverage of post-1890 developments: see Asa Briggs and Peter Burke, *A Social History of the Media: From Gutenberg to the Internet*, 2nd edn. (Cambridge: Polity, 2005); and Jane Chapman, *Comparative Media History: An Introduction: 1789 to the Present* (Cambridge: Polity, 2005).
4   Williams, *Get Me a Murder a Day!*, p. 2.
5   Ward, *Mass Communications and the Modern World*, p. 9.
6   Terry Flew, *Understanding Global Media* (Basingstoke: Palgrave Macmillan, 2007), pp. 206–7.
7   Manuel Castells, *The Rise of the Network Society* (Oxford: Blackwell, 1996); Manuel Castells (ed.), *The Network Society: A Cross-Cultural Perspective* (Cheltenham: Edward Elgar, 2004).

Chapter 2.   The Press as a Mass Medium

1   James Curran and Jean Seaton, *Power without Responsibility: The Press, Broadcasting and New Media in Britain*, 6th edn. (London: Routledge, 2003), p. 38.
2   Jeremy Black, *The English Press in the Eighteenth Century* (London: Croom Helm, 1987), p. 304.
3   Ibid., pp. 291, 301, 306.

4 Ken Ward, *Mass Communications and the Modern World* (Basingstoke: Macmillan, 1989), p. 38.

5 Ibid., pp. 26–7; see also Michael Emery, Edwin Emery, and Nancy L. Roberts, *The Press and America: An Interpretive History of the Mass Media*, 9th edn. (Boston: Allyn and Bacon, 2000).

6 Ward, *Mass Communications and the Modern World*, p. 35.

7 Emery et al., *The Press and America*, p. 230.

8 Curran and Seaton, *Power without Responsibility*, pp. 33–4.

9 Ibid., pp. 31–2.

10 Asa Briggs and Peter Burke, *A Social History of the Media: From Gutenberg to the Internet*, 2nd edn. (Cambridge: Polity, 2005), pp. 32–3.

11 J. Lee Thompson, *Northcliffe: Press Baron in Politics, 1865–1922* (London: John Murray, 2000), p. 35.

12 Francis Williams, *The Right to Know: The Rise of the World Press* (London: Longman, 1969), p. 79; Curran and Seaton, *Power without Responsibility*.

13 Ward, *Mass Communications and the Modern World*, pp. 41–3.

14 Ibid., pp. 41–2; Williams, *The Right to Know*, pp. 32–6.

15 Curran and Seaton, *Power without Responsibility*, p. 39.

16 Ward, *Mass Communications and the Modern World*, p. 42; Stefan Collini, "Lament for a Lost Culture," *Times Literary Supplement*, January 19, 2001, p. 4; J. Lee Thompson, *Politicians, the Press, and Propaganda: Lord Northcliffe and the Great War, 1914–1919* (Kent, OH: Kent State University Press, 2000), pp. xiv, 238.

17 Ward, *Mass Communications and the Modern World*, p. 31.

18 Briggs and Burke, *A Social History of the Media*, pp. 60, 61, 81–3.

19 David Paul Nord, *Communities of Journalism: A History of American Newspapers and their Readers* (Urbana, IL: University of Illinois Press, 2006); Mark Hampton, *Visions of the Press in Britain, 1850–1950* (Urbana, IL: University of Illinois Press, 2004).

20 Peter Young and Peter Jesser, *The Media and the Military: From the Crimea to Desert Strike* (South Melbourne: Macmillan Education, 1997), p. 23.

21 Williams, *The Right to Know*, p. 60; Ward, *Mass Communications and the Modern World*, p. 34.

22 Williams, *The Right to Know*, p. 63.

23 Ward, *Mass Communications and the Modern World*, p. 34.

24 Richard Allen Schwarzlose, *Newspapers: A Reference Guide* (Westport, CT: Greenwood Press, 1987), pp. xxix–xxx.

25 Stephen Badsey, "The Boer War as a Media War," in Peter Dennis and Jeffrey Grey (eds.), *The Boer War: Army, Nation and Empire* (Canberra: Army History Unit, Department of Defence, 2000), pp. 79, 83.

26 A. J. Anthony Morris, *The Scaremongers: The Advocacy of War and Rearmament 1896–1914* (London: Routledge and Kegan Paul, 1984).

27 Thompson, *Northcliffe*, p. 146.

28   See, e.g., Morris, *The Scaremongers*, pp. 365, 380–1; Ward, *Mass Communications and the Modern World*, pp. 58–9; R. Davenport-Hines, review of Thompson, *Northcliffe and Politicians, the Press and Propaganda* in *Times Literary Supplement* (June 2, 2000), p. 36; and S. Badsey, "The Missing Western Front: British Politics, Strategy, and Propaganda in 1918," in Mark Connelly and David Welch (eds.), *War and the Media: Reportage and Propaganda, 1900–2003* (London: I. B. Taurus, 2005), p. 50.
29   John Williams, *The Home Fronts: Britain, France and Germany 1914–1918* (London: Constable, 1972), p. 24.
30   Ward, *Mass Communications and the Modern World*, pp. 69–70.
31   Williams, *The Home Fronts*, pp. 258, 283. The quotation is from the *Rheinische-Westfalische Zeitung*.
32   Badsey, "The Missing Western Front," pp. 47, 60.
33   Young and Jesser, *The Media and the Military*, p. 33; Phillip Knightley, *The First Casualty: The War Correspondent as Hero and Myth Maker from the Crimea to Kosovo* (London: Prion, 2000); Miles Hudson and John Stanier, *War and the Media: A Random Searchlight* (Stroud: Sutton, 1997).
34   Peter J. S. Dunnett, *The World Newspaper Industry* (London: Croom Helm, 1988), p. 6.
35   Graham Murdock and Peter Golding, "The Structure, Ownership and Control of the Press, 1914–76," in George Boyce, James Curran, and Pauline Wingate (eds.), *Newspaper History from the Seventeenth Century to the Present Day* (London: Constable, 1978), p. 136.
36   Ibid., p. 130.
37   Emery et al., *The Press and America*, p. 293.
38   Ibid.
39   Ibid., p. 274; George H. Douglas, *The Golden Age of the Newspaper* (Westport, CT: Greenwood Press, 1999), p. 229.

Chapter 3.   The Development of the Film Industry

1   Quoted in Steven J. Ross, *Working-Class Hollywood: Silent Film and the Shaping of Class in America* (Princeton: Princeton University Press, 1998), p. 5.
2   Eric Rhode, *A History of the Cinema from its Origins to 1970* (New York: Hill and Wang, 1976), p. 16.
3   Charles Musser, *The Emergence of Cinema: The American Screen to 1907* (New York: Charles Scribner's, 1990), pp. 418–20.
4   Eileen Bowser, *The Transformation of Cinema 1907–1915* (New York: Charles Scribner's, 1990), p. 6; Russell Merritt, "Nickelodeon Theaters 1905–1914: Building an Audience for the Movies," in Tino Balio (ed.), *The American Film Industry* (Madison: University of Wisconsin Press, 1985), p. 86; Ken Ward,

Mass Communications and the Modern World (Basingstoke: Macmillan, 1989), p. 50; Kevin Williams, *Get Me a Murder a Day! A History of Mass Communication in Britain* (London: Arnold, 1998), p. 70; Klaus Kreimeier, *The Ufa Story: A History of Germany's Greatest Film Company, 1918–1945* (Berkeley and Los Angeles: University of California Press, 1999), p. 15.

5   Robert Sklar, *Film: An International History of the Medium* (New York: H. N. Abrams, 1993), pp. 47–8.

6   Quoted in Bowser, *Transformation of Cinema*, p. 3.

7   Lary May, *Screening out the Past: The Birth of Mass Culture and the Motion Picture Industry* (New York: Oxford University Press, 1980), pp. 147–66.

8   Sklar, *Film: An International History*, p. 63.

9   Victoria de Grazia, "Mass Culture and Sovereignty: The American Challenge to European Cinemas, 1920–1960," *Journal of Modern History*, 61 (1989), p. 61.

10   May, *Screening out the Past*, pp. 169–79; Neal Gabler, *An Empire of their Own: How the Jews Invented Hollywood* (New York: Doubleday, 1988).

11   Douglas Gomery, *The Hollywood Studio System* (New York: St Martin's Press, 1986), p. 9.

12   Ibid., p. 8.

13   Ibid., pp. 2, 12.

14   Ibid., pp. 14–23; Douglas Gomery, "Film and Business History: The Development of an American Mass Entertainment Industry," *Journal of Contemporary History*, 19/1 (1984), pp. 89–103.

15   Kristin Thompson, *Exporting Entertainment: America in the World Film Market 1907–34* (London: British Film Institute, 1985), pp. ix, 170; Ian Jarvie, *Hollywood's Overseas Campaign: The North Atlantic Movie Trade, 1920–1950* (Cambridge: Cambridge University Press, 1992), p. 18.

16   Susan Hayward, *French National Cinema* (London: Routledge, 1993), p. 20.

17   Thompson, *Exporting Entertainment*, pp. x, 100, 169.

18   John Grierson, "Notes for English Producers," quoted in Ian Jarvie and Robert L. Macmillan, "John Grierson on Hollywood's Success, 1927," *Historical Journal of Film, Radio and Television*, 9/3 (1989), p. 315.

19   Ross McKibbin, *Classes and Cultures: England 1918–1951* (Oxford: Oxford University Press, 1998), pp. 431–4. The quotation is from p. 431.

20   Hayward, *French National Cinema*, p. 20.

21   Quoted in Mark Glancy, "Temporary American Citizens? British Audiences, Hollywood Films and the Threat of Americanization in the 1920s," *Historical Journal of Film, Radio and Television*, 26/4 (October 2006), p. 468.

22   Quoted in Garth Jowett, *Film: The Democratic Art* (Boston: Little, Brown, 1976), p. 203.

23   Quoted in Jeffrey Richards, *The Age of the Dream Palace: Cinema and Society in Britain 1930–1939* (London: Routledge and Kegan Paul, 1984), p. 63.

24 Ruth Vasey, *The World according to Hollywood, 1918–1939* (Madison: University of Wisconsin Press, 1997), p. 7.

25 Ibid., p. 19.

26 Ibid., *passim*.

27 Ibid., pp. 51–5.

28 Kerry Segrave, *American Films Abroad: Hollywood's Domination of the World's Movie Screens from the 1890s to the Present* (Jefferson, NC: McFarland, 1997), p. 105.

29 Ibid.; Thomas Doherty, *Pre-Code Hollywood: Sex, Immorality, and Insurrection in American Cinema, 1930–1934* (New York: Columbia University Press, 1999), pp. 93–102; Thomas Cripps, *Hollywood's High Noon: Moviemaking and Society before Television* (Baltimore, MD: Johns Hopkins University Press, 1997), p. 87; Steven Carr, *Hollywood and Anti-Semitism: A Cultural History up to World War II* (Cambridge: Cambridge University Press, 2001), pp. 157–60.

30 Vasey, *World according to Hollywood*, pp. 89–90; Thompson, *Exporting Entertainment*, p. 121.

31 Quoted in Peter Kenez, *The Birth of the Propaganda State: Soviet Methods of Mass Mobilization, 1917–1929* (Cambridge: Cambridge University Press, 1985), p. 219.

32 Quoted in Garth S. Jowett, "Extended Images," in Raymond Williams (ed.), *Contact: Human Communication and its History* (London: Thames and Hudson, 1981), p. 193.

33 Jowett, *Film: The Democratic Art*, p. 475; Gregory D. Black, *Hollywood Censored: Morality Codes, Catholics, and the Movies* (Cambridge: Cambridge University Press, 1994), pp. 53–4; Frank Walsh, *Sin and Censorship: The Catholic Church and the Motion Picture Industry* (New Haven, CT: Yale University Press, 1996), p. 70.

34 Quoted in Doherty, *Pre-Code Hollywood*, p. 322. On the Payne Fund studies and the surrounding controversy, see Garth S. Jowett, Ian C. Jarvie, and Kathryn H. Fuller, *Children and the Movies: Media Influence and the Payne Fund Controversy* (Cambridge: Cambridge University Press, 1996); Jowett, *Film: The Democratic Art*, pp. 220–9; Robert Sklar, *Movie-Made America: A Cultural History of American Movies* (New York: Vintage Books, 1994), pp. 134–40; and Black, *Hollywood Censored*, pp. 151–5.

35 Quoted in Black, *Hollywood Censored*, p. 39; and John Trumpbour, *Selling Hollywood to the World: US and European Struggles for Mastery of the Global Film Industry, 1920–1950* (Cambridge: Cambridge University Press, 2002), p. 42.

36 See Vasey, *World according to Hollywood*, pp. 195, 205–10; and Sklar, *Movie-Made America*, p. 174.

37 Vasey, *World according to Hollywood*, pp. 197–8; Jowett, *Film: The Democratic Art*, pp. 272–3.

38   Vasey, *World according to Hollywood*, p. 196.

39   Ibid., pp. 202–6; Ross, *Working-Class Hollywood*, pp. 194–211.

40   Vasey, *World according to Hollywood*, pp. 49–62, 115–22, 140–93, 210–19; Allen L. Woll, "Hollywood Views the Mexican-American: From *The Greaser's Revenge* to *The Milagro Beanfield War*," in Robert Brent Toplin (ed.), *Hollywood as Mirror: Changing Views of "Outsiders" and "Enemies" in American Movies* (Westport, CT: Greenwood Press, 1993), pp. 41–52; Gina Marchetti, *Romance and the "Yellow Peril": Race, Sex, and Discursive Strategies in Hollywood Fiction* (Berkeley and Los Angeles: University of California Press, 1993).

41   Emmett J. Scott, quoted in Thomas Cripps, *Slow Fade to Black: The Negro in American Film, 1900–1942* (New York: Oxford University Press, 1977), p. 74.

42   See ibid., esp. pp. 170–202.

43   Ibid.; Vasey, *World according to Hollywood*, pp. 137–40.

Chapter 4.   The Growth of Radio Broadcasting

1   Susan J. Douglas, *Listening in: Radio and the American Imagination, From Amos 'n' Andy and Edward R. Murrow to Wolfman Jack and Howard Stern* (New York: Times Books, 1999), pp. 64–5.

2   Martin Shingler and Cindy Wieringa, *On Air: Methods and Meanings of Radio* (London: Hodder, 1998), p. 4.

3   Keith Geddes, with Gordon Bussey, *The Setmakers: A History of the Radio and Television Industry* (London: British Radio and Electronic Equipment Manufacturers' Association, 1991), pp. 12–13.

4   Hugh G. J. Aitken, *The Continuous Wave: Technology and American Radio, 1900–1932* (Princeton: Princeton University Press, 1985), p. 362; Susan J. Douglas, *Inventing American Broadcasting, 1899–1922* (Baltimore, MD: Johns Hopkins University Press, 1987), p. xxi. Geddes and Bussey, *The Setmakers*, provide a detailed account of the technical aspects of radio and television manufacturing, accompanied by excellent illustrative material; examples of analyses of social, commercial, and cultural aspects include works by Douglas, Hilmes, and Smulyan.

5   Susan Smulyan, *Selling Radio: The Commercialization of American Broadcasting 1920–1934* (Washington: Smithsonian Institution Press, 1994), pp. 8–9, 63.

6   Ken Ward, *Mass Communications and the Modern World* (Basingstoke: Macmillan, 1989, p. 81).

7   L. White, "The Growth of American Radio" and "Ragtime to Riches," in W. Schramm (ed.), *Mass Communications*, 2nd edn. (Urbana, IL: University

of Illinois Press, 1969); J. Fred MacDonald, *Don't Touch that Dial! Radio Programming in American Life, 1920–1960* (Chicago: Nelson Hall, 1979), p. 4.

8 Ward, *Mass Communications and the Modern World*, pp. 84–5; Smulyan, *Selling Radio*.

9 MacDonald, *Don't Touch that Dial!*, p. 63.

10 Ibid., p. 31.

11 Ibid., pp. 76–7.

12 Ibid., pp. 2, 25.

13 Smulyan, *Selling Radio*.

14 James Curran and Jean Seaton, *Power without Responsibility: The Press, Broadcasting and New Media in Britain*, 6th edn. (London: Routledge, 2003), pp. 109 ff.

15 Geddes and Bussey, *The Setmakers*, p. 16.

16 Ross McKibbin, *Classes and Cultures: England 1918–1951* (Oxford: Oxford University Press, 1998), p. 475.

17 Ward, *Mass Communications and the Modern World*, p. 87; Paddy Scannell and David Cardiff, *A Social History of British Broadcasting*, vol. 1, *1922–1939, Serving the Nation* (Oxford: Basil Blackwell, 1991), pp. 5–6.

18 Curran and Seaton, *Power without Responsibility*, pp. 111, 112.

19 Ibid., p. 121.

20 Ward, *Mass Communications and the Modern World*; Curran and Seaton, *Power without Responsibility*; Robert J. Brown, *Manipulating the Ether: The Power of Broadcast Radio in Thirties America* (Jefferson, NC: McFarland, 1998), p. 3.

21 Eric Hobsbawm, *Age of Extremes: The Short Twentieth Century 1914–1991* (London: Michael Joseph 1994), p. 197.

22 Alice Goldfarb Marquis, "Written on the Wind: The Impact of Radio during the 1930s," *Journal of Contemporary History*, 19 (1984), pp. 403–4; Lee De Forest, *Father of Radio: The Autobiography of Lee de Forest* (Chicago: Wilcox and Follett, 1950).

23 Stephen Barnard, *On the Radio: Music Radio in Britain* (Milton Keynes: Open University Press, 1989).

24 McKibbin, *Classes and Cultures*, p. 465.

25 Brown, *Manipulating the Ether*, p. 225.

26 MacDonald, *Don't Touch that Dial!*, p. 10.

27 Michele Hilmes, *Radio Voices: American Broadcasting, 1922–1952* (Minneapolis: University of Minnesota Press, 1997), p. 68; Gwenyth L. Jackaway, *Media at War: Radio's Challenge to the Newspapers, 1924–1939* (Westport, CT: Praeger, 1995).

28 Hilmes, *Radio Voices*, p. xiv.

29 Douglas, *Listening in*, p. 9.

30 Jean Seaton, "Writing the History of Broadcasting," in David Cannadine (ed.), *History and the Media* (Basingstoke: Palgrave Macmillan, 2004), pp. 141–59.

31 Brown, *Manipulating the Ether*, p. 1.
32 Douglas, *Listening in*, p. 5.
33 Ibid., p. 11; Scannell and Cardiff, *A Social History of British Broadcasting*.
34 Hilmes, *Radio Voices*, chs. 5–6.
35 Douglas, *Listening in*, p. 9.

Chapter 5.   The Rise of Advertising

1 Quoted in Daniel Pope, *The Making of Modern Advertising* (New York: Basic Books, 1983), p. 17.
2 Quoted in Raymond Williams, "Advertising: The Magic System," in *Problems in Materialism and Culture: Selected Essays* (London: Verso, 1980), p. 172.
3 See Susan Strasser, *Satisfaction Guaranteed: The Making of the American Mass Market* (New York: Pantheon, 1989), pp. 206–11.
4 Pope, *Making of Modern Advertising*, pp. 18–61; Williams, "Advertising," pp. 177–8; Olivier Zunz, *Why the American Century?* (Chicago: University of Chicago Press, 1998), pp. 80–5; Strasser, *Satisfaction Guaranteed*, p. 18.
5 Pope, *Making of Modern Advertising*, pp. 48–61; Williams, "Advertising," pp. 175–6; Strasser, *Satisfaction Guaranteed*, pp. 29–57; Michael Schudson, *Advertising, the Uneasy Persuasion: Its Dubious Impact on American Society* (London: Routledge, 1993), *passim*.
6 Pope, *Making of Modern Advertising*, pp. 112–83; Stephen Fox, *The Mirror Makers: A History of American Advertising and its Creators* (New York: Vintage, 1985), pp. 19–77; Strasser, *Satisfaction Guaranteed*, pp. 93–5.
7 Pope, *Making of Modern Advertising*, p. 26.
8 See Steven J. Ross, *Working–Class Hollywood: Silent Film and the Shaping of Class in America* (Princeton: Princeton University Press, 1998), p. 178; William E. Leuchtenburg, *The Perils of Prosperity, 1914–32* (Chicago: University of Chicago Press, 1958), p. 195.
9 Daniel Horowitz, *The Morality of Spending: Attitudes toward the Consumer Society in America, 1875–1940* (Baltimore, MD: Johns Hopkins University Press, 1985); William Leach, *Land of Desire: Merchants, Power, and the Rise of a New American Culture* (New York: Pantheon, 1993).
10 Roland Marchand, *Advertising the American Dream: Making Way for Modernity, 1920–1940* (Berkeley and Los Angeles: University of California Press, 1985), pp. 52–87; Jackson Lears, *Fables of Abundance: A Cultural History of Advertising in America* (New York: Basic Books, 1994), pp. 206–34; Zunz, *Why the American Century?*, pp. 57–62; Strasser, *Satisfaction Guaranteed*, pp. 155–9; Williams, "Advertising," pp. 179–80.
11 Marchand, *Advertising the American Dream*, *passim*, esp. pp. 9–24, 349–52; Lears, *Fables of Abundance*, pp. 162–95; Fox, *The Mirror Makers*, pp. 86–101;

Williams, "Advertising," pp. 179–81, 184–5; Susan Smulyan, *Selling Radio: The Commercialization of American Broadcasting 1920–1934* (Washington: Smithsonian Institution Press, 1994), pp. 88–91.

12   Marchand, *Advertising the American Dream*, pp. 88–94, 105–8; Smulyan, *Selling Radio*, pp. 68–71. The quotation is from ibid., p. 70.

13   Fox, *The Mirror Makers*, p. 154.

14   Ibid., pp. 150–62; Marchand, *Advertising the American Dream*, pp. 94–116; Smulyan, *Selling Radio, passim*; Susan J. Douglas, *Listening in: Radio and the American Imagination, From Amos 'n' Andy and Edward R. Murrow to Wolfman Jack and Howard Stern* (New York: Times Books, 1999), pp. 120–2.

15   Smulyan, *Selling Radio*, pp. 86–92; Marchand, *Advertising the American Dream*, pp. 66–9, 72; Charles McGovern, "Consumption and Citizenship in the United States, 1900–1940," in Susan Strasser, Charles McGovern, and Matthias Judt (eds.), *Getting and Spending: European and American Consumer Societies in the Twentieth Century* (Cambridge: Cambridge University Press, 1998), pp. 45–6.

16   McGovern, "Consumption and Citizenship," p. 46; Marchand, *Advertising the American Dream*, pp. 167–79, 186–8; David E. Nye, *Image Worlds: Corporate Identities at General Electric, 1890–1930* (Cambridge, MA: MIT Press, 1985), p. 129; Schudson, *Advertising, the Uneasy Persuasion*, pp. 182–97; Richard Kluger, *Ashes to Ashes: America's Hundred-Year Cigarette War, the Public Health, and the Unabashed Triumph of Philip Morris* (New York: Alfred A. Knopf, 1996), pp. 64–6.

17   Quoted in Nye, *Image Worlds*, pp. 130–1. See also Marchand, *Advertising the American Dream*, pp. 167–79.

18   Marchand, *Advertising the American Dream*, pp. 167–79; Lears, *Fables of Abundance*, pp. 183–92.

19   On the comparison with Europe, see Victoria de Grazia, "Changing Consumption Regimes in Europe, 1930–1970: Comparative Perspectives on the Distribution Problem," in Strasser, McGovern, and Judt (eds.), *Getting and Spending*, pp. 67–9.

20   Marchand, *Advertising the American Dream*, p. 218.

21   Ibid., pp. 63–83, 194–201, 217–22, 291–3; McGovern, "Consumption and Citizenship," pp. 47–8; Zunz, *Why the American Century?*, pp. 60–1, 94.

22   See Williams, "Advertising," p. 187.

23   Kluger, *Ashes to Ashes*, pp. 112, 129–31, 152.

24   See Lears, *Fables of Abundance*, pp. 206–10, 223–33.

25   Marchand, *Advertising the American Dream*, pp. 18–21; Fox, *The Mirror Makers*, pp. 97–8.

26   David M. Potter, *People of Plenty: Economic Abundance and the American Character* (Chicago: University of Chicago Press, 1954), pp. 166–88. The quotation is from p. 177. For critiques of the Potter thesis on advertising,

see Jackson Lears, "Reconsidering Abundance: A Plea for Ambiguity," in Strasser, McGovern, and Judt (eds.), *Getting and Spending*, pp. 454–5; and Schudson, *Advertising, the Uneasy Persuasion*, pp. 246–50. Galbraith's criticisms of advertising are set out in *The New Industrial State* (Boston: Houghton Mifflin, 1967), esp. pp. 203–10, 272–3.

27 Marcuse's argument on needs is developed in his *One Dimensional Man: Studies in the Ideology of Advanced Industrial Society* (London: Routledge and Kegan Paul, 1964).

28 For a clear statement of a Marxist interpretation of the history of advertising, see Stuart Ewen, *Captains of Consciousness: Advertising and the Social Roots of the Consumer Culture* (New York: McGraw-Hill, 1976).

29 Kluger, *Ashes to Ashes*, pp. 57–8, 60–2, 71–2, 76–9, 81–2, 85–8, 90–1.

30 Ibid., pp. 62–6; Schudson, *Advertising, the Uneasy Persuasion*, pp. 178–204. The quotations are from ibid., pp. 183, 197.

31 Marchand, *Advertising the American Dream*, pp. 63–6, 191–4; Zunz, *Why the American Century?*, pp. 59–62.

32 Nye, *Image Worlds*, p. 129.

33 See Patricia Springborg, *The Problem of Human Needs and the Critique of Civilisation* (London: George Allen and Unwin, 1981); and Schudson, *Advertising, the Uneasy Persuasion*, passim.

34 Schudson, *Advertising, the Uneasy Persuasion*, pp. 11, 240.

35 Ibid., p. 241.

Chapter 6.   Propaganda in Peace and War

1 Michael Balfour, *Propaganda in War 1939–1945: Organisations, Policies and Publics in Britain and Germany* (London: Routledge and Kegan Paul, 1979), pp. 421–2; David Welch (ed.), *Nazi Propaganda: The Power and the Limitations* (London: Croom Helm, 1983), p. 2.

2 Jacques Ellul, *Propaganda: The Formation of Men's Attitudes*. New York: Knopf, 1965; Garth S. Jowett and Victoria O'Donnell, *Propaganda and Persuasion*, 2nd edn. (Newbury Park, CA: Sage, 1992), p. 4.

3 Peter Kenez, *The Birth of the Propaganda State: Soviet Methods of Mass Mobilization 1917–1929* (Cambridge: Cambridge University Press, 1985), pp. 4, 8; Victoria E. Bonnell, *Iconography of Power: Soviet Political Posters under Lenin and Stalin* (Berkeley and Los Angeles: University of California Press, 1997), pp. 1–3.

4 Anne Applebaum, *Gulag: A History* (London: Penguin, 2003).

5 Ibid., p. 4.

6 Jeffrey Brooks, *Thank You, Comrade Stalin! Soviet Public Culture from Revolution to Cold War* (Princeton: Princeton University Press, 2000), p. 5.

7   Ibid.

8   Sheila Fitzpatrick, *Everyday Stalinism: Ordinary Life in Extraordinary Times; Soviet Russia in the 1930s* (New York: Oxford University Press, 1999), p. 21.

9   Directive quoted by Applebaum, *Gulag*, p. 221.

10   Richard Taylor, *Film Propaganda: Soviet Russia and Nazi Germany*, 1st edn. (London: Croom Helm, 1979), p. 71.

11   Richard Taylor and Derek Spring (eds.), *Stalinism and Soviet Cinema* (London: Routledge, 1993), pp. 55, 63, 71; David King, *The Commissar Vanishes: The Falsification of Photographs and Art in Stalin's Russia* (New York: Metropolitan Books/Henry Holt, 1997).

12   Ian Kershaw, *Hitler 1889–1936: Hubris* (New York: W. W. Norton, 1998), p. 133.

13   Z. A. B. Zeman, *Nazi Propaganda*, 2nd edn. (Oxford: Oxford University Press, 1973); William Sheridan Allen, *The Nazi Seizure of Power: The Experience of a Single German Town 1922–1945*, rev. edn. (New York: Franklin Watts, 1984), esp. ch. 13; George L. Mosse, *Nazi Culture: Intellectual, Cultural and Social Life in the Third Reich* (Madison: University of Wisconsin Press, 1966), p. 366.

14   Bullock, Alan, *Hitler: A Study in Tyranny*, rev. edn. (Harmondsworth: Penguin, 1962), p. 217.

15   Zeman, *Nazi Propaganda*, pp. 24, 30.

16   Ibid., p. 38; Taylor, *Film Propaganda*, p. 157.

17   Richard Taylor, "Goebbels and the Function of Propaganda," in Welch (ed.), *Nazi Propaganda*, pp. 29–44; Ian Kershaw, "How Effective Was Nazi Propaganda?" in ibid., pp. 180–205.

18   Zeman, *Nazi Propaganda*, pp. 44–5; David Welch, *The Third Reich: Politics and Propaganda*, 2nd edn. (London: Routledge, 2002), pp. 43–7; on Dietrich's role, see Jeffrey Herf, *The Jewish Enemy: Nazi Propaganda during World War II and the Holocaust* (Cambridge, MA: Belknap/Harvard University Press, 2006), pp. 22–6.

19   Herf, *The Jewish Enemy*, pp. 14, 28–31.

20   Welch, *The Third Reich*, p. 38.

21   Ibid., p. 42

22   Zeman, *Nazi Propaganda*, p. 49; Robert Jackall (ed.), *Propaganda* (New York: New York University Press, 1995), p. 188; Horst J. P. Bergmeier and Rainer E. Lotz, *Hitler's Airwaves: The Inside Story of Nazi Radio Broadcasting and Propaganda Swing* (New Haven: Yale University Press, 1997), p. 136.

23   See David Welch, "Nazi Film Policy: Control, Ideology, and Propaganda," in Glenn R. Cuomo (ed.), *National Socialist Cultural Policy* (New York: St Martin's Press, 1995), pp. 100–7; David Welch, *Propaganda and the German Cinema 1933–1945* (Oxford: Oxford University Press, 1983).

24   Welch, "Nazi Film Policy," p. 107; Welch, *Propaganda and the German Cinema*, pp. 30–8; Klaus Kreimeier, *The Ufa Story: A History of Germany's Greatest*

Film Company 1918–1945, trans Robert and Rita Kimber (New York: Hill and Wang, 1996).

25 See, e.g., Linda Deutschmann, *Triumph of the Will: The Image of the Third Reich* (Wakefield: Longwood Academic, 1991).

26 Welch, *The Third Reich*, p. 153.

27 See, e.g., Sarah Davies, *Popular Opinion in Stalin's Russia* (Cambridge: Cambridge University Press, 1997), pp. 32, 47, 118–19. Davies has used letters, diaries, memoirs, and summaries produced by the NKVD and party information departments on popular responses to particular events to substantiate her arguments about worker dissatisfaction, discontent, and "an autonomous current of popular opinion" under Stalin.

28 James von Geldern and Richard Stites (eds.), *Mass Culture in Soviet Russia: Tales, Poems, Songs, Movies, Plays and Folklore 1917–1953* (Bloomington, IN: Indiana University Press, 1995), p. xxvii; Davies, *Popular Opinion in Stalin's Russia*, pp. 9, 183; Sheila Fitzpatrick, *Everyday Stalinism: Ordinary Life in Extraordinary Times; Soviet Russia in the 1930s* (New York: Oxford University Press, 1999), p. 224.

29 Applebaum, *Gulag*, pp. 224–8.

30 Jochen Hellbeck, *Revolution on my Mind: Writing a Diary under Stalin* (Cambridge, MA: Harvard University Press, 2006); Catherine Merridale, *Night of Stone: Death and Memory in Twentieth-Century Russia* (New York: Penguin, 2002), and *Ivan's War: Life and Death in the Red Army, 1939–1945* (London: Faber and Faber, 2005).

31 Kershaw, "How Effective Was Nazi Propaganda?" pp. 180–205.

32 David Welch, "Nazi Wartime Newsreel Propaganda," in K. R. M. Short (ed.), *Film and Radio Propaganda in World War II* (Knoxville, TN: University of Tennessee Press, 1983), pp. 201–19

33 Ibid.; Herf, *The Jewish Enemy*, p. 232; Daniel J. Goldhagen, *Hitler's Willing Executioners: Ordinary Germans and the Holocaust* (New York: Alfred A. Knopf, 1996); Welch, *The Third Reich*, pp. 165, 170–1; Jo Fox, *Film Propaganda in Britain and Nazi German: World War II Cinema* (Oxford: Berg, 2007), pp. 6, 313–15.

34 See George H. Roeder, Jr., *The Censored War: American Visual Experience during World War Two* (New Haven, CT: Yale University Press, 1993), p. 2.

35 Richard Polenberg, *One Nation Divisible: Class, Race, and Ethnicity in the United States since 1938* (Harmondsworth: Penguin, 1980), p. 69.

36 Quoted in Clayton R. Koppes and Gregory D. Black, "Blacks, Loyalty, and Motion-Picture Propaganda in World War II," *Journal of American History*, 73/2 (1986), p. 383.

37 Garth Jowett, *Film: The Democratic Art* (Boston: Little, Brown, 1976), p. 310; Robert Sklar, *Movie-Made America: A Cultural History of American Movies* (New York: Vintage Books, 1994), p. 250.

38   On newsreels in the USA during the Second World War, see Thomas Doherty, *Projections of War: Hollywood, American Culture, and World War II*, 2nd edn. (New York: Columbia University Press, 1999), pp. 227–50.

39   Quoted in William T. Murphy, "The United States Government and the Use of Motion Pictures during World War II," in Abe Mark Nornes and Fukushima Yukio (eds.), *The Japan/America Film Wars: World War II Propaganda and its Cultural Contexts* (Chur, Switzerland: Harwood, 1994), p. 61. See especially David Culbert, " 'Why We Fight': Social Engineering for a Democratic Society at War," in Short (ed.), *Film and Radio Propaganda in World War II*, pp. 173–91.

40   See Thomas Cripps, *Making Movies Black: The Hollywood Message Movie from World War II to the Civil Rights Era* (New York: Oxford University Press, 1993), pp. 102–25.

41   Ibid., *passim*; Koppes and Black, "Blacks, Loyalty, and Motion-Picture Propaganda," pp. 383–406; Clayton R. Koppes and Gregory D. Black, *Hollywood Goes to War: How Politics, Profits, and Propaganda Shaped World War II Movies* (New York: Free Press, 1987), pp. 84–90, 178–84; Doherty, *Projections of War*, pp. 205–26.

42   Koppes and Black, *Hollywood Goes to War*, p. 179.

43   Thomas Cripps, "Racial Ambiguities in American Propaganda Movies," in Short (ed.), *Film and Radio Propaganda in World War II*, pp. 125–45.

44   Barbara Dianne Savage, *Broadcasting Freedom: Radio, War, and the Politics of Race, 1938–1948* (Chapel Hill, NC: University of North Carolina Press, 1999), p. 6.

45   Ibid., esp. pp. 106–42.

46   Roeder, *The Censored War*, pp. 7–25.

47   Nicholas Pronay, "The News Media at War," in Nicholas Pronay and D. W. Spring (eds.), *Propaganda, Politics and Film, 1918–45* (London: Macmillan, 1982), p. 183; Philip M. Taylor, *Munitions of the Mind: A History of Propaganda from the Ancient World to the Present Era* (Manchester: Manchester University Press, 1995), p. 212.

48   Quoted in Pronay, "The News Media at War," p. 182.

49   Ibid., pp. 186–96.

50   Ibid., p. 174.

51   Quoted in Balfour, *Propaganda in War 1939–1945*, p. 432.

52   Quoted in Paul Lashmar and James Oliver, *Britain's Secret Propaganda War* (Stroud: Sutton, 1998), p. 19.

53   See John Dower, *War without Mercy: Race and Power in the Pacific War* (New York: Pantheon, 1986); and Michael Renov, "Warring Images: Stereotype and American Representations of the Japanese, 1941–1991," in Nornes and Yukio (eds.), *The Japan/America Film Wars*, pp. 104–8.

54 Lynette Finch, "Knowing the Enemy: Australian Psychological Warfare and the Business of Influencing Minds in the Second World War," *War and Society*, 16/2 (1998), pp. 72, 83.

55 Quoted in Kay Saunders, " 'An Instrument of Strategy': Propaganda, Public Policy and the Media in Australia during the Second World War," *War and Society*, 15/2 (1997), pp. 85–6.

56 Ibid., pp. 86–7; Finch, "Knowing the Enemy," pp. 72, 83.

57 Koppes and Black, *Hollywood Goes to War*, pp. 100, 248–82; Doherty, *Projections of War*, pp. 122–48.

58 Dower, *War without Mercy*.

Chapter 7. Cold War and Communications

1 Quoted in Walter L. Hixson, *Parting the Curtain: Propaganda, Culture, and the Cold War, 1945–1961* (New York: St Martin's Press, 1997), p. 14.

2 Quoted in Frances Stonor Saunders, *Who Paid the Piper?: The CIA and the Cultural Cold War* (London: Granta, 1999), p. 148.

3 On ideology and US Cold War foreign policy, see John Fousek, *To Lead the Free World: American Nationalism and the Cultural Roots of the Cold War* (Chapel Hill, NC: University of North Carolina Press, 2000); Michael H. Hunt, *Ideology and US Foreign Policy* (New Haven, CT: Yale University Press, 1987), esp. pp. 125–98; W. Scott Lucas, "Beyond Diplomacy: Propaganda and the History of the Cold War," in Gary D. Rawnsley (ed.), *Cold-War Propaganda in the 1950s* (New York: St Martin's Press, 1999), pp. 11–30; and Scott Lucas, "Campaigns of Truth: The Psychological Strategy Board and American Ideology, 1951–1953," *International History Review*, 18 (1996), pp. 279–302.

4 Quoted in Hixson, *Parting the Curtain*, p. 24.

5 Quoted in Robert J. McMahon, *Colonialism and Cold War: The United States and the Struggle for Indonesian Independence, 1945–49* (Ithaca, NY: Cornell University Press, 1981), p. 43.

6 Richard Stites, "Heaven and Hell: Soviet Propaganda Constructs the World," in Rawnsley (ed.), *Cold-War Propaganda in the 1950s*, pp. 85–103; Martin Ebon, *The Soviet Propaganda Machine* (New York: McGraw-Hill, 1987), pp. 3–16.

7 Ellen Mickiewicz, "Images of America," in Everette E. Dennis, George Gerbner, and Yassen N. Zassoursky (eds.), *Beyond the Cold War: Soviet and American Media Images* (Newbury Park, CA: Sage, 1991), p. 28.

8 Stites, "Heaven and Hell," pp. 91–8.

9 Susan L. Carruthers, " 'Not Just Washed but Dry-Cleaned': Korea and the 'Brainwashing' Scare of the 1950s," in Rawnsley (ed.), *Cold-War Propaganda*

in the 1950s, pp. 47–66; Abbott Gleason, *Totalitarianism: The Inner History of the Cold War* (New York: Oxford University Press, 1995), pp. 89–107.

10   See Mark W. Hopkins, *Mass Media in the Soviet Union* (New York: Pegasus, 1970), p. 339; and Reinhold Wagnleitner, *Coca-Colonization and the Cold War: The Cultural Mission of the United States in Austria after the Second World War* (Chapel Hill, NC: University of North Carolina Press, 1994), pp. 60–1.

11   Michael Nelson, *War of the Black Heavens: The Battles of Western Broadcasting in the Cold War* (London: Brassey's, 1997); Hixson, *Parting the Curtain*, pp. 32–7, 46–52; Ellen Propper Mickiewicz, *Media and the Russian Public* (New York: Praeger, 1981), pp. 137–42.

12   Hopkins, *Mass Media in the Soviet Union*, pp. 336–7.

13   Stites, "Heaven and Hell," p. 101.

14   Larissa Fedotova, "The Image of the United States in the Soviet Mass Media: The Results of Sociological Surveys," in Dennis, Gerbner, and Zassoursky (eds.), *Beyond the Cold War*, p. 61.

15   Anne Applebaum, "After the Gulag," *New York Review of Books* (October 24, 2002), p. 40.

16   On the subject of loyalty to the Soviet state during the postwar years, including the loyalty of victims of the regime, see Catherine Merridale, *Night of Stone: Death and Memory in Twentieth-Century Russia* (New York: Viking, 2001); Nanci Adler, *The Gulag Survivor: Beyond the Soviet System* (New Brunswick, NJ: Transaction, 2002); Orlando Figes, *The Whisperers: Private Life in Stalin's Russia* (London: Allen Lane, 2007), esp. pp. 455–656; and Applebaum, "After the Gulag," pp. 40–2.

17   US Department of State, *Foreign Relations of the United States, 1950*, vol. 1 (Washington: US Government Printing Office, 1977), pp. 238–9.

18   See, e.g., Stephen J. Whitfield, *The Culture of the Cold War* (Baltimore, MD: Johns Hopkins University Press, 1991), pp. 154–63; Mark H. Van Pelt, "The Cold War on the Air," *Journal of Popular Culture*, 18 (1984), pp. 97–110; J. Fred MacDonald, *Television and the Red Menace: The Video Road to Vietnam* (New York: Praeger, 1985), pp. 58–100; and Nancy E. Bernhard, *US Television News and Cold War Propaganda, 1947–1960* (Cambridge: Cambridge University Press, 1999).

19   See Walter LaFeber, "American Policy-Makers, Public Opinion, and the Outbreak of the Cold War, 1945–50," in Yonosuke Nagai and Akira Iriye (eds.), *The Origins of the Cold War in Asia* (New York: Columbia University Press, 1977), pp. 55–6.

20   The point is well made in the context of the 1980s by Daniel C. Hallin, "Images of Self and Others in American Television Coverage of the Reagan–Gorbachev Summits," in Dennis, Gerbner, and Zassoursky (eds.), *Beyond the Cold War*, p. 58; and Daniel C. Hallin, *We Keep America on Top of the*

World: Television Journalism and the Public Sphere (London: Routledge, 1994), pp. 105–8.

21 See Thomas Powers, "The Plot Thickens," *New York Review of Books* (May 11, 2000), pp. 53–60.

22 Whitfield, *Culture of the Cold War*, pp. 163–4; Ken Ward, *Mass Communications and the Modern World* (Basingstoke: Macmillan, 1989), pp. 158–9; James L. Baughman, *The Republic of Mass Culture: Journalism, Filmmaking, and Broadcasting in America since 1941* (Baltimore, MD: Johns Hopkins University Press, 1992), pp. 64–5; David Halberstam, *The Fifties* (New York: Ballantine Books, 1994), p. 55; Bernhard, *US Television News*, pp. 156–77.

23 Quoted in Erik Barnouw, *A History of Broadcasting in the United States*, 3 vols. (New York: Oxford University Press, 1966–70), vol. 2, *The Golden Web, 1933–1953*, p. 251; and Lary May, *The Big Tomorrow: Hollywood and the Politics of the American Way* (Chicago: University of Chicago Press, 2000), p. 197.

24 Barnouw, *A History of Broadcasting*, vol. 2, pp. 253–73. The quotation is from p. 265.

25 See Thom Andersen, "Red Hollywood," in Suzanne Ferguson and Barbara Groseclose (eds.), *Literature and the Visual Arts in Contemporary Society* (Columbus, OH: Ohio State University Press, 1985), pp. 156–7.

26 Quoted in May, *The Big Tomorrow*, p. 177.

27 Whitfield, *Culture of the Cold War*, pp. 132–3; Bernard F. Dick, *Radical Innocence: A Critical Study of the Hollywood Ten* (Lexington: University Press of Kentucky, 1989), pp. 5–7; Ian Hamilton, *Writers in Hollywood 1915–1951* (New York: Harper and Row, 1990), pp. 284, 290.

28 Whitfield, *Culture of the Cold War*, pp. 146–9.

29 May, *The Big Tomorrow*, pp. 175–80, 202–4; Saunders, *Who Paid the Piper?*, pp. 284–95. Valuable studies of the Cold War's impact on Hollywood film content include May, *The Big Tomorrow*; Whitfield, *Culture of the Cold War*; Andersen, "Red Hollywood"; Les K. Adler, "The Politics of Culture: Hollywood and the Cold War," in Robert Griffith and Athan Theoharis (eds.), *The Specter: Original Essays in the Cold War and the Origins of McCarthyism* (New York: New Viewpoints, 1974), pp. 242–60; and Daniel J. Leab, "Hollywood and the Cold War, 1945–1961," in Robert Brent Toplin (ed.), *Hollywood as Mirror: Changing Views of 'Outsiders' and 'Enemies' in American Movies* (Westport, CT: Greenwood Press, 1993), pp. 117–37.

30 See MacDonald, *Television and the Red Menace*, pp. 101–45.

31 Ibid., p. 145; and Whitfield, *Culture of the Cold War*, pp. 162–3.

32 Brett Silverstein, quoted in George Gerbner, "The Image of Russians in American Media and The 'New Epoch'," in Dennis, Gerbner, and Zassoursky (eds.), *Beyond the Cold War*, p. 31.

33 Ibid., pp. 31–2.

34   On the concept of psychological warfare, see Christopher Simpson, *Science of Coercion: Communication Research and Psychological Warfare 1945–1960* (New York: Oxford University Press, 1994), esp. pp. 3–14, 31–51, 87–93; and Hixson, *Parting the Curtain*, pp. 2–4.

35   Hixson, *Parting the Curtain*, p. 10. On the Eisenhower administration's promotion of psychological warfare, see Kenneth Osgood, *Total Cold War: Eisenhower's Secret Propaganda Battle at Home and Abroad* (Lawrence, KS: University Press of Kansas, 2006).

36   Quoted in Hixson, *Parting the Curtain*, pp. 13–14.

37   Ibid., p. 21.

38   Paul Lashmar and James Oliver, *Britain's Secret Propaganda War* (Stroud: Sutton, 1998). On the IRD's influence on British cinema in the 1950s and 1960s, see Tony Shaw, *British Cinema and the Cold War: The State, Propaganda and Consensus* (London: I. B. Tauris, 2001), esp. pp. 66–7.

39   Gary D. Rawnsley, *Radio Diplomacy and Propaganda: The BBC and VOA in International Politics, 1956–64* (New York: St Martin's Press, 1996), p. 14.

40   Hixson, *Parting the Curtain*, pp. 37–46. The quotations are from p. 38.

41   Quoted in Nelson, *War of the Black Heavens*, p. 60.

42   Ibid., p. 37.

43   Rawnsley, *Radio Diplomacy and Propaganda*; Lashmar and Oliver, *Britain's Secret Propaganda War*, pp. 57–65.

44   For discussion of this question, see Hixson, *Parting the Curtain*, pp. 32–7, 46–52; Rawnsley, *Radio Diplomacy and Propaganda*, pp. 67–108, 166–82; Nelson, *War of the Black Heavens*, pp. 62–6; and Mickiewicz, *Media and the Russian Public*, pp. 137–42.

45   There is a substantial literature on the role of Western radio in the Hungarian uprising. See especially Rawnsley, *Radio Diplomacy and Propaganda*, pp. 67–108; Gary D. Rawnsley, "The BBC External Services and the Hungarian Uprising, 1956," in Rawnsley (ed.), *Cold-War Propaganda in the 1950s*, pp. 165–81; George R. Urban, *Radio Free Europe and the Pursuit of Democracy: My War within the Cold War* (New Haven, CT: Yale University Pres, 1997), pp. 211–44, 281–91; Hixson, *Parting the Curtain*, pp. 79–86; Nelson, *War of the Black Heavens*, pp. 69–84; Johanna Granville, "Radio Free Europe and International Decision-Making during the Hungarian Crisis of 1956," *Historical Journal of Film, Radio and Television*, 24/4 (2004), pp. 589–611; Johanna Granville, " 'Caught with Jam on Our Fingers': Radio Free Europe and the Hungarian Revolution of 1956," *Diplomatic History*, 29/5 (November 2005), pp. 811–39; and Charles Gati, *Failed Illusions: Moscow, Washington, Budapest, and the 1956 Hungarian Revolt* (Washington: Woodrow Wilson Center Press, 2006), *passim*.

46   Rawnsley, *Radio Diplomacy and Propaganda*, pp. 109–43.

47   On the fundamental shift in US propaganda approaches from the mid-1950s, see Hixson, *Parting the Curtain*.

48 Major studies of US cultural diplomacy during the Cold War include Hixson, *Parting the Curtain*; Wagnleitner, *Coca-Colonization and the Cold War*; Richard Pells, *Not Like Us: How Europeans Have Loved, Hated, and Transformed American Culture since World War II* (New York: Basic Books, 1997); Robert H. Haddow, *Pavilions of Plenty: Exhibiting American Culture Abroad in the 1950s* (Washington: Smithsonian Institution Press, 1997); Osgood, *Total Cold War*; and Jessica C. E. Gienow-Hecht, *Transmission Impossible: American Journalism as Cultural Diplomacy in Postwar Germany, 1945–1955* (Baton Rouge, LA: Louisiana State University Press, 1999). On the jazz tours, see Penny M. Von Eschen, *Satchmo Blows up the World: Jazz Ambassadors Play the Cold War* (Cambridge, MA: Harvard University Press, 2004).

49 See Saunders, *Who Paid the Piper?*; Hugh Wilford, *The CIA, the British Left and the Cold War: Calling the Tune?* (London: Frank Cass, 2003); and Volker R. Berghahn, *America and the Intellectual Cold Wars in Europe: Shepard Stone between Philanthropy, Academy, and Diplomacy* (Princeton: Princeton University Press, 2001).

50 Lashmar and Oliver, *Britain's Secret Propaganda War*; Wilford, *The CIA, the British Left and the Cold War*, pp. 48–81.

51 Quoted in Saunders, *Who Paid the Piper?*, p. 408.

52 Quoted in ibid., p. 409. On responses to the exposure of CCF links with the CIA, and on the ethical issues involved, see ibid., pp. 4–5, 367–416.

53 Simpson, *Science of Coercion*.

54 Hixson, *Parting the Curtain*, p. 223. See also Nelson, *War of the Black Heavens*.

Chapter 8.   Television and Consumer Societies

1 Quoted in James Curran and Jean Seaton, *Power without Responsibility: The Press, Broadcasting and New Media in Britain*, 6th edn. (London: Routledge, 2003), p. 173.

2 Raymond Williams, *Television: Technology and Cultural Form* (New York: Schocken Books, 1975), pp. 14–15.

3 Susan Briggs, "Television in the Home and Family," in Anthony Smith with Richard Paterson (eds.), *Television: An International History*, 2nd edn. (Oxford: Oxford University Press, 1998), p. 110.

4 See Williams, *Television, passim*.

5 Nancy E. Bernhard, *US Television News and Cold War Propaganda, 1947–1960* (Cambridge: Cambridge University Press, 1999), pp. 5, 47.

6 Les Brown, "The American Networks," in Smith with Paterson (eds.), *Television: An International History*, p. 147; James L. Baughman, *The Republic of Mass Culture: Journalism, Filmmaking, and Broadcasting in America since 1941* (Baltimore, MD: Johns Hopkins University Press, 1992), pp. 44, 92.

7   Baughman, *Republic of Mass Culture*, p. 46.

8   Stephen Fox, *The Mirror Makers: A History of American Advertising and its Creators* (New York: Vintage, 1985), pp. 210–11; William Leiss, Stephen Kline, and Sut Jhally, *Social Communication in Advertising: Persons, Products, and Images of Well-Being* (Toronto: Methuen, 1986), pp. 80, 86, 115.

9   Quoted in Erik Barnouw, *A History of Broadcasting in the United States*, 3 vols. (New York: Oxford University Press, 1966–1970), vol. 3, *The Image Empire*, p. 23.

10 Fox, *The Mirror Makers*, p. 213; Baughman, *Republic of Mass Culture*, p. 45.

11 Williams, *Television*, pp. 57–8.

12 Leiss, Kline, and Jhally, *Social Communication in Advertising*, pp. 88–9; Matthew P. McAllister, *The Commercialization of American Culture: New Advertising, Control and Democracy* (Thousand Oaks, CA: Sage, 1996), pp. 47–50; George Lipsitz, "Consumer Spending as State Project: Yesterday's Solutions and Today's Problems," in Susan Strasser, Charles McGovern, and Matthias Judt (eds.), *Getting and Spending: European and American Consumer Societies in the Twentieth Century* (Cambridge: Cambridge University Press, 1998), pp. 144–5.

13 Quoted in Barnouw, *The Image Empire*, pp. 197–8.

14 See Baughman, *Republic of Mass Culture*, p. 93.

15 Quoted in Stephen J. Whitfield, *The Culture of the Cold War* (Baltimore, MD: Johns Hopkins University Press, 1991), p. 166.

16 Baughman, *Republic of Mass Culture*, pp. 98–107; Brown, "The American Networks," pp. 153–5; Mary Ann Watson, *The Expanding Vista: American Television in the Kennedy Years* (Durham, NC: Duke University Press, 1994), pp. 36–54.

17 Kevin Williams, *Get Me a Murder a Day! A History of Mass Communication in Britain* (London: Arnold, 1998), p. 156; Lawrence Black, "Whose Finger on the Button? British Television and the Politics of Cultural Control," *Historical Journal of Film, Radio and Television*, 25/4 (2005), p. 552.

18 See Williams, *Television*, pp. 33–4, 38–9.

19 Curran and Seaton, *Power without Responsibility*, pp. 161–3; Williams, *Get Me a Murder a Day!*, pp. 151–4.

20 Quoted in Williams, *Get Me a Murder a Day!*, p. 162.

21 Black, "Whose Finger on the Button?," pp. 553–7; Asa Briggs, *The History of Broadcasting in the United Kingdom*, vol. 4, *Sound and Vision* (Oxford: Oxford University Press, 1979), pp. 885–936.

22 Curran and Seaton, *Power without Responsibility*, pp. 165–6, 169–70, 180.

23 See ibid., pp. 164–5.

24 Quoted in Williams, *Get Me a Murder a Day!*, p. 166. See also Black, "Whose Finger on the Button?," pp. 557–67.

25 Michael Tracey, *The Decline and Fall of Public Service Broadcasting* (Oxford: Oxford University Press, 1998), p. 96.

26 Tony Judt, *Postwar: A History of Europe since 1945* (New York: Penguin, 2005), p. 345; Ulf Jonas Bjork, " 'Have Gun, Will Travel': Swedish Television and American Westerns, 1959–1969," *Historical Journal of Film, Radio and Television*, 21/3 (2001), p. 310.

27 Judt, *Postwar*, pp. 345, 373; Anthony Smith, "Television as a Public Service Medium," in Smith with Paterson (eds.), *Television: An International History*, pp. 41–4; Bjork, " 'Have Gun, Will Travel'," pp. 309–21.

28 Baughman, *Republic of Mass Culture*, pp. 143–4; Brown, "The American Networks," pp. 157–8.

29 Leiss, Kline, and Jhally, *Social Communication in Advertising*, p. 88; McAllister, *Commercialization of American Culture*, pp. 45–7; Baughman, *Republic of Mass Culture*, p. 145.

30 Fath David Ruffins, "Reflecting on Ethnic Imagery in the Landscape of Commerce, 1945–1975," in Strasser, McGovern, and Judt (eds.), *Getting and Spending*, pp. 401–5.

31 Baughman, *Republic of Mass Culture*, p. 155.

32 James Ledbetter, *Made Possible by ...: The Death of Public Broadcasting in the United States* (London: Verso, 1997), pp. 3–4; Stephen Labaton and Elizabeth Jensen, "Official Resigns Public TV Post," *New York Times* (February 10, 2006); Rick Klein, "GOP Takes Aim at PBS Funding," *Boston Globe* (June 8, 2006).

33 Ledbetter, *Made Possible by ...*, p. 4.

34 Ibid., *passim*.

35 McAllister, *Commercialization of American Culture*, pp. 18–36.

36 Quoted in Daniel C. Hallin, "Commercialism and Professionalism in the American News Media," in James Curran and Michael Gurevitch (eds.), *Mass Media and Society*, 3rd edn. (London: Arnold, 2000), p. 234.

37 Gary Cross, *An All-Consuming Century: Why Commercialism Won in Modern America* (New York: Columbia University Press, 2000), pp. 206–13.

38 Ibid., p. 207; McAllister, *Commercialization of American Culture*, pp. 24–5.

39 Lipsitz, "Consumer Spending as State Project," p. 139. See also Leiss, Kline, and Jhally, *Social Communication in Advertising*, p. 89; and Williams, *Television*, pp. 70–1.

40 McAllister, *Commercialization of American Culture*, p. 110.

41 Michael Tracey, "Non-Fiction Television," in Smith with Paterson (eds.), *Television: An International History*, pp. 82–4; Daniel C. Hallin, *We Keep America on Top of the World: Television Journalism and the Public Sphere* (London: Routledge, 1994), pp. 178–9.

42 See, e.g., Robert Hughes, "Why Watch It, Anyway?," *New York Review of Books* (February 16, 1995), pp. 37–42; Godfrey Hodgson, "The End of the Grand Narrative and the Death of News," *Historical Journal of Film, Radio, and Television*, 20/1 (2000), pp. 23–31; Jürgen Kronig, "Elite versus Mass: The Impact of Television in an Age of Globalisation," ibid., pp. 43–9.

43   See Michael Massing, "Off Course," *Columbia Journalism Review*, 4 (July/ August 2005).

44   See Steven Johnson, *Everything Bad Is Good for You: How Today's Popular Culture Is Actually Making Us Smarter* (New York: Riverhead Books, 2005), pp. 62–115; and Geoffrey O'Brien, "A Northern New Jersey of the Mind," *New York Review of Books* (August 16, 2007), pp. 17–20.

45   David T. Z. Mindich, *Tuned Out: Why Americans under 40 Don't Follow the News* (New York: Oxford University Press, 2005), p. 15; Sam Roberts, "Who Americans Are and What They Do, in Census Data," *New York Times* (December 15, 2006); US Department of Labor, "American Time Use Survey Summary," June 28, 2007, http://www.bls.gov/news.release/atus.nr0.htm

46   Curran and Seaton, *Power without Responsibility*, pp. 185–203, 364–5; Williams, *Get Me a Murder a Day!*, pp. 171–5.

47   Curran and Seaton, *Power without Responsibility*, pp. 201–34; Williams, *Get Me a Murder a Day!*, pp. 185–90; David Welch, "News into the Next Century: Introduction," *Historical Journal of Film, Radio, and Television*, 20/1 (2000), pp. 5–13; Hodgson, "End of the Grand Narrative;" Kronig, "Elite versus Mass."

48   Georgina Born, *Uncertain Vision: Birt, Dyke and the Reinvention of the BBC* (London: Secker and Warburg, 2004), pp. 254–372.

49   Kronig, "Elite versus Mass," p. 46.

50   Tony Judt, "'Twas a Famous Victory," *New York Review of Books* (July 19, 2001), p. 27.

51   Curran and Seaton, *Power without Responsibility*, p. 202. On the problem of "dumbing down" on UK television, see Welch, "News into the Next Century;" Hodgson, "End of the Grand Narrative;" and Kronig, "Elite versus Mass."

52   Curran and Seaton, *Power without Responsibility*, pp. 232, 284.

53   Ibid., p. 233.

54   "Reaction to the BBC Green Paper," BBC News (March 2, 2005), http://news.bbc.co.uk/1/hi/entertainment/tv_and_radio/4311753.stm; "Who Will Replace BBC Governors?," BBC News (March 2, 2005), http://news.bbc.co.uk/1/hi/entertainment/4311895.stm.

55   Dietrich Berwanger, "The Third World," in Smith with Paterson (eds.), *Television: An International History*, p. 188; Junhao Hong, *The Internationalization of Television in China: The Evolution of Ideology, Society, and Media since the Reform* (Westport, CT: Praeger, 1998), p. 87.

56   Hong, *Internationalization of Television in China*, pp. 14–15, 82–6, 96–8, 120; Jeanette Steemers, *Selling Television: British Television in the Global Marketplace* (London: British Film Institute, 2004), p. 24.

57   See Curran and Seaton, *Power without Responsibility*, pp. 373–5; Tracey, *Decline and Fall of Public Service Broadcasting*; Michael P. McCauley,

Eric E. Peterson, B. Lee Artz, and DeeDee Halleck (eds.), *Public Broadcasting and the Public Interest* (Armonk, NY: M. E. Sharpe, 2003); Robert W. McChesney, *Rich Media, Poor Democracy: Communication Politics in Dubious Times* (Urbana, IL: University of Illinois Press, 1999), pp. 226–56.

58   Chris Barker, *Global Television: An Introduction* (Oxford: Blackwell, 1997), p. 49; Hong, *Internationalization of Television in China*, p. 18; Steemers, *Selling Television*, pp. 40–1; Kerry Segrave, *American Television Abroad: Hollywood's Attempt to Dominate World Television* (Jefferson, NC: McFarland, 1998).

59   John Sinclair, Elizabeth Jacka, and Stuart Cunningham (eds.), *New Patterns in Global Television: Peripheral Vision* (Oxford: Oxford University Press, 1996); Koichi Iwabuchi, "Feeling Glocal: Japan in the Global Television Format Business," in Albert Moran and Michael Keane (eds.), *Television across Asia: Television Industries, Programme Formats and Globalization* (London: RoutledgeCurzon, 2004), pp. 26–9; Steemers, *Selling Television*, pp. xiii–xv, 13, 33, 43; Tom O'Regan, "The International Circulation of British Television," in Edward Buscombe (ed.), *British Television: A Reader* (Oxford: Oxford University Press, 2000), pp. 309, 317.

60   Richard Pells, *Not Like Us: How Europeans Have Loved, Hated, and Transformed American Culture since World War II* (New York: Basic Books, 1997), pp. 207–9, 230–2, 259–62; Hong, *Internationalization of Television in China*, pp. 12–19, 89, 119.

61   Paul Hollander, *Anti-Americanism: Critiques at Home and Abroad 1965–1990* (New York: Oxford University Press, 1992), pp. 333–442; Pells, *Not Like Us*, *passim*; Jessica C. E. Gienow-Hecht, "*Shame on US?* Academics, Cultural Transfer, and the Cold War – A Critical Review," *Diplomatic History*, 24/3 (2000), pp. 465–94 (especially pp. 470–9).

62   Quoted in Ien Ang, *Watching Dallas* (London: Methuen, 1985), p. 2.

63   Pells, *Not Like Us*, pp. 273–4; Segrave, *American Television Abroad*, pp. 256–9.

64   Richard Pells, "Who's Afraid of Steven Spielberg?," *Diplomatic History*, 24/3 (2000), pp. 497–8. Pells's argument is developed at length in *Not Like Us*. Gienow-Hecht, "*Shame on US?*" is an excellent introduction to the literature.

65   Barker, *Global Television*, *passim*; John Tomlinson, *Cultural Imperialism* (Baltimore, MD: Johns Hopkins University Press, 1991), pp. 34–67; Pells, *Not Like Us*, pp. 230–5, 258–64, 279–82, 300–1; Hong, *Internationalization of Television in China*, pp. 6, 12, 24, 70–3, 122–3, 130; Richard Paterson, "Drama and Entertainment," in Smith with Paterson (eds.), *Television: An International History*, pp. 58–63; James Curran, *Media and Power* (London: Routledge, 2002), pp. 192–4.

66   Steemers, *Selling Television*, pp. 26, 150.

67   Iwabuchi, "Feeling Glocal," pp. 22–3.

68   Steemers, *Selling Television*, pp. 109–11.
69   Curran, *Media and Power*, pp. 179–80.
70   Steemers, *Selling Television*, pp. xiv, 14–15, 208–10.
71   Moran and Keane (eds.), *Television across Asia*; Steemers, *Selling Television*, pp. 34, 39–40, 42, 104–6, 109–45, 211–12; Albert Moran, "The Global Television Format Trade," in Michele Hilmes (ed.), *The Television History Book* (London: British Film Institute, 2003), pp. 118–21.
72   Judt, *Postwar*, p. 781. See also Steemers, *Selling Television*, pp. 18, 146–7, 152–3, 180–1, 183–4, 208–14.
73   Steemers, *Selling Television*, pp. 6, 9–10, 16–17; Curran and Seaton, *Power without Responsibility*, p. 307.
74   Richard Kuisel, "Americanization for Historians," *Diplomatic History*, 24/3 (2000), pp. 509–16. The quotation is from p. 510.
75   Joseph S. Nye Jr., *Soft Power: The Means to Success in World Politics* (New York: Public Affairs, 2004).
76   The expression is used by Tony Judt to describe the appeal of America to young people in postwar Europe. *Postwar*, p. 351.
77   Ross McKibbin, *Classes and Cultures: England 1918–1951* (Oxford: Oxford University Press, 1998), p. 524.
78   For a skeptical view of these polls, see Baughman, *Republic of Mass Culture*, pp. 160–2; and Hallin, *We Keep America on Top of the World*, p. 100.
79   Hallin, *We Keep America on Top of the World*, pp. 97–8; Baughman, *Republic of Mass Culture*, pp. 93–8; James T. Hamilton, *All the News that's Fit to Sell: How the Market Transforms Information into News* (Princeton: Princeton University Press, 2004), pp. 163–5.
80   Williams, *Television*, p. 46.
81   Ibid., p. 49.
82   See Hallin, *We Keep America on Top of the World*, pp. 91, 98, 100–1, 105, 136; Baughman, *Republic of Mass Culture*, pp. 98, 162; Williams, *Television*, pp. 46–8.
83   Daniel J. Leab, "*See it Now*: A Legend Reassessed," in John E. O'Connor (ed.), *American History/American Television: Interpreting the Video Past* (New York: Frederick Ungar, 1983), pp. 1–32; Thomas Rosteck, *See it Now Confronts McCarthyism: Television Documentary and the Politics of Representation* (Tuscaloosa, AL: University of Alabama Press, 1994); J. Fred MacDonald, *Television and the Red Menace: The Video Road to Vietnam* (New York: Praeger, 1985), pp. 54–7; Whitfield, *Culture of the Cold War*, pp. 164–6; Barnouw, *The Image Empire*, pp. 46–56; Robert J. Donovan and Ray Scherer, *Unsilent Revolution: Television News and American Public Life, 1948–1991* (Cambridge: Cambridge University Press, 1992), pp. 23–34.
84   Baughman, *Republic of Mass Culture*, pp. 95–6.
85   Hallin, *We Keep America on Top of the World*, pp. 87–92, 102–10.

86 Michael Massing, *Now They Tell Us: The American Press and Iraq* (New York: New York Review Books, 2004); Michael Massing, "The End of News?," *New York Review of Books* (December 1, 2005), pp. 23–7; Michael Massing, "The Press: The Enemy within," *New York Review of Books* (December 15, 2005), pp. 36–44.

87 BBC press release, "Veteran CBS News Anchor Dan Rather speaks out on BBC Newsnight tonight," http://www.bbc.co.uk/print/pressoffice/pressreleases/stories/2002/05_may/16/dan_rather.shtml

88 Ibid.

89 Massing, "The End of News?;" and "The Press: The Enemy within;" Barbie Zelizer and Stuart Allan, "Introduction," in Zelizer and Allan (eds.), *Journalism after September 11* (London: Routledge, 2002), pp. 10–15.

90 The Pew Research Center for the People and the Press, "The Media: More Voices, Less Credibility" (January 25, 2005), p. 42, http://people-press.org/commentary/display.php3?AnalysisID=105

91 David Barstow and Robin Stein, "Under Bush, a New Age of Prepackaged TV News," *New York Times* (March 13, 2005).

92 Don Hewitt, quoted in Baughman, *Republic of Mass Culture*, p. 165.

93 On the impact of untrammeled commercialism on American television journalism, the following are particularly instructive: Baughman, *Republic of Mass Culture*, pp. 216–18, 220; Hallin, *We Keep America on Top of the World*, pp. 176–80; Hallin, "Commercialism and Professionalism in the American News Media," pp. 218–37; S. Elizabeth Bird, "Audience Demands in a Murderous Market: Tabloidization in US Television News," in Colin Sparks and John Tulloch (eds.), *Tabloid Tales: Global Debates over Media Standards* (Lanham, MD: Rowman and Littlefield, 2000), pp. 213–28; Hamilton, *All the News that's Fit to Sell*, pp. 165–88; Leonard Downie Jr. and Robert G. Kaiser, *The News about the News: American Journalism in Peril* (New York: Vintage Books, 2003); Tom Fenton, *Bad News: The Decline of Reporting, the Business of News, and the Danger to Us All* (New York: Regan Books, 2005); Steve M. Barkin, *American Television News: The Media Marketplace and the Public Interest* (Armonk, NY: M. E. Sharpe, 2003); and Pew Research Center, "The Media: More Voices, Less Credibility."

94 Massing, "The End of News?;" Downie and Kaiser, *The News about the News*, pp. 145–6; Hamilton, *All the News that's Fit to Sell*, pp. 3, 106–9; Mindich, *Tuned Out*, pp. 57–8.

95 Philip M. Taylor, "News and the Grand Narrative: Some Further Reflections," *Historical Journal of Film, Radio, and Television*, 20/1 (2000), pp. 33–6; Welch, "News into the Next Century;" Kronig, "Elite versus Mass;" Downie and Kaiser, *The News about the News*, pp. 144–7.

96 Downie and Kaiser, *The News about the News*, p. 145; Pew Research Center, "The Media: More Voices, Less Credibility," pp. 42–5; Fenton, *Bad News*, p. 75; Barkin, *American Television News*, p. 4.

97   Mindich, *Tuned Out*; Pew Research Center, "The Media: More Voices, Less Credibility," pp. 45–7; Hamilton, *All the News that's Fit to Sell*, pp. 83–91.

98   For a range of views, see Curran, *Media and Power*, pp. 187–92; Richard Tait, "The Future of International News on Television," *Historical Journal of Film, Radio, and Television*, 20/1 (2000), pp. 51–3; Williams, *Get Me a Murder a Day!*, pp. 249–51; Hodgson, "End of the Grand Narrative;" and Kronig, "Elite versus Mass."

99   Curran, *Media and Power*, pp. 179–80, 189, 192.

100 See the discussion in ibid., pp. 187–92; and Tait, "The Future of International News on Television."

101 Williams, *Television*, p. 125.

102 See Elliot King and Michael Schudson, "The Myth of the Great Communicator," *Columbia Journalism Review*, 26 (1987), pp. 37–9; Baughman, *Republic of Mass Culture*, pp. 211–12; and Hallin, *We Keep America on Top of the World*, p. 105.

103 Williams, *Get Me a Murder a Day!*, pp. 251–4.

104 Tracey, "Non-Fiction Television," p. 81.

105 Mark Danner, "The Shame of Political TV," *New York Review of Books* (September 21, 2000), pp. 101–2; James Fallows, "Internet Illusions," *New York Review of Books* (November 16, 2000), pp. 29–30.

106 Danner, "The Shame of Political TV;" Lars-Erik Nelson, "Democracy for Sale," *New York Review of Books* (December 3, 1998), pp. 8–10.

107 See, e.g., Steven Barnett, *Games and Sets: The Changing Face of Sport on Television* (London: British Film Insitute, 1990); Garry Whannel, *Fields in Vision: Television Sport and Cultural Transformation* (London: Routledge, 1992).

108 See Joseph Turow, *Breaking up America: Advertisers and the New Media World* (Chicago: University of Chicago Press, 1997).

109 Curran, *Media and Power*, pp. 189–90. See also Curran and Seaton, *Power without Responsibility*, pp. 284–5.

110 Curran, *Media and Power*, pp. 190–1; Hamilton, *All the News that's Fit to Sell*, p. 3; Downie and Kaiser, *The News about the News*, p. 145.

111 Anthony D. Smith, *Nations and Nationalism in a Global Era* (Cambridge: Polity Press, 1995), pp. 42–5; E. J. Hobsbawm, *Nations and Nationalism since 1780* (Cambridge: Cambridge University Press, 1990), pp. 163–83.

112 Gregory Britton, "September 11, American 'Exceptionalism' and the War in Iraq," *Australasian Journal of American Studies*, 25/1 (2006), pp. 125–41.

113 Kronig, "Elite versus Mass," p. 41.

114 Roland Marchand, "Visions of Classlessness, Quests for Dominion: American Popular Culture, 1945–1960," in Robert H. Bremner and Gary W. Reichard (eds.), *Reshaping America: Society and Institutions 1945–1960* (Columbus, OH: Ohio State University Press, 1982), pp. 168–70; Lipsitz,

"Consumer Spending as State Project," pp. 142–3; Barker, *Global Television*, pp. 153–81.

115   Orhan Pamuk, "The Anger of the Damned," *New York Review of Books* (November 15, 2001), p. 12. See also Kronig, "Elite versus Mass," p. 43; and Benjamin M. Friedman, "The Power of the Electronic Herd," *New York Review of Books* (July 15, 1999), p. 40.

116   The following are of particular value on television and history: David Cannadine (ed.), *History and the Media* (Basingstoke: Palgrave Macmillan, 2004); Graham Roberts and Philip M. Taylor (eds.), *The Historian, Television and Television History* (Luton: University of Luton Press, 2001); Arthur Marwick, *The Nature of History*, 3rd edn. (Basingstoke: Macmillan, 1989), pp. 313–23; Steemers, *Selling Television*, pp. 123–33; Ian Jarvie, "History on Television," *Historical Journal of Film, Radio and Television*, 21/1 (2001), pp. 97–9; Judith Petersen, "How British Television Inserted the Holocaust into Britain's War Memory in 1995," *Historical Journal of Film, Radio and Television*, 21/3 (2001), pp. 255–72; Michael Nelson, "It may be History, but is it True?: The Imperial War Museum Conference," *Historical Journal of Film, Radio and Television*, 25/1 (March 2005), pp. 141–6; Stephen Badsey, "The Great War since *the Great War*," *Historical Journal of Film, Radio and Television*, 22/1 (2002), pp. 37–45.

117   On television history programs as vehicles for collective memory, see Petersen, "How British Television Inserted the Holocaust;" and Badsey, "The Great War since *the Great War*," p. 40. On the distinction between history and memory, see John Tosh with Seán Lang, *The Pursuit of History: Aims, Methods and New Directions in the Study of Modern History*, 4th edn. (Harlow: Pearson, 2006), pp. 1–27; Peter Novick, *The Holocaust in American Life* (Boston: Houghton Mifflin, 1999), especially pp. 3–4; and Judt, *Postwar*, especially pp. 829–31.

118   Novick, *The Holocaust in American Life*, pp. 209, 213–14; Jeffrey Shandler, *While America Watches: Televising the Holocaust* (New York: Oxford University Press, 1999), esp. pp. 155–78.

119   Quoted in Ian Buruma, "From Hirohito to Heimat," *New York Review of Books* (October 26, 1989), p. 40. See also Novick, *The Holocaust in American Life*, p. 213; and Judt, *Postwar*, p. 811.

120   See Williams, *Television*, pp. 126–8.

Chapter 9.   Media, Information, and Entertainment

1   Quoted in Garth Jowett, *Film: The Democratic Art* (Boston: Little, Brown, 1976), p. 349.

2   James L. Baughman, *The Republic of Mass Culture: Journalism, Filmmaking, and Broadcasting in America since 1941* (Baltimore, MD: Johns Hopkins University Press, 1992), p. 9.
3   Jowett, *Film: The Democratic Art*, pp. 473, 475.
4   Ibid., p. 482.
5   US Bureau of the Census, *The Statistical History of the United States: From Colonial Times to the Present* (New York: Basic Books, 1976), p. 400.
6   Baughman, *Republic of Mass Culture*, pp. 141–2.
7   On 1950s "teenpics," see Thomas Doherty, *Teenagers and Teenpics: The Juvenilization of American Movies in the 1950s* (Boston: Unwin Hyman, 1988).
8   See Gregory D. Black, *The Catholic Crusade against the Movies, 1940–1975* (Cambridge: Cambridge University Press, 1998); Frank Walsh, *Sin and Censorship: The Catholic Church and the Motion Picture Industry* (New Haven, CT: Yale University Press, 1996); and Leonard J. Leff and Jerold L. Simmons, *The Dame in the Kimono: Hollywood, Censorship, and the Production Code from the 1920s to the 1960s* (New York: Grove Weidendeld, 1990).
9   Charles B. Weinberg, "Profits out of the Picture: Research Issues and Revenue Sources beyond the North American Box Office," in Charles C. Moul (ed.), *A Concise Handbook of Movie Industry Economics* (Cambridge: Cambridge University Press, 2005), pp. 163–4; Gorham Kindem, "United States," in Gorham Kindem (ed.), *The International Movie Industry* (Carbondale, IL: Southern Illinois University Press, 2000), p. 327.
10   Sheldon Hall, "Tall Revenue Features: The Genealogy of the Modern Blockbuster," in Steve Neale (ed.), *Genre and Contemporary Hollywood* (London: British Film Institute, 2002), p. 22; Tino Balio, "'A Major Presence in all of the World's Important Markets': The Globalization of Hollywood in the 1990s," in Steve Neale and Murray Smith (eds.), *Contemporary Hollywood Cinema* (London: Routledge, 1998), p. 59; Kindem, "United States," p. 326; Motion Picture Association of America, "Research and Statistics," http://www.mpaa.org/researchStatistics.asp
11   Matthew P. McAllister, *The Commercialization of American Culture: New Advertising, Control and Democracy* (Thousand Oaks, CA: Sage, 1996), pp. 67–9, 81, 138–44, 161–8, 171–5.
12   Tino Balio, "Hollywood Production Trends in the Era of Globalisation, 1990–99," in Neale (ed.), *Genre and Contemporary Hollywood*, pp. 165–6.
13   Pauline Kael, "Why Are Movies So Bad? or, The Numbers," *New Yorker* (June 23, 1980); David Parkinson, *History of Film* (London: Thames and Hudson, 1995), p. 245; Nick Allen, "George Clooney: Hollywood has Lost its Sparkle," *Daily Telegraph* (February 7, 2008).
14   Balio, "'A Major Presence,'" pp. 58–9.
15   Figures on film production costs and earnings are from BOX OFFICE MOJO: http://www.boxofficemojo.com/

16 Mark Lawson, "A New Golden Age in Cinema," *Guardian* (February 1, 2008).

17 Greg Sheridan, "In a World of his Own," *Weekend Australian Magazine* (October 27, 2007), p. 28.

18 Thomas H. Guback, "Hollywood's International Market," in Tino Balio (ed.), *The American Film Industry* (Madison: University of Wisconsin Press, 1985), p. 481.

19 Tom O'Regan, "The International, the Regional and the Local: Hollywood's New and Declining Audiences," in Elizabeth Jacka (ed.), *Continental Shift: Globalisation and Culture* (Sydney: Local Consumption Publications, 1992), pp. 78, 80.

20 Weinberg, "Profits out of the Picture," pp. 167–8; Balio, " 'A Major Presence,' " pp. 58–60.

21 Kerry Segrave, *American Films Abroad: Hollywood's Domination of the World's Movie Screens from the 1890s to the Present* (Jefferson, NC: McFarland, 1997); Kindem, "United States," pp. 326, 328; Richard Pells, *Not Like Us: How Europeans Have Loved, Hated, and Transformed American Culture since World War II* (New York: Basic Books, 1997), pp. 219, 229.

22 There is room for uncertainty on the precise percentage of foreign films screened in the USA in the 1960s. Garth Jowett, citing the 1969 *Film Daily Yearbook*, states that imports accounted for more than two-thirds of films screened in the USA between 1961 and 1965. Jowett, *Film: The Democratic Art*, p. 430. It is not clear whether this figure includes Hollywood films produced abroad. Marcus Breen, citing a 1997 *Economist* article, states that foreign-language films represented 10% of the North American market in the 1960s – a figure that would suggest that the total proportion of foreign films (including English-language ones) was significantly more than 10% but less than 66%. Marcus Breen, "Australia," in Kindem (ed.), *The International Movie Industry*, p. 66.

23 Guback, "Hollywood's International Market," p. 479.

24 See ibid.; Peter Lev, *The Euro-American Cinema* (Austin, TX: University of Texas Press, 1993), pp. 24–5; and William H. Read, *America's Mass Media Merchants* (Baltimore, MD: Johns Hopkins University Press, 1976), pp. 56–7.

25 Quoted in the *Sydney Morning Herald* (May 12, 2001). On Hollywood's relationship to "national cinemas," see Albert Moran, "Terms for a Reader: Film, Hollywood, National Cinema, Cultural Identity and Film Policy," in Albert Moran (ed.), *Film Policy: International, National and Regional Perspectives* (London: Routledge, 1996), pp. 5–11.

26 For figures on leisure patterns in the USA, see Weinberg, "Profits out of the Picture," p. 169; and Motion Picture Association of America, "US Entertainment Industry: 2006 Market Statistics," p. 49, at http://www.mpaa.org/researchStatistics.asp

27   On these points, see Janet Wasko, "Critiquing Hollywood: The Political Economy of Motion Pictures," in Moul (ed.), *Concise Handbook of Movie Industry Economics*, pp. 17–19; and Moran, "Terms for a Reader," pp. 4–5. Moran cites the work of Thomas Guback and Thomas Elsaesser on the ideological content of American movies.

28   Leo Bogart, *Press and Public: Who Reads What, When, Where, and Why in American Newspapers*, 2nd edn. (Hillsdale, NJ: Lawrence Erlbaum Associates, 1989), pp. 15–24; Neil Henry, *American Carnival: Journalism under Siege in an Age of New Media* (Berkeley and Los Angeles: University of California Press, 2007), p. 24; Daniel C. Hallin, "Commercialism and Professionalism in the American News Media," in James Curran and Michael Gurevitch (eds.), *Mass Media and Society*, 3rd edn. (London: Arnold, 2000), p. 222; McAllister, *Commercialization of American Culture*, p. 30; Baughman, *Republic of Mass Culture*, p. 189.

29   Henry, *American Carnival*, pp. 24, 255 n. 5, 289 n. 24, 301 n. 107; David Lieberman, "Papers Take a Leap Forward, Opening up to New Ideas," *USA Today* (January 30, 2006); The Pew Research Center for the People and the Press, "The Media: More Voices, Less Credibility" (January 25, 2005), pp. 44, 49, http://people-press.org/commentary/display.php3?Analysis ID=105

30   Bogart, *Press and Public*, pp. 16–24; Baughman, *Republic of Mass Culture*, pp. 122–6.

31   Leonard Downie Jr. and Robert G. Kaiser, *The News about the News: American Journalism in Peril* (New York: Vintage Books, 2003), p. 68.

32   McAllister, *Commercialization of American Culture*, pp. 21–2; Baughman, *Republic of Mass Culture*, pp. 192–3.

33   Kevin Williams, *Get Me a Murder a Day! A History of Mass Communication in Britain* (London: Arnold, 1998), pp. 217–19.

34   Ibid., pp. 226–7; James Curran and Jean Seaton, *Power without Responsibility: The Press, Broadcasting and New Media in Britain*, 6th edn. (London: Routledge, 2003), pp. 76–9, 286; James Curran, *Media and Power* (London: Routledge, 2002), p. 231.

35   On press concentration in Western Europe, see Peter J. Humphreys, *Mass Media and Media Policy in Western Europe* (Manchester: Manchester University Press, 1996), pp. 66–110.

36   Joseph Man Chan, "Administrative Boundaries and Media Marketization: A Comparative Analysis of the Newspaper, TV and Internet Markets in China," in Chin-Chuan Lee (ed.), *Chinese Media, Global Contexts* (London: RoutledgeCurzon, 2003), pp. 161–4, 172; Perry Link, "China: Wiping Out the Truth," *New York Review of Books* (February 24, 2005), pp. 36–9.

37   James Button, "A Tough Crusader Falls," *Sydney Morning Herald* (October 14, 2006); Luke Harding, "Russian Journalist who Angered Country's

Military Falls to Death," *Guardian* (March 6, 2007); Andrew Kramer, "Back to the USSR: Putin Turns to Thought Control," *Sydney Morning Herald* (April 23, 2007); Anne Applebaum, "Why Putin Will Stop at Nothing to Smash the New Russian Revolution," *Spectator* (April 21, 2007).

38 "Inside Indonesia's Media," Australian Broadcasting Corporation Radio National (broadcast September 14, 2006), http://www.abc.net.au/rn/mediareport/stories/2006/1738747.htm

39 Jefferson to Edward Carrington, January 16, 1787, in Merrill D. Peterson (ed.), *The Portable Thomas Jefferson* (Harmondsworth: Penguin, 1977), p. 415.

40 Hallin, "Commercialism and Professionalism," pp. 219–21; Daniel C. Hallin, *We Keep America on Top of the World: Television Journalism and the Public Sphere* (London: Routledge, 1994), pp. 24–6, 170–2; Baughman, *Republic of Mass Culture*, pp. 13–14, 32–3, 118–20.

41 Baughman, *Republic of Mass Culture*, pp. 175–83; Robert J. Donovan and Ray Scherer, *Unsilent Revolution: Television News and American Public Life, 1948–1991* (Cambridge: Cambridge University Press, 1992), pp. 257–82; Hallin, *We Keep America on Top of the World*, pp. 25, 47–55, 170–6. The quotation is from ibid., p. 25.

42 Michael Massing, *Now They Tell Us: The American Press and Iraq* (New York: New York Review Books, 2004); W. Lance Bennett, Regina G. Lawrence, and Steven Livingston, *When the Press Fails: Political Power and the News Media from Iraq to Katrina* (Chicago: University of Chicago Press, 2007), pp. 13–45; Henry, *American Carnival*, passim.

43 "The *Times* and Iraq, From the Editors," *New York Times* (May 26, 2004); Howard Kurtz, "The *Post* on WMDs: An Inside Story," *Washington Post* (August 12, 2004).

44 Michael Massing, "The Press: The Enemy Within," *New York Review of Books* (December 15, 2005), pp. 36, 40; Bennett, Lawrence, and Livingston, *When the Press Fails*, pp. 10–11, 41, 62, 66–7, 168–9, 172, 187–8; Dean Baquet and Bill Keller, "When Do We Publish a Secret?," *New York Times* (July 1, 2006); "The Road Home," editorial, *New York Times* (July 8, 2007).

45 Massing, "The Press: The Enemy Within," p. 44. See also Bennett, Lawrence, and Livingston, *When the Press Fails*, pp. 72–107; Massing, *Now They Tell Us*, pp. 79–90; and Michael Massing, "Iraq: The Hidden Human Costs," *New York Review of Books* (December 20, 2007), pp. 82–7.

46 See Massing, "The Press: The Enemy Within," pp. 36–8; and Greg Palast, "US Media Have Lost the Will to Dig Deep," *Los Angeles Times* (April 27, 2007).

47 John S. Carroll, "Last Call at the ASNE Saloon," speech delivered at the 2006 American Society of Newspaper Editors Convention, Seattle, Washington, April 26, 2006, http://concernedjournalists.org/print/12

48   Quoted in Donovan and Scherer, *Unsilent Revolution*, p. 267. See also Ian Hargreaves, "Is There a Future for Foreign News?," *Historical Journal of Film, Radio, and Television*, 20/1 (2000), pp. 55–61; and Godfrey Hodgson, "The End of the Grand Narrative and the Death of News," *Historical Journal of Film, Radio, and Television*, 20/1 (2000), pp. 23–31.

49   Downie and Kaiser, *The News about the News*, p. 109.

50   Ibid., pp. 63–110; Carroll, "Last Call at the ASNE Saloon;" Russell Baker, "Goodbye to Newspapers?," *New York Review of Books* (August 16, 2007), pp. 8–10.

51   Curran and Seaton, *Power without Responsibility*, pp. 67–73. The quotation is from p. 70.

52   Ibid., pp. 74–5, 360.

53   Williams, *Get Me a Murder a Day!*, p. 224. See also Curran and Seaton, *Power without Responsibility*, pp. 90–7, 103; Hargreaves, "Is There a Future for Foreign News?;" Hodgson, "End of the Grand Narrative;" Shelley McLachlan and Peter Golding, "Tabloidization in the British Press: A Quantitative Investigation into Changes in British Newspapers, 1952–1997," in Colin Sparks and John Tulloch (eds.), *Tabloid Tales: Global Debates over Media Standards* (Lanham, MD: Rowman and Littlefield, 2000), pp. 75–90; and Dick Rooney, "Thirty Years of Competition in the British Tabloid Press: The *Mirror* and the *Sun* 1968–1998," in ibid., pp. 91–110.

54   See Curran and Seaton, *Power without Responsibility*, pp. 77–103; Massing, "The Press: The Enemy Within," pp. 36–40; and Ross McKibbin, "The Destruction of the Public Sphere," *London Review of Books* (January 5, 2006).

55   See Humphreys, *Mass Media and Media Policy*, pp. 102–7; and Paul Murschetz, "State Support for the Daily Press in Europe: A Critical Appraisal," *European Journal of Communication*, 13/3 (1998), pp. 291–313.

56   See Carroll, "Last Call at the ASNE Saloon."

57   On these points, see especially ibid.; and Downie and Kaiser, *The News about the News*, pp. 63–7.

58   Baughman, *Republic of Mass Culture*, p. 66.

59   Michael Emery, Edwin Emery, and Nancy L. Roberts, *The Press and America: An Interpretive History of the Mass Media*, 9th edn. (Boston: Allyn and Bacon, 2000), p. 372.

60   Susan J. Douglas, *Listening in: Radio and the American Imagination* (New York: Random House, 1999), p. 285.

61   Ibid., pp. 294–8, 347–54.

62   Ibid., pp. 284–327. The quotation is from p. 285. See also Michael P. McCauley, *NPR: The Trials and Triumphs of National Public Radio* (New York: Columbia University Press, 2005).

63   Williams, *Get Me a Murder a Day!*, pp. 246–7.

Chapter 10.   Media, War, and International Relations

1   Phillip Knightley, *The First Casualty: The War Correspondent as Hero and Myth Maker from the Crimea to Kosovo* (London: Prion, 2000), p. 452.
2   S. Badsey, "The Boer War as a Media War," in P. Dennis and J. Grey (eds.), *The Boer War: Army, Nation and Empire* (Canberra: Army History Unit, Department of Defence, 2000), p. 70; S. Badsey, "The Media, Strategy, and Military Culture," *Australian Army Journal*, 2/2 (2005), p. 193; Justin Lewis, Rod Brookes, Nick Mosdell, and Terry Threadgold., *Shoot First and Ask Questions Later: Media Coverage of the 2003 Iraq War* (New York: Peter Lang, 2006), p. 18.
3   Knightley, *The First Casualty*.
4   Peter Young and Peter Jesser, *The Media and the Military: From the Crimea to Desert Strike* (South Melbourne: Macmillan Education, 1997), pp. 40–1; J. Fred MacDonald, *Television and the Red Menace: The Video Road to Vietnam* (New York: Praeger, 1985), pp. 31–7; see also John E. Mueller, *War, Presidents and Public Opinion* (New York: John Wiley and Sons, 1973); and Knightley, *The First Casualty*.
5   R. Elegant, "How to Lose a War," in R. J. McMahon (ed.), *Major Problems in the History of the Vietnam War* (Lexington: D. C. Heath and Co., 1990), pp. 528–36.
6   D. C. Hallin, *The "Uncensored War": The Media and Vietnam* (New York: Oxford University Press, 1986), p. 213. Other critics included Knightley, *The First Casualty*; M. Mandelbaum, "Vietnam: The Television War," *Daedalus*, 3 (Fall 1982), pp. 157–69; W. M. Hammond, "The Press in Vietnam as Agent of Defeat: A Critical Examination," *Reviews in American History*, 17/1 (1989), p. 318; W. M. Hammond, *Public Affairs: The Military and the Media, 1962–1968, United States Army in Vietnam* (Washington: Centre of Military History, United States Army, 1988); W. M. Hammond, *Public Affairs: The Military and the Media, 1968–1973, United States Army in Vietnam* (Washington: Centre of Military History, United States Army, 1996); W. M. Hammond, *Reporting Vietnam: Media and Military at War*. Modern World Studies (Lawrence, KS: University Press of Kansas, 1998); and C. A. Thayer, "Vietnam: A Critical Analysis," in P. E. Young, *Defence and the Media in Time of Limited War* (London: Frank Cass, 1992), pp. 89–115.
7   Based on Mueller, *War, Presidents and Public Opinion*; see also Hammond, "The Press in Vietnam," p. 318; Thayer, "Vietnam," p. 107.
8   Hallin, *The "Uncensored War,"* p. 168.
9   Knightley, *The First Casualty*, p. 437; Hallin, *The "Uncensored War,"* pp. 175, 190, 214.
10   Valerie Adams, *The Media and the Falklands Campaign* (Basingstoke: Macmillan, 1986).

11 Young and Jesser, *The Media and the Military*, p. 98; see also Klaus Dodds, "Contesting War: British Media Reporting and the 1982 South Atlantic War," in Mark Connelly and David Welch (eds.), *War and the Media: Reportage and Propaganda, 1900–2003* (London: I. B. Taurus, 2005), pp. 218–35.

12 Robert E. Denton Jr., *The Media and the Persian Gulf War* (Westport, CT: Praeger, 1993), pp. 8–10; Thomas Rid, *War and Media Operations: The US Military and the Press from Vietnam to Iraq* (London: Routledge, 2007), p. 77.

13 Warren P. Strobel, *Late-Breaking Foreign Policy: The News Media's Influence on Peace Operations* (Washington: United States Institute of Peace Press, 1997), p. 41. See also Young and Jesser, *The Media and the Military*; and Philip M. Taylor, *War and the Media: Propaganda and Persuasion in the Gulf War* (Manchester: Manchester University Press, 1992).

14 Taylor, *War and the Media*; H. Smith (ed.), *The Media and the Gulf War* (Washington: Seven Locks Press, 1992); W. L. Bennett and D. L. Paletz (eds.), *Taken by Storm: The Media, Public Opinion, and US Foreign Policy in the Gulf War* (Chicago: University of Chicago Press, 1994).

15 John J. Fialka, *Hotel Warriors: Covering the Gulf War* (Washington: Woodrow Wilson Center Press, 1991); see also Denton, *The Media and the Persian Gulf War*.

16 e.g., Taylor, *War and the Media*.

17 Jonathan Mermin, *Debating War and Peace: Media Coverage of US Intervention in the Post-Vietnam Era* (Princeton: Princeton University Press, 1999); W. V. Kennedy, *The Military and the Media: Why the Press Cannot Be Trusted to Cover a War* (Westport, CT: Praeger, 1993); Young and Jesser, *The Media and the Military*.

18 M. Shaw, "Global Voices: Civil Society and the Media in Global Crises," in T. Dunne and N. J. Wheeler (eds.), *Human Rights in Global Politics* (Cambridge: Cambridge University Press, 1999), ch. 8, pp. 214–32; Strobel, *Late-Breaking Foreign Policy*.

19 Samantha Power, *"A Problem from Hell": America and the Age of Genocide* (London: Flamingo, 2002), pp. 356–75, 503, 508.

20 Philip M. Taylor, *Global Communications, International Affairs and the Media since 1945* (London: Routledge, 1997), pp. 145–92; Badsey, "The Media, Strategy, and Military Culture," pp. 193, 198; Lewis et al., *Shoot First and Ask Questions Later*, p. 18; Barry Richards, "Terrorism and Public Relations," *Public Relations Review*, 30 (2004), pp. 169–76; Mark Laity, "Straddling the Divide: Spinning for Both Sides," in Connelly and Welch (eds.), *War and the Media: Reportage and Propaganda, 1900–2003*, pp. 275–91.

21 Rid, *War and Media Operations*, pp. 105–6; Jean Seaton, *Carnage and the Media: The Making and Breaking of News about Violence* (London: Allen Lane/Penguin, 2005), p. 144; Susan L. Carruthers, "Missing in Authenticity: Media War in the Digital Age," in Connelly and Welch (eds.), *War and the*

Media: Reportage and Propaganda, 1900–2003; see also Susan L. Carruthers, *The Media at War: Communication and Conflict in the Twentieth Century* (Basingstoke: Macmillan, 2000); Oliver Boyd-Barrett, in Naren Chitty, Ramona R. Rush, and Mehdi Semati (eds.), *Studies in Terrorism: Media Scholarship and the Enigma of Terror* (Penang: Southbound, 2003), p. 49; Bradley S. Greenberg (ed.), *Communication and Terrorism: Public and Media Responses to 9/11* (Cresskill, NJ: Hampton Press, 2002); S. Hess and M. Kalb (eds.), *The Media and the War on Terrorism* (Washington: Brookings Institution Press, 2003); Pippa Norris, Montague Kern, and Marion Just (eds.), *Framing Terrorism: The News Media, the Government and the Public* (New York: Routledge, 2003); and David J. Whittaker, *Terrorists and Terrorism in the Contemporary World* (London: Routledge, 2004).

22 Stuart Allan, *News Culture*, 2nd edn. (Maidenhead: Open University Press, 2004), pp. 177–9, 182–3.

23 Philip Seib (ed.), *Media and Conflict in the Twenty-First Century* (New York: Palgrave Macmillan, 2005), p. 227; Mohammed El-Nawawy and Adel Iskander, *Al-Jazeera: The Story of the Network that Is Rattling Governments and Redefining Modern Journalism* (Cambridge, MA: Westview Press, 2003).

24 Andrew Hoskins, *Televising War: From Vietnam to Iraq* (London: Continuum, 2004), p. 72. See also Amy E. Jasperson and Mansour O. El-Kikhia, "CNN and al Jazeera's Media Coverage of America's War in Afghanistan," in Norris, Kern and Just (eds.), *Framing Terrorism*, pp. 51–5, 122–31; and Mohamed Zayani (ed.), *The Al Jazeera Phenomenon: Critical Perspectives on New Arab Media* (London: Pluto Press, 2005), p. 161.

25 Lewis et al., *Shoot First and Ask Questions Later*; Rid, *War and Media Operations*.

26 Rid, *War and Media Operations*, p. 150.

27 Lewis et al., *Shoot First and Ask Questions Later*, pp. 37, 40.

28 Stuart Allan, *Online News: Journalism and the Internet* (Maidenhead: Open University Press, 2006), pp. 102–3, 111; Allan, *News Culture*, pp. 184–5.

29 The Salam Pax blog "Where is Raed?" was published in 2003 by Atlantic Books in association with the *Guardian* newspaper as *The Baghdad Blog*; extensive material from "Riverbend" was published in two volumes, *Baghdad Burning: Girl Blog from Iraq* and *Baghdad Burning II: More Girl Blog from Iraq*, by Feminist Press in 2005 and 2006, the second volume covering the period to March 2006.

30 Allan, *News Culture*, pp. 190–1.

31 Nicholas Mirzoeff, *Watching Babylon: The War in Iraq and Global Visual Culture* (New York: Routledge, 2005), p. 67; Sean Aday, "The Real War Will Never Get on Television," in Seib (ed.), *Media and Conflict in the Twenty-First Century*, pp. 149–52; Douglas Kellner, *Media Spectacle and the Crisis of*

Democracy: Terrorism, War, and Election Battles (Boulder, CO: Paradigm, 2005), pp. 63–4; Lewis et al., *Shoot First and Ask Questions Later*, pp. 109–11, 195.

32 Nick Possum, quoted in "Who Killed Nick Berg?" *Sydney Morning Herald* (May 29, 2004). See also Wikipedia articles on Abu Ghraib and Nick Berg, http://en.wikipedia.org/wiki/Abu_Ghraib_torture_and_prisoner_abuse and http://en.wiikpedia.org/wiki/Nick_Berg, retrieved January 2, 2008.

33 Allan, *Online News*, pp. 143–55.

34 Ibid., 172.

Chapter 11.   The Rise of New Media

1   "Murdoch and China," *Observer*, August 24, 2003.

2   Peter Forman and Robert W. Saint John, "Creating Convergence," *Scientific American* (November 2000), pp. 34–5.

3   Henry Jenkins, *Convergence Culture: Where Old and New Media Collide* (New York: New York University Press, 2006), pp. 2–3, 282.

4   See, e.g., Wilson Dizard Jr., *Old Media/New Media: Mass Communications in the Information Age* (London: Longman, 1994), pp. xv, 2.

5   See Wikipedia entry on "New Media", http://en.wikipedia.org/wiki?New_media, retrieved January 2, 2008.

6   Martin Lister, Jon Dovey, Seth Giddings, Iain Grant, and Kieran Kelly, *New Media: A Critical Introduction* (Abingdon: Routledge, 2003, reprinted 2005), pp. 2, 13; Terry Flew, *Understanding Global Media* (Basingstoke: Palgrave Macmillan, 2007), pp. 22–4.

7   Gerard Goggin, *Cell Phone Culture: Mobile Technology in Everyday Life* (London: Routledge, 2006), p. 211.

8   Mark D. Pesce, "Three Billion," Keynote Address, in Franco Papandrea and Mark Armstrong (comps.), *Record of the Communications Policy and Research Forum* (Sydney: Network Insight Institute, 2007), p. 97.

9   Goggin, *Cell Phone Culture*, p. 2.

10 Christina Spurgeon, *Advertising and New Media* (London: Routledge, 2008), p. 2; Manuel Castells, "Communication, Power and Counter-Power in the Network Society," *International Journal of Communication*, 1/1 (2007), pp. 238–66.

11 Chris Barker, *Global Television: An Introduction* (Oxford: Blackwell, 1997), p. 149.

12 Dizard, *Old Media/New Media*, p. 42.

13 Gillian Appleton, "Converging and Emerging Industries: Video, Pay TV and Multimedia," in Stuart Cunningham and Graeme Turner (eds.),

The Media in Australia, 2nd edn. (St Leonards: Allen and Unwin, 1997), pp. 180–1.

14 Ray Eldon Hiebert and Sheila Jean Gibbons, *Exploring Mass Media for a Changing World* (London: Lawrence Erlbaum, 2000), ch. 15; see also Trevor Barr, *newmedia.com.au: The Changing Face of Australia's Media and Communications* (St Leonards: Allen and Unwin, 2000); Brian Winston, *Media Technology and Society: A History; From the Telegraph to the Internet* (London: Routledge, 1998); Terry Flew, *New Media: An Introduction*, 2nd edn. (Oxford: Oxford University Press, 2005); and Gary B. Shelly, Thomas J. Cashman, H. Albert Napier, Philip J. Judd, and Emily M. Kaufmann, *Discovering the Internet: Brief Concepts and Techniques*, 2nd edn. (Boston: Thomson Course Technology, 2008).

15 Many websites provide historical and current Internet use statistics; see, e.g., http://www.internetworldstats,com/stats.htm (2007 data retrieved January 7, 2008). See also James Curran and Jean Seaton, *Power without Responsibility: The Press, Broadcasting and New Media in Britain*, 6th edn. (London: Routledge, 2003), p. 270.

16 Curran and Seaton, *Power without Responsibility*, p. 262.

17 Korinna Patelis, "The Political Economy of the Internet," in James Curran (ed.), *Media Organisations in Society* (London: Arnold, 2000), pp. 95–8.

18 David A. Vise, with M. Malseed, *The Google Story* (London: Pan, 2006), p. 280.

19 Spurgeon, *Advertising and New Media*, p. 14.

20 Stuart Allan, *Online News: Journalism and the Internet* (Maidenhead: Open University Press, 2006), pp. 44 ff.; Stuart Allan, *News Culture*, 2nd edn. (Maidenhead: Open University Press, 2004), pp. 179–80, 184–90.

21 http://en.wikipedia.org/wiki/Blog, retrieved January 7, 2008; Dan Silkstone, "The Blogs that Ate Cyberspace," *Age*, April 7, 2007; Allan, *Online News*, p. 172; Sarah Boxer, "Blogs" [review article], *New York Review of Books* (February 14, 2008), p.16.

22 http://en.wikipedia.org/wiki/List_of_social_networking_websites, retrieved March 17, and April 23, 2008.

23 http://en.wikipedia.org/wiki/MySpace, retrieved January 4, 2008.

24 Spurgeon, *Advertising and New Media*, pp. 109–10.

25 Tom Hodgkinson, "Why You Should Beware of Facebook," *Age* (January 19, 2008).

26 http://en.wikipedia.org/wiki/Bebo, retrieved January 7, 2008.

27 Lister et al., *New Media*, pp. 219 ff.

28 Bernadette Luck, "Cyberbullying: An Emerging Issue," in Papandrea and Armstrong (comps.), *Record of the Communications Policy and Research Forum*, pp. 137–52.

29 http://en.wikipedia.org/wiki/YouTube, retrieved January 8, 2008.

30   *Age* (December 28–9, 2007).

31   Stevie Ryan, quoted by Paul Sheehan, *Sydney Morning Herald* (December 9–10, 2006); Allison Orr, "Why the Online Revolution Is Just Another Line," *Sydney Morning Herald* (January 1, 2007).

32   Mandy Salomon, "Virtual Worlds and the 3D Web: Australian Policy Debates in Second Life," in Papandrea and Armstrong (comps.), *Record of the Communications Policy and Research Forum*, p. 129.

33   Allan, *Online News*, p. 135.

34   Stacy Schiff, *Age*, A2 (December 2, 2006), p. 13; Jenkins, *Convergence Culture*, p. 254; Rachel Buchanan, *Age* (August 25, 2007).

35   Darren Sharp, "User-Led Innovation: A New Framework for Co-Creating Knowledge and Culture," in Papandrea and Armstrong (comps.), *Record of the Communications Policy and Research Forum*, pp. 103, 107.

36   Spurgeon, *Advertising and New Media*, p. 2; John Battelle, *The Search: How Google and its Rivals Rewrote the Rules of Business and Transformed our Culture* (New York: Portfolio, 2005).

37   On Google's history see Battelle, *The Search*; Vise, *The Google Story*; on Google and news, see Allan, *Online News*, pp. 175–9.

38   Gideon Haigh, "Information Idol: How Google Is Making Us Stupid," *Monthly* (February 2006), p. 33; Virginia Nightingale and Tim Dwyer (eds.), *New Media Worlds: Challenges for Convergence* (Melbourne: Oxford University Press, 2007), p. 334.

39   Vise, *The Google Story*, p. 261.

40   Ibid., p. 279.

41   Haig, "Information Idol," pp. 25–33; Patricia Edgar, "The Day the Television Died," *Age* (July 28, 2007).

42   Victor Keegan, "Searching for a Way to Rule Search," *Age* (February 23, 2008).

43   Nightingale and Dwyer (eds.), *New Media Worlds*.

44   Spurgeon, *Advertising and New Media*, pp. 16–17 (quoting Hartley, Jenkins, Toffler, O'Regan and Goldsmith, Banks, Bruns and Jacobs, Packard, Arvidsson).

45   Allan, *Online News*, pp. 123, 129–34, 184; Aaron Barlow, *The Rise of the Blogosphere* (Westport, CT: Praeger, 2007); Andrew Keen, *The Cult of the Amateur: How Today's Internet Is Killing our Culture* (Sydney: Allen and Unwin, 2007); Antony Loewenstein, *Sydney Morning Herald* (January 20–1, 2007).

46   Nightingale and Dwyer (eds.), *New Media Worlds*, pp. 20, 23, 332.

47   Claudia Eller and Dawn Chmielewski, *Sydney Morning Herald* (May 5–6, 2007).

48   Bobbie Johnson, "Tiny Music Machine Offers a New Angle on Architecture," *Sydney Morning Herald* (December 28, 2006).

49   Nick Miller, *Sydney Morning Herald* (January 13–14, 2007).

50 Lifelounge Urban Market Research 2007, cited in *Sydney Morning Herald: The Guide* (August 6–12, 2007).
51 Edgar, "The Day the Television Died."
52 Spurgeon, *Advertising and New Media*, p. 114.
53 Curran and Seaton, *Power without Responsibility*, p. 271.

Chapter 12. Globalization and Media

1 William A. Hachten and James F. Scotton, *The World News Prism: Global Media in an Era of Terrorism*, 6th edn. (Ames, IO: Iowa State Press, 2002), p. x; Manfred B. Steger, *Globalization: A Very Short Introduction* (Oxford: Oxford University Press, 2003), p. 13; Malcolm Waters, *Globalization*, 2nd edn. (London: Routledge, 2001), p. 5.
2 Terry Flew, *Understanding Global Media* (Basingstoke: Palgrave Macmillan, 2007), pp. 67–8.
3 See, e.g., Frank J. Lechner and John Boli (eds.), *The Globalization Reader* (Oxford: Blackwell, 2000), p. 1; Lee B. Becker, "Afterword," in David Demers (ed.), *Terrorism, Globalization and Mass Communication*. Papers presented at the 2002 Center for Global Media Studies Conference (Spokane: Marquette Books, 2003), p. 344.
4 Steger, *Globalization*, p. 84.
5 For the more skeptical view, see Jean Seaton, "Global Futures, the Information Society, and Broadcasting," in James Curran and Jean Seaton, *Power without Responsibility: The Press, Broadcasting and New Media in Britain*, 6th edn. (London: Routledge, 2003), pp. 297 ff.
6 John B. Thompson, "The Globalization of Communication," in David Held and Anthony McGrew (eds.), *The Global Transformations Reader: An Introduction to the Globalization Debate* (Cambridge: Polity, 2000), p. 210; Trevor Barr, *newmedia.com.au: The Changing Face of Australia's Media and Communications* (St Leonards: Allen and Unwin, 2000), p. 161.
7 Donna A. Demac and Liching Sung, "New Communication Technologies and Deregulation," in John Downing, Ali Mohammadi and Annabelle Sreberny-Mohammadi (eds.), *Questioning the Media: A Critical Introduction*, 2nd edn. (London: Sage, 1995), p. 281; Chris Barker, *Television, Globalization and Cultural Identities* (Buckingham: Open University Press, 1999), p. 50.
8 Hachten and Scotton, *The World News Prism*, p. 170; Eytan Gilboa, "Effects of Global Television News on US Policy in International Conflict," in Philip Seib (ed.), *Media and Conflict in the Twenty-First Century* (New York: Palgrave Macmillan, 2005), pp. 17, 22–3.
9 Nik Gowing, "Real-Time Television Coverage of Armed Conflicts and Diplomatic Crises: Does It Pressure or Distort Foreign Policy Decisions?," in Nancy

Palmer (ed.), *Terrorism, War, and the Press* (Hollis, NH: Joan Shorenstein Center on the Press, Politics and Public Policy, Harvard University/Hollis Publishing, 2003), pp. 139 ff; Philip Seib, *The Global Journalist: News and Conscience in a World of Conflict* (Lanham, MD: Rowman and Littlefield, 2002), p. 15.

10　Hachten and Scotton, *The World News Prism*, p. xii.

11　Flew, *Understanding Global Media*, p. 71 (drawing on *Financial Times* data, 2006).

12　C. Ann Hollifield, in "Current Issues in Transnational Media Management Research," in Demers (ed.), *Terrorism, Globalization and Mass Communication*, p. 53.

13　Kevin Williams, *European Media Studies* (London: Hodder Arnold, 2005), p. 25.

14　Ibid., p. 26.

15　Flew, *Understanding Global Media*, p. 88.

16　Sean MacBride and Colleen Roach, "The New International Information Order," in Lechner and Boli (eds.), *The Globalization Reader*, pp. 286–92.

17　John Sinclair, Elizabeth Jacka, and Stuart Cunningham (eds.), *New Patterns in Global Television: Peripheral Vision* (Oxford: Oxford University Press, 1996).

18　Stuart Cunningham and Elizabeth Jacka, *Australian Television and International Mediascapes* (Cambridge: Cambridge University Press, 1996); Lechner and Boli (eds.), *The Globalization Reader*, pp. 2–3. See also James Curran, *Media and Power* (Abingdon: Routledge, 2002), pp. 169 ff.

19　Sinclair, Jacka, and Cunningham (eds.), *New Patterns in Global Television*; Peter Block (ed.), *Managing in the Media* (Oxford: Focal Press, 2001), pp. 72, 81, 84.

20　Robert W. McChesney, "Corporate Media, Global Capitalism," in Simon Cottle (ed.), *Media Organization and Production* (London: Sage, 2003), p. 33.

21　Curran, *Media and Power*, pp. 171–4; John Tomlinson, "The Agenda of Globalization," *New Formations*, 50 (2003), 16.

22　Flew, *Understanding Global Media*, pp. 54–5, 58–65.

23　Curran, *Media and Power*, p. 78; Edward Herman and Robert W. McChesney, *The Global Media: The New Missionaries of Global Capitalism* (London: Cassell, 1997); see also Held and McGrew (eds.), *Global Transformations Reader*; and David Held, Anthony McGrew, David Goldblatt and Jonathan Perraton, *Global Transformations: Politics, Economics and Culture* (Cambridge: Polity, 1999).

24　Curran, *Media and Power*, p. 183; Steger, *Globalization*, p. 64.

25　McChesney, "Corporate Media, Global Capitalism," p. 35.

26　Lewis A. Friedland, "Covering the World," in Lechner and Boli (eds.), *The Globalization Reader*, p. 296.

27　Murdoch's statement quoted in Mark Wheeler, *Politics and the Mass Media* (Oxford: Blackwell, 1997), p. 176; Barr, *newmedia.com.au*, p. 163.

28 Internet Filtering in China in 2004–2005: A Country Study. http://www. opennetinitiative.net/studies/china/, retrieved May 5, 2007.

29 Philip Seib, *Beyond the Front Lines: How the News Media Cover a World Shaped by War* (New York: Palgrave Macmillan, 2004), p. 95.

30 Seib, *Beyond the Front Lines*, pp. 105, 110, 124; Mohamed Zayani (ed.), *The Al Jazeera Phenomenon: Critical Perspectives on New Arab Media* (London: Pluto, 2005), p. 29; Mohammed El-Nawawy and Adel Iskander, *Al-Jazeera: The Story of the Network that Is Rattling Governments and Redefining Modern Journalism* (Cambridge, MA: Westview Press, 2003), pp. x, 197.

31 Seib, *Beyond the Front Lines*, pp. 2–3; Seib (ed.), *Media and Conflict in the Twenty-First Century*, pp. 231–2; Hachten and Scotton, *The World News Prism*, p. xiv; Peter Steven, *The No-Nonsense Guide to Global Media* (Oxford: New Internationalist/Verso, 2003), p. 125.

32 See, e.g., Daya Kishan Thussu and Des Freedman (eds.), *War and the Media: Reporting Conflict 24/7* (London: Sage, 2003), pp. 122–4; Eric P. Louw, *The Media and Political Process* (London: Sage, 2005), pp. 124 ff.; Gilboa, in Seib (ed.), *Media and Conflict in the Twenty-First Century*, pp. 9, 17; Susan L. Carruthers, *The Media at War: Communication and Conflict in the Twentieth Century* (Basingstoke: Macmillan, 2000), p. 168; and Brigitte L. Nacos, "Mass-Mediated Terrorism in the New World (Dis)Order," in J. David Slocum (ed.), *Terrorism, Media, Liberation* (New Brunswick, NJ: Rutgers University Press, 2005), pp. 188, 204–5.

33 Seib (ed.), *Media and Conflict in the Twenty-First Century*, p. 232.

Chapter 13.   Conclusion

1 Raymond Williams, *Communications*, 3rd edn. (Harmondsworth: Penguin, 1976), pp. 24–7 (1st edn., Penguin, 1962).

2 Raymond Williams, "Retrospect and Prospect, 1975," in ibid., pp. 180–6.

3 Ibid., p. 188.

4 Benedict Anderson, *Imagined Communities: Reflections on the Origin and Spread of Nationalism*, rev. edn. (London: Verso, 1991).

5 E. J. Hobsbawm, *Nations and Nationalism since 1780: Programme, Myth, Reality* (Cambridge: Cambridge University Press, 1990), p. 142.

6 See David Farber (ed.), *What They Think of Us: International Perceptions of the United States since 9/11* (Princeton: Princeton University Press, 2007); Joseph S. Nye Jr., *Soft Power: The Means to Success in World Politics* (New York: Public Affairs, 2004), pp. 35–44; and "Public Diplomacy by the Numbers: Reports from Multi-National Opinion Surveys on US Standing, 2002–2007," http://www.publicdiplomacy.org/14.htm#Apr2007

Further Reading

General

Barnouw, Erik. *A History of Broadcasting in the United States*. 3 vols. New York: Oxford University Press, 1966–70.

Baughman, James L. *The Republic of Mass Culture: Journalism, Filmmaking, and Broadcasting in America since 1941*. Baltimore, MD: Johns Hopkins University Press, 1992.

Briggs, Asa. *The History of Broadcasting in the United Kingdom*. 4 vols. London: Oxford University Press, 1961–79.

Briggs, Asa, and Peter Burke. *A Social History of the Media: From Gutenberg to the Internet*, 2nd edn. Cambridge: Polity, 2005.

Cannadine, David (ed.). *History and the Media*. Basingstoke: Palgrave Macmillan, 2004.

Chapman, Jane. *Comparative Media History: An Introduction: 1789 to the Present*. Cambridge: Polity, 2005.

Cull, Nicholas J., David Culbert, and David Welch (eds.). *Propaganda and Mass Persuasion: A Historical Encyclopedia, 1500 to the Present*. Santa Barbara, CA: ABC-CLIO, 2003.

Curran, James. *Media and Power*. London: Routledge, 2002.

Curran, James, and Michael Gurevitch (eds.). *Mass Media and Society*, 3rd edn. London: Arnold, 2000.

Curran, James, and Michael Gurevitch (eds.). *Mass Media and Society*, 4th edn. London: Hodder Arnold, 2005.

Curran, James, and Jean Seaton. *Power without Responsibility: The Press, Broadcasting and New Media in Britain*, 6th edn. London: Routledge, 2003.

Emery, Michael, Edwin Emery, and Nancy L. Roberts. *The Press and America: An Interpretive History of the Mass Media*, 9th edn. Boston: Allyn and Bacon, 2000.

Hobsbawm, Eric. *Age of Extremes: The Short Twentieth Century, 1914–1991*. London: Michael Joseph, 1994.

Judt, Tony. *Postwar: A History of Europe since 1945*. New York: Penguin, 2005.

McChesney, Robert W. *Rich Media, Poor Democracy: Communication Politics in Dubious Times*. Urbana, IL: University of Illinois Press, 1999.

McKibbin, Ross. *Classes and Cultures: England 1918–1951*. Oxford: Oxford University Press, 1998.

Seymour-Ure, Colin. *The British Press and Broadcasting since 1945*, 2nd edn. Oxford: Blackwell, 1996.

Starr, Paul. *The Creation of the Media: Political Origins of Modern Communications*. New York: Basic Books, 2004.

Turow, Joseph. *Breaking up America: Advertisers and the New Media World*. Chicago: University of Chicago Press, 1997.

Ward, Ken. *Mass Communications and the Modern World*. Basingstoke: Macmillan, 1989.

Williams, Kevin. *Get Me a Murder a Day! A History of Mass Communication in Britain*. London: Arnold, 1998.

Williams, Raymond. *Communications*, 3rd edn. Harmondsworth: Penguin, 1976.

Chapter 2.   The Press as a Mass Medium

Black, Jeremy. *The English Press in the Eighteenth Century*. London: Croom Helm, 1987.

Boyce, George, James Curran, and Pauline Wingate (eds.). *Newspaper History from the Seventeenth Century to the Present Day*. London: Constable, 1978.

Cranfield, Geoffrey Alan. *The Press and Society: From Caxton to Northcliffe*. London: Longman, 1978.

Douglas, George H. *The Golden Age of the Newspaper*. Westport, CT: Greenwood Press, 1999.

Hampton, Mark. *Visions of the Press in Britain, 1850–1950*. Urbana, IL: University of Illinois Press, 2004.

Morris, A. J. Anthony. *The Scaremongers: The Advocacy of War and Rearmament 1896–1914*. London: Routledge and Kegan Paul, 1984.

Nasaw, David. *The Chief: The Life of William Randolph Hearst*. Boston: Houghton Mifflin, 2000.

Nord, David Paul. *Communities of Journalism: A History of American Newspapers and Their Readers*. Urbana, IL: University of Illinois Press, 2006.

Schwarzlose, Richard Allen. *Newspapers: A Reference Guide*. Westport, CT: Greenwood Press, 1987.

Thompson, J. Lee. *Northcliffe: Press Baron in Politics 1865–1922*. London: John Murray, 2000.

Thompson, J. Lee. *Politicians, the Press and Propaganda: Lord Northcliffe and the Great War, 1914–1919*. Kent, OH: Kent State University Press, 2000.

Chapter 3.   The Development of the Film Industry

Basinger, Jeanine. *American Cinema: One Hundred Years of Filmmaking*. New York: Rizzoli, 1994.

Black, Gregory D. *Hollywood Censored: Morality Codes, Catholics, and the Movies*. Cambridge: Cambridge University Press, 1994.

Bodnar, John. *Blue-Collar Hollywood: Liberalism, Democracy, and Working People in American Film*. Baltimore. MD: Johns Hopkins University Press, 2003.

Cripps, Thomas. *Hollywood's High Noon: Moviemaking and Society before Television*. Baltimore, MD: Johns Hopkins University Press, 1997.

De Grazia, Victoria. *Irresistible Empire: America's Advance through Twentieth-Century Europe*. Cambridge, MA: Belknap/Harvard University Press, 2005 (chapter 6).

Doherty, Thomas. *Pre-Code Hollywood: Sex, Immorality, and Insurrection in American Cinema, 1930–1934*. New York: Columbia University Press, 1999.

Gabler, Neal. *An Empire of their Own: How the Jews Invented Hollywood*. New York: Doubleday, 1988.

Gomery, Douglas. *The Hollywood Studio System*. New York: St Martin's Press, 1986.

Jarvie, Ian. *Hollywood's Overseas Campaign: The North Atlantic Movie Trade, 1920–1950*. Cambridge: Cambridge University Press, 1992.

Jowett, Garth. *Film: The Democratic Art*. Boston: Little, Brown, 1976.

Koszarski, Richard. *An Evening's Entertainment: The Age of the Silent Feature Picture, 1915–1928*. New York: Scribner, 1990.

May, Lary. *Screening out the Past: The Birth of Mass Culture and the Motion Picture Industry*. New York: Oxford University Press, 1980. Also published in paperback by University of Chicago Press in 1983.

Parkinson, David. *History of Film*. London: Thames and Hudson, 1995.

Puttnam, David. *The Undeclared War: The Struggle for Control of the World's Film Industry*. London: HarperCollins, 1997.

Rhode, Eric. *A History of the Cinema from its Origins to 1970*. New York: Hill and Wang, 1976.

Ross, Steven J. *Working-Class Hollywood: Silent Film and the Shaping of Class in America*. Princeton: Princeton University Press, 1998.

Segrave, Kerry. *American Films Abroad: Hollywood's Domination of the World's Movie Screens from the 1890s to the Present*. Jefferson, NC: McFarland, 1997.

Shindler, Colin. *Hollywood in Crisis: Cinema and American Society 1929–1939*. London: Routledge, 1996.

Sklar, Robert. *Movie-Made America: A Cultural History of American Movies*. New York: Vintage Books, 1994.

Sklar, Robert. *A World History of Film*. New York: H. N. Abrams, 2002.

Thompson, Kristin. *Exporting Entertainment: America in the World Film Market 1907–34*. London: British Film Institute, 1985.

Trumpbour, John. *Selling Hollywood to the World: US and European Struggles for Mastery of the Global Film Industry, 1920–1950*. Cambridge: Cambridge University Press, 2002.

Vasey, Ruth. *The World according to Hollywood, 1918–1939*. Madison: University of Wisconsin Press, 1997.

Chapter 4. The Growth of Radio Broadcasting

Aitken, Hugh G. J. *The Continuous Wave: Technology and American Radio, 1900–1932*. Princeton: Princeton University Press, 1985.

Albarran, Alan B., and Gregory G. Pitts. *The Radio Broadcasting Industry*. Boston: Allyn and Bacon, 2001.

Barfield, Ray E. *Listening to Radio, 1920–1950*. Westport, CT: Praeger, 1996.

Barnard, Stephen. *On the Radio: Music Radio in Britain*. Milton Keynes: Open University Press, 1989.

Briggs, Asa. *The BBC: The First Fifty Years*. Oxford: Oxford University Press, 1985.

Brown, Robert J. *Manipulating the Ether: The Power of Broadcast Radio in Thirties America*. Jefferson, NC: McFarland, 1998.

De Forest, Lee. *Father of Radio: The Autobiography of Lee de Forest*. Chicago: Wilcox and Follett, 1950.

Douglas, Susan J. *Inventing American Broadcasting, 1899–1922*. Baltimore, MD: Johns Hopkins University Press, 1987.

Douglas, Susan J. *Listening in: Radio and the American Imagination*. New York: Random House, 1999.

Geddes, Keith, with Gordon Bussey. *The Setmakers: A History of the Radio and Television Industry*. London: British Radio and Electronic Equipment Manufacturers' Association, 1991.

Hilmes, Michele. *Radio Voices: American Broadcasting, 1922–1952*. Minneapolis: University of Minnesota Press, 1997.

Jackaway, Gwenyth L. *Media at War: Radio's Challenge to the Newspapers, 1924–1939*. Westport, CT: Praeger, 1995.

MacDonald, J. Fred. *Don't Touch that Dial!: Radio Programming in American Life, 1920–1960*. Chicago: Nelson Hall, 1979.

Scannell, Paddy, and David Cardiff. *A Social History of British Broadcasting*, vol. 1, *1922–1939, Serving the Nation*. Oxford: Basil Blackwell, 1991.

Shingler, Martin, and Cindy Wieringa. *On Air: Methods and Meanings of Radio*. London: Hodder, 1998.

Smulyan, Susan. *Selling Radio: The Commercialization of American Broadcasting 1920–1934*. Washington: Smithsonian Institution Press, 1994.

Chapter 5.   The Rise of Advertising

Cross, Gary. *An All-Consuming Century: Why Commercialism Won in Modern America*. New York: Columbia University Press, 2000.

De Grazia, Victoria. *Irresistible Empire: America's Advance through Twentieth-Century Europe*. Cambridge, MA: Belknap/Harvard University Press, 2005 (chapter 5).

Fox, Stephen. *The Mirror Makers: A History of American Advertising and its Creators*. New York: Vintage, 1985.

Lears, Jackson. *Fables of Abundance: A Cultural History of Advertising in America*. New York: Basic Books, 1994.

Leiss, William, Stephen Kline, and Sut Jhally. *Social Communication in Advertising: Persons, Products, and Images of Well-Being*. Toronto: Methuen, 1986.

Marchand, Roland. *Advertising the American Dream: Making Way for Modernity, 1920–1940*. Berkeley and Los Angeles: University of California Press, 1985.

Nye, David E. *Image Worlds: Corporate Identities at General Electric, 1890–1930*. Cambridge, MA: MIT Press, 1985.

Pope, Daniel. *The Making of Modern Advertising*. New York: Basic Books, 1983.

Potter, David M. "The Institution of Abundance: Advertising," in *People of Plenty: Economic Abundance and the American Character*. Chicago: University of Chicago Press, 1954 (pp. 166–88).

Schudson, Michael. *Advertising, the Uneasy Persuasion: Its Dubious Impact on American Society*. London: Routledge, 1993.

Smulyan, Susan. *Selling Radio: The Commercialization of American Broadcasting 1920–1934*. Washington: Smithsonian Institution Press, 1994.

Williams, Raymond. "Advertising: The Magic System," in *Problems in Materialism and Culture: Selected Essays*. London: Verso, 1980 (pp. 170–95).

Chapter 6.   Propaganda in Peace and War

Applebaum, Anne. *Gulag: A History*. London: Penguin, 2003.

Balfour, Michael. *Propaganda in War 1939–1945: Organisations, Policies and Publics in Britain and Germany*. London: Routledge and Kegan Paul, 1979.

Brooks, Jeffrey. *Thank You, Comrade Stalin! Soviet Public Culture from Revolution to Cold War*. Princeton: Princeton University Press, 2000.

Carruthers, Susan L. *The Media at War: Communication and Conflict in the Twentieth Century*. Basingstoke: Macmillan, 2000.

Chapman, James. *The British at War: Cinema, State and Propaganda, 1939–1945*. London: I. B. Tauris, 1998.

Cuomo, Glenn R. (ed.). *National Socialist Cultural Policy*. New York: St Martin's Press, 1995.

Davies, Sarah. *Popular Opinion in Stalin's Russia*. Cambridge: Cambridge University Press, 1997.

Doherty, Thomas. *Projections of War: Hollywood, American Culture, and World War II*, 2nd edn. New York: Columbia University Press, 1999.

Dower, John. *War without Mercy: Race and Power in the Pacific War*. New York: Pantheon, 1986.

Ellul, Jacques. *Propaganda: The Formation of Men's Attitudes*. New York: Knopf, 1965.

Fitzpatrick, Sheila. *Everyday Stalinism: Ordinary Life in Extraordinary Times; Soviet Russia in the 1930s*. New York: Oxford University Press, 1999.

Hellbeck, Jochen. *Revolution on my Mind: Writing a Diary under Stalin*. Cambridge, MA: Harvard University Press, 2006.

Herf, Jeffrey. *The Jewish Enemy: Nazi Propaganda during World War II and the Holocaust*. Cambridge, MA: Belknap/Harvard University Press, 2006.

Jowett, Garth S. and Victoria O'Donnell. *Propaganda and Persuasion*, 2nd edn. Newbury Park, CA: Sage, 1992.

Kenez, Peter. *The Birth of the Propaganda State: Soviet Methods of Mass Mobilization 1917–1929*. Cambridge: Cambridge University Press, 1985.

Koppes, Clayton R., and Gregory D. Black. *Hollywood Goes to War: How Politics, Profits, and Propaganda Shaped World War II Movies*. New York: Free Press, 1987.

Roeder, George H., Jr. *The Censored War: American Visual Experience during World War Two*. New Haven, CT: Yale University Press, 1993.

Savage, Barbara Dianne. *Broadcasting Freedom: Radio, War, and the Politics of Race, 1939–1948*. Chapel Hill, NC: University of North Carolina Press, 1999.

Short, K. R. M. (ed.). *Film and Radio Propaganda in World War II*. Knoxville, TN: University of Tennessee Press, 1983.

Taylor, Philip M. *Munitions of the Mind: A History of Propaganda from the Ancient World to the Present Era*. Manchester: Manchester University Press, 1995.

Taylor, Richard. *Film Propaganda: Soviet Russia and Nazi Germany*, 2nd edn. London: I. B. Tauris, 1998 (1st edn., Croom Helm, 1979).

Taylor, Richard, and Derek Spring (eds.). *Stalinism and Soviet Cinema*. London: Routledge, 1993.

Welch, David (ed.). *Nazi Propaganda: The Power and the Limitations*. London: Croom Helm, 1983.

Welch, David. *Propaganda and the German Cinema 1933–1945*, 2nd edn. London: I. B. Tauris, 2001 (1st edn., Oxford University Press, 1983).

Welch, David. *The Third Reich: Politics and Propaganda*, 2nd edn. London: Routledge, 2002.

Chapter 7.   Cold War and Communications

Bernhard, Nancy E. *US Television News and Cold War Propaganda, 1947–1960.* Cambridge: Cambridge University Press, 1999.

Dennis, Everette E., George Gerbner, and Yassen N. Zassoursky (eds.). *Beyond the Cold War: Soviet and American Media Images.* Newbury Park, CA: Sage, 1991.

Doherty, Thomas. *Cold War, Cool Medium: Television, McCarthyism, and American Culture.* New York: Columbia University Press, 2003.

Hixson, Walter L. *Parting the Curtain: Propaganda, Culture, and the Cold War, 1945–1961.* New York: St Martin's Press, 1997.

Lashmar, Paul, and James Oliver. *Britain's Secret Propaganda War.* Stroud: Sutton, 1998.

MacDonald, J. Fred. *Television and the Red Menace: The Video Road to Vietnam.* New York: Praeger, 1985.

May, Lary. *The Big Tomorrow: Hollywood and the Politics of the American Way.* Chicago: University of Chicago Press, 2000 (chapter 5).

Mitrovich, Gregory. *Undermining the Kremlin: America's Strategy to Subvert the Soviet Bloc, 1947–1956.* Ithaca, NY: Cornell University Press, 2000.

Nelson, Michael. *War of the Black Heavens: The Battles of Western Broadcasting in the Cold War.* London: Brassey's, 1997.

Osgood, Kenneth. *Total Cold War: Eisenhower's Secret Propaganda Battle at Home and Abroad.* Lawrence, KS: University Press of Kansas, 2006.

Pells, Richard. *Not Like Us: How Europeans Have Loved, Hated, and Transformed American Culture since World War II.* New York: Basic Books, 1997.

Rawnsley, Gary D. (ed.). *Cold-War Propaganda in the 1950s.* New York: St Martin's Press, 1999.

Rawnsley, Gary D. *Radio Diplomacy and Propaganda: The BBC and VOA in International Politics, 1956–64.* New York: St Martin's Press, 1996.

Saunders, Frances Stonor. *Who Paid the Piper?: The CIA and the Cultural Cold War.* London: Granta, 1999. Published in the United States as *The Cultural Cold War: The CIA and the World of Arts and Letters.* New York: Free Press, 1999.

Shaw, Tony. *British Cinema and the Cold War: The State, Propaganda and Consensus.* London: I. B. Tauris, 2001.

Simpson, Christopher. *Science of Coercion: Communication Research and Psychological Warfare 1945–1960.* New York: Oxford University Press, 1994.

Taylor, Philip M. *Munitions of the Mind: A History of Propaganda from the Ancient World to the Present Era.* Manchester: Manchester University Press, 1995 (chapter 24).

Urban, George R. *Radio Free Europe and the Pursuit of Democracy: My War within the Cold War.* New Haven, CT: Yale University Press, 1997.

Von Eschen, Penny M. *Satchmo Blows Up the World: Jazz Ambassadors Play the Cold War*. Cambridge, MA: Harvard University Press, 2004.

Wagnleitner, Reinhold. *Coca-Colonization and the Cold War: The Cultural Mission of the United States in Austria after the Second World War*. Chapel Hill, NC: University of North Carolina Press, 1994.

Whitfield, Stephen J. *The Culture of the Cold War*. Baltimore: Johns Hopkins University Press, 1991.

Wilford, Hugh. *The CIA, the British Left and the Cold War: Calling the Tune?* London: Frank Cass, 2003.

Chapter 8.   Television and Consumer Societies

Barker, Chris. *Global Television: An Introduction*. Oxford: Blackwell, 1997.

Barnouw, Erik. *Tube of Plenty: The Evolution of American Television*. Oxford: Oxford University Press, 1982.

Baughman, James L. *Same Time, Same Station: Creating American Television, 1948–1961*. Baltimore: Johns Hopkins University Press, 2007.

Buscombe, Edward (ed.). *British Television: A Reader*. Oxford: Oxford University Press, 2000.

Doherty, Thomas. *Cold War, Cool Medium: Television, McCarthyism, and American Culture*. New York: Columbia University Press, 2003.

Donovan, Robert J., and Ray Scherer. *Unsilent Revolution: Television News and American Public Life, 1948–1991*. Cambridge: Cambridge University Press, 1992.

Downie, Leonard, Jr., and Robert G. Kaiser, *The News about the News: American Journalism in Peril*. New York: Vintage Books, 2003.

Hallin, Daniel C. *We Keep America on Top of the World: Television Journalism and the Public Sphere*. London: Routledge, 1994.

Hilmes, Michele (ed.). *The Television History Book*. London: British Film Institute, 2003.

Hong, Junhao. *The Internationalization of Television in China: The Evolution of Ideology, Society, and Media since the Reform*. Westport, CT: Praeger, 1998.

Ledbetter, James. *Made Possible by …: The Death of Public Broadcasting in the United States*. London: Verso, 1997.

Moran, Albert, and Michael Keane (eds.). *Television across Asia: Television Industries, Programme Formats and Globalization*. London: RoutledgeCurzon, 2004.

Sinclair, John, Elizabeth Jacka, and Stuart Cunningham (eds.). *New Patterns in Global Television: Peripheral Vision*. Oxford: Oxford University Press, 1996.

Smith, Anthony, with Richard Paterson (eds.). *Television: An International History*, 2nd edn. Oxford: Oxford University Press, 1998.

Steemers, Jeanette. *Selling Television: British Television in the Global Marketplace.* London: British Film Institute, 2004.

Tracey, Michael. *The Decline and Fall of Public Service Broadcasting.* Oxford: Oxford University Press, 1998.

Watson, Mary Ann. *The Expanding Vista: American Television in the Kennedy Years.* Durham, NC: Duke University Press, 1994.

Williams, Raymond. *Television: Technology and Cultural Form.* New York: Schocken Books, 1975.

Chapter 9.   Media, Information, and Entertainment

Bennett, W. Lance, Regina G. Lawrence, and Steven Livingston. *When the Press Fails: Political Power and the News Media from Iraq to Katrina.* Chicago: University of Chicago Press, 2007.

Bogart, Leo. *Press and Public: Who Reads What, When, Where, and Why in American Newspapers,* 2nd edn. Hillsdale, NJ: Lawrence Erlbaum Associates, 1989.

Dickenson, Ben. *Hollywood's New Radicalism: War, Globalisation and the Movies from Reagan to George W. Bush.* London: I. B. Tauris, 2006.

Donovan, Robert J., and Ray Scherer. *Unsilent Revolution: Television News and American Public Life, 1948–1991.* Cambridge: Cambridge University Press, 1992.

Douglas, Susan J., *Listening in: Radio and the American Imagination, From Amos 'n' Andy and Edward R. Murrow to Wolfman Jack and Howard Stern.* New York: Times Books, 1999,

Downie, Leonard, Jr., and Robert G. Kaiser, *The News about the News: American Journalism in Peril.* New York: Vintage Books, 2003.

Graham, Allison. *Framing the South: Hollywood, Television, and Race during the Civil Rights Struggle.* Baltimore: Johns Hopkins University Press, 2001.

Hallin, Daniel C. *We Keep America on Top of the World: Television Journalism and the Public Sphere.* London: Routledge, 1994.

Henry, Neil. *American Carnival: Journalism under Siege in an Age of New Media.* Berkeley and Los Angeles: University of California Press, 2007.

Jowett, Garth. *Film: The Democratic Art.* Boston: Little, Brown, 1976.

Kindem, Gorham (ed.). *The International Movie Industry.* Carbondale, IL: Southern Illinois University Press, 2000.

McCauley, Michael P. *NPR: The Trials and Triumphs of National Public Radio.* New York: Columbia University Press, 2005.

MacDonald, J. Fred. *Don't Touch that Dial! Radio Programming in American Life, 1920–1960.* Chicago: Nelson-Hall, 1979.

Massing, Michael. *Now They Tell Us: The American Press and Iraq.* New York: New York Review Books, 2004.

Moran, Albert (ed.). *Film Policy: International, National and Regional Perspectives.* London: Routledge, 1996.

Neale, Steve (ed.). *Genre and Contemporary Hollywood.* London: British Film Institute, 2002.

Neale, Steve, and Murray Smith (eds.). *Contemporary Hollywood Cinema.* London: Routledge, 1998.

Parkinson, David. *History of Film.* London: Thames and Hudson, 1995.

Puttnam, David. *The Undeclared War: The Struggle for Control of the World's Film Industry.* London: HarperCollins, 1997.

Rhode, Eric. *A History of the Cinema from its Origins to 1970.* New York: Hill and Wang, 1976.

Segrave, Kerry. *American Films Abroad: Hollywood's Domination of the World's Movie Screens from the 1890s to the Present.* Jefferson, NC: McFarland, 1997.

Sklar, Robert. *Movie-Made America: A Cultural History of American Movies.* New York: Vintage Books, 1994.

Sklar, Robert. *A World History of Film.* New York: H. N. Abrams, 2002.

Zassoursky, Ivan. *Media and Power in Post-Soviet Russia.* Armonk, NY: M. E. Sharpe, 2004.

Chapter 10.   Media, War, and International Relations

Adams, Valerie. *The Media and the Falklands Campaign.* Basingstoke: Macmillan, 1986.

Allan, Stuart. *News Culture,* 2nd edn. Maidenhead: Open University Press, 2004.

Allan, Stuart. *Online News: Journalism and the Internet.* Maidenhead: Open University Press, 2006.

Bennett, W. Lance, and David L. Paletz (eds.). *Taken by Storm: The Media, Public Opinion, and US Foreign Policy in the Gulf War.* Chicago: University of Chicago Press, 1994.

Carruthers, Susan L. *The Media at War: Communication and Conflict in the Twentieth Century.* Basingstoke: Macmillan, 2000.

Connelly, Mark, and David Welch (eds.). *War and the Media: Reportage and Propaganda, 1900–2003.* London: I. B. Taurus, 2005.

Denton, Robert E., Jr. *The Media and the Persian Gulf War.* Westport, CT: Praeger, 1993.

Fialka, John J., *Hotel Warriors: Covering the Gulf War.* Washington: Woodrow Wilson Center Press, 1991.

Gow, James, Richard Paterson, and Alison Preston (eds.). *Bosnia by Television.* London: British Film Institute, 1996.

Hallin, Daniel C. *The "Uncensored War": The Media and Vietnam.* New York: Oxford University Press, 1986.

Hammond, William M. *Reporting Vietnam: Media and Military at War*. Modern World Studies. Lawrence, KS: University Press of Kansas, 1998.

Hoskins, Andrew. *Televising War: From Vietnam to Iraq*. London: Continuum, 2004.

Hudson, Miles, and John Stanier. *War and the Media: A Random Searchlight*. Stroud: Sutton, 1997.

Knightley, Phillip. *The First Casualty: The War Correspondent as Hero and Myth Maker from the Crimea to Kosovo*. London: Prion, 2000.

Lewis, Justin, Rod Brookes, Nick Mosdell, and Terry Threadgold, *Shoot First and Ask Questions Later: Media Coverage of the 2003 Iraq War*. New York: Peter Lang, 2006.

Massing, Michael. *Now They Tell Us: The American Press and Iraq*. New York: New York Review Books, 2004.

Mermin, Jonathan. *Debating War and Peace: Media Coverage of US Intervention in the Post-Vietnam Era*. Princeton: Princeton University Press, 1999.

Norris, Pippa, Montague Kern, and Marion Just (eds.). *Framing Terrorism: The News Media, the Government and the Public*. New York: Routledge, 2003.

Rid, Thomas. *War and Media Operations: The US Military and the Press from Vietnam to Iraq*. London: Routledge, 2007.

Seaton, Jean. *Carnage and the Media: The Making and Breaking of News about Violence*. London: Allen Lane/Penguin, 2005.

Seib, Philip (ed.). *Media and Conflict in the Twenty-First Century*. New York: Palgrave Macmillan, 2005.

Strobel, Warren P. *Late-Breaking Foreign Policy: The News Media's Influence on Peace Operations*. Washington: United States Institute of Peace Press, 1997.

Taylor, Philip M. *War and the Media: Propaganda and Persuasion in the Gulf War*. Manchester: Manchester University Press, 1992.

Young, Peter, and Peter Jesser. *The Media and the Military: From the Crimea to Desert Strike*. South Melbourne: Macmillan Education, 1997.

Zayani, Mohamed (ed.). *The Al Jazeera Phenomenon: Critical Perspectives on New Arab Media*. London: Pluto Press, 2005.

Chapter 11.   The Rise of New Media

Barr, Trevor. *newmedia.com.au: The Changing Face of Australia's Media and Communications*. St Leonards: Allen and Unwin, 2000.

Cunningham, Stuart, and Graeme Turner (eds.). *The Media in Australia*, 2nd edn. St Leonards: Allen and Unwin, 1997.

Dizard, Wilson, Jr. *Old Media/New Media: Mass Communications in the Information Age*. London: Longman, 1994.

Flew, Terry. *New Media: An Introduction*, 2nd edn. Oxford: Oxford University Press, 2005.

Flew, Terry. *Understanding Global Media*. Basingstoke: Palgrave Macmillan, 2007.

Goggin, Gerard. *Cell Phone Culture: Mobile Technology in Everyday Life*. London: Routledge, 2006.

Held, David, and Anthony McGrew (eds.). *The Global Transformations Reader: An Introduction to the Globalization Debate*. Cambridge: Polity Press, 2000.

Hiebert, Ray Eldon, and Sheila Jean Gibbons. *Exploring Mass Media for a Changing World*. London: Lawrence Erlbaum, 2000.

Jenkins, Henry. *Convergence Culture: Where Old and New Media Collide*. New York: New York University Press, 2006.

Nightingale, Virginia, and Tim Dwyer (eds.). *New Media Worlds: Challenges for Convergence*. Melbourne: Oxford University Press, 2007.

Owen, Bruce M. *The Internet Challenge to Television*. Cambridge, MA: Harvard University Press, 1999.

Spurgeon, Christina. *Advertising and New Media*. London: Routledge, 2008.

Winston, Brian. *Media Technology and Society: A History; From the Telegraph to the Internet*. London: Routledge, 1998.

Chapter 12.   Globalization and Media

Barker, Chris. *Global Television: An Introduction*. Oxford: Blackwell, 1997.

Barker, Chris. *Television, Globalization and Cultural Identities*. Buckingham: Open University Press, 1999.

Barr, Trevor. *newmedia.com.au: The Changing Face of Australia's Media and Communications*. St Leonards: Allen and Unwin, 2000.

Branston, Gill, and Roy Stafford. *The Media Student's Book*, 2nd edn. London: Routledge, 1999.

Cottle, Simon (ed.). *Media Organization and Production*. London: Sage, 2003.

Cunningham, Stuart, and Elizabeth Jacka. *Australian Television and International Mediascapes*. Cambridge: Cambridge University Press, 1996.

Cunningham, Stuart, and Graeme Turner (eds.). *The Media in Australia*, 2nd edn. St Leonards: Allen and Unwin, 1997.

Curran, James (ed.). *Media Organisations in Society*. London: Arnold, 2000.

Demers, David (ed.). *Terrorism, Globalization and Mass Communication*. Papers presented at the 2002 Center for Global Media Studies Conference. Spokane: Marguette Books, 2003.

Flew, Terry. *Understanding Global Media*. Basingstoke: Palgrave Macmillan, 2007.

Hachten, William A. and Scotton, James F. *The World News Prism: Global Media in an Era of Terrorism*, 6th edn. Ames, IO: Iowa State Press, 2002.

Held, David, and Anthony McGrew (eds.). *The Global Transformations Reader: An Introduction to the Globalization Debate*. Cambridge: Polity, 2000.

342   *Further Reading*

Held, David, Anthony McGrew, David Goldblatt, and Jonathan Perraton. *Global Transformations: Politics, Economics and Culture*. Cambridge: Polity, 1999.

Lechner, Frank J., and John Boli (eds.). *The Globalization Reader*. Oxford: Blackwell, 2000.

Nacos, Brigitte E. *Mass-Mediated Terrorism: The Central Role of the Media in Terrorism and Counterterrorism*. Lanham, MD: Rowman and Littlefield, 2002.

Palmer, Nancy (ed.). *Terrorism, War, and the Press*. Hollis, NH: Joan Shorenstein Center on the Press, Politics and Public Policy, Harvard University/Hollis Publishing, 2003.

Rantanen, Terhi. *The Media and Globalization*. London: Sage, 2005.

Seib, Philip. *Beyond the Front Lines: How the News Media Cover a World Shaped by War*. New York: Palgrave Macmillan, 2004.

Seib, Philip. *The Global Journalist: News and Conscience in a World of Conflict*. Lanham, MD: Rowman and Littlefield, 2002.

Seib, Philip (ed.). *Media and Conflict in the Twenty-First Century*. New York: Palgrave Macmillan, 2005.

Sinclair, John, Elizabeth Jacka, and Stuart Cunningham (eds.). *New Patterns in Global Television: Peripheral Vision*. Oxford: Oxford University Press, 1996.

Slocum, J. David (ed.). *Terrorism, Media, Liberation*. New Brunswick, NJ: Rutgers University Press, 2005.

Thussu, Daya Kishan, and Des Freedman (eds.). *War and the Media: Reporting Conflict 24/7*. London: Sage, 2003.

Wheeler, Mark. *Politics and the Mass Media*. Oxford: Blackwell, 1997.

Winston, Brian. *Media Technology and Society: A History; From the Telegraph to the Internet*. London: Routledge, 1998.

Zayani, Mohamed (ed.). *The Al Jazeera Phenomenon: Critical Perspectives on New Arab Media*. London: Pluto, 2005.

Websites

BBC Online – History
http://www.bbc.co.uk/history/
The BBC Story: History of the BBC
http://www.bbc.co.uk/thenandnow/history/index.shtml
Box Office Mojo
http://www.boxofficemojo.com/
British Film Institute
http://www.bfi.org.uk/
Center for Media and Democracy
http://www.prwatch.org/
Columbia Journalism Review

http://www.cjr.org
Columbia Journalism Review – Who Owns What
http://www.cjr.org/tools/owners/
Committee of Concerned Journalists
http://www.concernedjournalists.org/
Film History by Decade
http://www.filmsite.org/filmh.html
Global Media Journal
http://lass.calumet.purdue.edu/cca/gmj/
Historical Journal of Film, Radio and Television
http://www.iamhist.org/journal/index.html
The International Association for Media and History
http://www.iamhist.org/
The Internet Archive
http://www.archive.org/index.php
The Internet Movie Database
http://www.imdb.com/
The Internet Society: Histories of the Internet
http://www.isoc.org/internet/history/
Media, Culture and Society
http://mcs.sagepub.com/
The Media Report, Australian Broadcasting Corporation Radio National
http://www.abc.net.au/rn/talks/8.30/mediarpt/
Media Resources Center, Moffitt Library, University of California, Berkeley
http://www.lib.berkeley.edu/MRC/
Media Shift, Public Broadcasting Service
http://www.pbs.org/mediashift/
Media, War and Conflict
http://mwc.sagepub.com/
Motion Picture Association of America
http://www.mpaa.org/AboutUs.asp
Nielsen Media Research
http://www.nielsenmedia.com
NOW on PBS
http://www.pbs.org/now/thisweek/archive.html
Pew Research Center
http://pewresearch.org/
University of Maryland Libraries: Library of American Broadcasting
http://www.lib.umd.edu/LAB/
University of Minnesota Media History Project
http://www.mediahistory.umn.edu/

Index